D1298015

BUSINESS AND PROFESSIONAL COMMUNICATION
IN THE GLOBAL WORKPLACE

BUSINESS AND PROFESSIONAL COMMUNICATION IN THE GLOBAL WORKPLACE

THIRD EDITION

H. L. Goodall, Jr.
Director of the Hugh Downs School of Human Communication
Arizona State University

Sandra Goodall

Jill Schiefelbein
Director of Online Programs, College of Liberal Arts and Sciences
Arizona State University

WADSWORTH
CENGAGE Learning

Australia • Brazil • Japan • Korea • Mexico • Singapore • Spain • United Kingdom • United States

WADSWORTH
CENGAGE Learning™

Business and Professional Communication in the Global Workplace, Third Edition
H. L. Goodall, Jr., Sandra Goodall, Jill Schiefelbein

Publisher: Lyn Uhl

Executive Editor: Monica Eckman

Editorial Assistant: Colin Solan

Associate Technology Project Manager: Jessica Badiner

Marketing Manager: Erin Mitchell

Marketing Coordinator: Mary Ann Payumo

Marketing Communications Manager: Christine Dobberpuhl

Content Project Manager: Jessica Rasile

Art Director: Linda Helcher

Production Technology Analyst: Jamison MacLachlan

Print Buyer: Sue Carroll

Permissions Editor: Mardell Glinski-Schultz

Production Service: Pre-Press PMG

Photo Manager: Don Schlotman

Cover Designer: Rokusek Design

Cover Image: © Brand X Pictures/Fotosearch

Global Profile for Success box icon © Julie Grondin; Thinking Globally box icon © Ong Kok Keat; Focus on Ethics box icon © Mark Stay; Skill Builder Workshop box icon © Murat Koc.

© 2010, 2006 Wadsworth, Cengage Learning

ALL RIGHTS RESERVED. No part of this work covered by the copyright herein may be reproduced, transmitted, stored, or used in any form or by any means graphic, electronic, or mechanical, including but not limited to photocopying, recording, scanning, digitizing, taping, Web distribution, information networks, or information storage and retrieval systems, except as permitted under Section 107 or 108 of the 1976 United States Copyright Act, without the prior written permission of the publisher.

For product information and technology assistance, contact us at **Cengage Learning Academic Resource Center, 1-800-423-0563**

For permission to use material from this text or product, submit all requests online at **www.cengage.com/permissions.** Further permissions questions can be e-mailed to **permissionrequest@cengage.com**

Library of Congress Control Number: 2008942755

Student Edition:
ISBN-13: 978-0-495-56738-7
ISBN-10: 0-495-56738-8

Wadsworth
20 Channel Center Street
Boston, MA 02210
USA

Cengage Learning products are represented in Canada by Nelson Education, Ltd.

To learn more about Wadsworth, visit **www.cengage.com/wadsworth**

Purchase any of our products at your local college store or at our preferred online store **www.ichapters.com.**

Printed in Canada
1 2 3 4 5 6 7 12 11 10 09

CONTENTS IN BRIEF

CONTENTS

PREFACE

We are very excited about the newest edition of *Business and Professional Communication in the Global Workplace (*formerly *Communicating in Professional Contexts: Skills, Ethics, and Technologies)*. Writing a new edition of a textbook offers unique challenges. Authors must parse reviews and suggestions received from adopters and students, and from them make changes that significantly improve the text. Authors should then look around them and see what is new and emerging within their area of expertise, asking themselves: what are people in the field concerned about? How has the field changed since the last edition of the book? Where is the field going? A successful new edition is a blend of subtle changes that address the concerns of current users and new information that incorporates the changes that have occurred in the field since the last edition. We think *Business and Professional Communication in the Global Workplace* addresses both of these needs.

WHAT HAS CHANGED

First, we would like to thank all of you who have reviewed, adopted, supported, and offered your suggestions for improving the first two editions of the book. Your generous gift of time and insights for improving the book for future audiences have been extremely valuable and greatly contributed to this edition.

The reviewers of the second edition felt that while students found the CCCD model—choose, create, coordinate, and delivery—used throughout the book to be helpful, it was perhaps too embedded in the examples and might be overemphasized. We felt this was a valid observation. We have kept CCCD. However, rather than using it as an overarching methodology, CCCD is now used simply to remind students of the steps in the communication process and how following the steps ensures a successful outcome. We have removed or simplified the CCCD charts to reduce the visual clutter within the chapters.

Another element that was prevalent in the first two editions of the book that received mixed reviews was the use of narratives at the beginning of each chapter. While many students and instructors enjoyed the narratives, others found them distracting and unnecessary. In this edition, we have either removed the narratives or incorporated them as case studies within the chapter. Instructors now have the choice to use the case studies as teaching tools or ignore them altogether. One note about the narratives: we received a few e-mails from instructors wondering about the veracity of the narratives. Often, authors use examples or stories within their text that reflect a perfect case or things as they should be in business. The narratives in this book are drawn from Sandra's actual experiences as an organizational consultant. The names and companies have been changed but the underlying circumstances, the situations, and the interactions are all accurate. Some of these examples depict messy, imperfect, and mindless (a term we use throughout the book) reactions to business situations. Many of the students using the book have found these less-than-perfect scenarios extremely educational. We hope you do too.

An important part of this edition has been the review and revision of each and every chapter. During this review, we streamlined the text, paying particular attention to dense paragraphs and identifying those we could break down using bulleted lists and additional headings. And, of course, we have updated the exercises, ancillaries, and other materials that accompany this text.

WHAT IS NEW

For many students, the term "global" when used in conjunction with the economy, workplace, markets, etc. may seem like nothing more than a buzzword. The world of business is a messy place. In the world of work, valid notions of fairness, political correctness, and gender and racial sensitivity are often at odds with generational, regional, and cultural understandings. The way we *should* treat one another in the workplace may not be the way we *do* treat one another. This is especially true of those who have not been taught how to communicate in the global workplace. Throughout the text, we provide tips, hints, and strategies for communicating in the global workplace. In each chapter, we offer examples taken from actual business situations to highlight what can happen when people communicate in the global workplace using mindless, rather than mindful, approaches to communication. And we emphasize communicating ethically, responsibly, and appropriately in the workplace. We encourage students to be sensitive and mindful when faced with different views of gender, culture, race, age, or religion in the global workplace. For this new edition, we have added three teaching tools that instructors can use to generate discussion and build on the concepts explored in each chapter. These tools include:

GLOBAL PROFILES FOR SUCCESS

To get students thinking globally, this new edition includes a *Global Profile for Success* feature in each chapter. We selected companies for these profiles that students might not immediately view as companies positioned in the global workplace or those that truly represent the global workplace. The companies profiled offer a unique perspective on the content in the chapter in which they appear. For example, in Chapter 5 we focus on interpersonal communication. The company selected for this chapter's profile is the Virgin Group, an internationally recognized company with operations in 29 countries. The Virgin Group's website emphasizes "responsible business practise [as] an integral part of the Virgin culture—ensuring it is part of every individual's role and responsibility." By highlighting the actual corporate policies and ideology espoused on corporate websites, students see that the techniques, strategies, processes, and concepts for communicating they read about in the pages of *Business and Professional Communication in the Global Workplace* are being practiced by the companies that they may work for someday.

FOCUS ON ETHICS

The *Focus on Ethics* boxes placed throughout the text pose ethical situations that students may encounter in the global workplace. We ask students to consider the situation from different viewpoints or perspectives. Instructors can use the situations as presented or incorporate additional elements to the situation to complicate it further. The *Focus on Ethics* scenarios can also be used as the base for writing, group, or impromptu speaking assignments.

THINKING GLOBALLY

The *Thinking Globally* boxes emphasize specific cultural situations that occur in the global workplace. For example, in Chapter 6, *Interviewing and Conscious Communication,* we ask students to imagine that they are interviewing for a job in a different country or with a company that is based in another country. To be successful, the student needs to learn about the interviewing practices of a particular country or culture. We provide an Internet site detailing interviewing practices by country. The *Thinking Globally* questions can also be used as the basis of a resume, writing, or group exercise.

CASE STUDIES

The detailed case studies we have included in each chapter allow students to put themselves in complex, workplace situations. At the end of each case study, we explain the significance of the case and walk students through a set of questions designed to expand the discussion beyond the facts presented so that students learn to consider communication situations from different viewpoints and look beyond the obvious. Students are then given options for putting what they have learned into practice.

Finally, some of you may have noticed that we have added a third author in the third edition. Jill Schiefelbein has extensive experience teaching the business and professional speaking course. She has designed an online business and professional communication course, and has developed online ancillary materials for the *Business and Professional Communication in the Global Workplace* text. She also provided input on many of the changes and revisions in this edition. Welcome, Jill.

WHAT IS INSIDE

Our goal throughout this text has been to incorporate the best academic approaches with the most up-to-date skill set on the market. We have found that students who receive basic instruction in researching, organizing, and delivering informative and persuasive presentations will find that they are far ahead of their peers in the workplace who lack this training. And while it is possible to learn how to interview, work in small groups or on a team, or communicate interpersonally on the job, those who develop these skills in this classroom will find themselves prepared to lead and succeed in the workplace, where others can merely follow. And of course, no instruction in business and professional communication would be complete without training in listening, verbal and nonverbal communication, the components of the communication process, and an introduction to communication theory.

In addition to introducing students to the topics listed above, we provide:

- a theoretical orientation to guide each chapter, derived from current research in *mindful* and *ethical* communication practices within a global context.
- a consistent model for guiding the communication process called CCCD— *choose* (a communication goal and strategy), *create* (the message), *coordinate* (with other people), and *deliver* (the message).
- integrated materials and examples of *cultural diversity* and *gender differences* in most chapters.
- a focus on *information technologies* to underscore how e-mail exchanges, cross-company networking, the use of the Internet to find information and conduct research, the use of PowerPoint to develop presentations, and the use of the telephone to conduct initial employment interviews intersect with everyday interpersonal, group, team, and presentational business contexts.
- a *focus on ethics* that combines a posed dilemma with discussion questions for each chapter
- an emphasis on practical exercises that come from actual business consulting experience

Welcome to *Business and Professional Communication in the Global Workplace*. It is our sincere hope that this book is a useful and valuable resource for the class and in the future. Good luck in the course and in all of your future endeavors in the global workplace!

H. L. "Bud" Goodall
Sandra Goodall
Jill Schiefelbein

ACKNOWLEDGMENTS

Books are rarely written without a strong support group in the background cheering on the author(s) and making space for their work. This is especially true when it comes to writing a third edition. We are very lucky to have in our lives a large and loud group of supporters. First, we would like to thank our editor, Monica Eckman, who championed a third edition of the book and enthusiastically supported its new "global" direction. And Kimberly Gengler, our assistant editor, whose patience and gentle prodding was as appreciated as the excitement she showed every time we sent her a new chapter.

We would also like to thank Bud's wonderful staff at ASU—Karen, Sue, Rosemary, Lynn, Heather, Barbara, Michele, Carol, and Jordon, Bud's technical wizard. While they may not have contributed directly to the writing, they do such a fantastic job every day and make it possible for Bud to carve out a bit of time to do what he loves—*write*. A special thanks to Belle Edson, the undergraduate director of the HDSHC, and to Angela Trethewey, for adopting the book and providing us with much needed input.

And to Sandra's unpaid, but no less appreciated support staff—THANKS! To our wonderful son Nic, who never hesitates to throw in a load of laundry or run the vacuum when he sees that we are working hard to meet a deadline. And to Mac and James, for helping Nic out and keeping him entertained. And to Seth, for being way too smart—good luck at Harvard! Thanks to Tori, who knows exactly when to break up the tedium with tales about life in Auburn, which she owns. Thanks too to Vikki, for offering examples from her practice and numerous cups of coffee along the way. And, to Martha and Clarence, who have encouraged us for the past twenty years to "keep writing" and "make some money."

Thanks to the Schiefelbeins—Paul, Claudia, and Scot, for sharing their workplace successes and frustrations, and for always being there to listen. And to Raul, who always helps me see both sides of any situation and is a constant source of support. And finally, thanks to my students, who, over the span of fifteen business and professional communication class offerings, provided the input that helped shape the content in this edition.

COMMUNICATION FOUNDATIONS

"Globalization isn't a choice. It's a reality. There is just one global market today, and the only way you can grow at the speed your people want to grow is by tapping into the global stock and bond markets, by seeking out multinationals to invest in your country and by selling into the global trading system what your factories produce."

Robert Rubin[1]

BREAKTHROUGH SKILLS FOR A GLOBAL WORKPLACE

CHAPTER **1**

You are at your desk, which was made in Sweden, sitting on a chair from Taiwan, and working on a laptop built with American ingenuity and parts from China, Singapore, Japan, and the U.S. You are typing an e-mail to a client in St. Paul, Minnesota, whose main office is located in London. You live and work in Tampa, Florida, for an engineering firm located in Rouen, France. You shop, blog, and play online games with people from all over the world. The global workplace affects everything you do as a worker, consumer of goods and entertainment, and inhabitant of the world.

Even if you never leave your 10×10 foot dorm room, your college campus, or your hometown, you still engage in the global workplace each and every day. What is the global workplace? Thomas Friedman, author of *The World is Flat (2005)*, optimistically describes the global workplace as a level playing field where competitors around the globe receive an equal opportunity to succeed. Friedman goes on to say that globalization evolved from the:

> democratizations of technology, finance and information—which have changed how we communicate, how we invest and how we look at the world—gave birth to all the key elements in today's globalization system ... They are what created the networks, which enabled each of us now to reach around the world and become super-empowered individuals. They are what blew away all the old ideologies, other than free-market capitalism. They are what created the incredible new efficiencies that every business either had to adapt to or die. They are what lowered the barriers to entry in virtually every business. They are what is forcing people to change from thinking locally first and then globally, to thinking globally first and then locally.[2]

---

[1] Quoted in Thomas L. Friedman, *The Lexus and the Olive Tree: Understanding Globalization,* (New York: Farrar, Strauss, and Giroux, 1999), 93.

[2] Friedman, 117.

3

In the global workplace, success can no longer be defined by geographical conquests or constraints or through references to national boundaries or borders. In the global workplace, we achieve success through conscious communication, applied technology, and strong knowledge and skill base. To achieve success in the global workplaces, individuals must develop a set of breakthrough skills that enable them to compete in an ever-expanding global environment.

What is a "**breakthrough skill**"? For business and professional communicators, it is a skill, or skill set, that allows people to act purposefully and competently with others in a global environment. Increasingly, traditional and emerging professions—law, accounting, architecture, nursing, engineering, education, design, and business—seek graduates who can "adapt quickly to organizational and technological change and understand the needs of the communities in which they work and live."[3] Those competing in the global workplace should develop breakthrough skills with four goals in mind:

- developing a global mindset
- practicing cultural agility
- managing relationships
- creating opportunity

Let's explore these goals in more detail.

Developing a Global Mindset. Having a **global mindset** means working in or leading global organizations that exist within a variety of different social, economic, and political environments. It also means demonstrating the ability to adapt to the communication needs and expectations of people from different cultures. In a global workplace and a world marked by difference, what you know *and how you communicate* determine your success.

Practicing Cultural Agility. Practicing **cultural agility** means recognizing that important communication differences exist among people from different cultures. It also means recognizing that how you communicate may, and probably will, differ from how others communicate. Acknowledging the gap that exists between your communication style and the communication style and expectations of others is one way to become more culturally agile. Another way to develop cultural knowledge and understandings of the **cultures** you encounter is to promote shared understanding. Developing knowledge of people from the cultures you work with allows you to be flexible, rather than sticking to a strict American style of communicating based on your own cultural expectations.

Managing Relationships. Managing relationships means collaborating with others in a way that ensures *everyone* involved achieves their professional goals. It also means promoting a healthy, productive, and agreeable work environment for that collaboration. One key element of managing communication in a global environment is having the ability to work with ambiguity and avoid the misunderstandings that often occur in a global workplace.

Creating Opportunity. Creating opportunity means identifying market trends, employee and customer needs, and ways to monitor costs and add value to what

---

[3] Excerpt from MIT website discussion of how MIT "must change" for MIT graduates to become future leaders of society, not just well-trained scientists. The website focuses on education for life and can be viewed at: http://www.web.mit.edu/committees/sll/f2.html.

Dynamic Graphics/Creatas Images/Jupiter Images

you do. One of the ways you add value is to improve how you communicate with suppliers, customers, employees, and management. It also means developing the ability to analyze opportunities that arise locally and globally.

Notice that the common theme among these four workplace goals is the ability to communicate globally. Global business and professional communication skills go beyond the ability to engage in casual talk within organizations. Trying to resolve business situations with the communication values you learned at home, or skills you routinely use with your friends, may backfire in the workplace. It is important at the outset to understand that business settings require specific communication skills and knowledge.

GLOBAL PROFILE FOR SUCCESS—FROM MILWAUKEE TO THE WORLD

Johnson Controls began in Milwaukee, Wisconsin, in1885 as a manufacturer and service provider for automatic temperature regulation systems for buildings. In 1978, Johnson Controls began to acquire several automotive component companies, positioning it as a leading manufacturer and service provider for automotive batteries, seating, plastics, and console interior components.

Thinking globally is not a new concept for Johnson Controls, which opened its first European sales office in 1910. Today, it has 1,300 offices worldwide and employs 140,000 people around the globe. If you go to work today as an engineer, salesperson, computer programmer, or marketing executive for Johnson Controls, it is a safe bet that you will need to think globally and have the skills needed to operate successfully in the global workplace.

Explore Johnson Controls' website: http://www.johnsoncontrols.com/publish/us/en/about.html.

What can you learn about thinking globally from the Johnson Controls website? What skills are necessary to succeed in the global workplace as a member of the Johnson Controls team?

THINKING GLOBALLY—WHY IS IT IMPORTANT TO KNOW HOW TO COMMUNICATE IN A GLOBAL WORKPLACE?

Many of you will be working nurses, designers, professionals in marketing or sales, architects, or engineers. You may be planning a career in law, politics, health care, or on Wall Street. How does developing the ability to communicate in a global workplace apply to your chosen career? Can you communicate effectively and be successful without these skills? As you move through the text, keep your chosen field in mind. Analyze each skill and piece of information introduced to see how it can benefit you within the global workplace you are preparing for.

WHAT IS BUSINESS AND PROFESSIONAL COMMUNICATION?

Business and professional communication is a shorthand term that refers to all forms of speaking, listening, relating, writing, and responding in the workplace, both human and electronically mediated. **Human communication** includes informal conversations, interviews, group and team meetings, informative briefings and speeches, sales pitches, and persuasive presentations. **Electronically mediated communication** includes phone conversations, text messages, satellite conferences, e-mail, instant messaging, personal and company web pages, and the use of the Internet for business communication through social networking and e-commerce. As you will learn, business and professional situations require communication skills that are both appropriate to and effective for the workplace and that address the internal and external audiences inherent in the global workplace.

We designed this textbook to provide you with the breakthrough skills, knowledge, and experiences required for successful global business and professional communication. Our goal is to help you understand the new professional standards for global communication competency and to help you develop the skills and confidence to move ahead in whatever business or profession you choose.

CASE STUDY 1 | **ANALYZING COMMUNICATION IN THE GLOBAL WORKPLACE**

Maria hurried down the hall, her arms full of papers, reports, and folders. She was nervous about her first teleconference with her new team. The team was working on a new design project for a chain of stores in Singapore. Maria, the newest addition to the team, analyzed the expanding market the new stores would fill and she was determined to make a good impression during her first meeting between the Singapore and Los Angeles team. When she entered the conference room, she was relieved to find no one else was there or had appeared online. Maria

spent the next fifteen minutes arranging her information on the table in front of her. She nervously checked her watch. A few minutes before 2:00 the members of the Singapore team appeared on the screen. At 2:00, Kiran, the team leader, began the conference from her office in Singapore. Maria was surprised to see that most of the members of the U.S. team had not shown up for the meeting. She listened as Kiran welcomed her and made a joke about how the American team members were often late and that is was refreshing to see one of them there on time. The rest of the U.S.

continued

CASE STUDY 1 | **ANALYZING COMMUNICATION IN THE GLOBAL WORKPLACE** *continued*

team straggled in as Kiran asked the team members to recap for Maria their assignment and the progress each of them had made.

Given how well she had prepared, Maria immediately cut her off. "No need, Kiran. I've read all of the progress reports from the past month." She pulled out the folder and waved it in front of the camera.

Kiran smiled. "I appreciate your efforts, but I think you'd benefit from hearing about the project firsthand from each team member, and learning a little more about who you are going to be working with first."

Maria, who would not be sidetracked, said, "Why don't I recap what I've read and you all can fill in any blanks? Although I'm sure you've all worked really hard on this project, I have a couple of ideas that might speed things along." Maria then launched into a twenty-minute recap of what she had read.

When she finished, Kiran smiled into her camera and said, "Thank you, Maria, for recapping all of the ideas we have already thought about and discarded for one reason or another. Now, Chan, would you begin filling Maria in on what wasn't in the memos and reports she read?"

Maria's face grew hot and red. She sank as far into her chair as she possibly could, obstructing her view of

the camera and hopefully the others' view of her. Wow, had she read the memos wrong! She spent the rest of the meeting pretending to make notes and avoiding eye contact with those in the room and across the globe. After the meeting, she gathered up the materials in front of her and fled back to her cube. She never got the chance to "meet" her new team members, but she definitely made an impression.

We include this case study to highlight how a lack of understanding of the fundamental goals of communication can be detrimental to one's success in the global workplace. Successful communicators realize that none of the fundamental goals of global communication—having a global mindset, practicing cultural agility, managing relationships, and creating opportunities—occurs in a vacuum. Successful communicators recognize that communication is a cumulative activity that builds understandings and relationships over time, rather than a series of snapshots that freeze understanding in place. Maria did not recognize the importance of these functions of business communication. One way Maria could have better understood and evaluated her situation would have been to become a more conscious communicator.

COMPONENTS OF CONSCIOUS COMMUNICATION

One of the comments we often hear from beginning students in courses such as this one is, "Why should I study communication? After all, I've been doing it all my life!" Our response is that although almost everyone is fortunate enough to acquire an ability to communicate, not everyone learns how to communicate effectively. Still fewer people acquire the knowledge and skill to develop communication competencies specific to the workplace.

To learn about communication means more than simply doing it. It also means studying it and acquiring knowledge about it. To study business and professional communication means to read and discuss the important ideas that have shaped our most advanced understandings about this vital skill. After careful study, application of this knowledge should help improve your communicative abilities. As a result of having successfully completed a course specifically designed to improve both your understanding and skills, you should be a more conscious communicator.

To help you begin our investigation of business and professional communication, and to help you begin to think more intelligently and consciously about

FOCUS ON ETHICS

What are ethics? Ethics is often described as the moral compass we use to guide our lives. How do personal and business ethics differ? How do individuals blend their personal ethics to the ethical principles espoused or implied by the companies they work for? Throughout the text, these breakout boxes highlight the moral or ethical problems that can arise in a business environment.

Did Maria handle her introduction to the team ethically? An important component of ethical communication is to assist others by providing the information needed to make informed choices. Were there things Kiran could have done to ease Maria's first meeting with the team? How would you have handled Maria's first meeting differently?

communication in the global workplace, we offer the following list of conscious-communication components:

- Conscious communication is mindful.
- Conscious communication displays awareness of communication as a process.
- Conscious communication respects diversity.
- Conscious communication requires balancing strategy, ethics, and outcomes.

Conscious communication is mindful. Communicating mindfully means that you take into consideration the needs and expectations of others, as well as contexts (Damasio, 1999; Langer, 1989). Mindful communicators recognize that while it is important to use strategic communication to reach goals, it is equally important to reach business and professional goals ethically.

Conscious communication displays awareness of communication as a process. Although we use the terms "episode" or "event" to describe an act of communication in the workplace, it is more accurate to think of communication as an ongoing process. One communication event leads into another, expanding the context of communication throughout an organization.

Conscious communication respects diversity. Sensitivity to others includes a profound awareness of **diversity**: cultural, gender, racial, religious, age, and socioeconomic differences. To be a mindful communicator means to research and respond intelligently to the differences you encounter in the workplace.

Conscious communication requires being strategic in your formulation of messages while also being aware of the ethical and business consequences of delivering your message. In today's global business environment, conscious communication is essential to success. Being conscious means that we are at once "an observer, a perceiver, a knower, a thinker, and a potential actor" (Damasio, 1999, p. 10). When we talk about **strategic communication**, we are referring to communication planned with specific audiences and specific intentions in mind, communication that is cognizant of individual and cultural differences. As we saw in the case study, Maria was unaware of her audience, she did not take the time to understand the goals of the meeting—having her team members bring her up to speed and allow her an opportunity to meet everyone she would be working with and be integrated into the team. Had she understood and focused on the team leader's goals during the teleconference, she would not have so severely limited her ability to communicate consciously during the meeting and in the future.

To successfully engage in conscious communication in a global environment, you need to choose, create, coordinate, and deliver your message. We will use this four-step choose, create, coordinate, and deliver (CCCD) process for conscious communication throughout the remainder of the book. Let's look at each of these components in more detail.

The CCCD Process			
Choose	**Create**	**Coordinate**	**Deliver**
a communication strategy	your message	the communication event	the message

FIGURE 1.1

STEP 1: CHOOSING A COMMUNICATION GOAL

Choosing an effective communication goal and identifying the objective you hope to achieve requires developing an awareness of the possible messages and *interpretations* of messages in any business situation. When we choose a goal, we analyze the possible outcomes of a communication situation. It is essential to apply a global mindset when choosing communication goals. In a global workplace we must be cognizant of the many different audiences or cultures that will encounter our messages. Different messages and different audiences require different communication goals designed to increase the likelihood of successful communication.

An appropriate goal for interpersonal communication might not be appropriate for a formal presentation. A goal that applies to an e-mail might be inappropriate for a team meeting. Individual goals might conflict with team or group goals. Let's look back at the example of the meeting with Maria and Kiran above, Kiran's goals for the meeting were to introduce Maria to her fellow team members and bring Maria up to speed on the project. Maria's goals were to show that she had reviewed the team's progress and had the answer to its problems. Was she successful? Might she have been more successful if she had started with the goal of becoming a good team member, or the goal of understanding the team's progress, rather than jumping straight to the goal of problem solving? Might Maria have fared better in the meeting if she had taken into consideration the difference in communication style between those in the Singapore office and those in the U.S. office? Maria's embarrassment was a direct result of not practicing conscious communication. She did not make a conscious effort to choose a goal that took into account the collaborative nature of teamwork or the team's communication history. Moreover, she skipped the creating and coordinating steps, both integral parts of conscious communication, and jumped to the end stage in the CCCD process: delivery. The result was negative for Maria and her team members.

Choosing a communication goal involves conducting a complete assessment of the following:

- Audience needs and expectations—what is the audience hoping to achieve by reading your e-mail, listening to your presentation, or engaging in a conversation? Do they need information, assurance, direction, or assistance? Or are they just having some fun? Do they expect solutions, problem solving, guidance, or an apology? Or just recognition of the creativity in their sense of humor?
- Likely communication outcomes—what outcome is the audience hoping for? What are the possible communication outcomes for the goal you have chosen? Could there be negative outcomes from pursing your goal? If so, you need to rethink your goal.
- The criteria against which you will measure your success—how will you know if you have been successful? What type of feedback do you expect from your audience?

Once you have chosen a goal, you can begin to create a message with your specific goal and audience in mind.

STEP 2: CREATING THE MESSAGE

Creating the message is the process of developing a plan designed to reach a specific audience and carry out the strategy you developed in Step 1. To a large extent, this part of the process is about organizing a message for a specific audience. You need to plan what you are going to say first, how to develop your ideas, and how to summarize and conclude your message with your audience's needs, expectations, outcomes, and feedback in mind. In Maria's situation, rather than create a message that portrayed her as a team player, she created a message that set her apart from the team, highlighting what the team had failed to accomplish. If Maria had spent more time creating a team-based message, the outcome for both Maria and the team would have been positive. Another option available to Maria in the first meeting was to simply listen. Listening is a powerful communication strategy and an important skill that we will discuss later in detail.

Creating a message, establishing the agenda for a meeting, or planning involves:

- Determining the best organization for your message, based on the goal set in Step 1: Choosing a Communication Goal.
- Developing support for each point within the message—a message should follow an organized plan. For each point you make in your message, you need to follow up with support for that point. We discuss how to establish main points, sub-points, and support in detail in later chapters.
- Crafting an introduction and conclusion, if appropriate. Successful communicators orient their audience to the topic and the points of discussion,

and offer a recap in their introductions and conclusions. We discuss how to establish introductions and conclusion in detail in later chapters.

Once you have created your message, it is important to coordinate with other members of your team, department, or organization.

STEP 3: COORDINATING WITH OTHERS

Conscious communication requires input from a variety of sources. It also requires a different way of thinking about success in organizations. The old model for success in business was the "Lone Ranger" model (James, 1996). The Lone Ranger rode in on a white horse to save a department or organization from disaster, and then rode back out of town into the radiant sunset. This model worked well when businesses operated in isolation from other businesses, but that does not work well in a global business environment. The new model for success in organizations is more akin to the Three Musketeers model: "All for one, and one for all." For this collaborative process to work, you and the other members of your organization must trust that you will keep one another informed, locally and globally. You must work to create an inclusive organizational community. Unfortunately, in the example above, Maria chose the Lone Ranger model, and did not understand the importance of coordinating with her new team members.

Coordinating is the act of bringing together everyone required to successfully deliver and evaluate the success of your message. Coordinating with others is an ongoing organizational activity and, in some cases, may take place concurrently with *Step 2: Creating a Message.* For example, once you have determined your goals, outcomes, and criteria, you may need to check with other members of the team to ensure presentations representing the team reflect the team's goals. Or, you may not have all the information you need to present an idea, so you may need to coordinate with other departments or team members to gather all the information needed. As you coordinate information, you will be creating and revising your message. Another important aspect of coordinating is checking to make sure that all the appropriate members of the organization are aware of the timing of a specific communication event. You should make sure everyone knows where and when the event is scheduled and that the information to be presented represents every aspect of the organization fairly. Coordinating is an activity that also involves making all the necessary room and equipment reservations well in advance and confirming those reservations before your event.

To avoid Maria's fate, and after completing Steps 1 and 2, you should follow these guidelines for coordinating with others:

- Assemble as much information as you can about how your agenda, plan, or position fits within the mission and goals of the organization.
- Ask the team or meeting leader if you are unsure about the purpose of a meeting, memo, or presentation.
- Communicate with other members of the organization (teams, departments, supervisors, and managers) your need for input and feedback.
- Respect the professional and personal boundaries of others.
- Adapt your message, episode, or event accordingly.

Now you are ready to deliver your message.

STEP 4: DELIVERING THE MESSAGE

Imagine if Maria had chosen a communication goal, created an effective message, and coordinated with her team leader. Her message would have been much better received! The final step in CCCD, delivery, is really *the* most crucial, because in many business situations, the payoff depends on the communication performance. Effective delivery requires the following:

- Practice
- Receiving and evaluating feedback
- Incorporating feedback into your delivery

You can apply the CCCD model—choosing, creating, coordinating, and delivery—to many communication situations. Following the CCCD model before a communication event allows you to maximize your communication options and effectiveness in global business and professional situations. We use the CCCD model throughout the text to enhance your understanding of the communication process and to emphasize that communication is a *process* that, while ongoing, consists of communication episodes which have a distinct beginning, middle, and ending. Omitting part of the process can result in miscommunication in the workplace.

SUMMARY

Chapter 1 introduces the idea of conscious communication in the global workplace. We began by exploring why communication is a "breakthrough skill" for the twenty-first century. We then discussed the components and the functions of communication in business and professional contexts.

Next, we outlined and provided a conceptual overview of the CCCD process for improving communication at work. Finally, we provided a list of the principles of conscious communication in an effort to begin organizing your understanding of business and professional communication.

 SKILL BUILDER WORKSHOP

We have all experienced moments of apprehension before giving a presentation. Even the most reticent speakers can learn to be more comfortable by following a few simple steps before giving a presentation or speaking up in team meetings. So, before you even begin preparing for your first presentation, we want to start you off with a checklist that will help you reduce your anxiety and increase your confidence as a speaker.

Know your topic: When choosing a topic to speak about, select one you know something about and that interests you. The better you know the topic, the more comfortable you will be presenting the information and answering questions after your talk.

The more interested in the topic you are, the easier it will be to speak with enthusiasm. If you are asked to speak on an unfamiliar topic, find a way to relate it to your experience, or use the Internet or library to research the topic to increase your knowledge of the subject matter and your comfort level.

Prepare your talk: Use the CCCD method described briefly above and in detail throughout this book to prepare your talk. CCCD will help you cover all the bases, from research to delivery. Knowing that you have developed a talk that includes all the elements of a good presentation will give you confidence before you even step up to the podium.

SKILL BUILDER WORKSHOP *continued*

Practice: One of the biggest mistakes people make when giving a presentation is to forget the vital element of practice. You can develop a perfect presentation with an amazing digital slideshow for support and have a superb introduction and closing, but if you haven't practiced, the presentation might not help you reach your goals. Practice, preferably in front of a few other people, allows you to see what points need to be honed, which lines work and which don't, and whether your great opening and closing resonate as well aloud as they did on paper or in your head. Practice also allows you to develop a naturalness with the material that removes the stiffness of words on paper and enlivens your presentation with the fluidity of the spoken word. Every time you practice, you gain more control over your presentation and increase your confidence.

Speech Builder Express Workshop

Jot down a few biographical notes about yourself for a speech of introduction for your class. Your speech should include three to five basic facts about yourself and at least two interesting aspects of your personality or background that might be surprising, given your biography. Give your speech to two of your classmates. Ask your classmates for feedback. What did you learn about your ability to give a speech? Did speaking off-the-cuff increase your nervousness? Were the "surprising" aspects of your life well received? Why or why not?

Now go to Speech Builder Express. Select Introductory Speech from the menu. Write a brief speech of introduction using the outline provided. Your speech should include at least three basic facts about who you are and at least two additional interesting facts that will help others remember you. Your speech should be no more than two minutes long. You should include the feedback you were given from your impromptu speech in class. Practice your speech at least three times before your next class. Present your new speech to two different students. How did following an organization plan and practicing your speech change your speaking experience? Were you less nervous and apprehensive about speaking when you had a plan? Did practicing your speech help boost your confidence?

COMMUNICATING IN PROFESSIONAL CONTEXTS ONLINE

All of the following chapter review materials are available in an electronic format on either the *Business and Professional Communication in the Global Workplace* Resource Center or the book's companion website. Online you'll find chapter learning objects, flashcards of glossary terms, InfoTrack® College Edition Activities, weblinks, quizzes, and more.

WHAT YOU SHOULD HAVE LEARNED

Now that you have read Chapter 1, you should be able to do the following:

- Discuss the evolution from a local to a global workplace.

- Discuss the role of culture in a global workplace.
- Describe the four goals of communicating in a global workplace.
- Discuss the relevance of studying business and professional communication.
- Provide a basic definition of *communication* in a business and professional context.
- Describe the four *breakthrough skills* and their relationships to communication in the global workplace.
- Discuss the example of Maria and the ways she could improve her communication and team performance.

- Outline the CCCD process and discuss how it might apply to interpersonal communication, team communication, or a formal presentation

- Discuss what *conscious communication* means and describe its three components.

KEY TERMS

breakthrough skill *4*
business and professional communication *6*
CCCD *9*

conscious communication *8*
cultural agility *4*
culture *4*
diversity *8*

electronically mediated communication *6*
global mindset *4*
human communication *6*
strategic communication *8*

WRITING AND CRITICAL THINKING

The following activities can be completed online or submitted to your instructor.

Choose one of the following activities:

1. Interview a manager, CEO, or business owner. Describe the course you are taking. Ask the person you are interviewing how important global communication skills are to his or her industry. Have the person rate the importance of interpersonal, organizational, team, speaking, written communication, and presentational skills for his or her employees. What did you learn?

2. Obtain a memo or report from an organization. This could be an e-mail or memo from your workplace or something available on the Internet. If you use an e-mail from an organization, be sure you have permission. Analyze the memo or e-mail using the information in this chapter. What did your analysis reveal? What steps in the CCCD process did the writer use? What steps were ignored? How could the memo be improved using CCCD?

3. Working with your classmates as a group, determine the communication strategy for the following scenario:

   Mary has worked hard for XYZ Corporation for five years. The last two years she has received outstanding performance appraisals by both her manager, Kim, and Kim's director, Jamie. A few months ago, the employees of XYZ Corporation received notice that the company had been acquired by an Australian-based accounting firm. At her annual review, Mary was elated to be promoted not one, but two steps. A few days after her promotion, Kim called her into her office and told her that because her salary was already in line with the senior tax analyst position at the new parent company, she could not give Mary a raise to go along with her recent promotion. She told Mary she had pleaded with Jamie, who in turn had "gone to bat" for Mary with the new company president, who responded with a firm "No." Mary likes her job, but she wants the raise she would have received if the companies had not merged.

   Given what you have learned in this chapter, what should Mary do to make her case?

4. The expansion of global markets since the beginning of the twenty-first century has increasingly affected relationships in the business and professional world. As sales manager of XYZ Corporation, you have been transferred to another region of the world to explore new sales opportunities. In preparing for your move, choose a country (other than the U.S.) and use the Internet to research and prepare a presentation for your class identifying the key aspects of the culture in your chosen country and how it could impact your interactions and sales strategy.

PRACTICING COMMUNICATION IN PROFESSIONAL CONTEXTS

Do you have the communication skills you need to survive in a global economy? Do you regularly use e-mail? Have you written memos or reports? Do you have specific research skills? How are your interpersonal skills? Are you prepared to communicate professionally? What are your strengths and weaknesses?

Office Team is one of the world's leaders in specialized administrative staffing, with more than two hundred offices internationally. They developed the following questionnaire to assess a candidate's ability to compete and communicate in the workplace (*Canadian Manager*, 1999). The following questions will help you determine if you have the necessary people skills to be successful. For some of the questions, you may agree with more than one response. However, try to select the answer you most agree with. Circle your answers below.

THE QUESTIONS

1. Your colleagues have been passed over for a promotion, and you've been informed that you got it. But the announcement date becomes delayed due to your supervisor's other priorities. In the meantime, there is growing speculation among the staff, and one of your coworkers asks if you've heard anything about it. What approach do you take?
   a. Tell the colleague that you got it, but ask that he or she be discreet about it.
   b. Wait it out until your supervisor is ready.
   c. Tell a few select coworkers that you got it, but ask that they be discreet about it.
   d. Tell all coworkers involved.
   e. Tell your supervisor there is a growing discussion and you've been asked about it.

2. Your primary method of organizing work is to:
   a. Continuously reestablish priorities as needed based on the requirements of the day.
   b. Complete yesterday's priority list before reviewing new assignments for the day.
   c. Try as best you can to complete one project before accepting another one.
   d. Prioritize each day's work and stick to it regardless of additional projects that may distract you.

3. Which one of the following statements best describes your beliefs or approach?
   a. I generally like to avoid conflict whenever possible.
   b. Allowing emotions to enter into business decisions is unavoidable.
   c. I'm good at logically thinking through a problem.
   d. Making a relatively quick decision is always better than waiting to make a decision.

4. Your supervisor has given you an assignment, but you're unfamiliar with certain aspects of the project in which others in the department have more experience. You:
   a. Spend whatever time necessary on your own, getting at least a cursory knowledge of the unknown areas.
   b. Seek the assistance of the other experts and, in turn, offer your expertise to them.
   c. Tell your supervisor up front that you are not familiar with those aspects.
   d. Suggest to your supervisor that you handle only the familiar part.

5. Which one of the following statements best reflects your beliefs or approach?
   a. Success seems to come more easily to some people than others.
   b. If my closest friends and family agree on what's best for my career, I usually rely on their advice.

c. My employer is in the best position to decide which career path is best for me.

d. Career success is a direct result of my own efforts, not the efforts of others.

6. The best way to manage people is to:
   a. Make it very clear that you're in charge.
   b. Solicit input from them before making major decisions.
   c. Share your expertise by offering your direct supervision to as many people as possible.
   d. Set your goals before you begin the project and communicate them loudly and clearly to the team before getting started.

7. Which one of the following statements best reflects your beliefs or approach?
   a. When managing a project, I like all the team members to remain on task with the original approach.
   b. People with greater seniority in a company are in the best position to generate useful ideas.
   c. When managing a project, I encourage people to share differing opinions.
   d. If the majority of people believe in a certain approach, it's probably the best one.

8. Which of the following best describes the ingredients of effective persuasion?
   a. Remaining steadfast in your beliefs and not wavering.
   b. Being forceful and vocal in your opinion.
   c. Being pleasant as much as possible.
   d. Having strong listening skills.

9. One of your closest friends is in a business that you rely on as one of several vendors. You inadvertently give a little more information to your friend than you give to the other vendors. You realize that you have now given her an unfair advantage. You:
   a. Explain to your friend that you shouldn't have released this information and ask her not to make it a factor in her bid.
   b. Take into consideration when evaluating the bids that your friend had more information.

c. Give other vendors the same information and run the risk of appearing disorganized.
d. Give information you did not give to your friend to other vendors so they also benefit.

10. Your supervisor praises you publicly on the results of a successful project. You received invaluable help on this particular assignment from a coworker who wasn't named. You:
    a. Approach the coworker later and apologize.
    b. Tell your boss that credit should also go to the coworker.
    c. Weigh how important it is to bring up the coworker's involvement.
    d. Write your coworker a thank-you note.

11. Which statement most accurately reflects your beliefs?
    a. Writing will become less important due to technological advancements.
    b. Writing is a skill that is innate, not learned.
    c. An experienced writer uses large words and long sentences.
    d. An experienced writer tries to use fewer words.

12. Describe your verbal communication abilities.
    a. I'd rather walk on hot coals than speak to a large group, but I do fine one-on-one.
    b. I'm a much better oral communicator than writer.
    c. When I speak to a group, people seem to grasp my point quickly.
    d. I'm relatively talkative and not shy.

13. Which of the following best describes your approach to brainstorm meetings?
    a. I'm a risk taker and generally don't like to "follow the pack" in my thinking.
    b. I'm good at building on the ideas of others.
    c. I've always implemented ideas well and had good follow-up.
    d. I'd rather offer a feasible, well-thought-out idea than just any suggestion.

14. Which of the following statements best reflects your beliefs or approach?
    → a. I believe that my employer should provide me with the training I need.
    b. I often use the Internet to research information during nonbusiness hours.
    ✗. I believe that a person's college/university education will provide a comprehensive source of knowledge for the balance of his or her career.
    d. If I rely heavily on my supervisor's expertise, I'll get the best training.

15. Which one of the following best describes you or your beliefs?
    ✗. When the going gets tough, I often make an effort to reduce tension through laughter.
    b. Good-natured teasing of others creates a less tense environment and encourages camaraderie.
    c. People who succeed in most companies tend to take their work very seriously.
    d. I've always been a good joke teller.

ANSWER KEY

Each question was designed to test a particular people skill. The skill tested by each question is listed below.

1. Diplomacy/Discretion
2. Organization
3. Problem-solving abilities
4. Team-player skills
5. Accountability/Initiative
6. Leadership
7. Open-mindedness/Flexibility
8. Persuasion
9. Ethics
10. Honesty
11. Written communication
12. Verbal communication
13. Creativity
14. Educational interests
15. Humor

1. Diplomacy/Discretion
a. Sorry; your supervisor wasn't ready and should make the decision on timing.
b. Problematic; your supervisor should be made aware of the staff's queries, as discussions and speculation will only grow.
c. Unfortunately, this could hurt the morale of others.
d. Very risky; it's your manager's responsibility, not yours.
e. Right! This is something your boss should be made aware of and be able to act on to everyone's benefit. In the 2009 office, you'll take a broader look at the company's overall welfare because you'll benefit more directly from it. Companies will offer such programs as performance-based pay and stock ownership to help retain highly skilled workers.

2. Organization
a. Bingo! If new projects come in, you must evaluate their importance relative to existing priorities. In 2009 there will be more instant communication and more projects to prioritize, so this skill is crucial.
b. Often tempting, but yesterday's work may have to wait if new projects are more urgent.
c. Sorry; multitasking will be key in coming years—focusing on one assignment will be a luxury rather than the norm.
d. Oops! Such rigidity will keep you from attending to potentially more urgent projects.

3. Problem Solving
a. Who could blame you? But as interaction and communication levels increase, so will the potential for conflicts. Get ready to practice better conflict-resolution skills.
b. Sorry; in 2009 you'll have to put emotions aside. Your professional analytical abilities will be put to the test.

c. Way to go! You have the ingredients of someone who can think clearly and analytically, which is beneficial as the pace of business increases.

d. Not necessarily; although speed and efficiency will be important attributes in 2009, you may need more time and information to evaluate the best course of action.

4. **Team-Player Skills**

a. Not a bad choice—this demonstrates initiative. However, you could have worked in conjunction with the others in a team-oriented manner, saving time for the overall task.

b. Correct! As we head toward 2009, the ability to approach and help team members will be valuable, because productivity depends on continual information exchange.

c. Sorry; to find out what you'll need to know in the office of 2009 you'll be expected to show resourcefulness and initiative.

d. Careful; you need to show your supervisors as well as your peers that you're a team player.

5. **Accountability/Initiative**

a. Sorry; those who believe their success rides on factors beyond their control may need to change their thinking. In 2009, those who take charge of their careers will have the greatest number of opportunities.

b. A tough one; you want to solicit input from those who care about you, yet your major career decisions should be based primarily on your own interests and goals. In 2009, being the CEO of your own career will be more important than ever.

c. Employers can help guide you, but the ultimate expert on your career growth and satisfaction is you.

d. Hurrah! Taking charge of your career, whether you're a full-time, part-time, or project worker, will bring the greatest challenge and financial rewards.

6. **Leadership**

a. Proceed with caution! The future office environment won't allow for a command-and-control management style; employees want to contribute to making decisions and offer creative solutions.

b. Right! Skilled employees will have many career options in 2009. They'll choose opportunities in which their ideas are heard. In an increasingly competitive business world, smart managers will encourage greater participation from team members.

c. Sorry; while this may seem benevolent, this choice could indicate micromanaging technologies.

d. Almost! Although sharing your vision is an admirable management trait, allowing participation in setting goals is characteristic of a good leader.

7. **Open-mindedness/Flexibility**

a. An understandable choice, but you may need to become less rigid and allow room for modification and improvements. In 2009, rapidly changing events will make flexibility a key attribute.

b. Not necessarily; whereas more senior employees have experience on their side, ideas from more recent recruits or even consultants may provide valuable, fresh perspectives.

c. Good! This approach will give you the best thinking from your team.

d. Nice try; unfortunately, peer pressure can make some employees follow the path of least resistance, not always the most productive path.

8. **Persuasion**

a. Careful; if you become too rigid in your arguments, the other individual may become defensive. You must show interest in the beliefs of others to create open lines of communication.

b. Sorry. Intimidation or being more vocal will not convince people to see things your way; it could backfire.

c. Being pleasant and courteous will certainly help your efforts, but listening carefully is an even more valuable skill in this instance.

d. Right! The most persuasive people are those who have taken on the challenge of actively listening to other individuals to best understand their perspective and motives. With increased business demands in 2009, you'll have less time to make your own case. Practice strong listening skills with coworkers and watch the results.

9. **Ethics**

a. Caution; this may be naive, and you're not being fair to other vendors.

b. Sorry; you're still not giving other vendors the full opportunity to compete fairly.

c. Right! This could be embarrassing, but you'll know you've avoided giving preferential treatment to your friend. Ethics in business will remain critical in 2009.

d. Problematic; if you give out different information, this still won't level the playing field.

10. **Honesty**

a. A good try, but you're still accepting full credit.

b. Excellent! Your honesty and sense of team play will be appreciated more than ever in 2009 as employees work more closely in teams and are given more autonomy to make critical judgment calls.

c. Almost; you're moving in the right direction, but if you have doubts about whether something is ethical, chances are it is not, and you should take immediate steps to remedy the situation.

d. A nice gesture, but you're still falling short of appropriately sharing the credit.

11. **Written Communication**

a. Oops! There will be more e-mails than ever in 2009. Clear communication and good grammar will help you become more productive.

b. Not really; with practice and initiative, you'll improve.

c. Sorry; this may seem impressive, but good writers communicate clearly, not necessarily with big words.

d. Terrific! Keeping your writing concise will make it easier to understand and will have a greater impact. As e-mail becomes more pervasive in 2009 brevity will be valued; verbosity, counterproductive.

12. **Verbal Communication**

a. Ouch! Time to practice speaking to groups of people. You might consider joining a Toastmasters group or looking for opportunities to give speeches at your company, volunteer group, class, or other venues.

b. A good try, but the better answer would be that you can articulate your point clearly and effectively.

c. Good! You're able to present a clear message orally, an invaluable trait in 2009 when you must think on your feet, whether in a small or large group or during a videoconference.

d. Close; you may have the necessary confidence to be a good verbal communicator, but making your point clearly and concisely is the next step.

13. **Creativity**

a. You got it! In 2009, risk takers with creative ideas will be highly valued as companies compete more fiercely to come to market with innovative products and services. Are you ready to make your contribution?

b. A step in the right direction, but innovative thinking will have to start with you.

c. Sounds good, but original thinking will take you far in 2009.

d. Sounds practical, but in 2009, you'll be highly valued for taking creative risks. Your thoughts may not be well defined, but they could inspire or develop into outstanding ideas.

14. **Educational Interests**
    a. Careful; companies in 2009 will invest more in training, but workers must take the initiative to constantly upgrade skills.
    b. Yes! You demonstrated the thirst for knowledge that will make you marketable in 2009.
    c. Close; a college education is certainly beneficial. But the most successful workers in 2009 will continually upgrade technical and "soft" skills.
    d. Sorry; in 2009 you'll advance more quickly if you take it upon yourself to enhance your skills and knowledge, inside and outside of the office.

15. **Humor**
    a. Good! You have an invaluable interpersonal skill that will help smooth tensions that may arise in an instant-information environment.
    b. Sorry; humor at the expense of others is counterproductive.
    c. Sounds like a valid concept, but one of the most important ingredients in career success is the ability to laugh at oneself, putting others at ease.
    d. Great for parties, but joke telling is not quite the same as light-heartedness that reduces stress in others and offers perspective on the big picture.

SCORING

Refer to the answer key above and add up your correct responses.

13–15 correct answers

Congratulations! Your outstanding people skills will be an important contributor to your career success in 2009.

10–12 correct answers

Great. You have solid "soft" skills that will facilitate your advancement in the office of the future.

6–9 correct answers

Pretty good, but your interpersonal and communication skills may need some work.

3–5 correct answers

Start concentrating on areas you are missing. You still have time!

0–3 correct answers

Now is the time to develop your people skills. Your career success will depend on it! Pay close attention to the information in this course that addresses these areas.

YOUR PERSONAL COMMUNICATION PROFILE

Begin building your communication profile by collecting examples of good communication. These could be memos, reports, or e-mails you are particularly proud of. You could create a journal detailing conversations you have had that went particularly well. Think about communication events that went exactly as you hoped they would. Read interviews by people you respect or wish to emulate. What communication strategies do they use in their talk? How could you adapt those strategies?

"Reality isn't what it used to be."

Steiner Kvale,
The Truth about Truth

"It is no accident that most organizations learn poorly…. The way we have been taught to think and interact … create(s) fundamental learning disabilities."

Peter Senge,
The Fifth Discipline

THE EVOLUTION OF COMMUNICATION IN A GLOBAL WORKPLACE

CHAPTER **2**

In this chapter, we explore the components of the communication process. We examine how these components interact to create a communication episode, and then link these components to the evolution of theories of organization, management, and communication. Earlier models of communication depicted communication as a linear process in which one person literally "transmits" a message to another person. More recently, models show communication as a transactional process, where both sender and receiver have an influence on each other as they interact within a global cultural context. The evolution of communication models is also evident when paralleled to the development of organizational communication and management theory. These theories provide a framework for understanding organizational cultures in a global context and the importance of communicating consciously in the global workplace.

COMPONENTS OF THE BUSINESS AND PROFESSIONAL COMMUNICATION PROCESS

Early models of business communication presented communication as simply the instructions (messages) given by a boss or manager (sender) to employees (receivers). (See Figure 2.1.) This model assumed that most business communication was top-down.

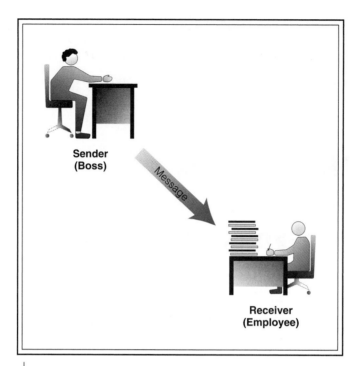

Sender
(Boss)

Message

Receiver
(Employee)

FIGURE 2.1 | TOP-DOWN MODEL OF BUSINESS COMMUNICATION

As our understanding of business communication improved, new models included the responses (feedback) employees give to bosses and to one another. (See Figure 2.2.) These newer models:

- Recognized the possibility for misunderstandings caused by disruptions (noise) in, or misinterpretations of, a message.
- Introduced the idea that messages are conveyed in different ways (channels), via airwaves (sound) or light waves (sight).
- Expanded the idea of "channel" to include electronically mediated methods of message delivery, such as radio, television, computers, and satellites, as well as the full range of print media, such as office memos and letters, newspapers, magazines, advertising flyers and brochures, and books.
- Added the physical, historical, and cultural environments (context) that inform a communication situation or episode.

Today, when we speak of the "components of a communication model," we include all of the terms: *sender, receiver, message, channel, noise, feedback*, and *context* in the communication model. (See Figure 2.3.) Let's take a look at these components in more detail.

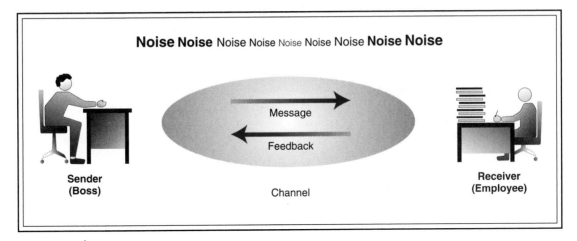

Noise Noise Noise Noise Noise Noise Noise **Noise Noise**

Message

Feedback

**Sender
(Boss)**

Channel

**Receiver
(Employee)**

FIGURE 2.2 | CURRENT MODEL OF BUSINESS COMMUNICATION

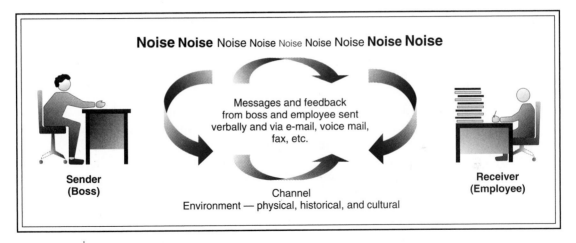

Noise Noise Noise Noise Noise Noise Noise **Noise Noise**

Messages and feedback
from boss and employee sent
verbally and via e-mail, voice mail,
fax, etc.

**Sender
(Boss)**

Channel
Environment — physical, historical, and cultural

**Receiver
(Employee)**

FIGURE 2.3 | UPDATED MODEL OF BUSINESS COMMUNICATION

SENDER

The **sender** is the originator or source of a message. In the earliest organizational models, the sender was a boss or a superior. We now realize that messages originate from a variety of sources, at all levels, both inside and *outside* an organization. For example, a customer making a complaint to a department store customer service representative is the sender—the originator of a message—to the customer service representative.

RECEIVER

The **receiver** is the person to whom the sender directs the message. In early organizational models, this person was an employee. Today we realize that everyone in an organization can and does receive messages. For example, the customer service representative in the example above is the receiver of the customer's complaint. However, the customer service representative may, in turn, report that complaint to any number of people in the organization—the manager of the customer service department, the manager of the department where the product was sold to the customer, coworkers in other departments. Indeed, the customer service representative may even "report" the complaint to those outside the organization, to friends and family members, when talking or texting about their day. Whoever receives an account of the exchange becomes a receiver—intended or unintended—of the message.

MESSAGES

The **message** is what the sender says and does during a communication episode. Messages are both verbal *and* nonverbal. Together, these message sources help us arrive at the meaning of a message. In our example, the customer's tone of voice, choice of words, general attitude, facial expression, gestures, and body posture all contribute to the customer service representative's interpretation of the message.

NOISE

Noise includes the physical, semantic, and hierarchical influences that either disrupt or shape the interpretation of messages. There are three types of noise that can affect a message:

- **Physical noise** may emanate from the environment: loud talking from the next room, opening and closing of doors, or sudden announcements over a loudspeaker that disrupts a conversation.
- **Semantic noise** refers to differences people have for the meanings of words. Semantic noise includes: misheard or misunderstood terms, gender bias (such as saying "he" when referring to all managers or "she" when referring to all child-care givers), the perception of racial undertones (such as a fear or anxiety expressed as something "dark"), in-house or professional jargon, and culturally derived metaphors (such as the predominance of sports metaphors in North American business).
- **Hierarchical noise** refers to the shadings in meaning we attribute to a message based on a person's rank or status within an organization. For example, a customer may insist on complaining to the customer service representative's supervisor rather than to the customer service representative, even though the manager will refer the message back down the chain of command. Introducing hierarchical noise may make the customer feel that the message is taken more seriously but it may also delay results or cause the message to be lost in the hierarchical shuffle.

FEEDBACK

Feedback is the activity of providing senders and receivers with responses to their communication, ideas, and identities. Initially, communication theorists viewed feedback in a very mechanical way. For example, a smile from our customer service representative could indicate acceptance of, and appreciation for, the customer's message. A frown could indicate confusion or disagreement. Quickly, however, communication researchers began to see the limitations of this either-or approach to discussing feedback. After all, a smile can be strategically deployed or faked. As researchers began studying feedback in business organizations, the complexity of the concept grew.

Feedback affects communication in an organization in a number of ways. Beyond responding to the specific words and actions of a sender, feedback can:

- Bring broader business and cultural implications to a conversation. It can help maintain the status quo through responses such as, "I'm sorry the salesperson told you something different, but that is not our return policy."
- Move a situation forward through responses such as "I apologize for the misunderstanding; let me see what I can do."
- Initiate change by fostering openness: "What can we do to restore your trust?"

Every exchange must be considered within the context of the specific communication episode. If a company is lagging behind in production or promised merchandise, feedback upholding the status quo might be considered negative. However, if a company has just undertaken a major change effort, confirming the status quo may be exactly what that company needs to do to remain successful. What might appear to be negative feedback in one situation or one culture, can be viewed as positive in another.

CHANNELS

A **channel** is the thoroughfare a message takes from sender to receiver. Channels have evolved from a simple choice between speaking and writing to complex choices available through numerous technological possibilities. By choosing a specific channel for communication the sender influences the timing, reception, and understanding of the message. For example, an unhappy customer could choose to:

- write a letter.
- send an e-mail.
- appear in person at the store.
- leave a voice message on an answering machine.
- post a comment or review on an Internet bulletin board or review sites like Epinions.com or Kudzu.com.
- call a media hotline.

Each channel may reach a different audience and therefore elicit a different outcome. As a result, the choice of channel provides the customer with varying levels of potential satisfaction and practical results.

CONTEXT

All communication occurs within a context. This context includes the physical arrangement of the space, the cultural context the participants bring to the situation, and the communication history that exists between the participants. Each of these factors can have an impact on the success of a message. Let's examine each of these influences on the context of a message in more detail.

Physical Situation   In the workplace, the physical situation comprises the following:

- influence of technology
- physical space, including temperature, humidity, and noise
- organization of the workspace, including placement of office furniture and displays of personal or professional items
- time and timing

Understanding how the physical situation influences communication allows you to avoid many of the pitfalls communicators encounter in the global workplace.

Influence of technology—In the global workplace, we can no longer assume that meetings will be face-to-face. Every day, people in the global workplace meet, conduct presentations, and communicate with one another across the globe using technology. Technology offers opportunities for communication when face-to-face meetings are not possible; however, technology also presents challenges to communication that affect both senders and receivers. We discuss technology and its impact on communication in detail in Chapter 6.

Physical Space—The physical space can impact communication partners and influence outcomes. Is the room large enough to accommodate everyone who was invited to a meeting? Are you discussing an intimate topic such as raises or reprimands in an open office space? Is the room too crowded with furniture? Is the temperature too warm or too cold for comfort? Are there distractions caused by excessive noise?

The size, location, organization, and comfort levels of the physical environment can make or break a deal, sidetrack negotiations, escalate conflict, or reduce the effectiveness of a presentation in a training program. If communication is impaired, or if distractions are present, people tend to focus on the physical distractions rather than the message. For example, imagine that you are giving a presentation to a group of potential clients. You spend weeks researching your group and honing your presentation. You book the "good" conference room two weeks in advance. The day of your presentation, you walk into the conference room to find the space is flooded because of a leak in the adjoining kitchen. The only option is a room with tattered chairs, a broken LCD panel, and a constant temperature of about 80 degrees. Chances are good that the condition of the room will negatively impact your feelings of confidence about the presentation, as well as your audience's ability to perceive you, your company, and your product favorably.

Organization of workspace—The organization of your workspace can have an impact on perceptions of your identity, culture, communication sensitivities, and professional competence. What does your workspace say about you? Is it a clean and neat area with well-organized shelves which hold carefully organized and aligned reference books and professional trade publications? Or is it a mess, complete with yesterday's half-eaten donut and long-cold cup of coffee? Does your desktop signal an organized approach to work, or is it the last resting place for a variety of personal objects, books, magazines, and piles of junk? Have you decorated your walls with tasteful photographs and signs of professional accomplishments, or with torn-out pages from sports magazines and personal fitness guides? Are there displays of items that could be offensive to others, such as questionable cartoons or calendars, or photographs that advertise overt sexuality?

The display of personal and professional items in a workspace creates impressions of your personal and professional identity. People enter your workspace and take account of it as a reflection of your interests, accomplishments, and sensitivity to a variety of cultural and gendered issues. Many businesses prohibit the display of personal items such as pictures of loved ones and pets because they believe it detracts from the business context of the workspace. In recent years, businesses have forbidden the display of suggestive sexual materials because it potentially constitutes an actionable offense under sexual-harassment laws. It is a good idea to become more conscious about the possible interpretations others may make of what you display in your workspace. Workspace displays are forms of nonverbal communication; they send clear messages about your understanding of your workplace culture and reflect on your ability to interpret and participate in that culture.

Time and timing—The time and timing of a message have dramatic effects on business and professional communication. As you undoubtedly know, some people are at their best in the morning, and others are night owls. Think about your own time preferences. Consider them when you plan a presentation or meeting or have to perform in an interview setting. Additionally, take into account the time and timing preferences of your audiences. Is it really a good idea to schedule that presentation right after the company lunch? Are meetings scheduled on Tuesday likely to accomplish more than those scheduled first thing Monday morning or late on Friday afternoons? The influences of time and timing help create the atmosphere and environment for communication.

Global Cultural Context   Business and professional communication occurs within a global cultural communication context: the thoughts and feelings we have in a situation, the history between the communicators, the similarities and differences between or among the organizational and national cultures we represent, and the relationship in which the communication occurs (Wood, 1996, p. 113). For example, our friend John took an executive position with the ABC organization, a small U.S. company located in the South. John is from Canada, where religion is rarely discussed or displayed at work. The company he works for frequently makes announcements about upcoming sales events, employee illnesses or hardships, and community needs, which are followed by the statement, "Any prayers you would like to offer would be appreciated." Prayer is not a requirement of the job at John's company, yet it sets a cultural context for communication within his organization.

John initially feared that, given the zeal of some religious organizations in the United States, he might have a difficult time adapting his communication to the workplace. As it turns out, he has been pleasantly surprised. Religion is certainly one context John encounters at work; however it is not the only context that influences his communication (see Figure 2.4).

John's experience at ABC changed his view on discussions about religion in the workplace. The owners of ABC companies did not force their religious views on John; rather, they incorporated a supportive, spiritual tone as part of the corporate culture. He has admitted that a few times, when faced with particularly tough sales challenges, it was comforting to think about everyone back in the office pulling for him. He has begun to view the religious undertones as a part of the organizational culture that reflects a caring team spirit. For others, however, any inclusion of religion, prayer, or discussions of spirituality may be intrusive and even offensive. Successful global communicators realize that communicating in global contexts requires flexibility and tolerance of everyone's beliefs.

John's example shows us that cultural contexts for communication are fluid. Our expectations about what is correct in a business environment changes as we move between organizations, cultures, and countries. Successful communicators gain insight and knowledge from each new experience and adjust their expectations for and communication within each new context they encounter.

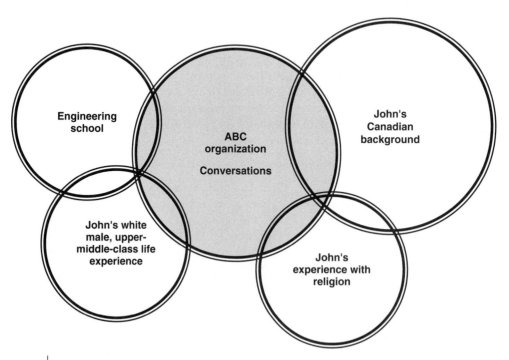

FIGURE 2.4   OVERLAPPING CONTEXTUAL INFLUENCES THAT INFORM A CONVERSATION

Thinking Globally—What is Culture?

Cultures are complex symbolic environments. **Organizational culture** consists of the histories, habits, values, and rules for conduct that make working in a particular organization or being part of a group of people feel unique. From a communication perspective, this means that it takes coordination, collaboration, and communication to produce a shared sense of culture—shared understandings and meanings. Add to this cultural context the uncertainties that always exist in any communication setting, and you begin to get an idea of why communication must be understood as an ongoing process that emerges from, and contributes to, organizational culture.

Think about the organizational cultures you are a part of—work, school, social groups, teams, etc. Create a diagram similar to Figure 2.4. Are you surprised at the influences on your personal communication? If each of us brings our own contexts to communication situations, is there any wonder that we need to learn skills and strategies that help us communicate successfully in a global workplace?

Communication History When we talk about **communication history**, we refer to the interpersonal history between two or more communication partners. Communication history includes factors such as:

- How long have you known each other?
- Where are you in your relationship?
- What has your experience together taught you about how each of you is likely to respond to situations?
- Have you had arguments or disagreements in the past?
- Are there topics you knowingly avoid?
- Are there issues you are likely to agree upon?
- What intellectual, social, and personal baggage does each of you bring to communication encounters?

Communication history can determine if you are open to the opinions and observations of a communication partner, or if you become defensive or closed-minded even before hearing what the other person has to say. Your shared communication history either creates a space for potentially open communication or closes the door to it. Yet, with each communication encounter, both positive and negative, your shared history changes. If, for example, a supervisor has a history of never asking for input at a weekly meeting and suddenly does, that one significant event alters the group's shared history from that point on. Shared history shapes our communication, and our communication constantly reshapes that history.

Our model of the global business and professional communication process provides a basic vocabulary for describing how communication "works." Each of the components contributes to the interpretation and meaning we give to messages, to our relationships, and to our respective cultures. In the following section we describe how these components may be combined with theories of organization, management, and communication.

THEORIES OF ORGANIZATION, MANAGEMENT, AND COMMUNICATION

Now that you understand the components involved in the communication process, let's discuss how these elements coalesced over time to create the theories of organization, management, and communication that govern much of business communication in the world. In this section we want to revisit a parallel evolution of two lines of thought that dominated the twentieth century: theories of organization and management, and theories of organizational communication. These theories form the basis of our understanding about how and why people communicate the way they do in organizations. As you will see, our theoretical understanding, as much as our understanding of communication best practices, evolved over time.

As students in an applied communication course, we know your first response to a discussion about theory is "Ugh!" However, having a basic awareness of the theory of organizational communication—how and why people act the way they do—will enhance your ability to communicate more effectively in the global workplace. This chapter also ties together two distinct areas of theory—business and communication—so you can see how organizational and management theory and communication theory are similar to and complement one another. To do this, we follow a more or less concurrent historical timeline that begins in the Industrial Revolution and ends in the present day. Using the timeline shown in Figure 2.5, we walk you through the evolution of theories of management and how these theories influenced theories of business and professional communication.

Organizational and Communication Theory Timeline

Classical Period—		Human Relations—	Human Resources—	Systems Theory	Cultural Theory	Learning Organizations—
Scientific Management and Bureaucracy		Hawthorne Studies and Maslow's Hierarchy of Needs	Maslow's Hierarchy of Needs			Five Disciplines
1900	1920	1940	1960	1980		2000
Communication as Information Transfer			Communication as Transactional Process	Networks	Power / Organizational Narratives	Dialogue

FIGURE 2.5 | EVOLUTION OF ORGANIZATIONAL MANAGEMENT AND COMMUNICATION THEORIES

If you are making an outline for this chapter, the following divisions should shape and inform your reading:

- Classical Management and Information Transfer
- Human Relations/Resources and Transactional Process
- Systems Thinking and Communication Networks
- Organizational Cultures, Communication, and Power
- Organizational Narratives and Dialogue

CLASSICAL MANAGEMENT AND INFORMATION TRANSFER

The classical period of management began at the height of the Industrial Revolution in the late 1800s and continued through the 1930s. The movement of people from the farm to the city and from the plow field to the factory highlighted this period. As more and more people entered the workplace, factory owners and store managers began to explore new and different ways to organize and manage people (Eisenberg, Goodall, and Trethewey, 2006).

Organizational charts from this period favored a strictly vertical, top-down arrangement. At the top was a board of directors; below was a president; below the president was a series of vice presidents; below the vice presidents were department managers; below them were the supervisors; and finally, at the very bottom of the chart, were the line workers. The term for this organization by rank and status is **hierarchy**.

Classical organizational structures assigned privileges according to one's rank and status in the organization. There were two important classical approaches to managing businesses and industries: *scientific management* and *bureaucracy* (Morgan, 1986). These two theories dominated the way organizations were structured and managed during the classical period.

SCIENTIFIC MANAGEMENT

Scientific management, defined by an engineer named Frederick Taylor (1913), emerged in the early 1900s. Taylor believed management was a true science governed by scientific principles, rules, and laws. He put forth the idea that owners and managers should operate factories and organizations as "efficient machines," modeled on the inner workings of a well-made mechanical clock. Inspired by this image of clockwork, he proposed conducting "time and motion" studies for every task in an organization. These studies encouraged business owners and managers to find "the one best way" (the method requiring the shortest amount of time using the smallest amount of motion) to complete tasks. The results established standards for every job, created an evaluation instrument that managers could apply equally to every worker, and established a reward (or punishment) system for workers based on their production or performance. Using Taylor's principles, managers divided tasks into discrete, measurable units, and trained workers to perform only one task, thus making replacement of sick or injured workers relatively easy. Workers became merely replaceable parts in the factory machine, and there was

Ford Assembly Line, March 1928

little if any room for learning or advancement. As Henry Ford, a proud scientific-management enthusiast, once put it, "Managers think; workers work."

What then did managers think about and do? During this same theoretical period, a Frenchman named Henri Fayol (1949) established the five functions of scientific management:

- planning
- organizing
- commanding (or goal-setting)
- coordinating
- controlling (or evaluating)

According to Fayol, it was the manager's job to plan the work, organize tasks, set goals, coordinate work, and control the workforce. A person hired as a manager would be trained to perform these duties, and *only* these duties. There was no allowance for encouraging managers to learn how to do their jobs better, or even differently. Certainly no thought was expended on "quality improvement" when it came to managerial tasks. A man (almost all the factory managers during this period in history were men) either knew how to do the job, or he didn't!

Although scientific management was, in principle, a good theory for organizing and managing repetitive tasks done in a mechanical environment, in practice it contributed to the dehumanization of the workplace. Workers, considered replaceable parts in a relentless machine, were often treated as less than human by business owners and managers. Working conditions during this period were unregulated, labor laws were virtually nonexistent, and management decisions were the final word. Managers could fire, hire, or reassign workers based on their sex, race, religion, attitude, or relationships to other workers.

BUREAUCRACY

Although it might not seem so today, the creation of a bureaucracy evolved as a more humane way of managing people in complex organizations. Max Weber, an observer of the rise of scientific management and a major sociological theorist of his day, saw bureaucracies as a means to overcome the problems of scientific management (1946). Weber believed that, managed correctly, using a set of universalisms or standards of fairness, bureaucracies would stamp out the harsh, inequitable, and often deadly conditions that arose from poor scientific management (Perrow, 1986). According to Weber (Scott, 1990), an ideal **bureaucracy** must have the following elements:

- a fixed division of labor
- a hierarchy of work responsibilities and authority
- a set of general operating rules that govern performance
- a separation of the personal lives of employees from their professional lives
- a selection process based on technical qualifications and equal treatment under the rules for operating the business

 ## COMMUNICATION AS INFORMATION TRANSFER

During the classical period, there arose an implicit theory of communication that would later be termed the **information transfer model**. Visualize a pipeline through which information or messages pass. On one end of the pipeline is a "sender," and on the other end is a "receiver." What you have just pictured is a representation of communication that contains one or more of the following assumptions about information transfer:

- Language transfers thoughts and feelings from person to person.
- Speakers and writers insert thoughts and feelings into words.
- Words contain the thoughts and feelings.

- Listeners or readers extract the thoughts and feelings from the words (Axley, 1984, p. 429).

The information transfer model, although simplistic in its characterization of management and communication, has had a lasting influence in bureaucracies worldwide. Moreover, academic interest in how people think and process information about task-oriented communication led to the development of sophisticated research programs aimed at explaining the gaps in this complex phenomenon. This research contributed to filling the gaps in the explanatory power of the information transfer model, which in turn created the questions that led to the emergence of human relation theories of management and a new perspective on communication in the workplace.

Scientific management and bureaucracy both relied on strict top-down authority structures, centralized decision making, and control of managerial power to govern the organization of work. They ignored the possibilities that workers could learn to manage, that managers could learn to become better at their jobs, or that managers and workers could learn from one another if they communicated more equitably.

HUMAN RELATIONS/RESOURCES AND TRANSACTION PROCESS

Although the 1920s had been a period of extreme affluence and growth in America, in the early 1930s, prosperity quickly gave way to closed factories, massive migrations, and widespread poverty and unemployment. With little to lose, workers began to make demands for better working conditions, fairer wages, and equal treatment. Labor unions grew in popularity and power.

The poverty of the Great Depression eventually gave way to a new cycle of expansion and prosperity. Driven by the production needs of World War II, by union-sponsored demands for fairer treatment of workers by managers, and by a desire among liberal-minded journalists, academics, and industrialists for a better way to get the job done, new theories of management emerged. These new theories of management grew out of what we now term the *human relations movement* (Eisenberg, Goodall, and Trethewey, 2006).

What made it different? The **human relations movement** viewed employees less as individual, replaceable machine parts and more as sources of group information and skill that could be developed through training and education by the organization. Two ideas were key to this movement; they were contained in the Hawthorne Studies and in Maslow's Hierarchy of Needs.

HAWTHORNE STUDIES

In the 1930s, Elton Mayo led a team of researchers to study the way people worked at Western Electric's Hawthorne Plant in Cicero, Illinois (Mayo, 1945). Using principles drawn from scientific management, Mayo's study altered lighting conditions to see if productivity in the plant improved. What he and his research team found surprised them. The changes in productivity they witnessed had nothing to do with the lighting, but everything to do with communication with and among the factory workers. Mayo found that increased attention to the workers led to improved morale, which in turn improved productivity, a finding that became known as the "Hawthorne Effect." The researchers also found that individuals are influenced by those around them and that those group interactions could have favorable effects on work.

These two insights became the basis for a gradual change from a strictly bureaucratic to a "human relations" approach to management. The core principles of the movement emphasized the following:

- the importance of open communication and supportive relations between managers and employees
- the need for managers to take into account employees' feelings

- the need for managers to respond to the developmental needs of workers, which might be incongruent with formal hierarchies and task specialization

MASLOW'S HIERARCHY OF NEEDS

During the 1940s and 1950s, a psychologist named Abraham Maslow developed the Hierarchy of Needs model to explain what motivates human behavior. The model represents a hierarchy of human needs that range from "lower order" needs, such as food, clothing, and shelter, to "higher order" needs, such as self-esteem and personal fulfillment ("self-actualization"). (See Figure 2.6)

Maslow argued that proper motivation of employees required understanding what they were thinking about and aspiring to in their lives. Owners and managers began to understand that although a paycheck can help fulfill the lower-order

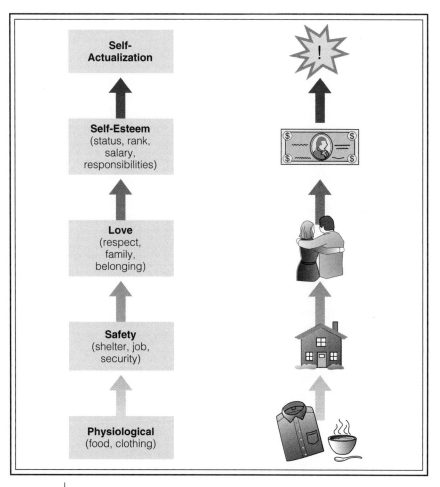

FIGURE 2.6 | MASLOW'S HIERARCHY OF NEEDS

needs, viewing workers as "human resources" by providing them with proper training and educational opportunities would help satisfy higher-order needs, thus making workers more productive.

Maslow's influence on managerial thinking cannot be overestimated. His work inspired other researchers to ask new questions about motivation and rewards, about the design and evaluation of performance, and about how "optimal performance" on the job might be accomplished. His work underscored the importance of what we now call "organizational learning" and "continuous improvement." He also set the academic stage for studies of "organizing for peak performance" (Eisenberg, 1990) that have led to insights about the necessary conditions for helping workers identify and meet challenges. In particular, Mihaly Cziksentmihalyi's theory of "flow" (1990, 1997) suggests that peak performances are gained when workers feel motivated to do a job that is a little above their skill level but have the training and resources to carry it out.

 ## COMMUNICATION AS A TRANSACTIONAL PROCESS

The **transactional process model** of communication emerged out of the failures of the scientific management and information transfer schools to provide a model for motivation, morale, and teamwork. Specifically, after the Hawthorne Studies, more attention was paid to the idea of communication as vital to manager–employee relations. As a result, clear hierarchical distinctions between bosses and workers were replaced with more equitable terms, such as *senders* and *receivers*. Additionally, these terms created an appreciation for how people at work perform those roles simultaneously. The transactional process model recognizes the following statements as true:

- All persons are engaged in sending and receiving messages (Wenberg and Wilmot, 1973).
- Each person is constantly affecting the other (Wenberg and Wilmot, 1973).
- Feedback, particularly nonverbal feedback, is a vital source of information (Anderson, 1999).
- The person receiving a message, rather than the person sending the message, is the source of meaning (Axley, 1984).

Communication as a transactional process was the dominant communication model informing advances in human relations, human resources, and human potential approaches to organization and management. In an evolutionary sense, you can see how what was once a top-down, "command and control" perspective on business and professional talk gave way to a more humane and complex view of verbal and nonverbal communication. Three major areas of academic research and business practice benefited from this model:

1. interpersonal communication in the workplace
2. team communication
3. leadership

The transactional process model provides a useful general approach to understanding interpersonal and team communication in the workplace, within which new findings and advances continue to be made. However, the evolution of new theories of organization, management, and communication created yet another new way of thinking about communication in the workplace. Verbal and nonverbal communication were not only viewed as a management function or as a component of team effectiveness, but they also became more broadly associated with the process for creating the organization and becoming the substance of management. These new theories are called the *systems* and *cultures* approaches to organization and communication.

SYSTEMS THINKING AND COMMUNICATION NETWORKS

The **systems thinking** theory of business organization combines holism and interdependence. It views an organization as a system of interconnected individuals and teams. A major claim of systems thinking is that for one member of a team or organization to succeed, all members of the team or organization must succeed (Goodall and Eisenberg, 2001). These days, in the early twenty-first century, to call a company's interlocking webs of communication a "system" is to use a language that most businesspeople readily accept and many understand. A system is a way to conceptualize the dynamic set of relationships that point to a new kind of order. This order is not one made of bureaucratic hierarchies and divisions of labor but instead consists of patterns of interaction among the system's components (Farace, Monge, and Russell, 1977; Senge, 1991).

An organizational system is often envisioned metaphorically as a "family of relationships," in which the organization equates with a family and each family member's communication has some effect on—is interconnected with—every other family member's understandings, meanings, and communication. The components of a system are as follows (Eisenberg, Goodall, and Trethewey, 2006):

- **Environment**: Organizations do not exist as isolated entities but as integral parts of the world.
- **Interdependence**: The organization, its environment, and the individuals and components within it are interrelated.
- **Goals** (what the system is organized to accomplish): Goals are negotiated between the individual components, with a large influence from the system's environment.
- **Feedback**: Feedback is an interconnected system of "loops" that connects communication and action. There are two kinds of feedback: negative, which corrects for deviations from the original goal, and positive, which finds new areas for growth and expansion.
- **Openness, order, and contingency**: These terms refer to the notion that there is no "one best way" to organize. To succeed, an organizational system must remain open and work within its environment, in an evolving and orderly way.

One of the major contributions to communication theory provided by systems thinking was the idea of communication networks. Another was the contingent nature of decision making. A third was the importance of feedback to the health and resilience of the organizational system. Let's examine why these ideas were so powerful and how they have influenced our business and professional communication.

Systems thinking has had a profound influence on theories of organization, management, and communication. Systems thinking is the core of Peter Senge's approach to using communication (in the form of dialogue) to build *learning organizations* (1994). But before we move into our discussion of conscious communication in learning organizations, we need to explain the influence of another powerful idea that has had tremendous impact on our understanding of business and professional communication: organizational cultures.

THE LINKS BETWEEN SYSTEMS THEORY AND BUSINESS AND PROFESSIONAL COMMUNICATION

There are three direct links between the components of an organizational system and communication in it: communication flow in networks, the contingent nature of decision making (interdependence), and the importance of feedback to the health and resilience of the system. Each of these links has a direct impact on how we communicate and interpret meaning in the workplace.

Communication Flow in Networks

When an organization is viewed as a communication system, two patterns stand out. First, some communication flows into and through the organization according to formal chains of command and through established groups and teamwork. For example, because of the devaluing of currency in the Asian economy, U.S. stock exchanges reacted swiftly and strongly. The CFO of XYZ Corporation responded to this shift in the economic environment by asking each group leader or department head to analyze how this shift would affect their products and customers. Department or group leaders worked together to incorporate their analysis into future corporate directions, which they presented to the CFO at their monthly status meeting.

Second, some communication flows into and through the organization using informal or social patterns of routine interaction that are not prescribed or authorized by the organization in a formal way. Informal patterns of interaction include talk around the water cooler and impromptu discussions in the employee lounge.

Together, these formal and informal patterns teach us a lot about how messages travel through an organization. For example, during the XYZ Corporation analysis, many employees and customers speculated on XYZ's ability to remain profitable. These conversations occurred over lunches, in parking lots, and during sales calls. Feedback from

these informal interactions enlightened the formal discussion, providing decision makers with additional sources of information. In turn, formal groups reported these concerns to their superiors, who engaged a consultant to help them through the period of potential crisis.

Contingent Nature of Decision Making

As you can see from these examples, viewing communication flow through networks in a system reveals the ongoing, dynamic nature of interaction and feedback. It also reveals why companies use a contingent approach to decision making. Rather than assume that once a decision has been made, the problem is solved, contingent decision makers understand the constant need to revise decisions based on new information and ongoing analysis of the effects of past decisions. This pattern of interaction that informs decision making is known as "interdependence." One of its major outcomes is organizational learning.

Feedback and the Health of a System

Maintaining open lines of communication is vital to the health and resilience of an organizational system. Open lines of communication ensure that feedback—both positive and negative (or corrective)—is available to make informed decisions and enhance the productivity of an organization. Lines of communication must remain open externally and internally. In the example above, the feedback received from customers was important for channeling customer concerns to the appropriate department and planning for communication back to the customers about future plans. One of the major outcomes of this kind of systems thinking is the development and use of continuous improvement models to monitor the quality of the organization, as well as its services or products.

USING FORMAL AND INFORMAL NETWORKS EFFECTIVELY

The systems perspective provides useful tips for communicating formally and informally in an organization. Let's examine ways you can use these concepts in your professional communication.

- Develop information and support contacts inside and outside of your workplace. Look for people who can help you plan the direction of your career and see opportunities that you might have missed if you stayed within an organizational shell.
- Keep the lines of communication with your contacts open at all times. To do so, you need to listen carefully, respond quickly to requests, seek information when unsure, and give credit where credit is due.
- Understand that decisions in organizations are subject to change and revision. Don't stake out a position and refuse to change because you

are relying on yesterday's information; tomorrow may require a shift in decision making.

- Never assume your company operates in isolation. Keep up with current events, changes in technology and the global economy, and shifts in your industry that will affect your company.
- Understand that in business, change is healthy. For most people, this requires a shift in thinking: change is healthy and stagnation unhealthy.
- Enter into all interactions from a conscious communication perspective. Be aware of the information value and potential effect of your communication on your identity, others' ability to act, and the organization's health and resilience.

ORGANIZATIONAL CULTURES, COMMUNICATION, AND POWER

Organizational culture, like a system, implies an intricate, interconnected, and purposeful pattern or order. Unlike systems, however, a culture's pattern is drawn from the metaphors and language of "community," which implies the following:

- a unique sense of place that both unites and divides members (Louis, 1979)
- histories and visions for the future, which may or may not be shared (Deal and Kennedy, 1982; Peters and Waterman, 1982)
- locally defined customs, rituals, rules, rites, and procedures (Pacanowsky and O'Donnell-Trujillo, 1983; Hofstede, 1983; Goodall, 1989)
- shared core values that, even when opposed by resistance factions, are recognized to exist (Ouchi and Wilkins, 1985; Kotter and Heskett, 1992; Shockley-Zalabak and Morley, 1994)

The culture of the organization includes the way employees dress, how they speak to superiors, the items they display in their office or cubes, and more. Culture appears to consist of the behaviors, customs, habits, stories, routines, and other meaningful events and processes that organize people (Putnam and Pacanowsky, 1983). However, cultural researchers stress the importance of understanding that culture is not a "thing," but a "happening" (Pacanowsky and O'Donnell-Trujillo, 1983).

Communication is the process by which culture is formed and transformed (Eisenberg, Goodall, and Trethewey, 2006; Kellett, 1999). The cultural approach teaches us that communication *is* the culture. The verbal and nonverbal messages that arise from the organization's culture create the *meanings* of behavior, customs, habits, stories, routines, events, and processes that organize and inform a group of people. As the anthropologist Clifford Geertz expressed it, "Humans live in webs of meaning that we ourselves have spun" (1973).

Studying organizational cultures allows us to expand our business and professional communication knowledge to include an understanding of power, organizational storytelling, personal narratives, and dialogue. Let's examine each of these forms of contemporary business and professional communication.

The Influence of the Cultural Approach to Power   One of the advantages of the organizational culture approach to communication is a new understanding of the role of communication in the creation of **power**—the sources of influence derived by an individual within an organization. In part, this new understanding of power was derived from looking critically at the advice about communication provided in previous models of organizing and managing (see Deetz, 1995; Conquergood, 1991; Conrad, 1991; Mumby, 1987). Before we can understand how the cultural approach challenged these theories of power, let's review how power functioned in previous models.

Classical Approach to Power   The classical approach to power provides what critics have labeled the *managerial view* of communication in organizations (Putnam and Pacanowsky, 1983). This means that our understanding of all communication practices, and especially of power, was rooted firmly in the idea that "rank has its privileges." Moreover, the expression of power was limited to structures created for, and functions carried out by, managers. French and Raven (1968) described the classic managerial forms of power:

- *Reward power:* A supervisor has reward power when a reward can be given—such as a bonus, time off, or an award—based on compliance with a directive.
- *Coercive power:* A boss has coercive power when employees perceive that negative things will happen if they don't comply with directives.
- *Referent power:* A boss has referent power when employees do what is asked of them because they seek to emulate her or him.
- *Expert power:* A boss has expert power when employees perceive a boss to have expert knowledge.
- *Legitimate power:* A boss has power simply because of his or her position within the hierarchy. Employees perceive the position to be legitimately held and therefore comply with directives.

As you can see, there are times when each of these forms of power may be appropriate and useful. Power should be applied consciously and after a mindful examination of the outcome you hope to achieve.

The Human Relations Approach to Power   In the transactional process model, the idea of power shifts from the manager's position within the hierarchy to the relationship between the manager and the employee. The employee gains power primarily by being encouraged to give feedback to the boss and to interpret his or her own meanings about the relationship and the work, and by negotiating with the organizational superior how, when, and with what resources the assigned work could be accomplished. The manager derives power from being more supportive, open, interested in the employees' feelings and thoughts, and trustworthy. Viewed this way, managers and employees use power cooperatively, and therefore more fairly.

The Systems Approach to Power   The systems perspective encourages us to see power less as a "thing" that organizational superiors have and subordinates don't have than as a system of relationships based only in part on an employee's status in the organizational hierarchy. Systems thinking helps us account for the available uses of power in everyday exchanges between and among equals (as well as between superiors and subordinates). For example, an entry-level computer programmer with deep knowledge of an operating system has a lot of potential power in a company that requires its operating system to be in place and up and running to do business. If the system goes down, so do company profits. The programmer's power is held in relation to every other employee's ability to do his or her job. Concurrently, the programmer's success may well depend on the input about the computer system she or he receives from other employees. Viewed systemically, everyone has some available power relative to everyone else's available power.

Similarly, employees who are interpersonally close to—and whose information (feedback) is trusted by—their managers tend to be able to exert influence despite hierarchical differences. Quality of relationships and the perceived value of information mediate and often negate overt power as defined by rank and status. This principle also helps us understand the power of rumors and gossip in an organization. As sources of informal communication, rumors and gossip serve to balance power by directing and controlling information and feedback within a larger organizational system.

The Cultural Approach to Power   The cultural perspective assumes that there is a constant struggle for power in every organization (Deetz, 1995). In organizations, people vie for attention, resources, rewards, influence, and dignity. From a cultural perspective, people and groups holding power are described as "dominant," and others seeking power are labeled "resistant" (Goodall, 1990a; Scott, 1990). One major contribution of this perspective is the study of power as it relates to and derives from gender, race, class, and sexual orientation in organizations.

Power and Difference   With the advent of the cultures perspective, the model for power expanded from *overt* hierarchy, information, and relationships to *covert*, or hidden, power (Conrad, 1983; Scott, 1990). Because of sociological research, power within companies came to be viewed in relation to power in societies. In societies marked by social and economic class divisions, where differences in opportunities and evaluations of one's abilities are often based on one's race, gender, or sexual orientation, the same patterns of influence and inequity manifest in businesses and professions. Furthermore, because sociologists and anthropologists teach us to see all cultures as localized sites of struggle between those who have power and those who don't, a new language of "resistance to domination" enters organizational analysis.

Power occurs "offstage" as well as "onstage" (Scott, 1990; Goodall, 1995), which means that the lines of power extend beyond face-to-face encounters, or even beyond the workplace. For example, disgruntled or alienated employees who feel wronged may turn their work worlds upside down, and therefore regain a sense of power and equity, by casting aspersions on their bosses. In the film *American Beauty* (1999), a character facing termination from his boring job in an advertising firm confronts his superior directly, turns the power equation inside out, and wins a large settlement. In real life this is unlikely, as resistance to domination typically occurs offstage. These offstage performances may occur in break rooms, in comic asides performed behind the boss's back, in nasty e-mails to friends, in "work-hate narratives" (Goodall, 1995), and during after-work or weekend gatherings.

Power and Democracy   Another way of understanding the cultural perspective on power is through the application of a cooperative (or democratic) model of influence. Although this is still the exception rather than the norm in business today, the concept bears examination. Stan Deetz created a model for power and democracy in the workplace using the "stakeholder organization" (1995), in which the success of the company depends upon shared decision making at every level. Deetz outlined four steps to create such a workplace (Eisenberg, Goodall, and Trethewey, 2006, pp. 166–167):

1. *Create a workplace in which every member thinks and acts like an owner.*
   When power is shared for decision making, stakeholders become more accountable to themselves, to one another, and to society.
2. *The management of the work must be reintegrated with the doing of work.*
   Empowering stakeholders to have control over how they perform their own jobs eliminates the need for managers or supervisors. Power is thus shared among equals.
3. *Quality information must be widely distributed.* Information is power, and power in a stakeholder organization must be shared equally. Additionally, by encouraging stakeholders to share only "real" information, this model discourages the meaningless proliferation of memos, faxes, e-mails, letters, and newsletters that reinforce existing power hierarchies.
4. *Social structure should grow from the bottom rather than be reinforced from the top.* Power is vested in all of the stakeholders, who determine every aspect of their jobs and workplace instead of taking orders from people paid to oversee and direct the work.

Now that we have studied the idea of power in relation to cultural theories of organization, let's examine two of the ways communication functions in a cultural model: *organizational narratives* and *dialogue*.

Focus on Ethics

Reflect on the definitions of power discussed previously. Which of these definitions of power make sense to you? How can power be manipulated or negatively applied in a global workplace? What are the ethical implications of using power in a negative way? What are the implications of unethical uses of power within a global context? Do these questions matter? Why?

ORGANIZATIONAL NARRATIVES AND DIALOGUE

All our experiences provide us with the raw materials to construct an ongoing "story of our lives" (Bochner, 1997; Goodall, 2008; Coles, 1989). Similarly, employees and managers in businesses and professions construct "organizational narratives" to re-create and retell the important events in their working lives (Boje, 1991, 1995; Mumby, 1987; Kellett, 1999).

Theorists have labeled this perspective the **narrative** view or paradigm (Bochner, 1994; Goodall, 2008; Fisher, 1987). The essential idea behind the narrative paradigm is that, communicatively, we live within the lines of the stories we tell others about our jobs, our lives, and ourselves. These narratives do not simply represent our experiences; they also help construct them. Our identities, goals, values, and passions derive from an ongoing narrative in which we each figure as a central character. How we make sense of situations and others is largely determined by the ways in which we can use the plots and lessons of our ongoing stories to render "the new" within a context of "the old" (Weick, 1995).

The four types of organizational narratives that emerge as forms of business and professional communication are:

- *Organizational stories* (Mumby, 1987; Goodall, 1989; Boje, 1991): Individual accounts of the workplace that reveal how events occurred, how problems were solved, how heroes and heroines were created, how legends were made, and how "things are done around here." Some of these stories reveal how power works; for example, accounts of "how things are done around here" tend to repress alternative ways of doing things.

- *Work-hate narratives* (Goodall, 1995): Individual accounts of harms, misdeeds, or violence done to employees. These stories are often told to regain equity in a situation, but they sometimes forecast acts of revenge.

- *Narrative recovery* (Kellett, 1999): As a consulting tool, these stories are collected publicly from all employees in a particular department or area to "recover" the history of the organization from a personal perspective. The consultant uses key questions to prompt the narratives, including: (a) What brought you to work here? (b) What are your personal joys and challenges? (c) Have there been any turning points in your relationship to this company? (d) What vision do you have for your future here?

- *Organizational change* (Ford and Ford, 1995; Kellett and Goodall, 1998; Kellett, 1999): Consultants, trainers, and managers all understand that productive change in organizations always begins in conversations. Because communication creates perceptions of reality, as well as constitutes systems and cultures, communication is responsible for bringing into existence ideas for change. Stories about those conversations emerge as part of the shared history—myths, legends, turning points—of any organization or profession.

DIALOGUE

Conceptually, **dialogue** refers to an ongoing, open, and dynamic process in which individual communicators have a balanced chance to speak and to be heard, and in which each person makes a conscious effort to understand and empathize with the perspective, experiences, and positions of the other (Buber, 1985; Eisenberg, Goodall, and Trethewey, 2006; Senge, 1991; Senge et al., 1994). The purposes of dialogue are to promote identity and community through empathetic understanding, to use communication to achieve mutual growth, and to search for meaningful patterns capable of effecting personal transformation and organizational change (Arnett and Cissna, 1996; Senge et al., 1994; Kellett and Dalton, 2001; Eisenberg, Goodall, and Trethewey, 2006). As you can see, dialogue represents a unique and powerful form of communication.

H. L. Goodall (2000), working from an earlier Peter Senge (1991) model for describing types of communication, developed a continuum for conceptualizing a range of the following everyday forms of talk:

- *phatic communication* (routine exchanges of small talk)
- *ordinary conversation* (discussion, gossip, or information exchange)
- *skilled conversation and professional communication* (interviews, negotiations, conflict management, informative and persuasive presentations, team presentations, argumentation and debate)
- *personal narratives* (stories)
- *dialogue* (deep conversation aimed at mutual growth that often requires risk taking, creativity, and suspension of critical judgment)

As this continuum reveals, dialogue is the most advanced form of communication. Viewed from an organizational perspective, dialogue requires that equitable communication opportunities are afforded to all employees (Eisenberg, Goodall, and Trethewey, 2006). However, merely having a right to speak doesn't adequately address the quality of communication exchanged during a dialogue.

The most conscious form of communication in an organization is dialogue. As you can see from Figure 2.7, the more conscious a communicator is of talk—the more open the exchange with the other person—the more dialogic the talk becomes. Let's examine the basis for this claim in greater detail.

Mindless Communication   Experience teaches us that we do not always behave mindfully at work or at home. Nor do we always behave in an ethical manner. In part, this is because many communication situations we face daily at work do not call for a lot of mental alertness or focused communicative activity. Communication researchers have termed these situations "phatic communication," or "small talk." In these situations, what is called for is not mindful, but "mindless" or automatic, often "scripted" responses (Greene, 1997; Goodall, 1996; Lodge, 1997).

Phatic Communication	Ordinary Communication	Skilled Talk	Personal Narratives	Dialogue
Routine, ritualized social talk	Exchanges of questions and responses, humor, ideas, and other forms of relational information	Interviews, negotiations, conflict management, presentational speaking, and teamwork	Autobiographical stories about the meaning of one's life experience	Creative, risk-taking, mutual quest for understanding and meaning

FIGURE 2.7 | COMMUNICATION CONTINUUM IN A LEARNING ORGANIZATION

Mindless communication—episodes of small talk or automatic talk—occurs most often in familiar situations. Why? Because when we are in familiar situations, speaking and listening to people we see every day, we often rely on past experiences, routines, rituals, or habits—what researchers call "scripted responses"—to guide our talk. We do not consciously select a strategy; we simply fall back on nonconscious routines we have used successfully. Below is a typical example of phatic communication:

Shavonda: Hi!

Rick: Hi.

Shavonda: So how are you?

Rick: Fine, and you?

Shavonda: Good.

Rick: So what's new in your department today?

Shavonda: Not much, and you?

Rick: The same. You know how it is. That's why they call it "work."

Shavonda: Yeah, I guess. Well, see you later.

Rick: Okay. See you.

Most of us repeat this form of small talk many times during an average day. Phatic communication is a necessary, although seldom sufficient, form of everyday business talk because it acts as a kind of social lubricant that encourages a surface level of collegiality and friendliness. Furthermore, cognitive researchers suggest that mindlessness is one way the brain conserves its energy for more challenging situations. In this way, "nonconscious behavior should not be viewed as an evil" (King and Sawyer, 1998, p. 334). By behaving "automatically," we make our mental energy available for other uses.

This is not to say that relying on phatic communication or small talk is a good thing. An overreliance on mindlessness diminishes our cognitive ability to develop new scripts or creative responses and to otherwise expand the repertoire of available communication strategies we bring to new situations (Goodall, 1996).

Communication ability is a skill, and like any skill, it requires practice. If all we do is rely on small talk and routine responses, we aren't using the full capacity of our communication potential. Likewise we are not getting much practice in developing the creative, mindful strategies that we need when phatic communication simply won't do. Nor are we always behaving ethically, because mindless activity does not allow for complex and difficult thoughts. This may help us account for why we inadvertently hurt others' feelings, or why we too often fail to appreciate how our routine actions have harmed or offended others. Finally, an over-reliance on small talk probably encourages others to perceive us as friendly, but boring. For these reasons, success in business and professional communication is unlikely to occur when mindless communication dominates our everyday interactions.

Improving our conscious communication—becoming more mindful in business and professional contexts—should be a major learning goal for anyone planning an organizational career. Many of the more popular books giving advice for business communication success can be understood as reflections of the basic assumptions about conscious communication afforded by the cognitive perspective. For example, Stephen Covey's *The Seven Habits of Highly Effective People* (1990) advocates becoming more goal-oriented, focused, and strategic in our dealings with others. Clearly, the knowledge and skills provided by this theoretical perspective on communication have direct relevance to developing important professional communication competencies. The next section discusses mindful, or more conscious, communication.

Mindful Communication   A mindful approach to talk enables us to view communication consciously, as a mental and relational activity that is both purposeful and strategic. We use our heads to come up with strategies that we encode into talk designed to help us achieve desirable ends with others. When we are conscious of our communication, we become more mindful (Langer, 1990; Motley, 1992). **Mindful communication** requires the following:

- analyzing communication situations
- thinking actively about possible communication choices available to us
- adapting our message to inform, amuse, persuade, or otherwise influence our listener or audience
- evaluating the feedback we receive as an indication of how successful we were in accomplishing our purpose

But what if what is desirable for us might hurt someone else? Researchers suggest that cognitively based communication is, or at least should be, ethical (Langer, 1989). This is because we are individually responsible for our choices, our modes of adapting to listeners and audiences, and the outcomes of our actions. Becoming more conscious as communicators, which is to become more mindful and strategic in our dealings with others at work, should help us become more ethical, as well.

Research shows that we can expect mindful communication to occur in specific situations (Motley, 1992):

- *When there is a conflict between message goals.* For example, an employee may knock on a supervisor's door to ask permission to perform a task but also to show the supervisor that he or she has taken the initiative to take on the task without being directed to do so. There is a conflict between the goals for the message—to demonstrate initiative, or to ask permission.

- *When undesirable consequences are expected from the use of a particular message.* For example, a technical writer knows that she must inform the manager that his deadline will not be met. She also knows that he will not be pleased with this information and will likely blame her for not accomplishing the job. She thinks this will harm her career, but she also feels obligated to tell him her work will be late.

- *During time delays between messages and mental processing difficulties, such as interpreting the meaning or intention of a message.* For example, two colleagues are having lunch together and one partner seems interested in taking the relationship, which until this time has been one of friendship and collegiality, to another, possibly romantic, level. The other partner pauses for a long time before answering her colleague's last statement about his "interest" in her. She is trying to figure out what he means. He is trying to figure out why she isn't answering him.

- *When communication situations are particularly troublesome or unique.* For example, a visiting computer engineer from Sweden arrives with gifts for the manager of a North American computer firm. The North American manager has no gifts to give in return and is clearly embarrassed. Both of them search for something to say to ease the situation.

WHY WE LEARN ABOUT THEORIES OF COMMUNICATION

Our experiences teaching business and professional communication courses over the years have taught us that some students, when confronted early on in the term with material in a chapter such as this one, wonder how it applies to developing their communication skills. It is a fair question, and one that we will answer for you.

To be practical, theories must be applied. You may have heard the expression, first coined by the mid-twentieth-century social scientist Kurt Lewin, that "nothing is so practical as a good theory." That statement is not just something an academic would say. It is a valuable expression that speaks to a profound human truth. A theory is best thought of as "equipment for living" (Burke, 1989), or as a tool to enhance our understanding. However, before you can apply theories or make them part of your intellectual equipment, you have to develop an understanding of the theories that have guided organizations.

By learning to think theoretically about communication in organizations, you acquire a language for describing and evaluating your personal experiences as a communicator at work. But you need to apply that language to your experiences in order to achieve the payoff. You have to incorporate what you have read into your everyday habits of mind. Use the theories as touchstones in your quest to understand the meanings of persons and things. Use them to become a more conscious, more informed communicator.

SUMMARY

Chapter 2 introduced the components of a global business and professional communication process and then explored the close connection between theories of organization and communication. The components provide a basic vocabulary to describe ideas essential to your understanding of communication. From these components, we then built your appreciation for how communication "fits" into the evolution of theories of organization, management, and more contemporary approaches to communication.

During the classical period, the ideal organization was a factory built on the model of "clockwork." Theorists such as Frederick Taylor, Henri Fayol, and Max Weber, using the concepts of scientific management and bureaucracy, built organizational structures ready-made for the top-down information transfer models of communication. As these tight organizational structures and top-down approaches to communication were challenged by the effectiveness of simple human contact and a concern for workers' morale, human relations/resources and transactional process models gradually replaced them. As organizations became more complex, technological and global systems thinking emphasized the importance of communication networks as a way of understanding the role of groups and teams—and later, dialogue and learning—in creating and maintaining healthy and resilient systems.

Finally, renewed interest in the human side of enterprise revealed that communication was a cultural product and that understanding an organization's culture afforded rich insights about everyday values, power, and the meaning of practices. Together, the concepts of systems thinking and organizational cultures reveal that communication is both formative and transformative.

COMMUNICATING IN PROFESSIONAL CONTEXTS ONLINE

All of the following chapter review materials are available in an electronic format on either the *Business and Professional Communication in the Global Workplace* Resource Center or in the book's companion website. Online, you'll find chapter learning objects, flashcards of glossary terms, InfoTrack® College Edition Activities, weblinks, quizzes, and more.

WHAT YOU SHOULD HAVE LEARNED

Now that you have read Chapter 2, you should be able to do the following:

- Define and understand the components of communication and how they interact with each other.
- Identify and define the two theories of management associated with the classical period of organizational management.
- Identify the communication theory that corresponds to the classical period.
- Identify and define the two studies associated with the human relations/resources period of organizational management theory.
- Identify the communication theory that corresponds to the human relations/resources period and the three areas of communication research derived from this period.
- Identify and define the components of a system.
- Distinguish between formal and informal networks.
- Define the term *organizational culture*.
- Identify at least one theory of culture in organizations.
- Discuss the different approaches to power and how our thinking about power in organizations has evolved.
- Discuss organizational narratives and the types of research associated with them.
- Discuss conscious communication, to include providing the continuum for communication from mindless to mindful communication.
- Distinguish between mindless and mindful communication.

KEY TERMS

bureaucracy   *33*

channel   *25*

communication history   *29*

dialogue   *44*

environment   *37*

feedback   *24*

goals   *37*

hierarchical noise   *24*

hierarchy   *31*

human relations movement   *34*

information transfer model   *33*

interdependence   *37*

message   *24*

mindful communication   *46*

mindless communication   *45*

narrative   *43*

noise   *24*

organizational culture   *29*

physical noise   *24*

power   *40*

receiver   *23*

sender   *23*

semantic noise   *24*

scientific management   *31*

systems thinking   *37*

transactional process
    model   *36*

WRITING AND CRITICAL THINKING

The following activities can be completed online or submitted to your instructor.

Choose one of the following activities:

1. Select a theory of organizational management. Describe the communication theory associated with the theory you selected. How are the theories linked? Link the tenets of the theory to your own organizational experiences.
2. Analyze a memorable conversation or dialogue from a current film. Look for points of theory described in the text. How does this exercise inform your understanding of the term *conscious communication?*
3. Working with your classmates as a group, select a theory discussed in this chapter that could help resolve the following situation:

    John has recently joined your team. He does not share the team's goal or vision for completing the project required by your instructor. He shows up for meetings without being adequately prepared,

and he doesn't talk unless directly spoken to. Every team meeting is a struggle to get John on board.

Which theory best describes this situation? What does the theory suggest as an intervention? Given what you have learned in this chapter, what might you and your team members do? What theories informed your answer?

4. Interview an employee in an organization and ask her or him to describe the following: What is the environment of the company? How does information flow through the company? How do decisions generally get made? What is the mechanism for employee feedback? What benefits do they perceive as an employee working for that company? Visit the web page of that same company and compare and contrast the profile presented by the employee with the one presented to the public on the web.

PRACTICING COMMUNICATION IN PROFESSIONAL CONTEXTS

Moving from Mindless to Mindful Communication

The next breakthrough skill offers a special challenge and opportunity for communication growth. Spend an entire day communicating mindfully. To do justice to this activity, you should follow these guidelines:

- *Avoid mindless communication.* Refrain from answering questions in ritualistic, routine ways. Rather than asking, "How are you?" ask, "How did your interview go yesterday?"
- *Connect with each person you meet in a sincere and interested way.* Don't allow your mind to wander to others in the room, the

things you need to do, what's happened to you in the past, or what you are going to have for lunch.

- *Don't give up.* When you find yourself communicating mindlessly, simply remind yourself of your goal and get back on track.
- *Communicate ethically.* Refrain from telling "little white lies" during your conscious communication.
- *Communicate authentically.* Do not say things just to please people if you don't mean them; speak your mind, from your heart.

- *Analyze each communication situation for the needs and expectations of others.* Think about possible communication choices before you speak. Adapt your communication to each listener or audience you encounter throughout the day.
- *Ask for and honestly evaluate the feedback you receive.* Use the feedback to determine how successful you were in accomplishing your purpose and as a source of corrective information capable of informing future communication choices.

YOUR COMMUNICATION PROFILE

While completing the above Practicing Communication in Professional Contexts activity, keep a journal of your "conscious communication day." Note the communication events that were conducted mindfully and those in which you lapsed into mindless communication. What did you learn from your experience?

INTERPERSONAL COMMUNICATION

THE POWER OF VERBAL AND NONVERBAL COMMUNICATION IN THE GLOBAL WORKPLACE

CHAPTER **3**

COMMUNICATION OF SELF IN THE WORKPLACE

In this chapter, we examine the relationship of communication to our work identities and how the concept of power influences our identity and the way we view others. What we say and do in the presence of others largely determines who we are, or our identities in the workplace. In turn, our identities determine how much power we have to influence others and outcomes. To develop positive identities and have influence at work, you need to understand the role verbal and nonverbal communication play in how others see you. As you will learn, issues of identity and power relate to how conscious we are of our presentation of self in verbal and non-verbal communication situations.

Identity is the response we get from others to what we say (verbal communication) and do (nonverbal communication) (Mead, 1934; Goodall, 1983; Wood, 1997). In this way, we can only partially control our identity at work. Those with whom we exchange verbal and nonverbal communication have a great deal of impact on our workplace identity. To gain more personal control over others' perceptions of our identity requires us to become more conscious of our communication.

How can we do that? By becoming more aware of the influence of our verbal and nonverbal communication in the workplace and choosing strategies for improving our image. Table 3.1 shows the connection between awareness and identity in the conscious communicator.

TABLE 3.1 | AWARENESS CONTINUUM

Verbal and Nonverbal Awareness Continuum		
Unaware	**Moderately Aware**	**Aware**
Communicator uses:	Communicator:	Communicator uses:
◆ unclear, ambiguous phrases.	◆ uses a mixture of clear and ambiguous phrases.	◆ clear, strategically unambiguous phrases.
◆ no strategies for upward and downward communication.	◆ attempts to apply upward and downward communication strategies.	◆ strategies for upward and downward communication.
◆ exclusive, disconfirming messages.	◆ uses a mixture of inclusive and exclusive messages.	◆ inclusive, affirming messages.
◆ unsupportive messages.	◆ attempts to use supportive messages.	◆ supportive messages.
◆ communication that detracts from professional credibility.	◆ uses communication that doesn't detract from professional credibility.	◆ conscious verbal communication that enhances professional credibility.
◆ communication that displays little or no awareness of the relationship between power and words.	◆ is aware of the relationship between power and words.	◆ communication that demonstrates the relationship between words and power.
◆ communication that displays no awareness of gender differences in talk.	◆ applies knowledge of gender differences in talk.	◆ communication that displays a respect for the differences in the way men and women communicate.
Mindless ⟶		**Mindful**

DEVELOPING AWARENESS IN THE WORKPLACE

As communicators, we need to become more conscious of our overall verbal and nonverbal impact in the workplace. We need to pay closer attention to our word choices, behaviors, appearance, and style of dress. We need to actively seek out feedback from others about our communication in interviews, interpersonal exchanges, group and team meetings, and presentations. By showing others that we are interested in their responses to what we say and do, we encourage them to share information with us about our identity at work.

We also need to become better monitors of the influence of our behaviors on others. By **monitoring**, we mean: (1) checking the accuracy of your perceptions regarding how the messages you sent were actually interpreted, and (2) questioning the cultural and contextual factors that may lead to different perceptions about your communication.

MONITORING OUR ASSUMPTIONS ABOUT COMMUNICATION

It may seem odd that we are often our own worst enemies when it comes to communicating mindfully at work. But the truth is that too often we operate mindlessly, allowing our stereotypes, cultural biases, assumptions about the meanings of words, and routine perceptual filters to control our daily communication.

GLOBAL PROFILE FOR SUCCESS—BREAKING GENDER BARRIERS

Archer Daniels Midland (ADM) began in 1902 as a linseed crushing business. Today, it is an international agribusiness specializing in milling, processing, specialty feed ingredients, specialty food ingredients, cocoa, nutrition, and more. ADM is headquartered in Decatur, Illinois. ADM has manufacturing, sales, and distribution facilities in 40 states and across the globe in Canada, Europe, Latin America, Asia, and Africa.

In 2006, ADM broke the gender barrier, naming Patricia A. Woertz CEO and president. In 2007, she was also named chairman of ADM. As chairman, CEO, and president, Ms. Woertz leads one of the world's largest agricultural processing companies.

Explore ADM's website: http://www.admworld.com/euen/.

What can you learn about thinking globally from the ADM's website? What skills are necessary to succeed in the global workplace as a member of the ADM team? What does having a woman as chairman, CEO, and president tell you about ADM?

Most of us operate mindlessly because we live as if our assumptions about verbal and nonverbal meanings are essentially the right ones. For example, we assume that we were brought up the right way, that our religious and political beliefs are correct, and that our thoughts and feelings about what others say are justified. It is as if we assume that our life—which is also to say our culture, gender, age, socioeconomic level, and race—is the center of the known universe and that everything and everyone essentially revolves around us. The problem with this belief in our assumed "rightness" is that it may lead us to treat others unfairly or to create inequity in the workplace.

THE PRINCIPLE OF WORKPLACE EQUITY

Equity is the principle that we should be treated fairly by others and, in turn, should treat them fairly. Think of equity as the golden rule that governs the choosing and creating of verbal strategies for workplace communication.

The concept of equity is based on four key assumptions (Walster, Walster, and Bershied, 1978; Wilson and Goodall, 1991):

1. *People work for rewards.* **Rewards** are what people derive from their work (money, identity, power, support, companionship, a skill set) in relation to what it costs them (physical labor, mental and emotional stress, loss of free time, time away from family, subordinating personal goals, dealing with difficult people, harassment). When what they get out of going to work balances with what it costs them to be there, they feel a sense of equity. Some days are better than others, but overall there is a sense of fairness, of justice in their work lives.

2. *People seek empowerment.* When people believe they are being rewarded fairly, they tend to do a good job and feel good about the work they perform. Workers who feel a sense of equity also tend to feel empowered. **Empowerment** is the process of enabling and motivating employees, mainly by removing obstacles, which builds feelings of personal effectiveness and control. When employees feel they are heard and their input is valuable, their performance improves. They actively seek better ways to perform tasks and get along with people because, in the end, what is good for the business is good for them.

3. *People become stressed when they feel they are treated unfairly.* When people find themselves in a state of inequity, they become stressed. Inequity may be caused by unequal pay for doing the same job as others, unfair treatment by coworkers or bosses, or a sense that the company doesn't care about the welfare of the worker as much as the worker cares about the welfare of the company. The stress brought on by feelings of inequity impairs the job being done. The more inequity felt, the more stress experienced, and the worse the job becomes.

4. *People who experience stress will try to restore equity.* When people experience stress brought on by feelings of inequity, they will try to restore equity in one of three ways: 1) *seeking mental equity* (making excuses for the bad treatment, forgiving the wrongdoer, assuming an attitude of moral or intellectual superiority); 2) *seeking actual restitution* (doing less work, slowing down the work of others, stealing property); or 3) *seeking narrative equity* (talking negatively about the workplace; engaging in gossip and rumors designed to lessen the influence of the perceived wrongdoer; telling work-hate stories).

In many ways, the equity principle can be applied directly to choosing communication strategies in the workplace. Your overall goal should be to select strategies that encourage others to treat you equitably and demonstrate your interest in treating others equitably.

Making Conscious Choices about Verbal Communication

Making conscious choices about communication is a central way in which you can become a better workplace communicator. It also may improve your communication skills at work. Why? Because most people's verbal communication at work can suffer from these types of problems:

- a lack of clarity or a misuse of ambiguity
- an inability to distinguish communication strategies for upward or downward communication in the organization
- a failure to distinguish between inclusive (affirming) and exclusive (disconfirming) message strategies
- a failure to distinguish supportive from nonsupportive messages
- an inability to conceive of verbal communication as a way of enhancing professional credibility
- a lack of awareness of the relationship of our words to power
- a lack of awareness of gender differences in talk
- a failure to recognize and/or respond to multiple cultural interpretations of a message

In the following sections we describe each of these verbal communication challenges in more detail.

Clarity and Ambiguity

Clarity means providing messages in the clearest, least ambiguous way. **Ambiguity** means expressing oneself in terms that are either unclear or open to multiple interpretations. One of the most frequently given pieces of advice for the workplace is to *always communicate clearly*. As you learned in Chapter 2, the underlying theory of communication informing this advice is the *information transfer model*. The idea, simply put, is that if a sender can find the clearest, least ambiguous way to say something, the chances are greater that the receiver will hear and understand it as it was intended. The problem with this conception of communication is that regardless of how clear the message may be from the sender's point of view, people listening to it may still interpret the meanings of words differently. This problem is even more profound when we take into account the differences in cultural interpretations of messages (Corman, Trethewey, & Goodall, 2008).

Does this mean that clarity shouldn't be a goal of effective communication? Absolutely not. It does mean that even if you choose and plan a message that you think is clear, your audience may not interpret exactly what you intended to communicate in the same way you intended it to be interpreted. For this reason, it is best to assume that *mis*communication is always a possibility, and ask for feedback on what message your listener actually received and interpreted. When you behave this way, you gain power over the meanings others attribute to your communication.

UPWARD AND DOWNWARD COMMUNICATION

A nationwide survey of employees who changed jobs points to a correlation between employee turnover and supervisor relationships. The majority of those surveyed cited a bad supervisor—not low pay—as the main reason for job change (*Greensboro News and Record*, May 30, 2000). We believe that at the core of the breakdown in the supervisor-employee relationship are poor communication skills and a lack of training in how to communicate in the global workplace.

Although a number of contemporary organizations have flattened older hierarchical structures and empowered employees, most companies still equate hierarchical position within a company with power. Put simply, the higher up you are on the organizational ladder in terms of title, position, seniority, or salary, the more authority you have to exert influence on those whose position is understood to be hierarchically lower. As you learned in Chapter 2, the power that is associated with a position in an organization is referred to as *legitimate* power.

In everyday communication, power among levels of legitimate authority in organizations is greatly influenced by choices made about the style and content of your message. This means that how you choose to speak, write, email, or text to organizational superiors (anyone higher than you on the ladder), organizational equals (anyone at the same level on the ladder), and organizational subordinates (anyone lower on the ladder) may determine how they respond to your identity, requests, directives, and commands.

Messages directed at organizational superiors are called **upward communication**. In general, the following communication choices tend to enhance employees' power and identity with superiors:

- balancing politeness with a clear task orientation
- balancing friendliness with respect and deference to authority
- balancing self-interest with company needs
- asking for feedback on the accomplishment of tasks
- avoiding sexist, racist, or classist remarks

Messages directed at organizational subordinates are called **downward communication**. In general, the following communication choices tend to enhance employees' power and identity with subordinates:

- listening openly to employees' communication
- responding honestly to inquiries and requests
- asking for information prior to evaluating a situation or problem
- providing feedback on tasks
- avoiding sexist, racist, or classist remarks
- balancing personal and professional respect with a task orientation and accountability

Messages directed at organizational peers is referred to as **lateral communication**. In general, the following communication choices tend to enhance your working relationships with your peers by:

- listening openly to employees' communication
- responding honestly to inquiries and requests
- asking for information prior to evaluating a situation or problem
- providing feedback on tasks
- avoiding sexist, racist, or classist remarks
- balancing personal and professional respect with a task orientation and accountability
- being guided by a sense of equity, helpfulness, and good will in all interactions

INCLUSIVE AND EXCLUSIVE MESSAGES

Organizations are *cooperative* settings. To work in an organization usually means to work with other people, using communication to coordinate objectives and activities and to share meanings. For this reason, your identity at work derives from generalized observations about how you deal with people. Are you open to the ideas of others? Do you seek feedback? Are you interested in what others think and feel about issues? Do you share credit (or blame)? Are you an interesting person? Do you have a good sense of humor?

Evaluations such as these reflect what communication scholars refer to as "inclusive and exclusive" message strategies. The basic idea is that how you treat others at work is part of an overall goal you have for using talk in your life. In political terms, one way to conceive of the difference is to think about democratic versus autocratic strategies. **Inclusive message strategies** are *democratic* because they reveal your interest in fitting in with the group or business culture, taking into account the thoughts and feelings of others, soliciting contributions from others, and actively valuing differences in opinion as a way of maximizing the available information needed to carry out a task. Examples of inclusive strategies include actively coordinating your goals with coworkers' goals, asking for and being willing to give feedback about tasks, soliciting the opinions of others on a project, and avoiding seeking sole credit for good ideas or work.

By contrast, **exclusive message strategies** reveal an *autocratic* communication style. Exclusive strategies are revealed in a "me first" pattern of behavior. Examples of exclusive strategies include seeking individual credit for ideas or work, requiring compliance from others, attempting to forge close allegiances with selected others who can advance your personal goals or career (often without feeling any equitable obligations or sense of reciprocity), pitting one group or person against another, and demonstrating a lack of interest in the opinions of others, particularly others whose opinions or background may differ from your own.

We choose to behave inclusively or exclusively. As a result, others evaluate our patterns of behavior accordingly. People who reveal an inclusive pattern tend to find that others work with them in achieving goals, affirm preferred identities, and cooperate with them in accomplishing tasks. They tend to be more integrated into formal and informal communication networks, thus improving their opportunities to gain and give feedback. They tend to be valued as team players by managers and coworkers. By contrast, people who demonstrate an exclusive pattern tend to find themselves more isolated from others in the workplace, which often translates into feeling less connected to formal and informal networks. Because they are not interested in the opinions of others and do not seek feedback, they leave themselves, their motives, and their actions open to suspicion, misinterpretation, and criticism. As a result, those who use exclusive message strategies tend to have less influence in the workplace and less control over interpretations of their identities.

CONFIRMING AND DISCONFIRMING MESSAGES

People are sensitive to the responses others give to their messages. One way in which we monitor our work identities is by evaluating the responses we get as being either confirming or disconfirming. Confirming responses support and enhance the identities we seek:

"I appreciate the work you did on this project."

"I think that's a great idea!"

"You're a wonderful employee."

Using the equity principle discussed earlier, you can see how positive, confirming messages influence coworkers, subordinates, and superiors to reciprocate. Confirming messages also may inspire them to repeat exemplary performances or even encourage them to believe they are capable of higher qualities of work.

By contrast, disconfirming messages attack the very heart of workers. Disconfirming messages deny or harm our identities:

"I can't believe anybody in this company would do such a stupid thing!"

"This is incompetent work."

"I'll never forget that you made this mistake."

"I can't believe I ever trusted you to carry out this task."

"You are a fool!"

Using the equity principle, you can see what is likely to happen when disconfirming messages are given to coworkers, subordinates, or superiors. The targeted individual will probably retaliate by seeking some form of restitution for the perceived harm done to her or his identity.

So is it possible to communicate effectively with people who have made mistakes on the job without being disconfirming? Yes. When engaging in corrective communication, it is important to limit the discussion to the task at hand and not attack the person's identity. In this way, you separate the mistake from the identity of the person who made it, and you show others that you treat people fairly and responsibly on the job. As you can imagine, these verbal choices will also enhance perceptions of *your* identity.

That said, sometimes emotions get the better of us. When stressed, many people say or do things they later wish they hadn't. Another important form of verbal communication in any workplace is the *sincere apology*, which is best communicated by (a) taking personal responsibility for your poor choice of behavior, and by (b) promising to not let it happen again. Equity may be partially restored when a sincere apology is given, but the proof of your sincerity will be tied to your future choices of behavior.

SUPPORTIVE VERSUS NONSUPPORTIVE MESSAGES

Closely related to inclusive and confirming message strategies is the mindful goal of using communication to provide support for others. As we have pointed out, because the workplace is a cooperative setting, people value others who try to support them. **Supportive messages** communicate concern and respect for others and indicate cooperation. Supportive messages include the following:

- offering to help out on a project
- listening
- doing thoughtful things for your coworkers
- showing respect for others' views and feelings, as well as for the general condition of the workplace
- demonstrating concern for the welfare of coworkers and their families

By contrast, the use of nonsupportive messages closely relates to exclusive, disconfirming communication. **Nonsupportive messages** are associated with an inflated ego and self-centeredness. They communicate disrespect of others and lack of cooperation:

- appearing aloof and behaving in a superior manner with coworkers
- refusing to be of assistance on a project when asked
- withholding information
- not listening
- disrespecting others and the condition of the workplace
- lacking concern for the welfare of coworkers
- not being a team player
- putting yourself and your needs ahead of everyone else's needs

Individuals who choose to be supportive in their dealings with others at work tend to encourage others to treat them equitably in return. Individuals who behave in supportive ways also encourage a sense of equity from others: supportive behavior tends to reap more benefits than does unsupportive behavior. In terms of constructing an identity in the workplace, supportive messages tend to encourage others to affirm your identity and, at the same time, provide corrective feedback when necessary. After all, being supportive sometimes means pointing out ways that communication may be improved or errors corrected. In this way, *support does not always mean affirmation*. Supportive messages, however, go a long way toward encouraging others to help you obtain your goals.

ENHANCING PERSONAL AND PROFESSIONAL CREDIBILITY

One of the first theorists of human communication, Aristotle, pointed out in his classic treatise, *The Rhetoric*, that the goal of all public talk should be the improvement of one's character with one's peers. Today, we describe that goal for talk as "the enhancement of personal and professional credibility."

Credibility refers to the authority and trust listeners or audiences give to speakers. If we believe that an individual is a good person, knowledgeable about a topic, and trustworthy, we tend to pay more attention to what he or she says. We also tend to be more easily influenced by that person. For this reason, advertisers promote their products with testimonies given by credible spokespersons. Credibility is often associated with celebrity, which may be a cultural by-product of living in a media-saturated age. However, the fact remains that we are persuaded most by people we find credible.

In the workplace, employees find that by developing their own personal and professional credibility, they also influence others to affirm their identities. Credibility is a goal for communication that is enhanced by the following actions:

- becoming informed and knowledgeable about the work assigned to you, which includes being an information resource for others, and providing people with the information they need when they need it
- behaving in a trustworthy manner by keeping secrets and confidences, looking for the good in situations and in others, and not spreading gossip and rumors
- being open, honest, and authentic in your dealings with everyone
- demonstrating that you are capable of being a friend as well as a coworker by showing respect and caring for others on the job
- doing what you say you will do, which means becoming reliable as a person and as a professional
- graciously accepting criticism and corrective feedback from others, and using these messages to improve your performance
- accepting personal responsibility for your actions and not blaming others for your problems, challenges, or mistakes

VERBAL COMMUNICATION AND PERCEPTIONS OF POWER

Communication is the basis for identity, and it is also the source of personal and professional power. Forms of organizational and institutional power are tied to one's status and hierarchical position at work. For example, a manager has the power to organize work teams, set objectives, and evaluate workers. Similarly,

THINKING GLOBALLY—GREETINGS IN THE GLOBAL WORKPLACE

Did you know that the thumbs-up gesture frequently used in America is considered an offensive gesture in Latin America, parts of Africa, Greece, and southern Italy? Every culture has an acceptable form of greeting. Each form of greeting accounts for issues of physical proximity, cultural traditions, and gender expressions. Many of you will work with people from different cultures or you may travel to different countries on business. Before engaging in business with people from other countries, you should review the traditions for greeting those from other countries.

There are numerous sources on the Internet covering this subject. To access these sources, do a search using these keywords: *gestures, culture, and business*.

A Short Course in International Business Culture by Charles Mitchell (World Trade Press, 1999) offers information for communicating in positive ways overseas. Books such as this one will help those of you who travel, or think you may travel, internationally for business to build a knowledge base for basic etiquette and manners in the global workplace.

forms of cultural power derive from an individual's wealth, perceived attractiveness, or family lineage.

But there is a form of power that is not tied to status or cultural hierarchies and that directly relates to communication. This is the communication power that refers to the perception others have of your ability to use words and actions to obtain workplace results that would not have occurred otherwise. In this way, communication power is a rhetorical or narrative quality attributed to you by listeners, audiences, coworkers, or managers because of what you say and do.

GENDERED TALK

Research has shown that women and men can differ in the ways they tend to communicate, construct meanings, and derive implications or evaluations from communication (see Tannen, 1994; Wood, 1997). For this reason, we say that all talk is "gendered." **Gendered talk** refers to the differences in the ways men and women tend to communicate.

Generalizing about gendered talk in the workplace is difficult. For every generalization, there are clear exceptions to the rule. There are also important cultural differences. However, research studies have shown the following to be true (Wood, 1997):

- Women generally use talk to build rapport in relationships; men generally use talk to make reports to others.
- Women's style of talk tends to be more expressive (rich with words intended to deepen understanding and meaning); men's style tends to be more instrumental (clipped responses, intended to provide direction).
- Women's communication style tends to be more tentative; men's style tends to reflect more certainty.
- Women tend to use talk to create and maintain relationships; men tend to use talk to gain control over situations and others.

VERBAL LIE DETECTORS

Do you know when someone is telling the truth? Here are some tips that may help you detect when someone is trying to deceive you.

- Response time—the time between the end of a question and the start of a reply. Liars take longer and hesitate more.
- Distancing—not saying "I," but talking in the abstract. For example, liars might say, "One might believe...."
- Uneven speech—stuttering while trying to think through the lie. Liars might also suddenly talk quickly, attempting to make a sensitive subject appear less significant.

- Gap filling—liars are too eager to fill in the gaps of conversation. Liars keep talking when it is unnecessary, as if a silence signifies that the other person does not believe them.
- Raised pitch—liars raise their voices unnaturally. Instead of the pitch dropping at the end of a reply, it is lifted in the same way as asking a question.
- Message insecurity–liars are unsure of their message, which leads to an increase in stuttering, slurring, and Freudian slips.

Adopted from Adrian Furnham, 1999, "Gesture Politics," *People Management* 6, 52.

For reasons that should be clear from the list of gendered differences, we suggest that women and men can improve their communication in the workplace by meeting halfway. For example, avoid the assumption that your intentions or meanings are clearly shared. Avoid talk that stereotypes another's talk or that connotes inferiority due to gender (such as "Only a woman would..." or "Guys always think..."). Think about the gender implications of communication *prior* to speaking. Lastly, be willing to switch styles when the situation calls for it.

Your workplace identity is based on the responses you get from others to what you say and do. However, you can have some control over how others respond to you by making wise choices about message strategies designed to help you accomplish your personal and professional goals. By communicating inclusively and affirming others' identities and efforts, by showing support for others, by striving to become credible as a person and as a professional, and by being more aware of cultural and gender biases in talk, you limit the possible negative responses others can make. You gain greater control over their perceptions of you and of your chances of reaching your goals with their help.

NONVERBAL COMMUNICATION AND PERCEPTIONS OF MEANING

Nonverbal communication is the natural counterpart of verbal communication. Nonverbal means "without words," and nonverbal communication refers to all of the resources beyond what you say that contribute to the meaning of a message. Unless you are physically removed from your listeners or audience (for example, talking on the phone or using e-mail), what is interpreted as meaningful in your interaction will be informed by what you say—and by how you look when you say it. Researchers have found that between 65 and 70 percent of the social meaning of communication is conveyed nonverbally (Birdwistell, 1970; Philpott, 1983). Researchers also have established that if there is a discrepancy between what you say and how you look when you say it, most listeners will believe your nonverbal actions over your verbal ones (Andersen, 1998).

In this section we want to examine the sources of nonverbal communication in business and professional contexts. Throughout our discussion, we want you to understand that although "actions speak louder than words," in most cases actions work *with* words to produce meanings. The discussion in this section is centered on the nonverbal communication that is commonly accepted within corporate America. If you find yourself dealing with other cultures, you should familiarize yourself with their nonverbal expectations and taboos.

YOUR WORKSPACE

In the global workplace, it is important to view your workspace as a reflection of the image you want to portray at work. Rather than risk offending your coworkers or clients, err on the side of caution and keep your work area neat, free from clutter, and clean. Limit the display of "artifacts." Artifacts are the "stuff" that populates a desk, office, or cubicle area; they serve to mark a territory as your own. We encourage the use of artifacts that attest to your accomplishments—diplomas, certificates, and awards. We discourage the display of too many personal items, and under no circumstances should you display anything that has suggestive sexual content. Our basic message is to treat your workspace as an extension of your professional self. Become conscious of the way your office area and artifacts communicate to others. To create the optimal workspace:

- Keep displays of your personal life to a minimum. One family photograph is enough. Don't clutter your office with items that may suggest you'd rather be doing something else.
- Prominently display diplomas, awards, certificates, and other professional accomplishments.
- Clear your desk and empty your trash prior to leaving work for the day.
- Be aware of the messages you are sending when you display personal items in your workspace. Keep personal collections at home. Your workspace is not the area to show off your car magazines, stuffed toys, or collection of cat photographs.

The books highlighted below will help you create your workspace. Putting time and effort into the appearance of your workspace sends a clear nonverbal message to those around you that you are considerate of others and that you take your work seriously.

- *Taming the Paper Tiger at Work*, by Barbara Hemphill (Kiplinger Books, 2005). This book is considered by many working in large companies to be the definitive book on organizing your workspace. Hemphill provides tips for managing a filing system, organizing your computer, using to-do lists, and knowing when to use piles. She also provides a list of essential tools for setting up your office files and tips for managing your voice mail.

- *Feng Shui Your Workspace for Dummies*, by Jennifer Lawler and Holly Ziegler (John Wiley and Sons, 2003). Feng shui is based on the principle that every space has energy, so that how you arrange your space either enhances or detracts from your energy. By positioning your desk and other materials in the optimal place, you can create an office that energizes you and helps you achieve your goals. Feng shui also addresses issues such as clutter, which many believe saps your energy and your ability to accomplish tasks and move forward.

CLOTHING AND PERSONAL APPEARANCE

You've undoubtedly heard the expression "You never get a second chance to make a good first impression." But have you ever asked why that is true? The answer is that most humans make initial evaluations of others based on stereotypes, and stereotypes are largely derived from the size and shape of our bodies, the clothing we wear, and perceptions of our level of physical attractiveness (Andersen, 1998). Of course we know we should avoid stereotyping and that evaluations made on the basis of stereotypes can be wrong, but most of us engage in it routinely every day. There is no place in our lives where stereotyping is more evident than in the formation of initial impressions. According to uncertainty-reduction theory (Berger and Calabrese, 1975), nonverbal cues are read and interpreted against stereotypes to reduce the uncertainty in initial interactions. In other words, as tennis star Andre Agassi put it, "Image is everything."

What does research about personal appearance teach us? For one thing, our culture values and rewards people who are tall, physically fit, appropriately dressed, well groomed, and physically attractive (Andersen, 1998, p. 31). Anyone who has watched television commercials can attest to the fact that the sale of body-building equipment, makeup, perfumes, clothing, beer, and even soft drinks depends on how well the ad communicates its messages of success, popularity, and happiness. Commercials rarely stress the intrinsic worth of being healthy, fashionable, or fit (Jhally, 1997). We live in a postmodern world that glorifies images rather than substance.

In business and professional settings, the norms for our cultural ideals also apply. Every few years, one of the major TV news programs does a segment on job interviews. Invariably, these shows pit a physically fit, well-groomed, attractive, and well-dressed applicant against an overweight, unkempt, unattractive, and sloppily dressed applicant. Both applicants have résumés reflecting exactly the same work experience and qualifications. Not surprisingly, the attractive applicant is consistently hired. The unattractive applicant is treated rudely and rejected on the basis of appearance. Noted communication theorist Peter Andersen has pointed out that "appearances can be deceiving, but that fact is almost beside the point. A communication perspective recognizes that subjective impressions by receivers are all that really matter" (1998, p. 31).

What should you do to "dress for success" on the job? Ethnographic studies have shown the advantages of researching the physical appearance, clothing, and hairstyles associated with people doing the job you are applying for (Goodall, 1989; Goodall and Phillips, 1985). Before applying for a position with a firm, ask for a company tour. Pay close attention to how people dress. Ask yourself if your appearance and clothing choices are a match for this organization. In most cases you will find that human resources people and managers tend to hire people who fit the attitude, appearance, and style of their company (Wilson and Goodall, 1991). Even in the "business casual" workplace, there are limits; going beyond those limits may send the wrong signal.

Once you are on the job, become more conscious of how your clothing choices fit into the norms of the organization. Unless you are interested in making a personal statement (perhaps at some risk to your career), it is a good idea to opt for a look that doesn't attract too much attention. To dress successfully in the global workplace:

- Never dress noticeably better than your boss or your peers. Your boss may wonder if you are moonlighting or going after his or her job. Your peers may feel you are trying to show them up.
- Savvy businesspeople understand that for men, casual dress means khakis or, depending on the organization, neat jeans with a nice golf shirt. Women have a harder time achieving a "business casual" look but should dress down without trying to look like "one of the boys." Avoid tight jeans, shorts, and other apparel that works against your ability to be taken professionally.
- Men and women should keep jewelry to a minimum. Too much jewelry can be distracting and, in some cases, physically limiting. The wrong kind of jewelry can alienate people.
- The reality is that everything in the competitive workplace counts. Our goal here is simply to make you aware.

Need help getting started on a work wardrobe? The books highlighted below will help you find a successful style for the workplace. Keep in mind every workplace is different and these sources are offered as starting points. Putting time and effort into your appearance sends a clear nonverbal message to those around you that you are in control and ready for whatever needs to be done.

- *Chic Simple Dress Smart for Men: Wardrobes that Win in the Workplace*, by Kim Johnson Gross and Jeff Stone (Grand Central Publishing, 2002). This book offers men a simple three-step process for dressing successfully on the job. For those who are wardrobe-challenged, the book includes photographs of shirt-and-tie combinations and more than forty work outfits. This is a practical, how-to guide for putting together looks to find a job, keep a job, or get a better job.
- *Chic Simple Dress Smart for Women: Wardrobes that Win in the Workplace*, by Kim Johnson Gross, Jeff Stone, and Kristina Zimbalist (Grand Central Publishing, 2002). If your goal is to dress in a corporate and traditional style, this book is a good guide. However, this is only one example of how to dress successfully in the workplace. Within the guidelines in the two books listed here, there is room for individuality and creativity. These books offer a good starting point for those who are not sure where to begin.

FOCUS ON ETHICS

Miranda has been working toward a big promotion for more than a year. She works hard, meets deadlines, stays late, and comes to the office early. Miranda is convinced there isn't anything that will hold her back.

Leona, Miranda's boss, respects her work and her work ethic. She recognizes that Miranda is the most dedicated researcher in the division. While she knows Miranda deserves the promotion she has worked so hard for, Leona isn't sure she can promote her to analyst. The promotion means that Miranda would have to meet with government officials and diplomats from other countries. Leona has no qualms about Miranda's ability to present crucial information; she just isn't sure how seriously others would take her. Miranda's entire wardrobe consists of sweaters with seasonal or holiday scenes on

them, khakis, and tennis shoes. While Miranda's work has evolved to the next level, her wardrobe hasn't. Leona doesn't feel Miranda dresses like someone with a high-security clearance who handles and analyzes sensitive government information.

As a researcher who rarely interacts with anyone outside the department, Miranda can wear whatever she wants, but as an analyst, Miranda needs to lose the theme sweaters and dress professionally. Does Leona have a responsibility to discuss an appropriate dress code with Miranda before she makes her decision? Should the way Miranda dresses hinder her career advancement? Is it ethical to deny someone a promotion simply because he or she needs a makeover? Does Miranda have a responsibility to dress in a professional manner?

VOICE

The human voice is a powerful instrument of meaning. Learn to listen critically to how you speak, and monitor the match between your vocal characteristics and the attitude, intention, or emotion you want to convey. Such monitoring is vital to communication effectiveness. How many times have you heard or used the expression "It's not what you said, it's how you said it"? What came across was not the words that were spoken, but an interpretation of the words derived primarily from the sound of the voice, or what communication theorists call *paralanguage*. Paralanguage is a powerful form of nonverbal communication because it conveys to listeners a communicator's attitude, intentions, and emotions. Consider the following list of sources of paralanguage in light of your own experiences in responding to others' speech:

- *pitch* (highness or lowness of the voice)
- *tempo* (speed at which the message is delivered)
- *intensity* (when words are vocally accented, or spoken softly, or with particular emphasis)
- *range* (the ability of the speaker to vary the pitch, tempo, and intensity of what is expressed verbally)
- *resonance* (richness or weakness of tone)
- *volume* (the loudness or softness of the voice)
- *articulation* (the precision with which words are spoken)
- *rhythm* (the relative flow and punctuation of the voice)

- *pauses* (the frequency and duration of silences between words, phrases, or sentences)
- *dysfluency* (punctuation of a message with expressions such as "er," "um," "you know," and "like")

Overall, these sources of paralanguage tell us a lot about the attitudes, intentions, and emotions we use to construct what we call the *meaning* of a message. Consider, for example, how we determine if someone is enthusiastic about a project or nervous about giving a presentation. Or whether someone we asked to carry out instructions will actually do so. In all of these cases, our evaluation is based on the articulation and tempo of the voice, the relative authoritative resonance we hear, smoothness or interruptions in flow, and whether there are too many or too few pauses. How we speak shapes how others interpret our messages.

There is a caveat. Although all of us believe we can evaluate a person's voice with great accuracy, research has revealed important cultural and gender differences. For instance, men who use a wide vocal range and often vary their pitch may be perceived as feminine and aesthetically inclined, whereas women using a similar pattern are perceived as dynamic and extroverted (Richmond and McCroskey, 1995). Similarly, some women and many young people tend to tag their sentences with vocal inflections ("uptalk") that turn a declarative statement into a question. For example, "I'm having lunch with Paul? We'll talk about the project?" may be intended as two statements of fact, but the vocal cues suggest they are two questions.

BODY MOVEMENT, FACIAL EXPRESSIONS, AND EYE CONTACT

The study of body movement, including facial expressions, eye contact, and gestures, is known as **kinesics**. The specific study of the eyes as a source of communication is called **oculesics**. Together, these forms of nonverbal communication dominate the research literature and provide interesting and useful resources for the conscious communicator in business and professional settings.

Of all of the forms of nonverbal expression, the most important source of information is the face, especially the eyes. Research shows that we seldom manifest distinct or recognizable facial expressions when we are alone (Kraut and Johnson, 1979). But the face becomes expressive when we are with other people, and humans have learned to be very attentive to even small differences in facial expression and eye contact.

We also learn how to manage our true feelings using our facial expressions. Researchers have shown that as we mature, we learn to "manage facial affect" by deploying five "display rules" (Andersen, Andersen, and Landgraf, 1985; Ekman, 1978; Bugental, 1982). Those display rules are as follows (from Andersen, 1998, p. 36):

- *simulation*: showing feelings when we have no feelings
- *intensification*: showing more feelings than we actually have
- *neutralization or inhibition*: showing no feelings
- *deintensification or miniaturization*: showing fewer feelings than we actually have
- *masking*: covering a feeling with an expression of a feeling we are not actually experiencing

Children do not learn to manifest these display rules until preschool or during their elementary school years. Mastery of them occurs only in adulthood.

One of the negative consequences associated with failing to express our true feelings is an increase in adverse psychological reactions, feelings of stress, and disease (Buck, 1979). In the workplace, we limit the ability of others to respond when we limit our nonverbal cues. By managing our facial cues, we deprive others of valuable communication information.

Oculesics   The eyes provide the clearest case of meaning associated with nonverbal communication. Why? Because when we talk to someone, we tend to locate their self right behind the eyes. We establish eye contact to make contact with others. According to research (Kendon, 1967), eye contact performs eight potential nonverbal actions:

1. Regulates interaction by signaling turn taking
2. Monitors interaction by receiving information from others
3. Signals cognitive activity, because eye contact is typically broken when individuals are thinking about complex issues
4. Expresses involvement in the interaction
5. Reveals intimidation through intensive staring, particularly when combined with negative facial expressions
6. Reveals flirtation
7. Reveals attentiveness
8. Displays the level of participative immediacy of listener involvement and attention

Researchers also have discovered that the eyes communicate through pupil dilation. Our pupils dilate (enlarge) when we are aroused by, interested in, or

BENEFITS OF MAKING EYE CONTACT

There are five benefits to making good eye contact:

1. It instills trust. Looking directly at the person you are speaking to sends a nonverbal signal that you are not trying to hide anything.
2. It signals confidence. Maintaining eye contact in a natural and confident way gives others confidence in you as a businesslike, serious, and self-assured speaker.
3. It allows you to appear engaged. Maintaining good eye contact provides you time to think and evaluate what you are hearing, while appearing engaged in the conversation.

4. It elicits feedback and encourages give and take. Demonstrating interest in your audience encourages your audience to give you feedback and to participate in the conversation.
5. It allows you to maintain control. Stopping a presentation and pausing until people have refocused their attention may not always be possible, but in some circumstances it maybe necessary to regain control. Wait until everyone's attention is refocused and then continue your talk. Use eye contact to remain connected with your audience so that you do not lose control of your presentation or your message.

attracted to another person (Andersen, Todd-Mancillas, and DiClemente, 1980). Most people are relatively unconscious of this signal and in many cases attribute positive responses to something else—a pleasant facial expression or a nice smile.

Eye movement is a controversial area of nonverbal communication research because results have been inconsistent. However, there is a general belief that the eyes move right or left during cognitive activity, and that there is a tendency, at least in males, to move the eyes to the left when employing visual or spatial right-hemisphere thought and to look right when employing linguistic cognition.

In business and professional settings, just as in everyday life, facial expression and eye contact communicate potentially useful information about ourselves and others. In our experience as consultants, we often find that people who display positive, affirming, and inclusive facial expressions and who maintain eye contact tend to win allies and gain a reputation for being good to work with or for. They are perceived as being easy to be around, and they seem to send a general nonverbal message of openness to and interest in others. How do they do this? In our experience, they are skilled in maintaining eye contact with listeners and using eye contact as a source of information about the emotional responses of others; using positive, affirming head nods to indicate they are listening to and appreciating the information being shared; and smiling easily and genuinely.

We tend to believe that the eyes are the source of truth about character and intention. Given that chronic liars tend to be very good at maintaining eye contact while telling lies, this is probably not as good an indicator of character as we believe it is. We also believe that smiles and affirming head nods are signs of interest, attention, and respect. However, in other cultures, such as Asian cultures, head nods merely mean that a message is being heard, not necessarily agreed with. These differences suggest that easy generalizations probably are not warranted.

Nevertheless, becoming a more conscious communicator means monitoring your own and others' facial expressions and eye contact. It is important to become aware of the nonverbal messages you may be sending others with your face, eyes, and body, as well as how these messages may be interpreted differently in diverse cultures. To do well in business and professional settings, you need to be mindful of the potential meaning of these nonverbal messages at least as much as you are mindful of your own and others' verbal content. You must also be mindful of cultural and gender differences that may affect your verbal and nonverbal communication with others.

SPACE

Proxemics is the study of interpersonal space and distance (Andersen, 1998). What do we know about the relationship of nonverbal communication to spatial relationships? Researchers have identified three broad categories of meaning: territoriality, crowding and density, and personal space.

Territoriality Humans are territorial creatures. Think about your desk in a classroom, or your room in your residence. How do you feel when someone invades your space? What do you do about it? Researchers have found that we use nonverbal communication to signal our boundaries, or markers of the edges of our territories (Sommer, 1969). We may leave our books or clothes on chairs or in rooms, or we may place backpacks on tables. In dating relationships, partners often leave behind personal items as if to signal to others that they are currently occupying this space, and perhaps to ward off potential intruders.

Crowding and Density   It has become a cultural cliché to say "I need my space." But in fact, research shows very clearly that this is true. When we feel crowded—in classrooms, rock concerts, or offices—we tend to become measurably stressed. In cases of extreme crowding, people have been shown to become pathological and engage in criminal conduct.

Personal Space   As we walk through life, we feel that we own a certain degree of space around us at all times. We call this area our **personal space**, and research indicates that we feel violated, uneasy, stressed, and potentially violent if anyone other than an intimate encroaches on it (Hall, 1968; Anderson, 1999). Our sense of the extent of our personal space varies from culture to culture—what a Canadian thinks is close may seem distant to someone from Turkey. Hall (1968) maintained that in North America we have four "zones of interaction":

- *Intimate zone*—from the edge of our skin to about eighteen inches away from our bodies. We allow into this zone only close friends, intimates, and family members.
- *Casual or personal zone*—from about eighteen inches to four feet away from our bodies. This is the space we reserve for most conversations and social engagements with friends and family members.
- *Social-consulting zone*—from four to eight feet. This is the zone we reserve for most business transactions with shop clerks and sales personnel, and with teachers, ministers, lawyers, and other professionals. This is also the zone we use most often in team or group meetings and with anyone with whom we want to signal a "business-only" relationship.
- *Public zone*—eight feet and beyond. This space is reserved for public speakers, celebrities, and executives.

Most people regard these distances as almost sacred. This means that we protect them, and we regard invasions of them to be culturally, if not personally, offensive. For people interested in becoming more conscious of their business and professional communication, it is wise to keep these distances in mind.

TOUCHING

The study of touching as a form of nonverbal communication is called **haptics**. Researchers (Heslin, 1974) have identified five basic types of touching behavior, which we have organized below from least to most intimate:

- *Functional-professional*. This is the form of touching that we expect from physicians, massage therapists, coaches, tailors, hairstylists, and other professionals who must invade our personal space and lay hands on us to do their jobs.

- *Social-polite.* The handshake is the most obvious example of this form of casual, yet meaningful, touching. Other forms include the social hug and the pat on the back, or placing a hand for a moment on the forearm of another person.
- *Friendship-warmth.* This category ranges from the outer limits of social-polite touching to the edge of love-intimacy touching, and for this reason it is the most common and most ambiguous in our culture. As Andersen put it, "Too much touch or touch that is too intimate conveys love or sexual interest, whereas too little touch may suggest coldness and unfriendliness and arrest the chance for relational escalation" (1998, p. 47).
- *Love-intimacy.* This is touching we reserve for those closest to us, and research indicates that it is unique to each person. Usually, this touching is nonsexual, but it may become sexual with the appropriate partner in the right setting. Studies show that when this type of touching occurs, the result is "increased psychological closeness and warmth" (Andersen, 1998, p. 47).
- *Sexually arousing.* This is the most personal and most intimate form of touching shared by humans. Research indicates that it is also the most arousing and most anxiety-producing form of human contact. For this reason, it requires "mutual consent, a high level of attraction, and a desire to stimulate and be stimulated by one's partner" (Andersen, 1998, p. 47).

As with other forms of nonverbal behavior in the workplace, it is important to become aware of the messages that may be communicated by touching. As a conscious communicator, you must be mindful of the potential meaning of such nonverbal messages.

 ## NONVERBAL LIE DETECTORS

Just as there are verbal indicators that someone is being less than truthful, nonverbal cues also may give liars away. Check the speaker's nonverbal behavior for the following:

- Too much squirming. Shifting around in one's seat signals a desire not to be there.
- Too much, rather than too little, eye contact—liars tend to overcompensate.

- Microexpressions—flickers of surprise, hurt, or anger that are difficult to detect.
- An increase in comfort gestures. These often take the form of self-touching, particularly around the nose and mouth.

From Adrian Furnham, 1999, "Gesture Politics," *People Management* 5, 53.

CASE STUDY 2 | BECOMING AWARE OF OUR VERBAL AND NONVERBAL COMMUNICATION IN THE WORKPLACE

Every morning on his way to work, Lawrence listened to the radio. He switched between a National Public Radio news-oriented program to keep up with current events and a local talk show featuring a feisty pair of hosts who engaged callers in a discussion of the "business question of the day."

Most mornings, the questions were about people's personal or work relationships, often focusing on personal relationships with coworkers. Lawrence listened to the talk show, because he believed it revealed how people really interacted in the workplace. Lawrence studied psychology, sociology, and communication as an undergraduate at his state university and was currently enrolled in a weekend MBA program. He worked as the assistant manager of human resources for a large bank, a job that allowed him to combine his interest in people with his love of business. His favorite books were of the self-help and motivational varieties, especially ones by best-selling authors who talked about how to deal with people at work and in personal relationships.

Lawrence saw himself as a positive, empathetic, high-energy person who excelled when working one-on-one with other employees, trying to help them solve work-related problems. He believed that he worked well in small-group or team situations, where he could use his knowledge of people to bring out the best in them. Because of his experiences as a college debater, he felt very comfortable and confident in presentational speaking situations. All in all, Lawrence considered himself a well-rounded communicator. Lately, however, his sense of himself as a good communicator who could handle any situation had been challenged at work. The previous week, he had overheard some coworkers talking about him in unflattering terms. They described him as being a person who is all flash and no real substance. They made fun of his positive attitude, his high level of energy, and his always-present smile. One coworker even joked about the way he dressed, calling his style "Esquire wannabe."

These comments stopped him cold in his tracks. Were they really talking about him? The more he overheard of their conversation, the clearer it became. Not only were they talking about him, they were making fun of the way he spoke and dressed. He stood in the hallway, hidden from view, with a growing sense of anger mixed with fear that gradually gave way to embarrassment. He walked back to his office alone and shaken.

With all his study of "how people are," with all his confidence about his communication skills, he didn't know what to do. Should he charge back down the hall and make a scene? Pretend he hadn't heard them? Act cool, as if nothing of importance had occurred? Try to get even?

As he reflected on his experience, he decided to use it to his advantage. He apparently needed to rebuild his image at work. If he was being perceived as a shallow person, all flash and no substance, what could he do about it? Maybe his clothing was part of the problem. And his big smile. On the other hand, maybe it was the other people who had the problem. After all, what was so bad about having a positive attitude at work? Or being well dressed? Or smiling? Why should he trust the opinions of people who talked badly about him behind his back?

The talk show he was listening to this morning featured the question, "What do your coworkers do that makes you nuts?" The first caller claimed that she wasn't being taken seriously by her coworkers. Lawrence turned up the volume. He listened for a while to her woes: she had good ideas, but other people stole them and she never got credit for the work she did. Within minutes, the hosts began imitating—cruelly, Lawrence thought—her high-pitched voice and her somewhat whiny conversation style. The caller became quiet, and Lawrence felt a little sorry for her.

The second caller complained that coworkers were spreading rumors about him in his organization but he was at a loss about what to do. He felt that if he denied the accusations, he would look guiltier. If he didn't say anything about them, he looked bad, too. Lawrence nodded. The hosts asked what the rumors were about. The caller hemmed and hawed, then finally admitted that the company was in the process of being bought out by a competitor. He was in charge of a department that was due to be downsized, and everyone thought he was negotiating a side deal with the new owners. "Well, are you?" asked one of the hosts. "Who, me?" came the reply. It was instantly apparent that the caller was not going to give a straight answer to the question—which probably

continued

meant, Lawrence mused, that the caller didn't give straight answers to any questions. That was his problem. His coworkers were spreading rumors because there was an absence of truth being told. Lawrence had seen it before.

The third caller reported that she was the victim of repeated sexual harassment at work, and that even though she had filed a complaint, nothing was being done about it. To make matters worse, everyone she worked with now gave her the silent treatment, as if she were the person who had done something wrong by reporting it. "Maybe they fear for their jobs if they associate with a whistle-blower," one of the hosts offered.

"Yeah, maybe," the caller replied. "I'm thinking about quitting," she admitted.

"Don't do that!" shouted one of the hosts. "You haven't done anything wrong!"

The caller sighed loudly. "You know," she said, "it just shouldn't be like this. I wish I knew what to do."

Lawrence, being well trained in dealing with sexual harassment issues, knew the woman was being unfairly treated and found himself aggravated that the human resources department at her company wasn't doing its job properly.

Finally, a woman called in to say that there was this nice guy at work, an assistant manager, whom everyone was down on lately. They talked about him behind his back. They made fun of how he dressed, how he talked, and even the books he read. This angered her, because she knew he was a dependable, hard worker who always had a smile on his face and a positive attitude toward his coworkers. She thought some of his coworkers were jealous of him because he was going back to school to get his MBA, which meant he would eventually get a big raise and

a promotion. She didn't know whether to tell him what was going on. She was also a bit ashamed that she hadn't spoken up to defend him when people were slamming the guy.

Lawrence froze. He recognized the caller's voice. This person worked down the hall from him, in computer services. He had no doubt whom she was referring to. She was talking about him! He listened to this show because it revealed "how people really are." Now he was hearing how he really was, or at least how some others saw him.

As Lawrence turned onto the avenue where his office was located, the hosts were saying it was "too bad" coworkers were acting that way, but they had to wrap up the show. They encouraged the caller to "talk to the man." Then, in their talk-show wisdom, they summed up the complaints they had heard during this hour as proof that "the people we work with are basically the same people we went to high school with, only older, uglier, bolder, and meaner." This line was accompanied by the standard laugh track, and then the show ended.

But for Lawrence, the day was just beginning.

We have included the example of Lawrence to highlight how your verbal *and* nonverbal communication can both undermine and boost your success in the workplace. Successful communicators realize that it isn't just what you say, but how you say it and what you look like when you say it. Successful communicators recognize that communication consists of both nonverbal and verbal messages that create understandings and connections. While Lawrence attempted to create a positive image in the workplace, some of his attempts backfired. If you were Lawrence's coworker, how would you help him improve his reputation at work? What verbal and nonverbal cues should he change?

HARASSMENT AND COMMUNICATION IN THE WORKPLACE

So far in this chapter, we have been concerned with functional forms of verbal and nonverbal interaction. In this section we describe a dysfunctional form of communication that is all too common in the workplace: harassment. In the United

Steven Lunetta/PhotoEdit

States, the Equal Employment Opportunity Commission (EEOC) tracks harassment and workplace discrimination resulting from: race, sex, national origin, religion, age, and disability. Based on EEOC guidelines, harassment includes slurs about sex, race, religion, ethnicity, or disabilities; offensive or derogatory remarks; verbal or physical conduct that creates an intimidating, hostile, or offensive work environment; and creating conditions that interfere with the individual's work performance. Please refer to the EEOC website for more information on this important topic: http://www.eeoc.gov.types/harassment.html.

One caveat. Not all cultures nor all governments recognize these forms of harassment. Once again, we urge you to familiarize yourself with the customs, habits, and laws governing appropriate workplace behavior in the specific country and/or region of the world where you do business.

In the remainder of this section, we will concentrate on sexual harassment, a form of harassment that is, unfortunately, prevalent in the workplace. However, much of the information and many of the tips provided in this section can be applied to the other forms of harassment listed above.

What Is Sexual Harassment?

In the context of the workplace, **sexual harassment** is any form of sexually explicit verbal or nonverbal communication that interferes with someone's work. The Civil Rights Act of 1964, additional legislation in Congress, and federal, state, and local court decisions have addressed two types of sexual harassment. The first type, **quid pro quo** ("this for that") harassment, is based on the threat of retaliation or the promise of workplace favoritism or promotion in exchange for dating or sexual favors. In recent years, this category has been interpreted to refer to suggestions and innuendoes as well as explicit quid pro quo comments. The second type of harassment, a **hostile work environment**, is created through sexually explicit verbal or nonverbal communication that interferes with someone's work or that is perceived as intimidating or offensive. It is important to note that the behavior doesn't have to be intentional to create or contribute to a hostile work environment. Offhand remarks or casual displays of sexually explicit materials count. So do remarks that the sender may think of as "compliments."

Sexual harassment can occur between people of the same sex or of the opposite sex. Although usually associated with the negative behavior and activities of men in the workplace, it also may be litigated when men are the alleged victims and women are the alleged perpetrators. (To view the latest statistics about sexual harassment from the Equal Employment Opportunity Commission, visit http://www.eeoc.gov/stats/harass.html.) Sexual harassment has become so pervasive in North American society that many for-profit and nonprofit companies, as well as most government agencies and schools, have implemented policies, mandatory seminars, and workshops to train employees in how to recognize and prevent it.

Sexual harassment, although clearly recognized as a problem in North American organizations and culture, is not viewed similarly in other cultures. Latin and Mediterranean cultures, for example, do not regulate physical contact or suggestive language usage in professional settings. Because of such differences, many intercultural misunderstandings can occur in the workplace. As we've pointed out already in this chapter, it is a good idea to understand that our assumptions about the rightness of our communication acts are largely culturally determined.

How Can Harassment Be Avoided?

The best defense against a sexual harassment charge is to carefully monitor your own verbal and nonverbal communication. Be courteous and polite at all times. Take other employees' feelings into consideration when you speak to them. Recognize that women and men often respond differently to comments about appearance, suggestions about behavior or attitudes, and sources of humor.

Do not engage in sexual commentary, jokes, or banter about others' appearance or clothing. Do not bring sexually explicit photographs, magazines, objects, or calendars to your workspace. While you should be especially careful about your conduct when you are around people you know to be especially sensitive to issues of harassment, the best practice is not to engage in activities that might be perceived by others as offensive. Trying to excuse yourself for an offensive statement or gesture is embarrassing and hurtful to your credibility at work; losing your job or having to spend months in litigation is far more damaging to your sense of self and career.

We all share an obligation to make the workplace a safe and productive environment for everyone. Toward this end, avoiding verbal and nonverbal communication likely to be perceived as offensive is the only right thing to do.

WHAT SHOULD YOU DO IF YOU ARE A VICTIM OF HARASSMENT?

Even though there are laws against sexual harassment, knowing exactly what you should do when you feel victimized is not always easy. One of the common problems experienced by harassment victims is the belief that either nothing will be done about it or that saying anything about it may cost them their jobs (Claire, 1998). Unfortunately, both of these scenarios can occur. The machinery of the judiciary is often slow, and victims of harassment may be forced to spend months or years in court trying to gain a settlement.

This does not mean you are defenseless. Nor does it mean that you should keep quiet about harassment. What you should do is be conscious of the steps the courts have determined a victim of harassment should pursue:

1. *Confront the harasser and ask him or her to stop the offensive behavior.* This advice is often the hardest to follow. If you fear the harasser, consider writing her or him a letter expressing your concerns or asking a friend to intervene on your behalf. However, it is vital to confront the person with the charge and to document the outcome. Failure to do so can result in a less viable legal position.
2. *Keep a diary in which you record the dates, times, and places of offensive or harassing actions.* In many cases, simply informing a harasser about the problem is enough to stop unwarranted comments or actions. However, if it persists, it is important to record, in as much detail as possible, further incidences of harassment. You are establishing a pattern of harassment, which is much harder for the harasser to defend against in court.
3. *Complain about the harasser within the channels prescribed for such action by the policies of your employer.* Become familiar with the policies regarding employee appeals in your organization. Follow them to the letter. Most companies ask that complaints against employees be made to a supervisor, who may then channel them to a personnel committee, union, or mediator for resolution. It is also important to decide what actions you want taken on your behalf. Will you be satisfied if the harasser stops harassing you? Or do you feel that additional remedies are required—a public apology, a job transfer, coverage of medical expenses?
4. *File a legal complaint with the federal EEOC or with your state agency for workplace discrimination.* You are entitled to file a complaint and to have legal representation. For people who elect to pursue this option, it is a good idea to schedule a meeting with an EEOC representative to discuss your case.

Sexual harassment is a crime. It is very serious business. It doesn't matter to the courts how you may personally feel about it, or whether your words were intended to offend or be complimentary, or how other people may have responded to similar jokes, suggestions, or touching. Being labeled as a convicted harasser will likely have lifetime negative consequences. Think carefully about these consequences *before* you engage in any activity that may be perceived as potentially harassing.

SUMMARY

This chapter explored the dimensions of verbal and nonverbal communication at work. We began by detailing the relationships among messages, identity, and power. In these sections we focused on how important it is to engage in conscious decisions about communication behavior, to monitor the effect of one's choices on others, and to be receptive to feedback about messages.

We then turned our attention to nonverbal communication. In these sections we focused on the powerful influences nonverbal actions have on the interpretation of meanings. We concluded this chapter with a discussion of sexual harassment as a special form of dysfunctional communication involving both verbal and nonverbal components.

BUSINESS AND PROFESSIONAL COMMUNICATION IN THE GLOBAL WORKPLACE ONLINE

All of the following chapter review materials are available in an electronic format on either the *Business and Professional Communication in the Global Workplace* Resource Center or the book's companion website. Online you'll find chapter learning objects, flashcards of glossary terms, InfoTrack® College Edition Activities, weblinks, quizzes, and more.

WHAT YOU SHOULD HAVE LEARNED

Now that you have read Chapter 3, you should be able to do the following:

- Discuss how we make conscious decisions about verbal and nonverbal communication in the workplace.
- Discuss the role of monitoring in conscious communication.
- Discuss the principle of workplace equity.
- Describe the difference between upward and downward communication.
- Explain the differences between inclusive and exclusive messages.
- Discuss the differences between supportive and nonsupportive messages.

- Explain how we can use verbal and nonverbal communication to enhance personal and professional credibility.
- Describe a few types of verbal power displays.
- Discuss differences in the ways men and women tend to communicate.
- List the types of nonverbal communication that may occur in the workplace.
- Discuss the impact of clothing and personal appearance on professional identity.
- Discuss how eye contact affects nonverbal communication.
- Discuss proxemics and why the concept of personal space is important to communication in the workplace.
- Discuss haptics and the types of touch that are appropriate and inappropriate in the workplace.
- Discuss the two types of sexual harassment recognized by the courts.
- Discuss ways to avoid sexual harassment.
- Describe what to do if you are a victim of sexual harassment.

KEY TERMS

ambiguity 56

clarity 56

downward communication 58

empowerment 55

equity 55

exclusive message
  strategies 58

gendered talk 62

haptics 71

hostile work environment 76

inclusive message strategies 58

kinesics 68

monitoring 54

nonsupportive messages 60

oculesics 68

personal space 71

proxemics 70

quid pro quo 76

rewards 55

sexual harassment 76

supportive messages 60

upward communication 57

WRITING AND CRITICAL THINKING

The following activities can be completed online or submitted to your instructor.

Choose one of the following activities:

1. Look at the area of your dorm room or apartment you use for studying, or your office, cube, or desk where you work. What nonverbal messages does your workspace send out? Are they the messages you want others to receive? Investigate the references in this book or go to the bookstore to find resources to help you get your work area in shape. Ask for books on clutter, feng shui, organizing, or space management.

2. Briefly write about a communication event that had a significant nonverbal component. The event you choose can be placed in either a professional or educational setting. What was memorable about the encounter? Did your behavior help or impair your ability to resolve the situation? What would you do differently now that you have read this chapter?

3. Spend a day of conscious, positive communication with the following goals in mind: clarity, inclusion, supportiveness. As you go through the day, be aware of how you use power and gender in your talk. Write a short essay about your experience. What did you notice? Did people respond to you differently? How did you feel at the end of your positive-communication day?

4. Select a country your current employer or a future employer might do business in. Research the business culture for the country you selected. Are there specific do's and do not's for nonverbal communication? How can you use what you learned to improve communication in the workplace?

PRACTICING COMMUNICATION IN PROFESSIONAL CONTEXTS

As a professional, you will be called upon to attend meetings of professional groups or civic organizations. These groups provide opportunities to network, gain information about the profession or industry, and practice communication skills.

Attend, either individually or with your group, a meeting of your local Toastmasters organization (or you may choose to attend another civic or professional meeting). You can use the Internet to locate meeting times and places in your community (for example, the Toastmasters International website is http://toastmasters.org).

This is your opportunity to be a "fly on the wall." Carefully watch the public and interpersonal communication events that occur during the meeting. What verbal and nonverbal cues did you notice people using to deal with communication diversity? How did males and females differ? What cues were used to deal with cultural diversity? How did the older members of the group communicate with the younger members of the group? What cues did you find yourself using?

YOUR COMMUNICATION PROFILE

Watch a film or a video of a speech with the sound turned off. Write down your impression of the nonverbal messages and emotions being conveyed by the speaker and your overall impression of the speaker based on nonverbal cues. Be specific in identifying the nonverbal cues that help form your impression. After writing down your impressions, rewind the video and replay it with audio. Consider the following:

- How accurate were your evaluations?
- Did the nonverbal message match the verbal message?
- If there was a discrepancy between the non-verbal behaviors and the spoken words, what suggestions would you give the speaker to enhance the connection between the verbal and nonverbal language?

Listening in a Multilingual World

CHAPTER 4

BECOMING A CONSCIOUS LISTENER

As we have seen in the previous chapters, often when we think we are communicating effectively, we may not be. This is equally true of **listening**, the process of hearing and interpreting messages. Listening is an integral part of the communication process. Think about it for a moment. How many of us truly listen? How many times has someone said to you, "You're not *listening* to me, are you?" One reason we haven't developed our listening skills is the fast pace of our culture. We don't seem to have time to listen; we're too busy talking, and if we aren't talking, we're formulating what we are going to say next.

Our failure to listen is also because of the lack of formal listening training we receive. Judith Pollack, president of Language at Work, has described the problem this way: "We spend 80 percent of our time communicating, but we only receive training in the speaking, reading, and writing aspects. We *never* really receive training in listening, except at the hands of our teachers and parents" (Jones, 1999, p. 15). Patrice Johnson, director of Spectra Incorporated in New Orleans, emphasized the importance of investing in listening training. She said, "I think listening is getting attention now because organizations don't have the luxury of redundancy. In the past, large dinosaur organizations had plenty of people to do rework, unnecessary work, and so forth. Failing to listen and the errors that it caused could be managed" (Salopek, 1999, p. 58). Now, however, many CEOs, training managers, and business owners think of listening as an important, even crucial, business skill.

Conscious listening, much like conscious communication, can be understood using a continuum (see Table 4.1). The continuum shows the spectrum of listening ranging from hearing to conscious listening, or "listening to the whole," which emerges out of dialogue (Senge et al., 1994, p. 20). Let's look at the listening continuum in more detail.

TABLE 4.1 | AWARENESS CONTINUUM

Hearing	Informational Listening	Critical Listening	Self-Reflexive Listening	Conscious Listening
Listener processes a signal from a speaker.	Listener identifies the signal as words. Moves from hearing to listening.	Listener deliberates on what is said, exploring the logic, reason, and point of view of the speaker.	Listener reflects on how what is said applies to his or her life.	Listener becomes open to the speaker's point of view.
Mindless Listening				➔ **Mindful Listening**

HEARING

Hearing is the passive and physical process of listening. We may hear a speaker's words, but we don't necessarily understand their meaning. Hearing is simply what happens when a message vibrates our eardrums and causes a signal to move to the brain. At the physical level, our ability to listen can be affected by outside elements that may hamper our ability to hear, including noise and physical and technological diversions.

Noise   Imagine you are at a job fair in a crowded hotel conference room. You finally have the attention of the head of personnel for a company you have been trying to interview with for months. However, the noise in the room keeps you from hearing the hiring information you need in order to target your résumé effectively. **Noise** is any sound that disrupts or interferes with the delivery of a message. Noise can cause a listener to become frustrated or confused, or to give up on the message altogether.

Physical Diversions   Have you ever tried to listen in a room that is too hot or too dark? A **physical diversion** is any physical element that disrupts or interferes with the delivery of a message. A few years ago, we were asked to sit in on training sessions at a software development company. The head of training had received a number of complaints from trainees about the material and the trainers. The head of training changed the trainers and revised the materials, but the complaints continued. Oddly enough, trainees complained only when the training was done at the home office. One hour into a training session there, we knew exactly why the trainees were unhappy. The room where the training sessions were held was a medium-gray color. The lights in the main part of the room were kept dim so that the trainees could see the large LCD screen at the front of the room. The temperature was a balmy 78 degrees. The problem wasn't the materials or the trainers. It was the room! The physical space lulled the trainees to sleep and kept them from listening or learning.

Technological Diversions   A **technological diversion** is any technological element that disrupts or interferes with the delivery of a message. How many times have you initiated a conversation, only to have the phone or doorbell ring? Because we work in a home-based office, this happens to us many times a day. After using call waiting for only two weeks, we called the phone company and canceled the service. This "revolution in the way people use the telephone" distracted and annoyed our callers. Even if we did manage to keep the first caller on the line, by the time we returned to the call, our listener was distracted or frustrated and no longer focused on our message.

INFORMATIONAL LISTENING

Informational listening describes the stage when a message begins to be interpreted by the listener. At this stage in the listening process, we assign meaning to the words we hear and we listen for information. Many people conduct much of their business communication at this stage of the listening process, getting caught up in a cycle of listening and responding, without moving on to the next stage, critical listening (see Figure 4.1).

At this level, our ability to listen and gain information can be influenced by internal elements, such as cultural, gender, and language differences. Another factor that may interfere with listening is our communication history with the person speaking. Let's look at each of these factors in more detail.

Cultural Differences Cultural differences affecting communication can include the slang used by a younger or older generation, the language and tonal accents used by another nationality or race, the regional differences in language style, and the jargon used in a certain profession or industry. All too often, we focus on the cultural differences of the speaker and forget to listen to the message itself. In business, where diverse cultures abound, this can become a serious communication problem.

 OVERCOMING BLOCKS TO HEARING

1. Hold conversations in spaces where noise is not a problem. If you are in a crowded or noisy space, try the following:
   - Move to a quieter space, if possible.
   - Make an appointment to call or see the person when you will be back in your office and can concentrate on the conversation. Be sure you have the person's contact information (phone number or e-mail address).
2. Make adjustments to the physical space:
   - Move closer to the front in dim rooms.
   - Adjust the temperature.
   - Hold the speaker or meeting manager accountable for the physical space. If you

attend regular meetings in the same room and every week you fall asleep or freeze during the meeting, bring it to the attention of the person who arranges the meeting.

3. Be conscious of technological distractions:
   - Don't take other calls, read your e-mail, or open your mail while someone is talking to you. Give others your full attention.
   - Be honest if someone begins a conversation during a time when you know you will be distracted. Tell the coworker, "This is not a good time for us to talk. I am really distracted right now and will not be able to give you my full attention. Can we schedule another time to talk about this?"

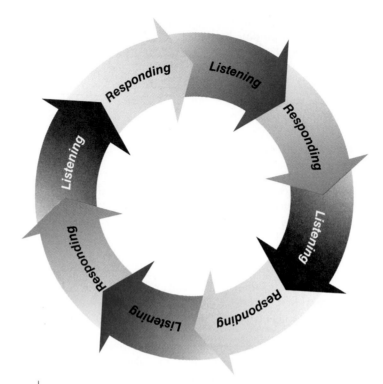

FIGURE 4.1 | THE LISTENING CYCLE

Cultural barriers also can present themselves in less obvious ways. An older male boss may ignore the suggestions of a younger male employee simply because he thinks the younger man is too inexperienced to know what he is talking about. Even clothes can present cultural barriers to listening. When talking to a sales clerk, have you ever found yourself distracted by the clerk's multiple earrings, or choice of earring location? Have you found others distracted by *your* nonverbal presentation of self? How you look and present yourself in a business setting can distract from your ability to communicate, by impeding others' ability to listen.

WORKING WITH NON-NATIVE SPEAKERS

- Pick one member of the group or team as the liaison for the non-native speaker.
- Encourage the non-native employee to put comments, suggestions, or other input in writing. Generally, non-native speakers have a better command of the written language.

- Repeat sentences back to the speaker, clarifying your understanding, one sentence at a time.
- Be patient. It is just as frustrating for the non-native speaker as it is for you. Becoming frustrated or angry will heighten the speaker's anxiety, which will make it more difficult for you to understand each other.

THINKING GLOBALLY—LISTENING IN THE GLOBAL WORKPLACE

We have learned that cultural differences can appear in different ways in the workplace. Consider the following example.

As a highly qualified, motivated programmer, Rasheed joined a development team that was working on a project. Rasheed was new to the United States, as well as to the company. Once he was up to speed on the project, he quickly became known for churning out more lines of code faster and more adeptly than almost all the other programmers on the project. When he spoke, however, his voice was barely above a whisper. In meetings, members of the development team would talk over one another, trading barbs and verbal jabs, excitedly working through ideas.

Rasheed struggled to be heard and after a few attempts to speak, he often he gave up out of frustration. He wasn't used to the team's raucous organizational culture, where everyone had to fight to be heard. Unfortunately, this meant the team lost out on a valuable perspective on the project. After a few weeks, Rasheed confided his concerns to the project manager. At the next meeting, she suggested to the team members that Rasheed raise a manila folder whenever he had a point to make. The tactic worked well. After hearing Rasheed's input, the team members were happy to give him space to talk. Not only did the team listen more carefully to Rasheed, ultimately they began to listen more carefully to one another.

Is it our responsibility as team members and coworkers to adjust our listening styles to those with cultural, gender, or other differences? Was the project manager's method for getting the other members of the team to listen to Rasheed effective? Are there other ways that the cultural barriers between hearing and listening can be addressed? Did the team members working with Rasheed have a responsibility to listen to Rasheed or, was it Rasheed's responsibility to make himself heard in his new organization? How would you handle this type of situation so that all team members are heard?

Gender Differences   We've all probably heard John Gray's statement, "Men are from Mars and women are from Venus." We know that numerous studies point to the differences in the way men and women communicate. Understanding why men and women communicate differently can go a long way toward explaining how men and women listen. Recent studies have shown that men and women use different parts of the brain during listening (Phillips, Lowe, Lurito, et al., 2000). This research shows that men primarily use the left side of their brain for listening, while women use both sides of the brain. So while we may not be from different planets, we certainly hear the world we inhabit differently.

Linguist Deborah Tannen has explained this difference in this way: "Men communicate to report, and women communicate to build rapport," (Tannen, 1990). If men are communicating to *report* knowledge, they probably are not as attuned to receiving feedback or gathering additional information or viewpoints. Men in business often view communication as a simple process of delivery, as one-sided communication events intended to impart knowledge.

If women are communicating to build *rapport* (create mutual understanding), they are more receptive to feedback and to the responses of others. Women generally are considered empathetic listeners. Not only do the words they hear affect them, so do the perceived feelings of the speaker. Openness to feedback and empathetic listening create a view of communication as conversation, as exchanges that are used to further relationships.

Gender differences also seem to occur in the way men and women process conversational cues. Women tend to use and process conversational cues such as "Oh, really?," "Hmmm," and "That's interesting" as means of moving the conversation along. These cues signal they are listening and engaged. For men, these same cues may signal agreement or submission. Men often view such cues as prolonging a conversation when only a quick decision is needed. Women become frustrated by most men's inability to listen, rather than react. Becoming aware of the gender differences in listening can help overcome gender-related misunderstandings and frustrations in the workplace.

Awareness is the first step toward a more effective global workplace. Reading one of the books or articles on gender communication suggested in the References will help you become even more aware of the differences that exist between the genders. You can also try some of the following communication suggestions:

- Be sensitive to the differences in communication. Listen carefully, regardless of a person's gender.
- Use summaries and questions to ensure that you have heard what was said.
- Don't assume that conversational cues such as "Hmm" or "Uh-huh" signal agreement.

Communication History   Have you ever noticed that you tune out certain people *before* they begin to speak? Have you ever considered why you respond this way? Chances are it is because of your **communication history**, the cumulative record of communication events between the participants in a conversation.

Communication history can interfere with listening in many ways. For example, some people just seem to waste your time. Others want to talk about issues you have no interest or stake in. Some people have the communication style of a battering ram; they hammer their point home over and over again. Others communicate only to complain. Their communication revolves around negative messages about how much work they have to do, how unfair the company is, or how bad their personal relationships are. Two distinct problems characterize these dysfunctional communication styles:

1. The speaker views the listener as a passive receptor who is there to absorb whatever message the speaker chooses to send.
2. The speaker assumes that talking is more powerful or important than listening.

As we will see later in this chapter, both of these positions weaken a speaker's ability to communicate effectively. Unfortunately, sometimes in business you have to communicate with these people to gain important information, which might mean wading through a certain amount of overload or negativity first. You can try the following suggestions to deal with communication history barriers:

- Begin any conversation by setting parameters. For example, "Gee, Mahona, I am sorry I can't talk. Hanna needs these figures for a meeting in fifteen minutes."

- Don't avoid someone who has information you need because of your communication history. Acknowledge your history and ask for the information. For example, "I know we normally talk about your job when we meet, but today I would like to focus on our project. If you need to talk about your job, we could schedule lunch later in the week."
- If communication history, or someone's communication style, continues to block your ability to get information, find a new source for the information, or discuss the problem with your boss. You may not be the only one dealing the problem; it might affect your entire team, department, or company.

CRITICAL LISTENING

Many people get bogged down in the cycle of listening and responding. Most of us are skilled in phatic communication and informational exchanges, but often we lack skill in **critical listening**—the ability of a listener to deliberate on what is said by exploring the logic, reason, and point of view of the speaker. It is only when we reach the critical listening stage that we can begin to reflect on the credibility of the speaker, the message, and the motivation behind the talk. Before we can reflect on the impact a message has on us personally, we have to evaluate the qualities of the message.

Speaker Credibility   When we examine a speaker's credibility, we are evaluating the personal and professional qualifications a speaker brings to a communication event. The qualifications a speaker needs in an interpersonal communication event may differ from those required for a formal presentation. For example, if your boss, a twenty-nine-year-old with an MBA from the Wharton School of Business and no actual work experience, offers you advice on dealing with a client you have been working with for five years, how would you view her advice? If the same advice came from an account executive who had worked with the client for eight years before you took over the account, would you view the suggestions differently? On the other hand, if the MBA boss presented a workshop on a new way of creating a monthly sales report that saves time, would you respond more positively to her advice?

Not all speakers are credible in every communication situation. Each situation, event, and speaker must be considered individually.

The Message   When we speak, it is important to back up what we say with support. When we listen, we are listening for the supporting evidence or data a speaker uses to add credibility to a message.

You should listen for the following:

- *Facts and statistics.* Are the facts and statistics offered reliable? Do they come from respected sources? Do they support the speaker's claims, or have they been used simply for effect?
- *Examples.* Are the examples clear and relevant? Or have they been added to make the material seem more interesting? Do you recognize an example as something that holds true for the topic? Can you identify with the example?

- *Personal appeals.* Are the personal appeals used to gain your compliance appropriate for the message and the speaker? Are the appeals being used in place of a strong and clear factual appeal?

Motivation   **Motivation** is the force or reason that drives us toward an action. All talk is rooted in the motivation to reach a goal. For example, we may speak to take up a department's cause, support a program slated to be cut, or move a group to action. Even passing along task information is rooted in a motivation—the need to ensure that a job gets done.

When you evaluate a speaker's motivation, you must listen for the speaker's stake in the message. What does the speaker have to gain? Is the speaker's motivation similar to yours? Or is the speaker acting from a selfish position?

When you speak, evaluate your own motivation. What do others hear you say when they listen to your message? Are your motivations appropriate for the message? Will you be perceived as working for the good of the team, or only for yourself?

SELF-REFLEXIVE LISTENING

So far, our listener has heard what was said, mined the message for useful information, and evaluated the credibility of the person speaking. Now it is time to reflect on the message. **Self-reflexive listening**—listening for how what is said applies to a listener's life—allows us to integrate and then move beyond the first three stages of the listening process. By reflecting on what is said and how it will affect us, we move closer to conscious listening. When we listen self-reflexively, we are listening for the ways a message reflects our identity at work, our personal goals, our understanding of an issue or problem, and our sensitivity to the needs of others.

Identity   When we listen self-reflexively, we hear and reflect on the meanings of what others say about us. Listening to what others say about us, our work, our values, and our work ethic provides us with insight into who we are in the workplace. The words and metaphors people use to describe us—"He's a real go-getter"; "She's the brightest bulb in the accounting department"; or "That's the toughest team I've ever had to work with"—create our work identity. How do people at work describe you? What are the adjectives commonly used when people talk about you or your work? Does this talk accurately reflect who you are or want to be in the workplace?

Personal Goals   Listening for the personal goals of the speaker gives us insight into the speaker's motivation. Listening self-reflexively allows us to think about how our personal goals align with those of the speaker. Is this a person you want to do business with, or are the speaker's personal goals outside of your personal or ethical boundaries? Are your personal goals aligned in such a way that together you could bring about change or close a sale that you could not accomplish separately? Listening for personal goals helps you identify people who can help you succeed and those who do not share your ethical, moral, or business values.

Understanding   Listening self-reflexively provides you with an opportunity to evaluate how well you understand a person, problem, or situation. Too often in business situations, we are concerned with how well *other* people understand a problem. It is much easier to be critical of another's position without really evaluating our own understanding. Listening self-reflexively allows us to listen to the verbal cues that signal *our* understanding of a problem or situation. Cues from others, such as "I really think you are on the right track" or "I'm not sure you see the whole problem," signal how well we grasp their message and intention.

Sensitivity   Listening with **sensitivity** means taking into consideration the differences between you and your communication partners. Becoming a sensitive listener requires listening for, and awareness of, the differences that arise from racial, gender, cultural, socioeconomic, and other factors that contribute to how we evaluate meanings and messages. It means that we are aware of how these differences affect our ability to listen and integrate the message into our thinking.

CONSCIOUS LISTENING

The final stage on the listening continuum is **conscious listening**, openly listening to the speaker's point of view, which emerges out of dialogue. Conscious listening occurs when all of the communication partners involved in a communication episode or event listen for and reflect on how talk affects the whole group, team, or company. Peter Senge has described this conscious listening as the "deeper patterns of meaning that flow through a group that build a subtle awareness of collective thought that profoundly transforms our experience of what is possible" (Senge et al., 1994, p. 20).

Conscious listening transforms us from individuals into relational partners or a collective group moving forward together. Conscious listening, like dialogue, takes into account the shared vision, goals, and values of a relationship, group, team, or organization. Conscious listening results in new alternatives that we would not have seen had we not listened consciously.

GLOBAL PROFILE FOR SUCCESS—LISTENING IS KEY

Terex Corporation is a $2 billion manufacturer of construction, infrastructure, and mining equipment that does business around the globe. Terex is based in Westport, CT.

In an article in *The Chief Executive* (2001), Terex CEO Ronald M. DeFeo emphasized the importance of listening in the workplace. He provided the following insight, "If you listen with a purpose when people talk to you, you will learn from what they have to say, but you will also learn whether you've been *heard*. If you haven't gotten your message

through, you need to construct a method to communicate more directly or more effectively."

Explore Terex's website: http://www.terex.com/main.php.

What can you learn about listening from the Terex website? What skills are necessary to succeed in the global workplace as a member of the Terex team? There is a section on the website about integrity. How does Terex define integrity? Can you meet the standards of integrity set by companies like Terex if you aren't a good listener?

Conscious listening is a vital business skill. It opens us to the views of others, presents possibilities we would not see if we didn't listen consciously, and creates a level of understanding that helps move our relationships, teamwork, and the organization forward. Now that we have a better understanding of listening in the workplace, let's look at what that means in terms of skills and specific business contexts:

- Stop talking. You cannot listen at any level if you are talking.
- Stop reacting. You cannot listen consciously if you are focusing on what you are going to say next.
- Listen for feelings. It is easier to be empathetic if you understand how someone feels. Rather than focus on the content, take a minute to focus on the feelings of the speaker.
- Listen for cues about yourself. What is the listener saying about you? Does it ring true?
- Listen for motivation. What motivates the speaker to feel this way, react this way, take this position?
- Listen for intention. What does the speaker really want to happen as a result of having spoken?
- Listen for position. Is compromise possible, or is the speaker unmovable?
- Listen for benefits. How will this benefit you, your company, or your client?
- Recap what was said as calmly as possible. Use phrases such as "I heard you say that..." or "It seems that you want...."
- Ask for confirmation. Ask questions such as "Do you feel I have a handle on the situation now that we've talked?"
- Suggest alternatives that work for both the individual and the whole. "We could ask Paula to reschedule the meeting so that you will have more time to

---

CASE STUDY 3 | **LEARNING TO LISTEN IN THE WORKPLACE**

Six months into a major development project, the management team had spent a large sum of money and had little to show for it. Everyone involved—the end users, the management team overseeing the new software development, and the programmers—were frustrated with how little progress had been made. The team called Sandra in to see if she could discover what was causing the delays and get the project back on track. After meeting with the management team and the programmers, she assembled a group of end users together and asked what they needed. Over a series of interviews and meetings, a clear picture emerged of what the users needed from their new software. It also became clear that the project's programmers,

management, and the end users were having trouble listening to one another. For six months, the programmers thought they had been giving the users what they wanted and needed, but what the users needed and what management wanted turned out to be very different things. It was only after Sandra sat with the users and watched their daily routine, questioning them as they went, and listening to their ideas for how each process should be improved in the new system, did she understand what their needs were. Then, she met with the managers to find out what their goals were for the new system. By listening, she learned where the gaps existed between the users' needs, the managers' expectations, and the system the programmers were developing.

continued

We have included the example from Sandra's consulting experience to highlight how important listening is in the workplace. Successful communicators realize that it isn't what is said, but what you hear that is important and that makes effective listening a key factor in communication. While the programmers on the project were very good at coding, they were less than attentive to listening to the needs of their users. If you were part of the management team Sandra worked with, what processes would you put in place for future development? What does this example tell you about the relationship between management and the employees who would use the software? Who was more responsible for the lack of progress on the project—the management team overseeing the project or the programmers? Why did it take bringing in an organizational communication consultant before progress could be made?

prepare. Or we could tell the group that your report is preliminary, because you were given the assignment yesterday, but they can begin to analyze the information. And let's go ahead and let everyone know your final report will be available on Friday."

THE IMPORTANCE OF LISTENING IN BUSINESS AND PROFESSIONAL CONTEXTS

Developing conscious listening skills should be a goal for anyone in business. In fact, in many business situations we discover that listening is our job. How well we listen in these situations, the level at which we listen, and the outcome of our listening will all have a direct impact on our success in our chosen business or profession. This section addresses the role of listening in a few typical business situations.

LISTENING IN MEETINGS

Meetings require a combination of listening skills. Although in meetings we listen mainly for information, it is also important that we follow the listening continuum up through critical, self-reflexive, and conscious listening. How well we listen can provide us with important information and an opportunity to share knowledge and receive feedback. To listen effectively in meetings:

- Set a positive example. Sit up, be quiet, and take notes. There is nothing worse than someone whispering, squirming, talking, or otherwise disrupting a meeting, class, or presentation.
- Don't pass judgment. You will continue to encounter your share of boring, disorganized, or unskilled speakers. Your job, however, may depend on the information you get from the speaker. Listen for information; downplay the presentation style.
- Take good notes. Outline the speech or talk using the CCCD components (Chapter 1). Try to determine the speaker's purpose, thesis, preview, main points, support, and conclusion.

- If possible, review the material later with the speaker or other members of the audience to verify or modify what you heard.
- Follow up on any points that need clarification or action.

LISTENING IN CONFLICT SITUATIONS

Listening in conflict situations requires well-developed listening skills, along with patience. Often when we find ourselves in conflict situations, we become defensive. However, the conflict may be situational, not personal. We need to learn to listen to the speaker's reactions and feelings about the situation, rather than concentrate on our own anger, defensiveness, or need to counterattack. To listen in conflict situations:

- Relax and take a few deep breaths. Step back from the person who is speaking so that you gain control over your personal space. Stepping back physically can also help us step back mentally.
- Don't become defensive when the speaker focuses on you rather than on the situation. Keep your thoughts and words focused on the situation, not the person. Remember, not everyone knows how to listen consciously.
- Acknowledge the conflict. If you know in advance that a conflict is brewing, begin the conversation with, "I know we have different views. I would like to hear yours before we go any further. Then please listen to what I have to say."
- Listen for areas of compromise. Most conflict resolution arises out of compromise, not consensus.
- Listen for signs of escalation of the conflict. If this happens, say, "I think we are becoming overly emotional. Perhaps we should meet later to discuss this."
- Recap what the speaker said. Show you were listening critically by recapping the speaker's motives, supports, and appeals. Show you were listening self-reflexively by acknowledging your role, from the speaker's perspective, in the conflict. Show you were listening consciously by pointing out the areas of compromise and alternatives for moving forward.

 ## FOCUS ON ETHICS

Sarah's manager, Louis, requires everyone to attend a weekly meeting to discuss the status of their department. Sarah admires and respects Louis and views him as an excellent manager and mentor, she can't stand the tedious weekly meetings. Louis reads each person's status report out loud and then asks if anyone has any questions or concerns about what each person is working on. Sarah understands the importance of everyone working together and knowing what other members of the team are doing. But she wonders if there is a better way of communicating everyone's status other than reading to them.

Should Sarah voice her concerns to Louis? Would you speak to Louis directly? Would you discuss the problem with everyone in the department and then confront Louis at the next meeting? Or would you simply head to the nearest coffee shop before the meeting, try to stay awake during the meeting, and keep your thoughts to yourself?

Are barriers to good listening the responsibility of the listener, or the speaker?

LISTENING TO COMPLAINTS

One of the things Kanika disliked most about working for a company was the amount of time she had to spend listening to coworkers, managers, and clients' complaints and problems. Now that she works as an independent consultant, she finds she gets much more accomplished because she doesn't have disgruntled people streaming into her office every day. Kanika's attitude might appear negative at first, but it is important to understand the difference between someone in the workplace who has a legitimate complaint and the chronic complainer who nibbles away at our time and energy.

Legitimate Complaints Legitimate complaints come from clients, customers, or members of your organization and address specific issues or problems. These types of complaints should be received with care and handled quickly and efficiently. To handle a legitimate complaint, follow these steps:

1. Listen carefully. Allow the person to have his or her say.
2. Remain neutral. When listening to a complaint, keep in mind that the complaint is not an attack; it is a request for acknowledgment.
3. Listen empathetically. Think about how the situation or problem has affected the person.
4. Repeat the person's statement of the problem. Let the person know that you understand the problem or situation from his or her perspective.
5. Ask what the person would like to have happen.
6. Explain your position.
7. Follow up in any reasonable way to ensure the person's satisfaction.

Chronic Complainers Chronic complainers complain about everything: the company, their manager, their assignments, and their coworkers. They rarely ever take action on a problem. Instead, they spend their time complaining. Listening to chronic complainers can zap our energy, create feelings of distrust toward group or team members or the organization, and take time away from important organizational activities. To deal with chronic complainers in the workplace:

- Acknowledge their complaints and their feelings about the situation.
- Explain that although you understand the situation must be frustrating, you cannot spend any more time discussing it.
- Offer positive actions the complainer can take to resolve the situation.
- When confronted by the complainer again, explain that you are in the middle of a task and now is not a good time to discuss the problem. After you refuse to listen to the complaints a few times, most complainers will get the message and either begin complaining to someone else or take action.

LISTENING WHEN ASKED FOR HELP

Occasionally, whether you are a manager, coworker, or team member, someone will come to you for help on a project or for career advice. When this happens, listening is the most vital skill you can use to ensure you give the best help possible.

How we listen can determine how well we understand the problem, the person's needs, and the feelings that may be contributing to the situation.

Try to understand what people expect from you. Are they looking for advice, a sounding board, a chance to vent, or the information they need to make an informed decision? Often people will come to you for help and their words will say one thing but what they want is something entirely different. Listening can help you pick up on the clues that are vital to understanding exactly what someone needs.

We have discussed the differences in communication styles between men and women. These differences also apply to the way men and women tend to approach requests for help. Men generally listen to the problem and then immediately provide a course of action. Women generally listen to the problem, ask questions, and ask how the speaker feels about what is happening. Women tend to be concerned about the feelings of the person asking for help, whereas men tend to be concerned with addressing the problem and moving on. Each style has its benefits; each gender can learn from the other.

You should follow certain procedures when people ask for your help:

- Let them speak. Don't interrupt or offer quick solutions.
- Ask them what form they want the help to take. Ask if they want advice, assistance, analysis, a solution, or simply your support.
- Offer the help they ask for if you feel comfortable giving it.
- Keep the conversation to yourself. When people ask you for help, they are doing so because they trust you. Don't abuse their trust by telling others about their request if it should be kept private.
- Offer support after the conversation is over. Follow up with their request and see how they are doing.

SUMMARY

Learning to be a conscious listener is important for two reasons: listening can help you avoid mistakes and misunderstandings, and it can help move your business and professional relationships forward. Listening allows us to gather important information, empathize with coworkers and clients, gain a deeper understanding of situations, and reflect on our place within a specific communication context.

In this chapter, we discussed listening as a skill vital to the workplace. We introduced the conscious listening continuum and the types of listening: hearing, informational listening, critical listening, self-reflexive listening, and conscious listening. We learned that although listening occurs in many forms, conscious listening is the kind of listening we should all strive to do in our business and professional interactions. We also offered a number of tips for dealing with specific listening situations and contexts.

BUSINESS AND PROFESSIONAL COMMUNICATION IN THE GLOBAL WORKPLACE ONLINE

All of the following chapter review materials are available in an electronic format on either the *Business and Professional Communication in the Global Workplace* Resource Center or the book's companion website. Online you'll find chapter learning objects, flashcards of glossary terms, InfoTrack® College Edition Activities, weblinks, quizzes, and more.

WHAT YOU SHOULD HAVE LEARNED

Now that you have read Chapter 4, you should be able to do the following:

- Identify and define the five types of listening.
- Explain the conscious listening continuum and provide two important characteristics of each type of listening.
- Explain why listening is a skill that is vital to the workplace.
- Distinguish between hearing and listening.
- Describe possible blocks that may keep someone from hearing a message.
- Draw the listening cycle associated with informational listening.
- Describe the four barriers that may occur with informational listening.
- Describe the qualities you should evaluate when listening critically.
- Discuss the four components of self-reflexive listening.
- Explain conscious listening and why it is important in the workplace.
- Follow the tips for listening in meetings.
- Listen in conflict situations.
- Listen to legitimate complaints and handle chronic complainers.
- Listen when asked for help.

KEY TERMS

communication history *86*

conscious listening *89*

critical listening *87*

hearing *82*

informational listening *83*

listening *81*

motivation *88*

noise *82*

physical diversion *82*

self-reflexive listening *88*

sensitivity *89*

technological diversion *82*

WRITING AND CRITICAL THINKING

The following activities can be completed online or submitted to your instructor. Choose one of the following activities:

1. Spend an entire day focusing on your listening skills. Take the time, for each communication event you encounter, to go through each stage of listening. Listen for information critically, self-reflexively, and finally consciously. Write down your listening experiences. What did you learn?
2. Evaluate a specific listening situation. What was the context? What were the speaker's motives? Was the speaker credible? What did the person want?

3. In your group, share an experience where either conscious listening or a lack of good listening skills had an impact on your personal or professional life. Ask your group members for feedback. What would they have done differently in the situation?
4. An unknown author once said, "I know that you believe you understand what you think I said, but I'm not sure you realize that what you heard is not what I meant." Prepare a short discussion on how this quote relates what you have learned in this chapter.

PRACTICING COMMUNICATION IN PROFESSIONAL CONTEXTS

Moving from Mindless to Mindful Communication

Working in a group, complete the following exercise. This process allows you to work

consciously through the exercise at an experiential level, then at an evaluative level.

The Process

1. Pick one member of the group to tell the story narrated below. (If your class is not working in groups, read the story to a friend and complete the remaining steps of the exercise.)
2. Go around the group and give each person three minutes to expand the story.
3. As each person speaks, listen to the personal narratives, facts, history, and other elements interjected into the story.
4. After the last person has spoken, leave the group without discussing the story further.
5. Write an essay describing what you heard and your listening experience. (See additional instructions below.)

The Story

Enrique was excited about his promotion to area sales manager at GHS. He had worked hard to reach his goal of becoming a sales director by age thirty. The company was growing and expanding, which meant he had more opportunity ahead of him. Shortly after his promotion, the regional

sales director, Hal, asked him to fly to the home office in Tampa for a regional sales meeting. The meeting would be on Monday; however, Hal wanted Enrique to fly in on Saturday so that he could go "golfing and hang out with the guys."

Later that day, when Enrique was talking to Mary, the area sales manager of another district, he mentioned that he was arriving in Tampa on Saturday. Mary asked why, and Enrique told her Hal had invited him to go golfing. Mary ...

In your groups, finish the story by having:

- Group member one speaks for one minute, adding to the story.
- Group member two speaks for one minute, adding to the story.
- Continue until all the group members have added to the story.

Outside of class, write a three- to five-page paper about your experience. How did gender, language, culture, and communication history affect what you heard? How did listening play a part in the development of the story?

YOUR PERSONAL COMMUNICATION PROFILE

Think about someone you come in contact with regularly who is a constant complainer. This might be a friend, a coworker, or a relative. Rather than handle the conversation with this person as you have in the past, script the conversation ahead of time, using the tips you have learned in this chapter for dealing with chronic complainers. How did your experience change? Were you able to cut off the person's complaints or channel them into a more productive direction? How will this experience help you handle complainers on the job?

Exploring Interpersonal Communication

In a practical sense, the "creating" stage of relational communication is about how we make decisions that will guide our word choices and actions in the workplace. From first impressions to last goodbyes, the work we do to manage our relationships involves balancing strategies for obtaining our goals with the ethical dimensions of workplace conduct. This begins with first impressions.

FIRST IMPRESSIONS

How do we form first impressions of people? The term we use to describe this complex process is *perception*. **Perception** refers to how we process and interpret cues from a person's outward appearance, voice, and language usage.

How does perception work? According to cognitive psychologists and communication scholars (see Andersen, 1993), we use **schemata,** or mental pattern recognition plans, that "help us identify and organize incoming information" (Trenholm, 2000, p. 50). Sarah Trenholm, a communication scholar, suggests that we use three basic patterns to develop first impressions: person prototypes, personal constructs, and scripts.

PERSON PROTOTYPES

We tend to characterize individuals by their physical and behavioral resemblance to an existing category of person. These categories are **person prototypes**. In everyday usage, we call person prototypes *stereotypes*. For example, we can recognize "student," "college professor," "politician," "business person," "cowboy," "artist," or "evangelist." If you can quickly form a mental representation of a type of person, you are relying on the person prototype schema.

Although stereotypes help us identify people by their relationship to our idealized images of a role or category, they also encourage us to ignore or miss important details that separate uniqueness among individuals from categorical generalizations. Because sterotypes form a basis for first impressions, they also influence how we choose to communicate with others. We tend to seek out contact with people who fit stereotypes that we associate with positive images and roles, and we avoid contact with people we associate—fairly or unfairly—with negative images and roles. Although it is true that you should "never judge a book by its cover," we often do.

PERSONAL CONSTRUCTS

If stereotypes represent basic patterns of person and role definition, **personal constructs** may be thought of as representing specific evaluations we make of others based on our assessment of their personal communication habits and behaviors. For example, we tend to evaluate others as being "hard charging" or "easygoing," as "neat and clean" or "sloppy," as "nice" or "mean."

The important thing to remember about personal constructs is that they are our personal preferences. Of the wide variety of clues we can pay attention to, each of us typically uses only a few to figure out others. For this reason, two people may meet a third person and come away from the interaction with different interpretations of the third person's identity and behavior.

SCRIPTS

First impressions often occur during *phatic communication*, the patterned sequences of talk that we use every day. Another term for phatic communion is **scripts**. Scripts allow us to behave effortlessly, mindlessly, while we appear to be engaged in a conversation. Because we know how to act during a scripted performance, we tend to evaluate others based on their compliance with—or alteration from—our preferred lines in the script.

However, we need to be careful about applying our script to others and thereby denying them opportunities for creativity and uniqueness of expression. To counter this powerful influence, we need to become more mindful during these scripted performances.

Several strategic choices enhance the impression we make during our first encounters with others. Follow these guidelines when meeting someone for the first time:

- Establish eye contact, smile, and offer a firm handshake, if culturally appropriate.
- Speak clearly and avoid using nicknames during initial encounters. This holds true whether you are introducing yourself or someone else.
- Listen carefully for the other person's name when being introduced. Repeat the name to yourself a couple of times or use a mnemonic device to remember name. For example, you can remember someone named McDonald if you think of the restaurant chain or the children's song.

THINKING GLOBALLY—DISCLOSURE IN THE GLOBAL WORKPLACE

Americans are quick to disclose. We have generated an industry of tell-all books, TV shows, and websites. We are quick to discuss the intimate details of our health, our finances, and our relationships. We may not be aware that people within our own culture and those from other cultures may not be comfortable with our high level of disclosure. Disclosure also has a gendered element. Men are less likely to be as comfortable with disclosure until a relationship has progressed.

Research the issue of disclosure and culture. Talk to people you work with who may be from other cultures. Ask them how they feel about the level of disclosure you and your fellow employees engage in at work. Think about how your disclosure can work in your favor or against you. Learn to adjust your level of personal disclosure so that those around you are comfortable in the workplace.

- Listen carefully to what is being said and respond clearly and succinctly when asked a question.
- Maintain a positive business attitude.
- Have a sense of humor. Smile and be pleasant.
- Maintain an appropriate social distance during the interaction. Do not be a close talker. Keep space between you and the other person.
- Exchange business cards for future contact, if appropriate.
- Leave when the conversation is over; professional people have work to do.

ESTABLISHING EXPECTATIONS AND BOUNDARIES

Although first impressions set the patterns of communication, how we construct our relationships is heavily dependent on the way we interpret the contexts and boundaries surrounding a communication event. To complicate things further, these interpretations are influenced by our experience, which in turn defines our expectations, which in turn limits our communication because of the limits of those perceived boundaries. In many ways, our ability or failure to communicate effectively in interpersonal communication events is a vicious circle. (See Figure 5.1.)

Expectations and boundaries have an effect on peer relationships in the workplace. Research suggests that we use three general categories to define peer relationships at work (Fritz, 1997; Kram and Isabella, 1985):

- *Information peers*: people of more or less equal status with us but with whom we share low levels of trust and disclosure, little emotional support, and little personal feedback.
- *Collegial peers*: people of more or less equal status with us and with whom we share a moderate level of trust, disclosure, and expression of self. For example, with these peers we may engage in "career strategizing, job-related feedback, friendship, some information sharing, confirmation, and emotional support" (Fritz, p. 30).

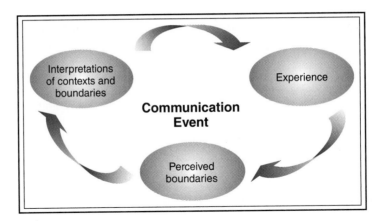

FIGURE 5.1 | THE CYCLE OF INTERPERSONAL COMMUNICATION

- *Special peers*: people of more or less equal status with us and with whom we share high levels of disclosure, intimacy, and confirmation. With our special peers, we feel free to express ourselves fully, openly, and directly.

Our perceptions of the people we work with, and our responses to them, may be limited by the peer categories we place them in. For example, we have a higher level of self-disclosure with collegial peers than we have with information peers, and our highest level of self-disclosure is reserved for the people we consider our special peers.

Organizational relationships are also limited by rules, policies, and cultures (Gilsdorf, 1998):

- **rules:** assumptions and formal pronouncements about proper communication among employees.
- **policies:** explicitly developed guidelines regarding conduct in the workplace. Often these guidelines are stated in a company's policies and procedures manual.
- **cultures:** evolved standards for communication practices that may be unique to the organization and must be acquired through observation and experience.

BEHAVING ETHICALLY

Knowing that organizational relationships are defined by expectations and limited by boundaries, policies, rules, and cultures can help you become more strategic and ethical in your selection of communication practices. You improve strategic skills by focusing communication goals on what individuals can fairly provide, and by being mindful of the limits that operate within your relationship. You improve ethical skills by communicating within these established boundaries.

Although it may appear obvious that relationships in the workplace—and the workplace itself—should be governed by conscious ethical decision making, the fact is that the harsh realities of a global marketplace often pit the ethical interests *against* the business interests of organizations. There are numerous examples of companies that, when faced with a choice between making a profit and doing the right thing, chose to fatten the bottom line. Tobacco company executives, for example, admitted they knew the health risks associated with cigarette smoking, yet for many years they continued to cover them up.

However, public vigilance via the Internet, combined with investigative reports from responsible journalists, encouraged more ethical conduct from organizations. Furthermore, "whistle-blowers" (Redding, 1993) are more willing to speak publicly about unethical, immoral, and illegal business activities.

Unfortunately, ethical decisions are seldom easy. This is because "doing the right thing" often depends on where you stand in relation to an issue or problem. The main character in the film *Working Girl* engages in what many would consider unethical conduct, but she sees her choices as necessary because women from working-class backgrounds have limits placed on their opportunities in American corporate life. The maniacal sales manager in *Glengarry Glen Ross* believes harsh methods are required to motivate a sales force because his own job depends on their performance. As some economic philosophers (such as Milton Friedman) have pointed out, if the point of running a business is to make money for investors, then shouldn't our ethical code be derived solely from that primary objective? If so, wouldn't *any* decision that reduced profits for investors be considered an *unethical* decision?

Ethical decision making and conduct can be rendered even more problematic on a global economic scale, because an organization's cultural values may also be shaped by national norms. For example, North American firms often complain that they are disadvantaged when dealing with companies from nations that allow—and even encourage—the payment of bribes or the giving of expensive gifts to enhance business opportunities. On the global stage, what may seem obvious and ethical in one culture may well be illegal or unethical in another. Is it better to lose business while maintaining high ethical standards, or to compromise those standards by paying bribes and giving gifts that may enhance profits?

Communication ethicists point out that in reducing arguments about ethical conduct to "the ends justify the means" reasoning, people fail to acknowledge Gandhi's truth: "Means are ends in the making." The "ethical urgency" that ought to be used to guide decisions about conduct is, therefore, that you don't know how things are going to turn out (Bracci, 1999). In *Working Girl*, the main character's decisions may seem acceptable because of how things turned out for her, but in everyday business life, we cannot predict the results of our actions. We should therefore make decisions about ethical conduct based on what the consequence of behaving this way is likely to be.

To do that, we need to build our ethical practices on a solid foundation of core communication values. Ethical communication practices begin with an organization's need to clarify its underlying workplace values within the context of national norms and practices. For example, research indicates that in North American business culture, there are a number of desirable organizational values associated with ethical communication practices (Harshman and Harshman, 1999, p. 30):

- Trust one another.
- Treat others with respect.
- Recognize the value of each individual.
- Keep your word; do what you say you will do.

- Tell the truth; be honest with others.
- Act with integrity.
- Be open to change.
- Risk failing in order to get better.
- Learn; try new ideas.

The above list of productive organizational values reinforces the central notion that relational ethics are part and parcel of our everyday communication in organizations. There is no communication event or episode that does not reflect an ethical attitude or stance, or a strategic decision that cannot be informed by a conscious consideration of its ethical implications. For this reason, the National Communication Association (NCA) has adopted the following ethics code.

Balancing strategies for creating effective relationships at work with the appropriate ethical standards is a constant challenge for all communicators. In our view, learning to think of ethical conduct in terms of likely relational outcomes rather than solely as an "ends-means" justification is a good way to practice conscious ethical conduct. These principles hold true whether you are communicating face-to-face, in a conference call, or over the Internet.

 ## NCA CREDO FOR ETHICAL COMMUNICATION

Adopted November 6, 1999

Questions of right and wrong arise whenever people communicate. Ethical communication is fundamental to responsible thinking, decision making, and the development of relationships and communities within and across contexts, cultures, channels, and media. Moreover, ethical communication enhances human worth and dignity by fostering truthfulness, fairness, responsibility, personal integrity, and respect for self and others. We believe that unethical communication threatens the quality of all communication and consequently the well-being of individuals and the society in which we live. Therefore we, the members of the National Communication Association, endorse and are committed to practicing the following principles of ethical communication.

We advocate truthfulness, accuracy, honesty, and reason as essential to the integrity of communication.

We endorse freedom of expression, diversity of perspective, and tolerance of dissent to achieve the informed and responsible decision making fundamental to a civil society.

We strive to understand and respect other communicators before evaluating and responding to their messages.

We promote access to communication resources and opportunities as necessary to fulfill human potential and contribute to the well-being of families, communities, and society.

We promote communication climates of caring and mutual understanding that respect the unique needs and characteristics of individual communicators.

We condemn communication that degrades individuals and humanity through distortion, intimidation, coercion, and violence and through the expression of intolerance and hatred.

We are committed to the courageous expression of personal convictions in pursuit of fairness and justice.

We advocate sharing information, opinions, and feelings when facing significant choices while also respecting privacy and confidentiality.

We accept responsibility for the short- and long-term consequences for our own communication and expect the same of others.

Focus on Ethics

A number of websites devoted to personal accounts of ill treatment of employees have popped up. These sites provide employees strategies for whistleblowing and for overturning sources of corporate hierarchy and domination. The question is, are their recommendations ethical? Is it ethical to "rat" on your company and air your dirty laundry in public? What if your company's actions were unethical? Does that justify whistle blowing?

CREATING MESSAGES THAT REFLECT SELF, OTHER, AND CONTEXT

To create strategic messages in the workplace, we make use of the following concepts:

- equity
- self-disclosure
- risk taking
- feedback
- dialectics
- dialogue
- conflict resolution

Let's examine each of these concepts in detail.

EQUITY: PRINCIPLES OF EVERYDAY EXCHANGE

In Chapter 3, we introduced the idea of equity as a principle that guides most workplace interactions. We defined equity as the principle that we should be treated fairly by others and in turn should treat them fairly. We asked you to think of equity as the golden rule governing the choosing and creating of verbal strategies for workplace communication.

To refresh your memory, let's reexamine the four key assumptions that inform equity theory (Walster, Walster, and Bershied, 1978; Wilson and Goodall, 1991):

1. *People work for rewards.* We all attempt to maximize our outcomes. In relationships at work, we try to obtain our personal, social, and professional goals by gaining the cooperation and support of others.
2. *People seek equity.* We all want a sense of fairness and justice to guide our relationships with others.
3. *People become stressed when they feel they are being treated unfairly.* If we find ourselves in an inequitable relationship, we feel tension, stress, frustration, or even anger. We cannot overcome these ill feelings until we restore equity in the relationship.
4. *People experiencing stress will try to restore equity.* We may restore equity mentally, socially, or physically.

As you can see, the equity principle can be applied directly to the communication strategies you choose in the workplace. Your overall goal should be to select ethical strategies that encourage others to treat you equitably and that demonstrate your interest in treating others equitably. When you do so, you uphold the principle of *reciprocity*.

Sources of inequity in workplace relationships include the following:

- lying, cheating, or stealing
- misrepresenting yourself, your goals, or your methods
- not speaking up for a colleague who is wrongly accused or who is held accountable for something that isn't her or his fault
- not supporting the work of someone who regularly supports you
- allowing someone else to pick up the check for lunch or dinner without offering to do the same for them next time
- failing to volunteer to help someone meet a deadline even though this person has volunteered to help you in the past
- failing to disclose your personal feelings about an issue or idea after you have asked someone else to disclose their personal feelings
- being chronically late for meetings and events
- trying to claim sole credit for work done by a group or team
- ingratiating yourself with superiors at the expense of others with whom you work
- withholding information from others that may benefit them
- spreading rumors or gossip about others
- telling someone else's secrets

Once we recognize equity as a powerful tool for building rewarding professional and business relationships, we can tip the scales toward ethical and equitable behavior. We also can use this new knowledge of equity as a way of evaluating and critiquing our own and others' communication choices.

Case study four highlights how interpersonal conflict can develop into a career threatening situation. Successful communicators realize that it isn't just what you say, but how you *react* to others in the workplace that keeps rumors from forming or spreading. While Raina was well within her right to avoid or ignore Blake's question, her lack of disclosure and the way she responded confirmed Blake's assumptions. How would you have handled Blake's question? Should Raina have disclosed that her parents were from India and were Hindu, not Muslim? Would this have made any difference to someone like Blake? Should Raina disclose her conversation with Blake to her boss? What responsibility do Raina's superiors have for ensuring that LP is free from rumors and innuendos? What steps should be taken by Raina, Jeff, or by others in the company? What other factors may have led to Blake's behavior?

SELF-DISCLOSURE AND RISK TAKING

George Caspar Homans (1961) proposed that all human relationships can be partially understood as exchanges of goods, services, sentiments, and time. Ideally,

CASE STUDY 4 | SPREADING RUMORS IN THE WORKPLACE

Shortly after 9/11, Raina found herself the subject of a whisper campaign at work. As the youngest area manager for a pharmaceutical company, Raina had worked incredibly hard over the past few years to achieve her goal of becoming a regional manager before she turned thirty. She had received numerous awards and raises over the four years she worked for Life Pharmaceuticals (LP). Her superiors spoke highly of her and supported her with additional training opportunities and outside leadership courses.

Just last summer, her manager sent her to a week-long planning and development seminar at the Center for Creative Leadership. At the seminar she met the up-and-coming managers from the other areas of the company. Most of the people she met were pleasant and easy to get along with, furthering her impression of LP as a great place to work.

On the third night of the seminar, the area managers from the Southeast region went to dinner together. The group settled on a local restaurant overlooking one of the many lakes in the area. Among the group, was Blake, the area manager who represented the Tennessee and Kentucky region. Raina had bested Blake in the last sales competition. As the evening progressed, Blake started a loud conversation at one end of the table about

9/11 and Iraq. Throughout the conversation, he stared at Raina. Since 9/11, Raina, whose parents were from India, had dealt with comments and looks like those Blake was giving her. For the most part she chose to ignore them. However, later that evening, when Blake cornered her and asked her where she came from, Raina reacted negatively and told Blake her background was none of Blake's business. She immediately regretted dismissing his question when she heard him mutter, "That's what I thought" under his breath.

A week after the seminar, Raina's manager, Jeff, asked her to set aside time for a meeting that Friday, when she was at the regional office in Memphis. Raina and Jeff had a good working relationship and he had always treated Raina very fairly, so Raina always looked forward to meeting with Jeff. After exchanging pleasantries, Jeff got right to the point, informing Raina that someone in the company had been spreading the rumor that Raina was a Muslim and supported the 9/11 attacks. Jeff assured her he did not believe the rumors, but some people in the home office found them troubling and had asked him to look into them. Jeff was clearly uncomfortable even talking about the matter. After getting over her initial shock, Raina realized she knew exactly where the rumors were coming from.

---

these exchanges should be equitable, because relative value for goods, services, and sentiments is always understood between people as something that should be fairly traded, and it is generally understood that the amount of time one person puts into a relationship needs to be reciprocated by the other partner.

Given this theoretical framework, self-disclosure and risk taking have commodity value in workplace relationships:

- If I offer disclosures about myself to you, I expect that you will, in return, disclose something about yourself to me.
- If I take risks in our relationship, I am also encouraging you to take risks in our relationship.

As if guided by a marketplace metaphor, we "trade commodities" in our relationships. We understand the values we attach to those commodities. We operate under a principle of reciprocity and equity in making those trades or exchanges.

However, it is important to point out that self-disclosure and risk taking, although potentially powerful resources for building close relationships, can create risks in business and professional relationships. **Self-disclosure** means providing personal information within a conversation. It can also mean posting information and images to a social networking site or in an e-mail. Regardless of the medium selected for the message, selling your coworkers the intimate details of your life provides them with ways of understanding how your personal history informs and shapes your workplace identity. It also provides information to people who may not have your best interests in mind. Imagine, for a moment, if the details of your most reckless behavior on a weekend or vacation became common knowledge at work. Before you disclose, think about whether or not you really want your coworkers—and your superiors—to know these things about you. Chances are you probably don't. To monitor disclosures consider the following suggestions:

Your Disclosures

- Disclose personal information only to people you know well and trust. Remember, trust must be earned.
- Before you disclose something, stop and think about how information you disclose might be used.
- Never disclose personal information to anyone who may use it against you.
- Never disclose anything that may be interpreted by others as potentially damaging to your reputation or character, nor encourage others to. This includes all potentially illegal, immoral, or unethical conduct, no matter how it was motivated, how funny it was, or what the outcome may have been.
- Don't disclose information someone told you in confidence.

Responding to Disclosures

- Keep in mind that you are not a licensed therapist or counselor. If people who need emotional support begin disclosing unwanted or troubling information to you, the best thing you can do for them is help them find their way to a trained professional.
- If someone you work with begins disclosing personal information at a level you are not comfortable with, say, "I'm sorry, but there are some things about you I'd rather not know." Or "While I sympathize with your situation, I would like to keep our relationship on a professional level."
- Remember that self-disclosure is expected to be reciprocal. If others disclose information about themselves to you, they will expect you to disclose information about yourself to them.

When communicating in the global workplace, you should bear in mind that people from other cultures may be uncomfortable with the level of self-disclosure and risk taking that many North Americans routinely offer. Your goal when creating messages should be to adapt your talk to the needs and expectations of others.

ASKING FOR AND GIVING FEEDBACK

Feedback means providing others with an evaluation of the effectiveness of their actions. Feedback is a valuable source of information that allows communicators to

PhotoDisc, Inc.

adjust their talk to situations and to other people. Skilled communicators seek out feedback because it provides them with an evaluation of how well their messages achieved their goals, what modifications may need to be made, and what they may want to consider doing to become more effective. Asking for feedback is an important tool for the development of your communication skills. Giving feedback, however, can be problematic. Not everyone wants feedback. This may be because most people are simply not skilled in providing good feedback, so our reactions to feedback tend to be negative.

Research by Trenholm and Jensen (1992) suggests the following five rules for giving feedback:

- *Own your message.* Use the pronoun "I" to begin statements that evaluate the performance of others. Avoid using generalizations such as "everyone thinks" or "we all know" to preface your remarks. As long as you make it clear that *you* are the one providing the feedback, you are showing ownership (and responsibility) for what you say.

- *Avoid apologizing for your feelings.* Don't preface feedback with a disclaimer such as "It might just be me, but I thought what you said in the meeting was ill-timed." This sort of disclaimer gives the impression that you are apologizing for the feedback, or that you are the one at fault, not the person to whom you are offering the feedback. You are also downplaying the corrective effect of the message, which may be counterproductive. Say what you mean. Notice how different the impression would be if the sentence started, "I thought what you said in the meeting was ill-timed."

- *Make your message specific and behavioral.* Don't mask your feedback by being vague or ambiguous. The idea is to give someone useful information about their communication. To do that means specifying precisely what behaviors are being targeted. Focus on behaviors that may be modified or changed rather than on general mental states or attitudes. For example, you could say, "You didn't return my call yesterday, and as a result I didn't get the information I needed to finish the budget report." This kind of statement explains the behavior that caused the problem and opens up possibilities for a discussion of what needs to be done in the future.

- *Verbal and nonverbal behaviors should support each other.* Avoid trying to smile while expressing frustration, anger, or resentment, because the message your expression gives may be quite different from what you say. As we pointed out in Chapter 3, when there is a discrepancy between nonverbal and verbal messages, we tend to believe the nonverbal.

- *Avoid evaluating and interpreting your communication partner unless he or she asks you to.* Useful feedback avoids promoting defensiveness. Unsolicited feedback can easily be viewed as criticism, thereby encouraging your partner to become defensive or to argue against what you are offering.

DIALECTICS AND DIALOGUE

Dialectics generally refers to the interaction of two arguments that are by nature oppositional. The term *relational dialectics* (Rawlins, 1984; Baxter, 1988; Baxter and Montgomery, 1996) refers to the interaction of two opposing arguments or forces—called *tensions*—operating within the boundaries of the same relationship. Interpersonal researchers have identified three primary sources of relational dialectics:

- *Autonomy-togetherness dialectic.* To be in a relationship often means to spend time and to share information together. However, no matter how much you enjoy spending time with another person, sometimes you just want or need to be by yourself.

- *Novelty-predictability dialectic.* All relationships form patterns. In time, these patterns become predictable. Because relationships are at least in part predictable, they can be safe and comfortable and serve as islands of sanity in an otherwise stressed world. However, we also want our relationships to be novel, to offer excitement, adventure, and opportunities to experience and learn from new places, people, and things.

- *Expressive-protective dialectic.* This dialectical tension informs how we make decisions about sharing information about ourselves with our relational partners and coworkers. There are times when we freely disclose, and there are times when we prefer not to share what we consider private.

With all of these sources of dialectical complexity operating in our relationships, how can we make space for dialogue? More importantly, how do we make space for talk within the autonomous, predictable, and protective environments of the workplace?

Dialogue is communication that focuses on mutuality and relational growth rather than on self-interest. Dialogue is "more concerned with discovering than with disclosing, more interested in access than in domination" (Anderson, Cissna, and Arnett, 1994, p. 2). Peter Kellett (1999) has applied the idea of relational dialectics to creating dialogue in organizations:

- *Focus on mutuality*. Both partners in a dialogue should use the experience to learn and to grow; each communicator should consciously try to help the other person.
- *Discover rather than disclose*. Communicators should ask questions aimed at improving understanding of the other's position, standpoint, and perspective. Avoid unnecessary self-disclosures that deflect attention from mutual growth.
- *Be more interested in access than in domination*. Communicators should avoid strategies designed to one-up or demean the perspective offered by the other person. Each person should remain open to differences of opinion, values, and beliefs. The exchange of talk should be aimed at uncovering those differences for the purpose of mutual understanding and growth.

WORKING THROUGH RELATIONAL CONFLICT

Conflict refers to the feelings or perceptions of imbalance that arise in a relational setting. A number of strategies help us temporarily avoid or postpone a confrontation, but they will not help resolve the Conflict (from D. Johnson, 1993, pp. 205–207):

- *withdrawing*: walking away, changing the subject, or ignoring the conflict
- *accommodating*: giving in immediately simply to end the conflict
- *compromising*: giving up part of what you want in exchange for your communication partner also giving up part of what he or she wants
- *avoiding or postponing*: failing to engage in communication designed to address the conflict, or suggesting that the conflict be addressed later

Although each of these strategies may be appropriate in a given context, each provides a less than optimal way of working through the conflict. For example, by withdrawing, avoiding, or postponing conflict, relational partners may build up resentments that surface in other situations. By accommodating and compromising, relational partners may create an imbalance in their relationship that influences other aspects of their talk and work. Of all the strategies available for working through a conflict, only a problem-solving dialogue stands a good chance of producing a win–win situation.

That said, it is also true that "conflicts experienced in organizations are often related to deeper processes" (Kellett and Dalton, 2001). For example, conflicts can be based on deeper systems of meaning related to the politics in an organization (Cheney, 1995), differing perceptions of "the reality" of an issue that inform

GLOBAL PROFILE FOR SUCCESS—BREAKING GENDER BARRIERS

The Virgin Group was conceived in 1970 by founder Sir Richard Branson. The Virgin Group has 200 companies operating worldwide and employs 50,000 people in 29 countries. These companies, bearing the Virgin brand, engage in a wide range of businesses, including mobile telephones, transportation, travel, financial services, leisure, music, holidays, publishing, and retail.

On the Virgin Group's website, there is a section detailing Virgin's responsibilities and addresses environmental and ethical issues. This statement reads:

> Today's heightened interest in the role of business in society has partly been prompted by increased sensitivity to and awareness of environmental and ethical issues. Issues such as environmental damage and the improper treatment of workers have been

highlighted in the media and the pressure on business to play a role in social and environmental issues is bound to grow ... At Virgin, we've always tried to act sensitively and responsibly. Project Aware is a renewal of our effort to make responsible business practice an integral part of the Virgin culture—ensuring it is part of every individual's role and responsibility.

Explore Virgin's website: http://www.virgin.com/Companies.aspx.

What can you learn about thinking ethically from Virgin's website? What skills are necessary to succeed in the global workplace as a member of the Virgin Group? What does the above statement about individual responsibility tell you about the work environment at the Virgin Group?

competing values and narratives (Mumby, 1993), or deeper organizational processes and themes (Smith and Eisenberg, 1987). To get at these systemic or cultural conflicts, it is helpful to ask the following questions (from Kellett and Dalton, 2001):

- *Where does the conflict come from?* Who and what is producing the disagreement? Is there a history of disagreements between the communicators?
- *How is it being managed?* Who avoids it, and who wants to engage in it? What goals are being sought by the participants?
- *How do other people react to the conflict?* Is it perceived as "something new" or "nothing new"? What negative work-related consequences can be associated with the conflict? What personal consequences follow from it?
- *How does it affect key organizational functions?* How does the conflict influence productivity? How does it influence openness? Honesty? Learning? Dialogue?
- *How does it manifest systemically in other organizational practices?* Are stress levels higher for those with similar conflicts? Are discussions routed around these key participants? Is there a loss of potential important feedback? Are denial and blaming strategies spread to other conflicts? If the conflict is based on gender, class, or race, are other work relationships negatively impacted? How?

Conflict is often described as a "neutral" organizational term (Eisenberg and Goodall, 2001). This is because some level of conflict is natural to all group- and team-based activities (Fisher, 1984) and because conflict, when properly managed, can lead to productive, insightful, and creative learning opportunities (Goodall, 1990). Managing a conflict requires admitting you have one and then being willing to work through it using a problem-solving approach. By contrast, conflicts that are hidden, repressed, avoided, or denied tend to build resentment and frustration, as well as create additional problems within the organization.

MAKING RELATIONAL COMMUNITIES WORK

Today's global workplace poses new challenges for communicators. Interpersonal relationships require careful coordination and attention to cultural and gender differences in the workplace. In previous chapters, we discussed the cultural and gender implications of listening, verbal, and nonverbal communication. Now, we will examine how we negotiate interpersonal aspects of culture and gender.

NEGOTIATION OF CULTURAL DIFFERENCES

As Lovitt and Goswami (1999) have pointed out, until very recently, most textbooks and training tools for multinational business environments stressed the importance of learning as much as possible about other cultures. This included studying the history, politics, religion, economic structure, education, linguistics, and technology of a culture, as well as the "do's and taboos" of communicating with people representing that culture. More recent research (Scollon and Scollon, 1995; Perkins, 1999) indicates that only certain cultural factors, such as "ideology, face systems, forms of discourse, and socialization" (Scollon and Scollon, p. 126), actually influence business and professional communication. Moreover, shared language usage and standards for evaluating communication among professional categories—engineers, accountants, technical writers, technicians—may outweigh other cultural factors (Webb and Keene, 1999).

The important thing to remember is that learning about other cultures is a good way to build a repertoire of intercultural and cross-cultural communication skills, and allows you to show respect and appreciation for other cultures. Educating oneself about world cultures is a rich enough subject to last a lifetime, but there are some practical ways to begin exploring how cultural differences may influence communication. With this goal in mind, we would like to begin with a basic difference between individualist and collectivist cultures (Triandis et al., 1988).

Individualist cultures, such as the dominant culture of the United States, revere the individual person and expect individuals "to make their own decisions, develop their own opinions, solve their own problems, have their own things, and, in general, learn to view the world from the point of view of the self" (Samovar, Porter, and Jain, 1991, pp. 73–74). People in individualist cultures value democratic relationships and are less influenced by status or hierarchy when dealing with others. *Collectivist cultures*, such as the dominant culture of China, revere the common good over self-interest, value group and family identity over individual achievement, and tend to respect vertical status hierarchies. As you can well imagine, relationships between representatives of these distinct cultures could be very difficult. However, each partner learning more about the communication rules and cultural norms of the other person can significantly reduce the negative influences of these cultural differences. Table 5.1 outlines several rules or strategies for collectivist-individualist interaction.

Arthur Bell (1992), Jurgen Bolten (1999), and Judi Brownell (1999) have built on the work of Triandis and others to suggest that when persons from different cultures interact, a "third" or "transaction" culture is created. Bell elaborated:

> When you and your own cultural background come into contact with persons of another culture, something new emerges—a middle ground, called a "transaction culture."

TABLE 5.1 | RULES FOR COLLECTIVIST-INDIVIDUALIST INTERACTION

Rules Collectivists Should Follow When Interacting with Individualists	Rules Individualists Should Follow When Interacting with Collectivists
1. Don't expect to be able to predict an individualist's attitudes and behavior on the basis of group affiliations. Although this works in your country, individuals have their own ideas.	1. Expect collectivists to abide by the norms, roles, and obligations of their groups. If group membership changes, expect members' values and personal styles to change, as well.
2. Don't be put off when individualists take pride in personal achievement, and do not be too modest yourself.	2. Do not disclose personal information unless asked. Feel free, however, to disclose your age and salary.
3. Expect individualists to be less emotionally involved in group affiliation than is the norm for you. Do not interpret this as coldness or as a personal defect.	3. Do not criticize collectivists or openly refuse their requests. Expect them to be more sensitive to loss of face than you are.
4. Do not expect persuasive arguments that emphasize cooperation and conflict avoidance to be as effective as they are in your culture. Do not be offended by arguments that emphasize personal rewards and costs.	4. Persuasive arguments based on authority appeals or on the good of the group will be more effective than those based on personal rewards.
5. Do not interpret initial friendliness as a signal of intimacy or commitment. Expect relationships to be good-natured but superficial and fleeting according to your own standards.	5. Spend a great deal of time getting to know others. Be patient, expect delays, and do not adhere to a rigid timetable.
6. Pay attention to written contracts. They are considered binding.	6. Do not be surprised if plans are changed after everything was seemingly agreed upon. Do not be surprised if negotiations take a lot longer than you consider necessary.
7. Do not expect to be respected because of your position, age, sex, or status. Do not be surprised if individualists lack respect for authority figures.	7. Let others know your social position, job title, and rank. A collectivist has a strong need to place you in an appropriate niche in the social hierarchy.
8. Expect individualists to be upset by nepotism, bribery, and other behaviors that give in-group members an advantage over others.	8. Gift giving is important, but do not expect to be paid back immediately.
9. Do not expect to receive as much help as you would in your own country. After initial orientation, you may be left to do things on your own.	9. Remember that for collectivists, family and social relationships are extremely important. Expect collectivists to take time off from work for family matters.
10. Do not expect an individualist to work well in groups.	10. Do not expect to be afforded as much privacy as you may be used to.

Source: From Harry C. Triandis, Richard Briskin, and C. Harry Hui, "Cross-Cultural Training across the Individualism-Collectivism Divide," *International Journal of Intercultural Relations* 12 (1988), pp. 269–98.

In this new middle ground, sensitive and often unstated rules and understandings guide behavior. That is, if a member of Culture A interacts with a member of Culture B, neither the cultural rules of A nor those of B are the sole guide for behavior. Instead a mixed set of rules—middle Culture C—develops for the purposes of the interaction.

For example, consider the cultural rules that would guide a business conversation between you and a manager from Japan. You would not speak and act entirely as you would when conversing with American coworkers, nor would the Japanese manager hold fast to Japanese conversational rules and behaviors. Both of you would consciously and subconsciously bend your own cultural habits and assumptions to accommodate the communication needs of the others. (Bell, pp. 452–53)

NEGOTIATION OF GENDER DIFFERENCES

By the end of the twentieth century, the proportion of female managers in the United States was 45 percent, an increase of 35 percent since 1984. Women now account for almost half of all managers. Management is no longer a male-intensive occupation, making it possible that the managerial role is no longer associated with predominantly masculine characteristics (Powell and Graves, 2004).

As you learned in Chapter 3, women and men often exhibit differences in communication styles. Confusion about these styles can interfere with the message. Learning to coordinate your communication style with that of the opposite gender can help you to negotiate a successful outcome.

Recall that women tend to use what Deborah Tannen has called a "rapport-building" style, whereas men tend to use a "report-making" style. These differences in style, as well as differences in language and meaning, contribute to relational communication challenges in the workplace. For example, the fact that men tend to interrupt women speakers may be explained by research findings, but research findings should not be used to excuse this form of rude behavior. Similarly, the fact that some women tend to use more qualifiers ("I think maybe"; "I guess"; "maybe just a little bit"; "kind of"), disclaimers ("It might be beside the point, but ..."; "Don't get upset with me, but ..."), and tag questions ("You know?") should not diminish the need for users of these qualifiers to more carefully monitor their speech.

Another relational challenge occurs because not all women and men adhere to these gross stereotypes. Some women are report oriented, and some men are rapport oriented. Some men use tag questions, and some women routinely interrupt anyone who happens to be speaking. Simply categorizing individuals by these general findings can be very misleading. Labeling a pattern as a "genderlect" (a gender dialect) may help us to understand these differences, but it doesn't necessarily help people communicate more effectively with each other.

Most communication scholars agree that the single most important skill for us to develop is *flexibility* (Wood, 1997; Tannen, 1994; Trenholm, 2000). When we become aware of the way we talk and learn effective strategies for communication, we begin to override our automatic impulses and replace bad communication habits with habits that will serve us better in the workplace (Tannen, 1990, p. 95). Doing this makes us more mindful communicators.

IMPROVING RELATIONSHIPS AT WORK

Delivery of interpersonal messages can be viewed as dramatistic or pragmatic (Eisenburg and Goodall, 2001). Viewed dramatistically, all relationships are cultural performances, and the delivery of your communication role in those performances is central to the ongoing story, or narrative, of the workplace. Viewed pragmatically, how well we learn to adapt our communication to the needs and expectations of relational partners will determine the quality of those relationships and our levels of satisfaction within them. Either way, skill in building relationships at work means becoming mindful of our continual need to learn from those relationships and to improve them.

To become a more mindful communicator in workplace relationships, we recommend that you do the following:

- Become more conscious of your goals for communicating with others and their goals for communicating with you.
- Recognize that communication has consequences—avoid mindless talk, careless comments, gossip, rumors, sexual banter, and innuendos.
- Always be mindful of the equity principle in workplace relationships—always be conscious of the exchanges and commodity values that operate within them.
- Accept responsibility for your own communication in relationships—own what you say and do.
- Be open to feedback from others—use the feedback to improve your relational performance.
- Accept conflict as a natural part of any human relationship—when it occurs, try to use problem solving to resolve it, but recognize that not all conflicts are resolvable.
- Treat others with respect and honesty—take into account the ethical dimensions of your decisions and the influence those actions may have on your relationships and communities.
- Be mindful of cultural and gender differences in relationships.
- Use communication to build flexibility and freedom into your interactions with others.
- Always be on the lookout for ways to improve your communication with others—never stop learning.

SUMMARY

In this chapter, you learned how to organize interpersonal communication. We examined the process of choosing strategies that further goals while communicating ethically. We also examined the importance of first impressions and learned ways to improve the impressions we give and monitor those presented by others. Next we discussed expectations and boundaries and how we rely on these elements to help us define interpersonal situations and our responses to them.

Throughout this section, we discussed the ethics of interpersonal communication. By listing the ethical practices we believe are important in the workplace, we laid a foundation for developing ethical responses in the workplace. We discussed tools for creating ethical messages while maintaining equity in relationships, and we learned to balance self-disclosure in our communication.

We discussed dialectics in the workplace and ways to use dialogue to resolve issues of dialectics. In our discussion of conflict, we talked about the typical responses to conflict and provided a list of questions designed to help you manage conflict in the workplace.

We then discussed how cultural and gender differences affect coordinating a message in the workplace. Finally, we discussed delivery of a message as a way to improve work relationships. The goal of this chapter was to help you communicate more effectively in your personal relationships in the workplace.

BUSINESS AND PROFESSIONAL COMMUNICATION IN THE GLOBAL WORKPLACE ONLINE

All of the following chapter review materials are available in an electronic format on either the *Business and Professional Communication in the Global Workplace* Resource Center or the book's companion website. Online you'll find chapter learning objects, flashcards of glossary terms, InfoTrack® College Edition Activities, weblinks, quizzes, and more.

WHAT YOU SHOULD HAVE LEARNED

Now that you have read Chapter 5, you should be able to do the following:

- Explain the importance of first impressions.
- Discuss how person prototypes and personal constructs affect your first impressions.
- Explain how scripts undermine opportunities for creative or unique expression.
- Use information about expectations and boundaries to improve your relationships.
- Explain how rules, policies, and culture impact our communication.
- Discuss the importance of communicating ethically.
- List ways that we can communicate ethically.
- Define *equity* and how it is applied in the workplace.
- List sources of inequity in the workplace.
- Discuss how risk taking and self-disclosure enhance communication.
- Explain the concept of feedback and how it can be used to improve communication.
- Discuss the concepts of dialectics and dialogue.
- List negative reactions to conflict.
- Discuss how conflict can be handled in the workplace.
- Explain how we can adjust our message delivery for cultural or gender differences.

KEY TERMS

conflict *109*	perception *97*	schemata *97*
cultures *100*	person prototypes *97*	scripts *98*
dialectics *108*	personal constructs *98*	self-disclosure *105*
dialogue *109*	policies *100*	
feedback *106*	rules *100*	

WRITING AND CRITICAL THINKING

The following activities can be completed online or submitted to your instructor.
Choose one of the following activities:

1. Think about a communication situation you recently experienced that resulted in unresolved conflict. How did you handle the situation? Based on the conflict section in this chapter, how could you have handled the situation differently? Write a narrative of the situation, using what you have learned.

2. Ask the members of your group, friends, or peers at work to describe their first impression of you. Make a list of the words that recurred in the descriptions. Is this the impression you want to project? Develop a plan for changing the first impression that others form of you.

3. In your group, ask each person to disclose something about himself or herself that the group didn't previously know (e.g., the story behind her or his first name; something that is contained in his or her wallet, etc.). Be careful about what you disclose. Reread the section on disclosure and think carefully about what you want this group to know about you. How did the disclosures change your impression of your group members? Was the information disclosed appropriate?

Why? Has your impression of each group member grown more or less favorable? Discuss the nuances of disclosure in your group.

4. Write an essay identifying the strategy you most often use in conflict. Can you identify it as any of the behaviors listed in the chapter? If so, consider and identify some of the factors that may have contributed and continue to contribute to this. These may include factors such as culture, gender, family background, position of power, rewards, and punishment. What do you see as your strengths and your challenges in employing your conflict behaviors? Are the outcomes typically satisfactory, or unsatisfactory? If unsatisfactory, what strategies can you use to create a more positive outcome?

Practicing Communication in Business and Professional Contexts

Form groups of four or more people. Have each group member prepare a three-minute talk about him or herself. Keep in mind the principles covered in this and the preceding chapters. In your group, take turns giving your talks. As group member talk about themselves, take notes about what each person says in relation to the principles covered so far. Be prepared to provide feedback. Your feedback should follow these guidelines:

- Use the word "I" so that you own your message.
- Avoid apologies.
- Be specific.
- Avoid conflicting verbal and nonverbal behaviors.

This exercise is designed to prepare you for the group and presentation exercises to come.

CAREER FUNDAMENTALS

INTERVIEWING AND CONSCIOUS COMMUNICATION

CHAPTER 6

CONDUCTING CONSCIOUS INTERVIEWS

Interviewing assumes there is a back-and-forth, give–give exchange of ideas, questions, and information on the part of the interviewer and interviewee. In many ways, watching a good interview is like watching a good tennis match. Each participant is responsible for upholding his or her end of the game. Each must return information in order for the interview to continue. The worst interviews happen when one or both participants drop the ball. Game over. Nobody wins.

In this chapter, we examine how the CCCD process—choosing, creating, coordinating, and delivering—works in a variety of interviewing contexts. While the main example is that of an employment interview, other examples, tips, and questions will be presented to explore the different types of interviewing you may encounter in the workplace. The basic types are indicated in the conscious communication and interviewing continuum provided in Figure 6.1.

Before you begin an interviewing process, it is important to identify the type of interview you are conducting. Are you trying to fill a position, solve a problem, or gather information? Let's examine the types of interviews in more detail.

INTERROGATION

From the perspective of the conscious communication continuum, with its scale of mindless to mindful communication, the most mindless form of interviewing is **interrogation**. An interrogation is a one-sided interview that usually concentrates on the negative aspects of a situation or an employee's behavior. Although interrogation may sound ominous and out of character in the business world, you might be surprised how often managers interrogate rather than interview employees when there is a problem. While there may be a rare occasion when an interrogation

119

Interrogation	Persuasive or sales interview	Informational interview or focus groups	Employment interview	CONSCIOUS COMMUNICATION CHOICES
Interviewee is grilled about a grievance filed by a customer or a co-worker. Typically one-sided and biased.	Interviewer appeals to the values and needs of the interviewee to make a convincing pitch or appeal. Typically one-sided, can be manipulative.	Employee will receive and respond to messages only at prescribed times.	Employee thinks about the best channel for messages but doesn't always follow through.	Give and take of information by participants who are informed and goal oriented.

Mindless Interviewing → **Mindful Interviewing**

FIGURE 6.1 | CONSCIOUS COMMUNICATION AND INTERVIEWING CONTINUUM

would bring results, we don't recommend using this technique if your goal is to build rapport, gain information, or develop consensus.

PERSUASIVE OR SALES INTERVIEWS

At its core, a **persuasive interview** is a sales call. Most people recognize it as such. How many times have you been sitting home in the evening and received a call from a telemarketer who first apologizes for disturbing you and then rushes to inform you,

Royalty-Free/Corbis

"This is not a sales call; I only want to ask you a few questions." The first time you hear this pitch you think, "Sure, I can answer a few questions," but then you find yourself listening to a ten-minute sales pitch. The persuasive or sales interview is usually one-sided and can be manipulative.

PERFORMANCE REVIEWS

A **performance review** is a review or critique of an employee's work and job performance. Performance reviews are designed to give employees feedback on their performance, reward good performance, set expectations for improvement, and solve any problems that an employer thinks may be inhibiting good job performance. While they are often classified as interviews, rarely are performance appraisals conducted in the give–give manner of a true interview. Nor should they be. The performance review is the employer's, manager's, or team leader's opportunity to let employees know how they are doing. Although there should always be room for a brief question-and-answer period in a performance review, the manager imparts most of the information, and the employee listens and takes notes. After the employee has had an opportunity to evaluate the information provided in the review, the employee should be allowed to offer additional information or evidence, if necessary.

TIPS FOR PERFORMANCE REVIEWS

Employer

Before the Review
- Ask for a written evaluation from the employee of his or her performance.
- Carefully read the employee's evaluation before you complete your evaluation.
- Review (if a record exists) the employee's past two performance reviews.
- Outline the areas of the employee's performance that exceeded expectations, met expectations, and fell short of expectations for the appraisal period.
- Indicate areas that have fallen below expectations over the past two review periods.
- Outline a course of action for the employee to follow that will meet expectations.
- Document the course of action in a memo for both you and the employee to sign.

During the Review
- Present the evaluation to the employee beginning with areas that exceeded expectations, 2 followed by those that met expectations, and ending with those that were below expectations.

Employee

Before the Review
- Prepare a written evaluation of your work prior to the manager's evaluation.
- If you are not asked for a self-evaluation, check with your manager two weeks before your review date and request the opportunity to provide a self-evaluation.
- In your evaluation, give an honest assessment of your performance. Include the areas where you believe you went above and beyond the requirements of the job and the areas where you need improvement.
- Outline goals for the next review cycle. The goals you outline should reflect your individual and team goals.
- Submit a well-thought-out, well-reasoned, organized appraisal of your work.

During the Review
- Listen, listen, listen. By now, your manager knows what you think. Listen carefully to everything he or she has to say.
- Take notes.

(continued)

Employer

During the Review (continued)

- Keep the focus on the employee's job performance and team and group interactions.
- Avoid making vague references to the employee's "attitude" or other subjective references.
- Present the course of action for improvement.
- Ask the employee if he or she has questions.
- Offer the employee a brief period to think about the evaluation and respond either in writing or in person.
- Ask the employee to sign the review memo documenting the course of action. Indicate that you will expect the memo to be signed by the employee by a specific date and that a nonresponse on the part of the employee indicates agreement with the memo as is.

After the Review

- Follow up on the memo if the employee has not signed it by the date specified.
- Continue to document problems as they arise, but don't harp on problems that have been discussed and solved.
- Praise the employee for changes and progress made.
- Follow up with additional reviews as needed at three-month intervals.

Employee

During the Review (continued)

- Be gracious when given praise or high marks for doing well.
- Acknowledge areas you know need improvement.
- Ask for a period to reflect on and respond to areas that may be in dispute.
- Walk away from the review without being defensive, negative, or closed to suggestions offered by your manager.

After the Review

- Spend some time honestly thinking about your review.
- Don't talk about the review with coworkers.
- Submit a well-thought-out, well-reasoned, organized assessment of your review if you believe any areas were unfair.
- Indicate areas of agreement and areas that seem unfair or too harsh. Suggest ways to remedy the disagreement. Indicate that you are willing to work on your performance as well as working toward an amicable conclusion.
- Give your manager an opportunity to respond.

INFORMATION INTERVIEWS OR FOCUS GROUPS

A person, group, or organization uses an information interview to gather specific information, further understanding, or test a concept or idea. Information interviews can take the form of exit interviews, legal investigations, medical histories, surveys, polls, news interviews, research interviews, or personal or organizational histories. A focus group is a group assembled to help explore an idea or test a product or concept.

Information interviews can be one-on-one or with a group:

- One-on-one: for example, a team leader interviews an employee who has quit to determine if there were problems on the team, or a sales manager interviews a customer about changes to a product.
- With a group: for example, focus groups can be used to explore a new Internet concept, or professional groups can be polled at a meeting about regulatory changes.

TIPS FOR INFORMATION INTERVIEWS

Interviewer

- Determine the purpose of the interview.
- Conduct any research necessary to familiarize yourself with the interview subject.
- Set clear goals for the interview.
- Create limits for the interview, including the number of participants, the questions to be asked, and the time frame for the interview.
- Select participants for the interview who have knowledge of or experience with the subject.
- Develop a clear structure for the interview.
- Prepare the interviewees by explaining the process you will use for conducting the interview.
- Follow up with a thank-you e-mail, phone call, or note. Or, if appropriate, send the interviewee a thank-you gift.
- Prepare the final report.
- Present the final report.

Interviewee

- Confirm the purpose of and the process for the interview before the interview begins, if the interviewer does not provide an orientation.
- Think carefully about your answer before speaking.
- Don't elaborate unless you are asked to.
- Don't be an interview hog. If you are a member of a focus group, don't always be the first to speak. The interviewer is interested in everyone's opinion.
- Don't try to be funny or entertaining. Focus groups are expensive to conduct, and interviewers will not appreciate wasting time.
- Don't attempt to bias the other members of the group. Each member of a focus group is selected to provide a balanced view of the product, concept, or service under investigation. It is not your job to sway the members of the group to your side.

The goal, the purpose of the interview, the persons interviewed, and the limits of the interview should be clearly defined before the interview begins. Information interviews that stray beyond these set limits are rarely effective and can be frustrating for the persons being interviewed.

EMPLOYMENT INTERVIEWS

Employment interviews are the most common form of interviews. Many of you have already experienced an employment interview—or you soon will. The employment interview's purpose is to create a match between a potential employee and the employer that satisfies all or most of the goals each party brings to the table. Thus the participants must do the following:

- spend time clearly defining their goals and expectations prior to the interview
- be honest about their goals and expectations to ensure a good fit
- approach the interview from an informed position that allows information to flow back and forth
- make an informed choice based on all the available information

The goal of an employment interview should never be to "find a body to fill the position" or to "get a job, any job." If these are the goals, the outcomes will surely be dismal for both parties.

The remainder of this chapter focuses on using the CCCD process—choosing, creating, coordinating, and delivering to conduct successful and ethical employment interviews.

CHOOSING: SETTING THE PARAMETERS FOR THE INTERVIEW

Goals help you determine the qualifications you are looking for in job candidates, along with factors such as the number of team members required, the job title for each position, and the mix of team members. Job descriptions help you tailor the skill set and experience to the specific job—for example, the number of years of experience a person must have, the types of experience needed, or the specific tools required. These elements allow you to develop a framework for a positive and productive interview for you and the applicants.

SETTING THE GOALS FOR THE INTERVIEW

If you are the interviewer, an obvious goal is to find the best-qualified person to fill the position. However, you may also find that a number of secondary goals, once identified, will help you narrow the field of applicants and result in a better fit for your organization. For example, are you looking for a spit-and-polish professional, or someone who is more a khaki-pants-and-golf-shirt type? Do most of your team members have four-year or graduate degrees, or is the team a mix of interns and technical and degreed people? What qualities do you or your team members value most—hard work, a sense of humor, creativity? What have previous team members lacked that kept them from fitting into either the team or the organizational culture? These are the types of questions to examine during the choosing phase of interviewing.

DEVELOPING A JOB DESCRIPTION

Large corporations usually develop detailed **job descriptions** that minutely specify all of the individual duties and responsibilities that make up a particular job. Smaller companies may not go into such detail. A job description for an open position usually includes experience and education requirements and the salary range for the position. This brief description is the basis for the job announcement that will appear in print ads or online job boards. These job announcements or brief job descriptions set the tone for the questions asked during the interview, establish the criteria for selecting a successful applicant, and allow potential applicants to determine if there is an initial match with the company.

Just as the résumé is the first impression you have of a job applicant, the job description you place in the newspaper, trade publications, or on the Internet is the first impression prospective employees have of the job and your company. When you write a job description for a job announcement, you should follow these guidelines:

- Keep the description as short but informative as possible.
- Provide a list of at least three qualifications for the position.
- Identify the city and state the job is located in. Online job banks allow users to search by city and state. Not providing this information may narrow your

GLOBAL PROFILE FOR SUCCESS—VIRTUAL INTERVIEWS

Second Life is a 3D virtual world that opened online in 2003. Since its inception, government, educational, and corporate organizations have used Second Life to bring people together from around the globe for a myriad of purposes. One popular and growing use of Second Life is to host virtual job fairs and conduct interviews. Companies like Verizon, Microsoft, and Hewlett-Packard have participated in Second Life job fairs.

To participate in Second Life, you create an online persona called an avatar. In Second Life, you can be anything you want to be—an animal or a taller, thinner version of yourself. However, those interviewing for a job might want to stick to a realistic version of themselves.

Explore Second Life's website: http://secondlife.com/.

What can you learn about virtual interviewing from the Second Life website? Create an avatar and practice interviewing in the virtual world. Would you be comfortable conducting a virtual interview in Second Life? What are some of the pros and cons of interviewing in this virtual environment?

---

pool of candidates. Providing this information may help eliminate applicants who will not relocate to your area.

- Provide a clear contact for the applicant, along with contact information. If you are using an online job bank, be sure to provide an e-mail address. If you don't want to use your own e-mail address, have your company establish one that is used specifically for job applications—for example: applications@bilin.com.

Here's an example of a job description that uses these guidelines:

Job Description: Documentation and Training Team Leader

Description: Internet startup located in Greensboro, NC, is looking for an enthusiastic individual to join our growing company. We are seeking a team leader with 5 to 7 years of team, leadership, and knowledge-based experience. The D&T team leader will be responsible for hiring, leading, and developing a team of 5 to 7 writers, curriculum developers, and trainers. Primary responsibilities will be to determine the documentation and training set and schedule for each release, schedule training for new clients, provide ongoing internal training for the organization, and manage the training facility.

Send resumes to: applications@bilin.com. Please put D&T *leader in the subject line.*

POSTING THE JOB

Once you have written your job description, it is time to post the description so that potential employees can view the description and chose whether or not to apply. Jobs can be posted in a variety of places. Traditionally, ads were placed in local newspapers or with college recruitment centers. Headhunters, professional associations, and trade publications, along with online job databanks, provide technically savvy job hunters with additional venues for their job search.

Local Newspapers An ad in the local paper typically limits the applicants to the delivery area of the paper. The advantage of this option is that you will receive applications from people living in the immediate area who will not have to arrange a move to take the job, which means less lag time and no moving expenses. This is also a relatively inexpensive option for placing announcements. A disadvantage is that a large number of qualified people in your industry may not live in your area, so you may be choosing from a limited pool of applicants.

University Career Placement Centers   Career placement centers are a great place to locate entry-level and experienced applicants who have returned to college to pursue a degree. Concentrating on colleges in your area ensures that the applicants will be readily available to interview or to accept a position without incurring travel costs. Many colleges also have an online job database where you can post an ad or search for a job.

Professional Associations and Trade Publications   Organizations such as the Society for Technical Communication, the Internet Developers Association, the International Television Association, and the American Academy of Audiologists all provide job databanks that help pair job applicants with organizations. The advantage of placing an announcement with a professional organization is that you are targeting a very specific group of people with very specific skills. The disadvantage is that chances are slim the person you find will be located in your city, which means you may have to pay moving expenses for higher-level positions.

Online Job Resources   Online services such as those found at http://www.monster.com and http://www.careerbuilder.com provide a wide range of announcement opportunities. Some of the online services serve a specific industry or profession. For example, http://www.interec.net/ focuses on engineering jobs, salaries, and other resources for the job seeker and searcher. The cost for placing an announcement with an online databank varies. The advantages are that you reach a broad range of potential applicants very quickly. In many cases, as soon as you hit the "enter" key on the form, the job announcement is online. The disadvantage is the same as with professional organizations and trade publications; the ideal candidate may not live in your area.

Headhunters   With this option, you essentially pay someone to screen potential applicants. Headhunters can save you a tremendous amount of time, but their services are very expensive. They often charge as much as 25 to 30 percent of the position's annual salary if they place someone with your company.

CREATING: SCRIPTING THE INTERVIEW

Good interviews put participants at ease and allow information to flow between participants. The success of the interview requires a well-established interview plan or script. An **interview script** is a plan of questions used for the interview. An interview script should contain questions that accomplish the goals listed on page 127.

Once the general script is created, it will need to be adapted to each individual interviewee. This type of interview is called a *semi-structured interview*. The interview script establishes the main questions that will be asked within each segment of the interview, but it leaves the interview process open for follow-up and response questions.

SAMPLE INTERVIEW SCRIPT

Establish rapport

These questions should put the interviewee at ease and break the ice. Examples are:
- How was your flight?
- Did you have trouble finding us?

Define the interviewee's experience

These questions arise from the cover letter, résumé, and references. Examples are:
- I see that you majored in communication. How has your major prepared you for this job?
- Tell us a little about your current position.
- What are two things about your current job that you find challenging?
- What are two things about your current job that you dislike?
- What has been your biggest accomplishment at your current position?
- What will you miss most about the company you work for?
- Of all the jobs you have had, which has been the best fit, and why?

Clarify the requirements for the position

These questions zero in on the requirements for the position. Examples are:
- This position requires hiring and developing a team of writers and trainers. How would you go about doing that?
- In this position, you will be required to manage a team. What qualities do you think are important in a team environment?
- As a manager, you will be required to report the progress of your team. How do you feel about providing regular status reports?
- An important function of this position is liaison to other teams. What skills do you have that will facilitate this function?
- How would this position further your career goals?

Present the organization

These questions open a discussion of the organization. Examples are:
- What do you know about Bilin.com?
- How do you feel about working for an Internet startup, coming from such an established company?
- Bilin is a small, young company and we can't offer the benefits some organizations can. Is that a problem?
- We have just signed three major contracts, which has tripled our deliverables overnight. To meet our schedules, we know that we have to work extremely long hours. Is there anything to prevent you from working long hours when necessary?

Provide closure

These questions signal the end of the interview and allow for a final opportunity to clarify information. Examples are:
- Do you have any additional questions?
- If offered the position, when could you start?

ETHICAL INTERVIEWING

The interview script should not contain illegal or inappropriate questions. It should not ask questions that require an interviewee to justify his or her race, marital status, religion, age, sex, or sexual orientation. The chart given below describes some of the questions you can and can't ask.

 ## ETHICAL INTERVIEWING

Topic	What You Can't Ask	What You Can Ask
Marital Status	Are you married or single? How long have you been married? Are you divorced? Do you go by your maiden name? Does your husband (or wife) mind your traveling?	This position requires a good bit of travel. Is there any reason you cannot travel? Have you ever used another name for any reason?
Children	How many children do you have? How old are your children? Is day care a problem for you?	Our company has an excellent onsite daycare program. Would you like to visit the daycare center?
Citizenship	Are you a U.S. citizen? What country were you born in? How long have you lived in the United States? Do you have a green card?	Do you speak any languages other than English? Your Arabic is very good. How long have you spoken the language? Our company requires employees to provide proof of citizenship or legal work papers after they are hired. Will this be a problem?
Race	You have the nicest eyes. Are you Asian?	There are no questions in this area that are appropriate.
Age	How old are you? When did you finish high school? I love getting my AARP discount. Have you applied for your card yet?	There are aspects of this job that require the operator to be over 18. Can you provide proof of age?
Physical Attributes	How long have you had a weight problem? Is your height a problem in your current job?	This position requires a lot of physical activity. Do you have a handicap or physical condition that would keep you from performing any part of the job? Do you require special equipment or accommodations?
Military Service	Have you ever served in the military?	I see that when you were in the Navy, you were a telecommunications expert. How do you think these skills apply to this position?
Criminal Record	Have you ever committed a crime? Have you ever been arrested?	Have you been convicted of a felony? Before you answer, I need to inform you that the information you provide may disqualify you for this position.

FOCUS ON ETHICS

You are conducting a joint interview with a colleague who keeps asking inappropriate questions. The colleague asks gender-based questions, directly asks an interviewee his age, and implies that overweight applicants are a waste of his time. What do you do? Is your primary ethical obligation to the interviewee, your colleague, or your company?

COORDINATING: SETTING UP THE INTERVIEW

When a team member is hired, he or she will work with people throughout the organization. It is important that new hires fit within the organizational culture and meet the expectations of those outside, as well as inside, the group. To ensure a good fit throughout the organization:

- Inform those who might interact with the position that you are interviewing candidates for the position.
- Give the mangers from other departments an opportunity to meet with each candidate for the position.
- Take their recommendations and concerns into consideration when making your final decision.
- Inform those within the organization who need to know whom you have hired and when he or she will be starting.
- Make sure the new employee has an opportunity to meet with those he or she will be working with throughout the organization before he or she attends formal meetings, if possible.

THINKING GLOBALLY—INTERVIEWING CUSTOMS AROUND THE GLOBE

The website http://www.jobera.com/job-interviews/international-job-interviews/international-job-interviews.htm allows you to select a country and learn about the interview customs that are common for the country selected. If you are interviewing for a job overseas or for an overseas company with offices in the United States, it is important that you are aware of the cultural differences that may present themselves during the interview.

Compare the interview tips for each country. Which expectations are the most surprising? What can you learn about conducting interviews with people from other countries from this and other websites of this type?

DELIVERING: READY, SET, INTERVIEW

Before the interview, be sure you have all the necessary information in front of you. You should have a file for each interviewee that contains the following information:

- application (if one was required)
- résumé
- letters of recommendation
- notes on calls to references
- a copy of the job description
- the interview schedule for the interviewee
- writing or other samples if provided
- additional information about the job, salary, travel, etc.
- any documentation the interviewee might need to sign—non disclosure forms, travel reimbursement, etc.

You should begin the interview by establishing rapport with the interviewee and then follow the interview script you developed in *Creating: Scripting the Interview* on page 127.

CASE STUDY 5 | **CONDUCTING VIRTUAL INTERVIEWS**

Ling sat at his desk, surprised at how much better he felt now that he had contracted with a consultant to help him staff the new technical writing department he was responsible for developing. As director of customer service for Bilin.com, an Internet startup, Ling handled everything that "impacted customers both internally and externally." Two weeks ago, he found out this included the documentation, on-line help, and training materials required for the various software systems Bilin.com develops and uses. The problem was that, Ling didn't know anything about writing documentation or hiring technical writers.

Carmen, the head of the quality assurance group, soon came to the rescue. In her previous job at a different company, Carmen had worked with a technical communication consultant, Valerie, who helped her define and staff the documentation and training group there. She gave Ling the consultant's name and number and suggested he give her a call.

Sitting at his desk after his meeting with Valerie, Ling thought about the consultant he had just hired. "What a strange interview," Ling thought. "I feel like I was the one being interviewed! I have to get better at this now that I have all this responsibility."

On the way back to her office, Valerie thought about her newest consulting job. She was excited to be working for a smaller company again, doing what she did best—hiring and training writers and building a department. Yet she could tell from her meeting with Ling that this was going to be a lot of work. Ling didn't have a clue about interviewing, the job requirements for technical writers or trainers, the requirements for a documentation department, the components of a documentation set, or anything else that would be needed to get the department up and running. That was the downside. The upside was that Ling seemed to be a nice, easygoing guy who didn't mind admitting when he didn't know something. He was honest about his inability to hire and

continued

CASE STUDY 5 | **CONDUCTING VIRTUAL INTERVIEWS** *continued*

develop a writing staff on his own. He had been very up front about the budget and staffing resources that were available. Valerie found that honesty a big plus.

A few weeks later, Ling and Valerie were ready to conduct their first interview. They started with Anna, whose strong résumé highlighted her twelve years of documentation and training experience. She currently worked as part of a D&T team that, on paper, appeared similar to the team Ling hoped to develop. Ling had placed her at the top of the list. Valerie, however, had a couple of reservations. Anna's job experience appeared complete, yet she had changed jobs frequently in the past seven years. Missing from her skill set were some software products that Valerie thought were key for the position. They set up a phone interview with Anna for 2:00 the next day.

Ling and Valerie met in the conference room equipped with a speakerphone so that they both could hear Anna and speak to her. Anna answered the phone, saying "Hello" in a soft voice.

"Anna, I am here with Valerie, our consultant," Ling said, after introducing himself.

"Hi, Anna," Valerie said.

"Hi," Anna said softly.

Ling jumped right in, asking Anna about the information on her résumé and the duties of her current job. Anna answered each of his questions completely, but very softly and offered very limited information. A couple of times, Ling had to ask her to speak up or repeat what she had said. And he and Valerie had to follow up every question with a more detailed question to draw additional information out of Anna.

Valerie asked Anna about some of the software she used on various projects and then asked her about software she didn't see on Anna's résumé. Anna explained that most of her positions had used the same software over the years and she really didn't need additional tools. She felt that sticking to what she had always used was more efficient.

Ling then addressed the issue of job changes. Anna explained that she had worked in the textile industry and been downsized a couple of times. She then found a job with a company that made machine engines. She was doing technical writing, but the work was very limiting and she felt she was writing the same thing over and over. She felt stuck. So after only thirteen months in her current position, she was looking again. She was very eager to find a position with a growing company in a growing industry.

Ling thanked Anna and told her they would be in touch. After hanging up, Ling asked Valerie what she thought.

"Well, I'm not sure if she doesn't like talking on the phone or if she is always that timid, but I found listening to her very trying. I can't believe you had to ask her to speak up four times. What did you think?" Valerie asked.

"I hate to say it, but I knew after the first four questions that she wasn't going to work out," said Ling. "The programmers will run all over her if she is that timid in person. We really need a go-getter in this position and she just didn't come across that way on the phone."

We have included the example of Ling and Anna to highlight how difficult an interview can be for both parties. Often we see the interview process from the side of the interviewee, but preparing for and conducting an interview is equally as challenging and stressful. Successful interviewers recognize that time spent in preparing for the interview pays off when they find exactly the right person for a job. While Ling and Valerie attempted to give Anna every opportunity to perform well in the interview, Anna's timid nature came through loud and clear over the phone. Are phone interviews fair? Are there people who simply do not have good phone skills, yet in person communicate smoothly and effectively? Should this be Anna's only shot? Ask your friends, relatives, and coworkers to gauge your phone skills. What do you need to improve before participating in a phone interview? If you find yourself scheduled for a phone interview for a job you really want, remember to practice, practice, and practice before the interview. Also, be sure to smile! You can hear a smile over the phone and smiling will keep you from getting tense and shutting down. Review the tips on page 132 for conducting a phone or video interview.

TIPS FOR PHONE AND VIDEO INTERVIEWS

- Make sure that there are no distractions when you conduct or participate in a phone or video interview.
- Reserve a conference room so that you will not be interrupted.
- Turn off call waiting! The last thing you want to do is ask the interviewee to hold while you answer another call.

- Speak clearly and loudly enough to be heard, especially if the call is being conducted over a conference phone.
- Wait until each speaker finishes before beginning to speak.
- Clarify any responses you don't understand.
- Smile. When you smile, your voice is friendlier and it puts everyone at ease.

CONDUCTING PHONE AND VIDEO SCREENING INTERVIEWS

Phone interviews are an excellent way of narrowing down the possible candidates for a job. From a phone interview, you can get a general idea of an individual's personality, energy level, and knowledge base.

An alternative to a phone interview is the video interview. With oil prices and air fares rising, companies are turning to video interviews as a way to cut costs. Video interviewing allows companies to reduce travel expenditures for interviewees and have verbal and visual interaction with job candidates. Video interviews have other advantages. Tapes of the interview can be saved and reviewed later by those unable to attend the initial interview or those in remote offices who will be interacting with the candidate if he or she is hired. For more information about video interviews see: http://jobsearch.about.com/od/jobinterviewtypes/a/videointerv.htm.

SUMMARY

This chapter examined the different types of interviews and the uses for each. It also introduced the concept of conscious interviewing and used the employment interview as an example of how we can implement conscious interviews, primarily from the interviewer's perspective. We also followed the interview process by developing goals, a job description, and an interview script.

The chapter reviewed the importance of asking questions that are fair and nonintrusive but that elicit the information needed to qualify a candidate for a position. Finally, we discussed phone and video interviews. The next chapter examines the interviewing process from the interviewee's perspective.

BUSINESS AND PROFESSIONAL COMMUNICATION IN THE GLOBAL WORKPLACE ONLINE

All of the following chapter review materials are available in an electronic format on either the *Business and Professional Communication in the Global Workplace* Resource Center or the book's companion website. Online you'll find chapter learning objects, flashcards of glossary terms, InfoTrack® College Edition Activities, weblinks, quizzes and more.

WHAT YOU SHOULD HAVE LEARNED

Now that you have read Chapter 6, you should be able to do the following:

- Describe the major types of interviews.

- Discuss the difference between a mindful and mindless interview.
- List the steps in conducting a performance review.
- Discuss the do's and don'ts for information interviews.
- Discuss the choices that need to be made for a conscious employment interview.
- Create a job description.
- Set goals for an interview.
- Create a script for the interview.
- Establish an interview schedule.
- Conduct a phone or video interview.

KEY TERMS

employment interviews *123*	interview script *126*	performance review *121*
interrogation *119*	job descriptions *124*	persuasive interview *120*

WRITING AND CRITICAL THINKING

The following activities can be completed online or submitted to your instructor.

Choose one of the following activities.

1. Write a job description for your current job or a job you previously had. If you haven't had a job, write a job description for your ideal job.
2. Write an interview script for the job description you wrote in Activity 1.
3. In pairs, answer the interview questions for the job description and interview script.

Or have a friend ask you the interview questions.

4. You are working for an international company with offices in Europe and Asia. Visit http://www.jobera.com/job-interviews/international-job-interviews/international-job-interviews.htm, and select a country in each of those areas. Make a list of the cultural considerations you need to take into account for interviewing candidates in each area. How are they different from interview customs that you are used to?

PRACTICING COMMUNICATION IN PROFESSIONAL CONTEXTS

Handling Team Interviews

Often, you will be asked to conduct an interview with two or more people. Let's consider the following scenario:

Ling and Valerie ask Tom, the implementation manager, to sit in on an interview with a prospective employee. The applicant, Jan Chin, is a young Asian American woman who is well qualified for the position. During the interview, Tom asks questions that are both illegal and inappropriate, many having nothing to do with Jan's ability to perform the job. Which of the following should Ling and Valerie do?

a.   Ignore Tom and continue the interview.
b.   Apologize for Tom, make excuses about how hard he has been working, and continue the interview.
c.   Stop the interview, ask Tom to leave, and continue the interview.
d.   Stop the interview, leave the room with Tom and ask him not to return, then continue the interview without him.

After the interview, which of the following should Ling and Valerie do?

a.   Forget about what happened.
b.   Confront Tom about his behavior during the interview.
c.   Speak to Tom and then Tom's boss about his behavior.
d.   Bring up their concerns with the human resources manager.

Select the answer you think is the best action for each situation. Write an explanation for your choices. Discuss your choices with the class or within your group.

The Job Search and Conscious Communication

CHAPTER 7

CONDUCTING A CONSCIOUS JOB SEARCH

Every day, people across the world look for jobs. As the global economy continues to change, competition for many positions gets harder. Some job seekers will accept the first job they are offered. Some will accept a job that they aren't thrilled about, figuring it's better than what they have been doing. Some will search for a job consciously and find a *great* job.

What makes the difference between the person who takes the first job offered and the person who finds a great job? The conscious job search. In this chapter, we outline the process for conducting a conscious job search, including preparing for and participating in an interview. But first, look at the job search continuum in Figure 7.1 to see the difference between mindless and mindful job searches.

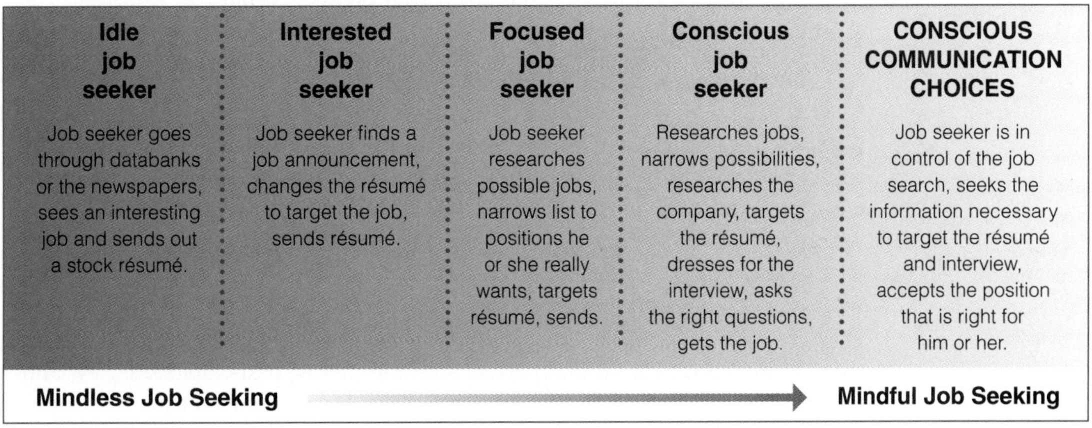

Idle job seeker	Interested job seeker	Focused job seeker	Conscious job seeker	CONSCIOUS COMMUNICATION CHOICES
Job seeker goes through databanks or the newspapers, sees an interesting job and sends out a stock résumé.	Job seeker finds a job announcement, changes the résumé to target the job, sends résumé.	Job seeker researches possible jobs, narrows list to positions he or she really wants, targets résumé, sends.	Researches jobs, narrows possibilities, researches the company, targets the résumé, dresses for the interview, asks the right questions, gets the job.	Job seeker is in control of the job search, seeks the information necessary to target the résumé and interview, accepts the position that is right for him or her.

Mindless Job Seeking ⟶ **Mindful Job Seeking**

FIGURE 7.1 | CONSCIOUS COMMUNICATION AND JOB SEEKING CONTINUUM

Before beginning the job search and interview process, it is important to identify the type of position you want. Are you looking for a management position, or a trainee job? Do you need flexible hours? Are you hoping to travel? The first step in the conscious job search, like the first step in any communication situation, is to choose your job goals. The job search is like many other communication situations. Applying the CCCD process can help you engage in conscious communication.

CHOOSING: SETTING YOUR JOB GOALS

The choosing process helps you set the parameters of your job search. Before you write your résumé, apply for a position, or schedule an appointment for a job interview, you must set **job goals**. Job goals can be expressed as the type of position you want and the outcomes you want from your employment. You can start by identifying the following elements:

- types of positions you would enjoy
- benefits you expect from a position
- your salary requirements
- types of employers you would like to work for
- types of industries you would like to work in
- lifestyle you expect from the position

Keep in mind, these are basic parameters. Be careful not to narrow your job search to the point where few if any jobs meet your goals.

JOB RESEARCH

The research stage is crucial for finding not only a job, but the *right* job. Without research, you are not aware of the job possibilities available or the limitations and benefits of a particular position. How do you begin a conscious job search? How do you know which job is right for you? How do you know which company will be a good fit? How do you set clear job goals? The first step is research. However, job seekers often overlook this crucial step in the job search process. What can research do?

- *Focus or broaden the types of jobs you are applying for.* Often, seasoned job seekers will continue to apply for the same job over and over, thinking, "That is what I do." Rather than use research to find related jobs or a similar job in a related industry that might be more fulfilling and interesting, they continue to do the same old thing; only the company actually changes. At the other extreme, some new job seekers attempt to apply for anything and everything without a lot of thought for the duties, responsibilities, or salary associated with a particular job. Research helps you focus on the types of jobs you really want to do, eliminating those that don't fit your expectations.
- *Provide you with important job parameters.* Knowing important parameters such as the education and experience requirements, associated salaries, and travel requirements for a particular type of job will save you the time of applying for jobs you are under- and over-qualified for and will keep you from omitting crucial elements from your résumé.

- *Help you identify potential industries and employers.* Often, job seekers fail to target industries and employers that may offer great job opportunities. Research helps you identify industries or employers you may not have realized need your services.
- *Help you define what you can contribute to a specific company.* The bottom line with interviewers is the question, "What can you do for us?" At the heart of this question lies a second question, "How will you make my job and life easier?" Without research, you cannot sell yourself to a prospective employer.
- *Impress an interviewer.* Interviewers are impressed when you take the time to research their company. Speaking intelligently about a company's products and services shows interviewers that you are interested in not just a job, but a job with *their* company. We recommend coming to an interview prepared with questions to ask the interviewer. These questions demonstrate your desire to ensure that the job and company are a good fit for you and your qualifications.

How do you begin? There are a number of starting places to use for job research:

- the Internet—to find job boards, view a company's website, view online profiles and prospectuses, locate news articles, and consult professional organizations
- company employees, friends, and relatives—to gather insider information on a specific organization
- company tours—to gather information on work habits, dress code, and departmental interaction
- campus recruitment office—to determine the success rate of other grads who have been placed with a particular company or to research and schedule appointments with companies that are interviewing on campus

You can use one or more of these tools to effectively research possible jobs.

Internet Research   The Internet has revolutionized the job search process. Using the Internet, you can search for job openings, research a company and its key employees, gather details about the products or services an organization provides, locate examples of résumés targeted to a particular industry or specialty, and determine if you and the company are a good fit.

First, consult a few of the hundreds of job boards that have sprung up on the Internet, such as Monster.com or Jobs.com. Some of these boards offer a wide variety of jobs that cut across a variety of industries—medical, technical, high-tech, retail, and many others. Other job boards offer postings specific to a particular industry. For example, a number of them provide listings only for high-tech development positions. Within the high-tech area, there are boards that list jobs only for JAVA programmers.

Another online resource is the wide variety of social networking sites that connect people for a common purpose. LinkedIn (http://www.linkedin.com) is one site that connects job seekers with opportunities to collaborate with others, find a job, start a new project, get recommendations, or connect with professionals in the field they are interested in.

Company Employees, Friends, and Relatives   Company employees, friends, and relatives are a valuable source of information. If you know someone working in a company or industry that interests you, give him or her a call. Take the employee to lunch and ask questions about the company. Here are some areas to ask about:

- organizational structure
- departmental ties, conflicts, and strengths
- work environment
- company future
- dress codes
- programs to enhance work-life balance

However, when talking with current company employees, it is important to keep in mind that you are gaining only one person's perspective. It may be necessary to balance what is said with the other information you gather about the company. You may know someone working for the company you want to work for. Or, you may live in a city or town where there are only one or two large companies. Friends and relatives working in these companies can provide a wealth of knowledge about the company, the industry, and the people you might be working with someday.

Company Tours   Company tours are often available at large companies such as CNN, BMW, and Warner Brothers. Even some smaller companies—the ice cream maker Ben & Jerry's, for instance—offer daily tours. These public tours can be very useful for gathering information about an organization to help you determine if this is a place where you want to work. While on a tour, pay close attention to the interaction of employees, the dress code, and the working environment.

If a public tour is not offered, you might call the human resources department and ask for a tour of the organization. You can explain that you are interested in the company as a potential employee. Many organizations will not provide a tour, however, because of the private nature of their products or services. For example, many banking and financial institutions would view a request for a tour with suspicion and would deny your request. If a tour request is not a viable option, you can always ask the human resources department for suggestions on getting to know the company. Knowing your audience and being conscious of your communication can help you avoid any awkward requests.

Campus Recruitment Office   The campus recruitment office at your college or university can be an excellent source of information about prospective employers, dressing for an interview, targeting résumés, and more. College students looking for a job should visit their college recruitment office at least once. The college recruitment office may be able to put you in touch with alumni working for a company that interests you. Further, many colleges offer résumé and cover letter help, as well as online job databases where employers looking for college students post available positions.

GLOBAL PROFILE FOR SUCCESS—JOB SEARCH GOLD

Monster.com began in the 1990s as a career website designed to link employers and employees. Since then, it has expanded to provide career services around the globe. In 2004, Monster.com became the only pan-European recruitment website and has since expanded by launching Monster Mexico and providing services in the Middle East region.

Monster.com has expanded from a job database website to providing job seekers with company research and career advice, which includes significant information on interviewing.

Explore Monster's website: http://www.monster.com/.

Monster.com offers job seekers the opportunity to look at job postings around the world. View some of the postings for jobs in Europe or Mexico. What skills are necessary to succeed in the global workplace? Did you find jobs that you might not have known about or considered before viewing the postings on Monster.com?

HINT

If a job listing interests you but does not include the company name or contact information, send a general inquiry letter or e-mail. This allows you to elicit more information from the company before sending a résumé. For example:

Hello!
I just finished reading your posting on monster.com. I am very interested in the position you posted. However, I would like more information before submitting my résumé. Any additional information you could provide about the position and the company would be greatly appreciated.

Sincerely,
Shannon Green

CREATING: PUTTING TOGETHER A WINNING RÉSUMÉ AND COVER LETTER

Let's start this section with a personal story. After Sandra finished her graduate program, she decided to stay at home with our son Nic. Four years later, after Nic started school, Sandra found that she had a good bit of free time and little to fill it. One afternoon, H.L. came home ranting about how difficult it was to get a job and how his students were really struggling in the slow job market. Sandra challenged his point of view and boldly said, "Oh, come on! I could get a job tomorrow if I wanted, and I've been staying at home with a child for the last four years." Of course H.L. took Sandra up on her challenge. He dared her to find a job in such a tight market.

A few days later, Sandra found a job announcement on the Internet that matched her experience and her goals. A consulting firm located in Tampa, Florida, was looking for someone to develop documentation and training materials for a client in South Carolina. She researched the company, targeted her résumé, wrote a snazzy cover letter that included an explanation for her absence from the job market, and faxed the résumé to the number on the announcement. Exactly one day later, the president of the company called Sandra. He loved her cover letter and résumé. Her past experience spoke for itself, and he was also impressed that she clearly understood the changes that had occurred in the marketplace and that she was equipped to adjust to those changes. He informed Sandra that although the project manager in South Carolina was looking for a technical writer for a specific customer, *he* was looking for someone to develop a documentation and training department for the entire organization. This was something, according to Sandra's résumé, that she had done in the past. After lengthy phone interviews with the president and other key members of the management team, Sandra was offered a position as Director of Training and Development. The salary and stock participation blew her away, and best of all, she could work from home. She immediately accepted the job.

We tell you this story for two reasons:

1. Bad résumés and cover letters get thrown in the trash; good résumés and cover letters will get you an interview; great résumés and cover letters can make an important lasting impression.
2. Well-written résumés and cover letters *can* open doors you may not know exist within an organization.

TARGETING YOUR RÉSUMÉ

A **résumé** is a formal statement of who you are. It is part autobiography, part work history, and part sales presentation. The primary goal of a résumé and cover letter is to compel the reader to contact you for an interview. If you currently have résumés out and you aren't receiving requests for interviews, revise your résumé immediately. There are two components to creating a winning résumé: selecting the information and selecting your format.

Years ago, before computers became so widely available, we would spend hours on our résumés, have professionals review them, and pay to have the final résumés typeset. We would get twenty or thirty copies printed and send them out. Not anymore. Now, because computers, high-quality printers, and electronic transmission of information are so prevalent, there is no excuse for *not* tailoring a résumé to a specific job or employer. Even job seekers with little or no experience will benefit from tailoring their résumés. Tailoring the résumé may require you to do the following:

- Change the format based on the type of industry or organization you are applying to. For example, a technical writer applying to an engineering firm might use a traditional format; however, that same writer might use a contemporary format for an Internet firm and an artistic format to apply for a position at a new magazine.
- Highlight accomplishments that match the job requirements.
- Change the language of the résumé to match the jargon of the industry you are applying to.
- Change the tone of the résumé from informal to formal, based on the type of industry you are applying to.

Tailoring your résumé will only go so far if your information is not well organized. There are three basic tiers of information organization in each résumé: headlines, highlights, and details.

- **Headlines** are where the reader's eye should be drawn first. In a standard résumé, this is done by using a slightly larger font, or bold-face type. Headlines are categories that emphasize the areas of your résumé that stand out the most. The first headline on most résumés is your name. Other common headlines include *Education, Work Experience, Awards and Honors*, etc. If the job you are applying for specifically asks for you to detail your computer skills, for example, one headline in your résumé could be *Computer Skills*.
- **Highlights** are the most important facts that you want emphasized under each headline. Under an *Education* headline, for example, you would want to list your degree first, not your school, as in most cases your field of study is more important to your application than where the degree was obtained. Under a *Work Experience* headline you would want to list the position and/or title first, and then the company.
- **Details** allow you to expand upon the highlights and describe and explain each experience. The details area is a great place to tailor your résumé to the qualifications and specifications that the employer is requesting.

TWO WORDS NEVER TO USE ON A RÉSUMÉ

Entry-level. These words raise red flags for those who are in charge of the screening process. You will be screened, never to be heard from again. Avoid using these two words, not only on your résumé, but also in your job search language, written and spoken. Companies are not looking for entry-level employees. They are looking for employees who can contribute to the growth and development of the organization.

Adapted from Job Search Info at www.collegegrad.com (2000).

THINKING GLOBALLY—BEING READY TO GO AT A MOMENT'S NOTICE

Throughout this book, we have emphasized the pan-global structure of most American and international companies. If you went to work for a company that expected you to travel internationally, could you? Do you have a passport? After June 1, 2009 passports will be required for travel to Canada and Mexico. Consider applying now for a passport. A passport costs $75.00. It can take 4–6 weeks for a passport application to be processed. While it is possible to expedite a passport application, expedition still takes up to two weeks. Imagine your employer asks you to travel to Europe. You have to leave in three days and you don't have a passport. Not only do you have to pass on a great opportunity, you have to pass on a free trip to Europe.

Go to http://travel.state.gov/passport/passport_1738.html to learn more about applying for a U.S. passport.

SELECTING A RÉSUMÉ FORMAT

Now that you've decided on what information you are going to include in your résumé, the next step is to decide how to organize that information, which means selecting the appropriate format. There are four formats for résumés:

- traditional
- contemporary
- artistic
- scannable

The uses for each format and examples are shown below.

Traditional Format   The traditional format is very conservative and straightforward. It is the least creative résumé style. This format should be used for very conservative organizations, such as law firms, banks, and accounting companies. An example is provided for your reference (Figure 7.2).

Contemporary Format   The contemporary format leans toward the conservative, but it allows the writer to include accomplishments that deserve mentioning. This format works well for managers or those who wish to move into a management position. This is also a good résumé for advertising, marketing, and high-tech professionals. An example is shown in Figure 7.3.

Artistic Format   The artistic format is used by job seekers who need to display their creative or individual talents. It allows the writer to highlight talents or creative abilities, which may be difficult to fit into a traditional or contemporary format. This format works well for artists, musicians, and actors who need to showcase their creative side. An example is shown in Figure 7.4.

Scannable Format   A scannable résumé is one that an optical scanner can read easily and accurately. Employers using scannable résumés conduct a search of all the résumés that have been scanned and stored in a database computer. The search returns those applicants whose résumés match the skills specified for a particular job. Because searches are based on keywords, it is important to include key terms and industry specific acronyms and jargon that accurately describe your skills and experience. An example is shown in Figure 7.5.

While scannable résumés contain the same basic content and headlines as traditional résumés, they are formatted for scanning. Follow these guidelines for creating a scannable résumé:

- Left justify your text.
- Use Arial or Times New Roman fonts in 11 to 14 point size.
- Avoid any kinds of graphics or shading.
- Keep formatting simple. Use all caps for major headings, but avoid bolding, italicizing, and underlining.
- Do not use bullets or lines.

Shannon Green

790 Snowgoose Cove
Middletown, MD 25678
210-555-5555
sgreen@middletown.com

Goal: To find a writing position with an established engineering firm that allows me to use my experience and education to the fullest.

Education

1993–1996   Master of Science in Communication from the University of Maryland.

1989–1993   Bachelor of Arts in English from Maryland State.

Work Experience

May 1996–current   *Computer Consultants, Inc.*
Senior Technical Writer   *Middletown, MD 25678*

Duties include developing documentation, online help, and training materials for a variety of companies. Work required learning a number of custom software packages and developing custom materials.

June 1993–May 1996   *First Bank of Maryland*
Technical Writer   *Middletown, MD 25678*

Duties included developing documentation, online help, and training materials for teller software packages.

June 1990–June 1993   *The Graduate School*
Work Study   *Maryland State*

Duties included preparing graduate student packages for prospective graduate students and editing masters theses.

References available upon request.

FIGURE 7.2 | TRADITIONAL FORMAT

Shannon Green

Home   **Business**
790 Snowgoose Cove   Computer Consultants, Inc.
Middletown, MD 25678   Middletown, MD 25678
210-555-5555   210-555-5552, ext. 789
sgreen@middletown.com   shannon.green@ccinc.com

Goal: To find a writing position with a growing Internet company that allows me to grow and develop my
skills and move into a management position.

Professional Experience

May 1996–current Senior Technical Writer	***Computer Consultants, Inc.*** *Middletown, MD 25678*
	Duties include developing documentation, online help, and training materials for a variety of companies.
Accomplishments:	Learned over 35 software packages in the last four years to develop customer documentation and training. Guided the development and delivery for the last nine projects including: selecting the writing and training team, developing the project plan, assigning the resources, and delivering documentation and training. Each project was delivered on time and within budget.
	Received five outstanding reviews and pay raises over the last four years.
June 1993–May 1996 Technical Writer	***First Bank of Maryland*** *Middletown, MD 25678*
	Duties included developing documentation, online help, and training materials for teller software packages.
Accomplishments:	*Received TIP (Team Initiative and Performance) award from three separate branches for the training I wrote.*
June 1990–June 1993 Work Study	***The Graduate School*** *Maryland State*
	Duties included preparing graduate student packages for prospective graduate students and editing master's theses.
Accomplishments:	*Asked to remain on in a full-time position after graduation.*

Education

1993–1996   Master of Science in Communication from the University of Maryland. GPA 4.0
1989–1993   Bachelor of Arts in English from Maryland State. GPA 3.8

References available upon request.

FIGURE 7.3 | CONTEMPORARY FORMAT

Shannon Green

Home
790 Snowgoose Cove
Middletown, MD 25678
210-555-5555
sgreen@middletown.com

Business
Computer Consultants, Inc.
Middletown, MD 25678
210-555-5552, ext. 789
shannon.green@ccinc.com

Goal: To find a writing position that allows me to mix my creative talents and professional expertise.

Agent: Marilyn Timmons, 17000 Park Avenue, New York, NY 10028.

Writing Competitions and Awards

New York Literary Magazine   Juried Award, Short Story Competition
May 2000

Maryland Writing Contest   Juried Award, Short Story Competition
December 1999

Coyote Journal   Judges Award, Short Story Category
June 1999

Books and Publications

I currently have one book, *Tales From My Heart,* and three short stories with my agent.

Professional Experience

May 1996–current   **Computer Consultants, Inc.**
Marketing Writer   *Middletown, MD 25678*

Duties include writing and editing the company newsletter and marketing and public relation articles for a variety of business and trade publications.

Senior Technical Writer   Developed documentation, online help, and training materials for a variety of companies.

June 1993–May 1996   **First Bank of Maryland**
Technical Writer   *Middletown, MD 25678*

Duties included developing documentation, online help, and training materials for teller software packages.

June 1990–June 1993   **The Graduate School**
Work Study   *Maryland State*

Duties included preparing graduate student packages for prospective graduate students and editing master's theses.

Education

1993–1996   Master of Science in Communication from the University of Maryland. GPA 4.0
1989–1993   Bachelor of Arts in English from Maryland State. GPA 3.8

References available upon request.

FIGURE 7.4 | ARTISTIC FORMAT

SHANNON GREEN
790 Snowgoose Cove
Middletown, MD 25678
Phone: 210-555-5555
E-mail: sgreen@middletown.com

OBJECTIVE

To find a writing position that allows me to grow and develop my skills and move into a management position.

QUALIFICATIONS SUMMARY

Several years' experience and education in technical writing and communication, leading to the development of communications, client relations, order processing, interpersonal, accounting, marketing, health policy, leadership, and management skills.

SYSTEMS SKILLS

Microsoft Office, HTML/Web publishing, WordPerfect, PageMaker

EDUCATION

M.S., University of Maryland, Communication

B.A., Towson State University

–Major: Communication

–Minor: Technical Writing

PROFESSIONAL EXPERIENCE

–Senior Technical Writer, Computer Consultants, Inc.

–Technical Writer, First Bank of Maryland

ACCOMPLISHMENTS

–Guided the development and delivery for the last nine projects, including: selecting the writing and training team, developing the project plan, assigning the resources, and delivering documentation and training.

–Delivered each project on time and within budget.

–Learned over 35 software packages in the last four years to develop customer documentation and training.

REFERENCES
Available upon request.

FIGURE 7.5 | SCANNABLE FORMAT

WRITING A COMPELLING COVER LETTER

Recently, we did an Internet search on the phrase *résumé and cover letters*. The search returned over 1,860,000 hits. That's almost two million websites with information about résumés and cover letters. Before you begin your résumé, look at the examples on some of these sites. You should also look at the example in Figure 7.6. Borrow the best formats, wording, and styles you find. You don't have to reinvent the wheel. Just make sure that whatever you borrow is appropriate for the type of job you are applying for.

SHANNON GREEN

790 Snowgoose Cove
Middletown, MD 25678
210 555-5555
sgreen@middletown.com

May 10, 2006

Ling Cyan
Bilin.com
555 Frontage Road
Greensboro, NC 27485

Mr. Cyan,
After reading your posting on the Society for Technical Communication job board, I knew I had to submit my resume. I have been considering a change since receiving my master's degree a few months ago. The job you posted resonated closely with many of the goals I have established for myself.

I am a motivated and experienced technical writer with over ten years of experience. For the past four years, I have worked for a consulting company creating documentation and training materials for a variety of companies and industries, developing a broad range of technical and writing knowledge. I have led a number of project development teams and I know how to motivate writers and trainers. I have developed documentation and training sets for both internal and external training audiences, determined schedules, and managed training facilities for a number of clients.

I am looking for a position with a fast-growing company. I enjoy the change and challenge that are part of the Internet experience. I am looking forward to discussing my qualifications with you. You can contact me at the above number or e-mail address.

Sincerely,

Shannon Green

FIGURE 7.6 | COVER LETTER

Think of a cover letter as your first impression. A good cover letter introduces you to a prospective employer and highlights your credentials. A poorly written cover letter will get you eliminated from the running without a second glance. Excellent cover letters draw the reader in and show that the cover letter's author has taken the time to:

- target the letter to specific audience
- attend to the basics
- sell themselves with confidence
- proofread, proofread, proofread

Target the Letter to a Specific Audience   Often, job announcements will contain the name and/or title of the person who placed the announcement and is responsible for the hiring process. If not, you will have to track it down. First, call the company and ask for the person's name and correct title. While you're on the phone, verify the address. Some companies use a dummy e-mail or title in their announcements. You might avoid having your résumé sit in a pile waiting to be sifted through, simply by asking if the person has a direct e-mail address or postal address you can use. If the company has explicitly said no phone calls, do not call.

If a phone call doesn't work, don't be discouraged. It might be possible to find the information you need at the company's website. While you're there, learn as much about the company as possible. This information can be used in the cover letter and later at an interview.

Attend to the Basics   Follow standard letter writing formats. Microsoft Word has a template for business letters. Be sure to include your name, your address, and additional contact information. Keep your letter short. A cover letter should highlight your experience; it shouldn't duplicate your résumé. A cover letter shouldn't *ever* be longer than one page. Put your reason for submitting the résumé in the first or second line.

If you are responding to a particular announcement, state the position title exactly as it appears in the announcement. If you are interested in a position with a particular company but aren't sure whether there are specific openings, explain why you believe you would be a valuable addition to the organization.

Sell Yourself   If you don't sell yourself, no one will. The cover letter is an opportunity to tell your audience why you are the perfect person for the job. Refer to the job announcement and highlight places where your experience and the employer's needs coincide. For example, if the job announcement is for someone to develop training materials for a bank, you might say, "I have extensive experience developing online help systems and training materials for the financial market" and provide information on one specific experience that best highlights your experience in this area. Remember, the cover letter is not used to regurgitate your resume, but rather to highlight and narrate your experiences most pertinent to the desired position.

When you highlight your experience, focus on your *accomplishments*. If you've led a team, exceeded sales goals, initiated a program, or developed a product, include that in your cover letter. Use action words that depict a positive, goal-oriented achievement. Using active versus passive voice infuses your cover letter with energy. For example:

Passive: Profits were increased by 17 percent because of the new sales plan.
Active: The new sales plan resulted in a 17 percent increase in profits.

Job Title:	**Documentation and Training Team Leader**
Description:	Internet start-up located in Greensboro, NC, looking for enthusiastic individual to join our growing company. We are seeking a documentation and training team leader with 5–7 years of team leadership and knowledge-based experience. The D&T team leader will be responsible for hiring, leading, and developing a team of 5–7 writers, curriculum developers, and trainers. Primary responsibilities will be to determine the documentation and training set and schedule for each release, schedule training for new clients, provide ongoing internal training for the organization, and manage the training facility.
Contact:	Send résumés to applications@bilin.com. Please put D&T leader in the subject line.

Look carefully at the phrases highlighted in the sample e-mail cover letter shown below. Compare those to the phrases highlighted in the job description. Notice anything? The job seeker, Shannon Green, worked the phrases from the job description into her cover letter. The phrases give her cover letter punch. Shannon targeted her cover letter specifically to the job description for the company she is applying to, Bilin.com. Just as the résumé is customized, so is the cover letter, using the keywords and phrases from the job description.

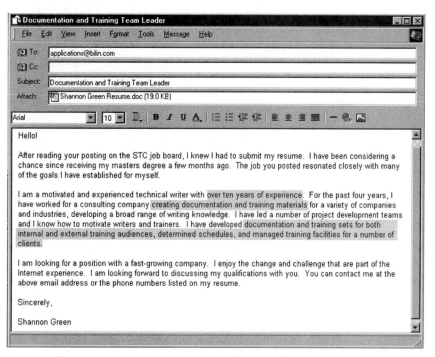

FIGURE 7.7   E-MAIL EXAMPLE OF COVER LETTER THAT INCORPORATES LANGUAGE FROM THE JOB DESCRIPTION

FOCUS ON ETHICS

Shannon feels confident that she has a great résumé. There's only one small snag: a few years ago, she took a short assignment with an Internet startup. She was let go after six weeks because the company couldn't afford to pay her. She found her current position within a week of losing the job. Rather than get into a discussion about what Shannon sees as a brief, unfortunate experience, she has chosen to leave the six weeks with the startup off her résumé.

Is Shannon's omission unethical? Is she required to include *all* of her job experience on her résumé? Is an omission the same as lying?

Proofread, Proofread, Proofread! You would be amazed at how many people toil over their résumé and then send out a cover letter with glaring mistakes. Misspelling the company's name or, worse, the name of the person you are sending the cover letter to are sure ways to have your résumé placed in the "No!" file. Proofread your cover letter and résumé carefully and then ask someone else to check it over before you send it.

SUBMITTING RÉSUMÉS AND COVER LETTERS

In this age of Internet and high-tech job searches, you have some decisions to make about how you submit résumés and cover letters. This can be a delicate call for some positions and organizations, but how you submit your résumé and cover letter can determine whether or not you get an interview. To ensure that your résumé is seen, you need to match the method of submission with the type of organization and the job posting. Here are a few things to keep in mind:

- Conservative or traditional organizations (law firms; accounting firms; large, established organizations with long histories): Submit your résumé by mail, on good-quality, cream-colored paper, using a traditional layout. Use a matching, legal-size envelope. Do not handwrite the envelope. Use a word processing program to create address labels that you can print out, or set your printer to print the return address and mailing address on an envelope. However, if you are applying to a conservative organization that provides only an e-mail address, by all means use e-mail.
- High-tech, Internet, and progressive organizations: Submit your résumé via e-mail. In most fact-paced organizations, managers are e-mail, not snail mail, oriented. Your résumé may sit unopened on the manager's desk while someone else's résumé is read immediately because it appeared in his or her e-mail inbox.
- Artistic and creative organizations: Submit your cover letter, résumé, and supporting materials by mail, unless your supporting materials are contained in files that can be sent over the Internet or the organization explicitly says to apply via e-mail. Likewise, in the Internet age, many people are using online portfolio sites to provide easy access to their artistic work. These sites are setup by the individual to showcase examples of their work. If you want to learn more about creating an online portfolio, visit: http://www.smashingmagazine.com/2008/03/04/creating-a-successful-online-portfolio/.

COORDINATING: THE INTERVIEW PROCESS

When it comes to coordinating your interview it is important that you are flexible, but not foolish. Make sure you are comfortable with the schedule, accommodations, and travel arrangements. In most cases, the person who will interview you or the human resources department at the company where you are interviewing will coordinate your travel. If the interview is in your town and doesn't require travel, there is little to coordinate other than the time and location of the interview. If the interview is out of town you need to coordinate:

- travel to and from the place of the interview
- lodging
- meals
- rental car or local means of transportation
- additional time either before or after the interview to see the area
- reimbursement for meals, cab fare, and other reasonable out-of-pocket expenses

If you don't think the interview schedule allows you adequate travel time, say so. If you are uncomfortable with the accommodations, speak up. You cannot be at your best for an interview if you can't sleep the night before or if you haven't eaten because the schedule didn't leave time for lunch.

Make reasonable, not ridiculous requests. If you are a vegetarian, it is reasonable to ask the human resources person if there is a vegetarian restaurant near your hotel or request a vegetarian option for any meals during the interview. It is ridiculous to ask for a suite, a luxury car, or a first-class seat on the plane unless you are interviewing and qualified for a CEO position.

Be understanding, but not gullible. Occasionally, you will encounter a small company or a startup that will ask you to pay for your travel and they will reimburse you later. If you can afford to pay, you really want the job, and you can afford not to be reimbursed, say yes. If you can't, ask if other arrangements are possible, acknowledge that you realize travel budgets are tight, be honest about your inability to pay for your travel, and suggest a phone or video interview. In most cases, the company will work something out. Be sure that you keep all your receipts so that you will have a record of your expenses later.

TIPS FOR PREPARING FOR INTERVIEWS

All Interviews

- Have information on the job, the company, and a copy of your résumé in front of you (for a phone interview) or on hand for interviews in person.
- Before the interview, make a list of three to five key characteristics, skills, or accomplishments you feel you bring to the job and be sure to highlight those attributes when given the opportunity.
- Make a list of questions to ask the interviewer. Interviewees who come to an interview showing an interest in learning more about the company they are interviewing with, impress interviewers.

- Practice, practice, practice! Go over the questions in the *Practicing the Interview* section in the following section.
- Get plenty of rest before the interview.
- Eat a light breakfast or lunch before the interview. Avoid heavy meals and garlicky or spicy foods.
- Get to the interview (or be waiting by the phone) ten minutes before the interview is scheduled to begin so you have time to focus before the interview begins.

Phone Interviews

- Secure a quiet area where you will not be interrupted.
- Make sure the phone you are using allows you to adjust the speaker volume so you can hear a soft-spoken interviewer.
- Speak clearly and directly into the phone.

RESEARCHING INTERVIEWS

Google is known for having an intense and unique interviewing process. If you do an Internet search for "interviewing at Google" you will get over 500,000 hits. Reading some of the articles and blogs about interviewing at Google tells you a lot about the process. *Not* reading at least a few of the articles and blogs before interviewing at Google would be a big mistake. The same is true for many of the companies you will interview with. Here are a few of the searches we did:

- Interviewing at Nordstrom (high-end retailer) over 200,000 hits
- Interviewing on Capitol Hill (politics) over 400,000 hits
- Interviewing with the CIA over 800,000 hits
- Interviewing at Chandler Regional Hospital (Arizona) over 40,000 hits

While not all of the hits returned from these searches contain the type of information you might be looking for, many of them do. Even the search on Chandler Regional Hospital returned over 40,000 hits, and a quick scan of some of the links indicates that a candidate interviewing for a nursing or staff position can learn a great deal about the interviewing process by reviewing these sites.

DRESSING FOR SUCCESS

Coordinating what to wear for an interview used to be so easy. Back in the day, men and women wore a conservative blue or gray suit. If you were a man, you wore a conservative tie. If you were a woman, you wore hose and conservative pumps. Today, however, things are not quite as simple. Depending on the job and the industry, you may find yourself sitting across the table from someone in khakis and a golf shirt, or someone in jeans and a Hawaiian shirt, wondering who the stiff is in the suit.

How do you know what to wear? Ask! Ask the person arranging the interview or call the human resources department. If you call human resources, tell them who you are interviewing with and give them the name of the department, and ask about the dress code. Then use common sense. Can you wear jeans and a Hawaiian shirt if you know that's how the interviewer dresses? No! But, you can dress less conservatively than a suit and tie and still look professional. Follow the same rules as with cover letters and résumés: a conservative company means conservative dress; a progressive company means lean toward business casual. The important thing is to do your homework, plan ahead, and be prepared. Waiting until the morning of an important interview to decide what to wear often ends in disaster.

The chart below shows some of the basic do's and don'ts for creating a positive appearance at a job interview.

DRESS FOR SUCCESS: DO'S AND DO NOT'S

Do

- Match your level of dress to the type of company you are interviewing with.
- Wear conservative clothes for interviews with conservative companies; wear professional clothes for all other interviews.
- Think about what you will wear a few days in advance. Make sure everything is dry cleaned, pressed, and ready for the interview.
- Make sure your nails are well groomed; people notice the small things.
- Carry a professional briefcase or portfolio rather than a manila folder, school book bag, or crazy purse.

Don't

- Wear clothing to a job interview that you would wear out on a date, to a club, or to hang out with friends.
- Wear distracting jewelry. The focus should be on your experience and skills not on your accessories.
- Chew gum, smoke, or eat during the interview.
- Wear heavy makeup. This can be a distraction during the interview. Keep your makeup simple and unnoticeable.
- Wear heavy cologne or perfume. Your interviewer may have allergies you don't want to trigger during an interview.

DELIVERING: THE SUCCESSFUL INTERVIEW

While interviews produce anxiety, they really aren't that surprising. Most interviewers use the same basic list of questions. Occasionally, you will encounter a company or interviewer who is proud of a unique interviewing process, which is why we encourage you to research the interviewing process beforehand. While a few interviews follow a unique and unpredictable process, most interviews are conducted in either an informal or formal style. To be on the safe side, you should practice interviewing for both styles.

INFORMAL INTERVIEWS

In an **informal interview**, the questions will be unstructured and will cover a wide variety of topics. Informal interviews make use of **open questions**—questions that require more than yes or no responses and that allow you a good bit of room to discuss your experience or perspective.

The advantages of this type of interview are that you can showcase your experience, expound on your accomplishments, and display your ability to speak clearly and confidently. The disadvantage is that people who are not confident speaking off the cuff may have a difficult time. The interviewee bears most of the responsibility in informal interviews, which means you have to have something to say. Otherwise the interview doesn't tend to be very fruitful.

FORMAL INTERVIEWS

Formal interviews are structured and centered on questions designed to gather specific information. These interviews tend to be tightly scripted in advance. They frequently make use of **closed questions**—questions that require specific, concrete answers and that provide little opportunity to elaborate.

The advantages of the formal interview are that it works well for interviewers who don't know a great deal about interviewing. It allows the interviewer to learn from the interviewee without giving away how little he or she knows about the interview process. The disadvantage is that a formal interview doesn't allow the interviewer to get to know the interviewee. It provides a very flat, one-sided view of the person.

In a formal interview, you might be asked questions like these:

- This position requires a good bit of travel. Is travel a problem for you?
- How many days of work did you miss last year?
- Do you have plans to return to school?
- Will relocating be a problem?
- We are a much smaller company than you have been working for. Have you thought about how that might affect your plans for promotions?

PRACTICING THE INTERVIEW

To ensure that you don't have problems knowing what to say during an interview, practice responding to the following questions and prompts. Most of them are the kinds of open questions you would be asked in an informal interview. We have included practice answers for each question.

- *Tell me about yourself.* Plan an answer to this question in advance, and keep your answer focused on the job and the interview. The interviewer is not interested in your family, friends, hobbies, or dog unless these things somehow relate to the position you are applying for. Stick to the details of your résumé and focus on your college courses and work experience. Find a theme that unites the decisions you have made into a cohesive plan, ending with why you decided to apply for this position.

  "I have always believed it is important to do something you enjoy, and I really enjoy public relations. I like working on a variety of projects and I work well with people from different industries and backgrounds. I am best when I have a lot of irons in the fire, which this position seems to require. And I work really well in a team environment."

- *How did you decide to enter your current field of employment?* Few people grow up knowing what they want to be, and some never make a clear and conscious choice to major in something in college. However, you don't want a prospective employer to think that you just fell into your current job, selected your career only because you could make a lot of money, or because your parents told you to become an accountant.

"I took a communication class my freshman year and immediately knew I wanted to be in the communication field. When I was a junior, I interned at an advertising agency and worked in the public relations department. By the end of my internship, I knew that was what I was going to do."

- *Where do you want to be in five years?* Refrain from saying, "I want your job." Do, however, map a future plan that includes realistic, achievable goals without outwardly threatening the interviewer.

"I've been giving this a lot of thought lately, and I know that my next position will greatly influence my plan. I know that I am ready for a leadership position. I am very eager to develop a department and watch it grow—which should keep me busy for at least five years. Beyond that, I have thought about consulting, but I expect I need at least five more years of corporate experience first."

- *Why do you want to leave your current job?* This is a big red-flag question. The interviewer is looking for problems you might have with coworkers, your boss, authority figures, or your ability to do the job. Focus on the opportunities associated with the position you are interviewing for, rather than the disappointments of your current position. Do not, under any circumstances, knock your current employer.

"Until six months ago, I was very happy in my current position. Then my manager, Lisa, went on maternity leave and I was charged with managing the department while she was gone. I found the new responsibilities challenging but extremely rewarding, and the department performed really well during that period. When Lisa returned, I realized that it was time for me to begin looking for a management position."

- *Describe your dream job.* Most of us have dreams of being paid to write the great American novel or an award-winning screenplay. Is that what your prospective employer is looking for? No! Nor should you say, "This is my dream job," if you are applying for a training or junior management position. Keep your answer focused on a logical career path for the position you are applying for.

"My dream job is one that allows me to use my skills and experience to work with a variety of clients, but also allows me to grow and learn. It would have to include working with people I can learn from and who in turn look to me for specific expertise.

- *Why do you want to work for us?* Here is where your research pays off. Let the interviewer know you have researched the company.

"I am really impressed with the clients you have attracted. The mix of business, celebrity, and non-profit clientele offers a challenging opportunity. I think I could learn a lot working with these types of clients. Also, the fact that PR Inc. named your company as one of the top five companies to work for is very impressive."

- *Why should I hire you?* If you paint yourself as someone who can do anything and knows everything, you run the risk of being a big letdown if you get the job. That is, if the interviewer doesn't view your answer as a huge ego trip. When answering this question, be confident and keep your answer focused on your job and education.

"I am very motivated. I enjoy my work and work well with almost everyone. I have the project leadership skills you are looking for and the knowledge base the job requires. I'm ready for the work that is in front of whoever takes this position."

- **What are your greatest strengths and weaknesses?** The trick with this question is to be modest about your strengths and to turn a weakness into a plus.

"I strive to accomplish all of my assignments on time and within budget. Doing this often requires that I go beyond what is expected, and I expect those around me to do the same. Occasionally, I will find myself overworked rather than confront a team member who isn't pitching in as they should."

- **What makes you a good leader?** Try to avoid clichés or trite phrases. Make your answer concrete, and focus on actual experiences.

"Recently, I was asked to lead a team tasked with developing a new PR campaign for a celebrity golf tournament that would benefit a local children's hospital. After the tournament, I got an e-mail from the company president thanking me for putting the campaign together so quickly and informing me that the event raised more money than it had in the past ten years."

- **Do you have any questions?** Begin by focusing on the position and its fit within the organization. After a few questions about the organization, you can inquire about salary and benefits. However, don't delve too deeply into this area until you are offered the job.

CASE STUDY 6 | SUCCESSFUL INTERVIEWING

"Ling," Valerie said, "I have a résumé I want you to look at."

Ling groaned. "Do I have to? So far we've seen seven great résumés, but when we talk to these people, they aren't anything like what they seemed on paper."

"Why don't I give this one a call and do a phone screening?" Valerie offered. "If I think she's worth it, then we'll bring her in."

"Fine," Ling said. "If you like her, set something up for Monday and coordinate it with the interviewing team."

"No problem."

Valerie hoped Shannon would interview better than the last two candidates she and Ling had brought in for interviews. When she returned to her office, she decided to call Shannon to schedule a phone interview. She could send an e-mail, but she had a good feeling about Shannon and wanted to speak to her as soon as possible.

"Shannon, this is Valerie Shaw with Bilin.com. We received your résumé, and I would like to set up a time to conduct a phone interview."

"That would be great," Shannon said. "I was hoping I would hear from you. When would you like to do the interview?"

"Well, I know I called your work number and this is probably not a good time. Is there a time either later today or tomorrow that we could talk for an hour or so?"

"Sure," said Shannon. "I picked up clients at the airport this morning at 6:30, so I planned to leave a bit early. Could I call you around 4:00 Eastern time?"

"That would be great," Valerie replied.

"Thanks for calling," said Shannon. "I'm really eager to hear more about the job and the company. Bye."

"'Bye," Valerie said, smiling. Even in that short exchange, she had heard enthusiasm and ease that the other candidates lacked.

The phone interview went extremely well and Valerie asked if Shannon could fly to Greensboro on Sunday evening and have her interview on Monday morning.

The next morning Keisha, the human resource manager for Bilin.com, called Shannon with the details.

continued

CASE STUDY 6 | **SUCCESSFUL INTERVIEWING** *continued*

"Shannon, this is Keisha. Valerie asked me to give you a call and work out the details for your interview," Keisha said.

Shannon would fly out of Baltimore at 6:00 p.m. on Sunday and arrive in Greensboro at 7:42 p.m. She would be staying at the Greensboro Hilton. The Hilton had an airport shuttle, and it was only a couple of blocks from the office. A number of restaurants would be close by for dinner Sunday evening. At 8:30 Monday, Valerie and Ling would meet her in the lobby. Keisha would send her the itinerary for the rest of the day via e-mail. Her flight home would leave at 5:30 that evening, and Valerie would take her to the airport.

"Any questions?" Keisha asked.

"Actually, I was hoping to be able to see a little of the city. I've done a good bit of research on the company, and I'm impressed. But the location will have a lot to do with my decision, should I be offered a job. Would it be possible for me to fly in on Saturday so I'll have a chance to look around?" Shannon was a little nervous about asking, but she didn't want to take a job without seeing the city, and Valerie had indicated they would need an answer quickly.

"Sure! If you fly on Saturday, we can save money on the airfare, so I can get you a rental car. Let me check the flights for Saturday and I'll call you right back."

An hour later, Shannon had received the final itinerary from Keisha by e-mail. Her flight would leave on Saturday at 9:00 a.m. and she would be in Greensboro before lunch. Keisha had arranged for a realtor to meet her for lunch and drive her around for the afternoon. Sunday, she was on her own. Shannon immediately started surfing the Net for information on Greensboro.

On Saturday, Shannon flew to Greensboro. She met with the realtor she had contacted beforehand and looked at a few apartments, condominiums, and townhouses. By the end of the day, she had found exactly the right loft apartment in the downtown area, should she be offered the job. Sunday, she ate brunch and drove around the city on her own. She liked what she saw. Now it was time to go back to the hotel and practice for her interview.

In her hotel room, Shannon reviewed her notes and looked over her answers to practice interview questions. She also took out her laptop and Googled "interviewing at Bilin.com." She read over a few of the sites to see what she could learn. She checked her outfit for the interview and turned in early. The next morning she got up early, ate a light breakfast, and headed to her interview.

Valerie met her in the lobby and walked her to the conference room where Ling was waiting and made the introductions.

Ling: "How do you like Greensboro?"

Shannon: "From what I've seen, I really like it. I was surprised at the number of parks there are and how green everything is. I was also really pleased by the variety of housing choices."

Ling: "Would leaving Maryland be difficult for you? I see from your résumé that you went to college in Maryland and then remained in the state. You must have deep ties to the area."

Shannon: "Actually, I'm an army brat. I've lived in Maryland longer than I've ever lived anywhere. Settling in a new place has always been something I do easily."

Valerie: "Tell Ling a little about your current position. I know we have already covered a good bit of this, but I would like him to hear it from you."

Shannon: "I am currently a senior technical writer. But that title doesn't really do my duties justice. We have a philosophy that everything flows from documentation. Which means that the documentation and online help should be the basis for our training. When a client goes through training, we refer back to the online help and documentation, so we are constantly reinforcing both. When clients return to their office, they know where to get the answers to their questions in the documentation, online help, or training materials. Using this philosophy, we have reduced support calls by 38 percent.

"Because everything flows from the documentation, I am often in the position of team leader. I bring together the documentation writers, the curriculum developers, and the trainers for each project. I am responsible for the schedules, the resources, the deliveries, and the training classes."

Ling: "Sounds like you have your hands full. What are two things about your current job that you find challenging?"

continued

CASE STUDY 6 | **SUCCESSFUL INTERVIEWING** *continued*

Shannon: *"The most challenging thing about my job is leading the project team. Often, people we hire come from very different environments from ours and occasionally we have a case where a trainer or curriculum developer wants to run the show. It is my job to explain the department philosophy and keep that vision on track. At the same time, I strive to recognize each person's contribution to the project.*

"I also find the variety of clients we work with challenging. Each customer is a bit different, as is each delivery. That keeps me interested and learning."

Ling: *"What are two things about your current job that you dislike?"*

Shannon: *"One of the reasons I am looking for a new position is the lack of room for growth. It is both a curse and a blessing having a great, competent boss. However, I don't see the department or the organization expanding any time soon.*

"There is also a bit of resistance to new ideas and technology. I have introduced a number of ideas for distance training, upgrading our current computer-based training, and creating web-based online help, but most of these ideas have fallen flat. I feel that I keep growing and learning, but I can't seem to apply many of these skills in my current position."

Valerie: *"What has been your biggest accomplishment at your current job?"*

Shannon: *"My biggest accomplishment was stepping in for my boss, Lisa, during her maternity leave. I kept the projects on track and developed new projects without our department missing a beat. I took a lot of pride in how seamlessly we operated while she was on leave. I attribute a good bit of this to how well she trained me and prepared me to assume a leadership role."*

Ling: *"What will you miss most about the company you work for?"*

Shannon: *"I will miss the people I work with. We have a great team and we work really well together. I helped hire a number of the people I work with, so I feel very connected to them."*

Ling: *"Interesting that you mentioned hiring people. This position requires hiring and developing a team of writers and trainers. How would you go about doing that?"*

Shannon: *"I think working with Valerie is a very smart move. She will help make this part of the job a lot easier. I would continue to tap the STC and training and development websites, and I would attend the local STC meetings to see if anyone within the organization is actively looking for a new position. This has been a great source of networking for us. I would have to investigate it further, but I imagine that the Raleigh-Durham Research Triangle area has a very strong STC organization, so I would attend one of their meetings, as well.*

"When hiring trainers, it is important to do interviews and to have them do some stand-up training. We have avoided some potential mistakes this way. Some of the applicants with great résumés were not so great in front of the classroom.

"Finally, I would work the Internet job boards for both groups. A lot of people are putting out their résumés, and even though the job boards are time-consuming up front, they can save time in the long run."

Ling: *"In this position, you'll be required to manage a team. What qualities do you think are important in a team environment?"*

Shannon: *"I think that even though you are working in a team environment, everyone needs to feel that their contributions matter. You have to maintain a balance between the needs of the team and the needs of the individuals on the team. Team members need to understand the goals and direction of the team and use their individual talents to help the team succeed. It's the team leader's job to give them the resources to ensure that happens."*

Ling: *"Okay, I'm a stickler for knowing what is going on. I like status reports, but right now I have two team leaders who hate doing them. As a team leader, you will be required to report the progress of your team. How do you feel about providing regular status reports?"*

Shannon: *"What I do with my current manager is to meet with her on Monday and Thursday. We go over what has been accomplished in the past week and what we will be working on in the next week. We work through any problems, issues, and snags. After the status meeting, I send her an e-mail recapping what we have discussed. How would that work?"*

Ling: *"That sounds good. I've been trying different things, and this mixes an informal reporting process*

continued

CASE STUDY 6 | **SUCCESSFUL INTERVIEWING** *continued*

with something formal I can use for my own status reports."

Valerie: "As the documentation and training team leader, you would be the liaison to other teams. What skills do you have that would facilitate this function?"

Shannon: "As a communication specialist, I understand the need for gathering and disseminating information. I am good at targeting the information people need and what I need to do my job. I have a real belief in sharing information. I think it makes everyone's life and job easier."

Ling: "How would this position further your career goals?"

Shannon: "Well, as I've said, I am looking for a position that will allow me to use the leadership skills I've developed in my current position. I am ready for this type of challenge and feel strongly that it is the next logical step in my career."

Ling: "What do you know about Bilin.com?"

Shannon: "I've done a good bit of research on the company through articles on the Internet, and I have spent time looking at your website. What I don't know is what it's like to work for Bilin.com and what challenges face the company. Can you tell me a bit about that?"

Ling: "I'm glad you asked. Our public image is that of a growing organization rocketing to the top of the Internet dotcoms, and to some extent, that is true. Organizationally, we are a group of mostly nice people who want to see this company succeed at the highest level. Overall we have a lot of fun, work really hard, and have our fingers crossed most of the time. In the next year, we have to grow up. Right now, we are still a small company. We need a formal training program, we need to deliver solid documentation and online help, we need to develop the support area, and we need to deliver what we promise to our customers. If you ask someone else, you will get a different answer, but to me, these are the important things."

Valerie: "How do you feel about working for an Internet startup, coming from such an established company?"

Shannon: "I'm excited about it. In some ways, I feel that I've missed out by staying with a more traditional company. I think it would be interesting and challenging."

Ling: "Bilin is a small, young company and we can't offer the benefits some organizations can. Is that a problem?"

Shannon: "To be honest, I would need to know more about what you do and don't offer. I need to have a medical plan, but dental isn't as important. I would like to participate in some form of retirement through a 401(k) or profit sharing, but being vested in a stock option plan would certainly offset the lack of a 401(k). Can you tell me more about the benefits?"

Ling: "I could, but I'm sure I would leave something out. Keisha has a presentation planned for you later today. Can we table this until then?"

Shannon: "Sure. I may have additional questions by then."

Valerie: "Bilin has just signed three major contracts, which has tripled the company's deliverables overnight. To meet our schedules, we need to hire someone as quickly as possible. If offered the job, when could you start?"

Shannon: "I could start in two weeks. I would need at least a week to move and wrap things up in Maryland."

Ling: "Sounds great! Do you have any additional questions?"

Shannon: "Yes. Can you tell me a little about who I will be interviewing with the rest of the day?"

Throughout the day, everyone was impressed with Shannon. By the end of the day, Ling had gotten back in touch with everyone and was drafting an offer letter when Valerie brought Shannon by Ling's office to wrap up.

"Hi! How's it going?" Ling asked.

"Great! Everyone is so nice. Thanks for giving me the opportunity to come down and meet everyone," Shannon said.

"I'm so glad to hear it. I need to meet with Keisha and work out the details, but I would like to have a formal offer for you by tomorrow," Ling said, smiling. "If everything works out, could you start the first of next month? That gives you two and a half weeks to wrap things up in Maryland."

"Wow! I knew you were in a hurry, but I didn't expect you to make a decision this quickly. Yes, if everything works out, I'm sure I could start on the first. Thanks!"

continued

CASE STUDY 6 | **SUCCESSFUL INTERVIEWING** *continued*

We have included this example of the interview process to highlight how important it is follow all of the steps covered in this chapter for a successful job search. Successful communicators realize that it isn't enough to create a basic résumé and cover letter. Job searches should be targeted and thoroughly researched. You should prepare and practice for interviews in advance. How would you change or improve on Shannon's performance? How can you apply the information in the case study to your own job search? Shannon mentioned "STC" in her interview. The Society for Technical Communication is an important professional organization for technical writers. What technical or professional societies should you join to keep up-to-date within your field? Make a list of the tools you need to conduct a successful job search before you begin.

SUMMARY

In this chapter, we went through the process of conducting a conscious job search. We discussed the elements of a conscious search and applied the CCCD process to seeking a job. We began with choosing job goals. Without setting clear goals, chances are you will end up in a position that isn't right for you. We also emphasized how important research is in the job search process. We walked through the process of conducting research on the Internet, through company employees and tours, through friends and family, and through your campus recruitment office.

We then concentrated on the process of creating a résumé. We reviewed the formats you can use for a résumé and when to use each type. We talked about using the words from the job description when you are creating your résumé and cover letter.

In the section on coordinating, we provided tips for participating in a phone interview. We also talked about how to coordinate the travel arrangements for out-of-town interviews and how to decide what you will wear on your interview.

The delivery section explained the differences between informal and formal interviews. We emphasized how important it is to practice before you go for an interview. We also provided possible answers to standard interviewing questions. Finally, we walked through a typical interview, providing you with a script you can use to prepare for future interviews.

BUSINESS AND PROFESSIONAL COMMUNICATION IN THE GLOBAL WORKPLACE ONLINE

All of the following chapter review materials are available in an electronic format on either the *Business and Professional Communication in the Global Workplace Online* Resource Center or the book's companion website. Online you'll find chapter learning objects, flashcards of glossary terms, InfoTrack® College Edition Activities, weblinks, quizzes, and more.

WHAT YOU SHOULD HAVE LEARNED

Now that you have read Chapter 7, you should be able to do the following:

- Establish goals for your next job.

- Conduct research on possible jobs, potential companies, and career information.
- Use a job description to create a résumé and cover letter.
- Select the appropriate information and format for your résumé.
- Participate in a phone interview.
- Make arrangements for out-of-town interviews.
- Select the appropriate clothing for an interview.
- Use the practice interview questions to structure answers for an interview.
- Do well during an in-person interview.

KEY TERMS

WRITING AND CRITICAL THINKING

The following activities can be completed online or submitted in hard copy to your instructor.

1. Find a job description for a job you might be interested in. Develop a résumé that is geared toward the job description. Justify the information and format you choose.
2. Review the questions listed in the section "Practicing for the Interview." Prepare answers for five of the questions.
3. Go to the college recruitment office at your school. Ask about the services it offers. Look at the current list of corporate job openings. Select three job announcements that fit your career goals.
4. Below are three sets of interview situations. Working in groups of three, one person is designated the interviewer, the second person the interviewee, and the third the observer (or the class can act as observers). Using suggested questions from the chapter and other questions found in researching on the web, the interviewer develops a set of questions to be asked during the interview. After the interviewer and interviewee have completed the role-play, the observer provides feedback to both to the interviewer and the interviewee. Switch roles until all members of the group have played each role. If possible, videotape the interviews and write a short critique of each interview (or 'your interviews').

Situation 1
You have had a public relations internship at XYZ Corporation for the past six months, and you are aware that a full-time, entry-level position will be available in the PR department at the time of your graduation. During your internship, you have been responsible for filing and copying press releases. You want the challenge of the new position and feel you are qualified, but you worry that if you are hired, you will be perceived as the intern who does everyone's filing and copying. Based on the questions asked, you will have to convey confidence in your ability to take on a PR position.

Situation 2
During a job fair at school, you and other classmates have been invited to interview for the same position in XYZ Technology Corporation. Although your technical skills are adequate, they are not as sharp as those of several of your classmates who will also be interviewed. You do, however, have excellent leadership and organizational skills learned from the community service work you have been doing as part of your curriculum. Based on questions asked, you will need to convince the interviewer you are a viable candidate and equally valuable to the company as someone with more technical skills.

Situation 3
A job has recently become available at XYZ Corporation, and you have been invited to go in for an interview. Your qualifications match perfectly with the job description, and your friend who works for the company has assured you that you would be a great fit for the position. However, you are aware that the company has a long history of promoting from within, and at least two internal candidates have also applied for the position.

PRACTICING COMMUNICATION IN PROFESSIONAL CONTEXTS

A smooth interviewing style can come only with practice. This exercise is designed to give you control over the interviewing situation so that you can concentrate on developing a confident interview style.

1. Select a job description for a position you would like to interview for.
2. Using the job description, prepare a résumé and a cover letter.
3. Prepare an interview script (you may use the questions provided in and this chapter).
4. Prepare the answers for your questions.
5. Select a friend, family member, or class member to interview you.
6. Provide the friend, family member, or class member with the interview script. (Do not include the answers you have prepared.)
7. Schedule the interview.
8. Have the friend, family member, or class member conduct the interview.
9. Ask them to critique your performance using the following criteria:

    *   Did I provide adequate answers to the questions?
    *   Did I show knowledge of and enthusiasm for the position I selected?
    *   Was I sincere?
    *   Did my answers reflect the practice I have done?
    *   Was I confident?
    *   Would you hire me?

If possible, you should practice your answers at least three times before the interview, dress as you would for an actual interview, and have the interview videotaped so that you can review your performance.

TEAM BUILDING

INFORMATION TECHNOLOGY AND CONSCIOUS COMMUNICATION

CHAPTER **8**

This chapter is about information technology and how to use it consciously and wisely in the global workplace. We aim to help you begin thinking about information technology as a communication *tool* and improve the way you use it on the job. Your goal in reading this chapter, then, is to gain more control over your use of technology so that you can succeed in the global workplace.

We begin by framing the positives and negatives of information technology, and how different cultures view technology. We move on to a brief discussion of the types of information technologies currently in use in organizations. Next we discuss how to

Jose Luis Pelaez/Iconica/Getty Images

use our conscious-communication approach (CCCD) to make better decisions about using them. We then offer a practical section on doing web-based research. We conclude this chapter with some words of advice about how much technology you need and what information about technology you really need to know.

INFORMATION TECHNOLOGY AND COMMUNICATION

Let's begin our exploration of information technology with an intriguing thesis developed by an information scientist named Dan Lacy (1995). According to Lacy, if we view world history from a communication perspective, we will see that the societies that communicated information the farthest and the fastest gained power and dominated each era. Human communication has evolved from, as Lacy puts it, "grunts to gigabytes." Hunters who could gesture and grunt in ways that gained the cooperation of other hunters were able to pool their resources, hunt larger game, and better organize themselves for survival. Similarly, we can see how the invention of the Phoenician alphabet and rules for grammatical usage led to the Phoenicians' dominance in their epoch and to the later ancient Greek system of logical reasoning. In turn, these advances led to the systematization of conduct and laws for most societies.

Power and domination of a given society were not solely gained, nor maintained, by peaceful means. Roman generals and Chinese warlords used messengers to hand deliver plans of attack to their armies, thus greatly improving their ability to coordinate battles. The printing press, radio, television, computers, and satellites have significantly improved the widespread distribution of information and the speed with which it can travel, and they have determined which nations or multinational corporations control our destinies. As Lacy has put it, the nation or company that can send messages the farthest and the fastest wins. Companies know this and so they value and recruit employees who are technically savvy.

THE DOWNSIDE TO INFORMATION TECHNOLOGY

One downside to Lacy's worldview is that there are losers in every era—those people, nations, or companies that cannot compete. They fall behind in their ability to access and process important information. They do not learn at the same speed and from the diverse cultural sources required to maintain current knowledge and skills. These days, because information is a commodity of primary value in a global economy, the effects of falling behind in information technology have never been more potentially devastating. As Barnet and Cavanaugh (1994) expressed it, we are rapidly becoming a world made up of Global North and Global South, where those in the northern hemisphere have access to information technology and economic resources for the development and deployment of information, and many of those in the southern hemisphere don't. Companies with well-developed information technology systems and the economic resources to train people to use them become more powerful, and those who rely on outdated modes of accessing and processing information find they can no longer compete.

Simply having technology systems is unlikely to be enough. We must also provide intelligent ways of deciding which technologies are needed to carry out meaningful tasks, and which technologies are less useful or merely redundant. We must combine our ability to provide material resources with better instruction about becoming more conscious and ethical in our professional uses of those resources.

To do that means acquiring a new perspective on the relationship of information technology to business and professional communication.

REVISING OUR APPROACH TO INFORMATION TECHNOLOGY

Do you ever feel controlled by technology? Do you feel overwhelmed by the sheer number of voice mail or e-mail messages you have to respond to? Or by the pressure to respond to all of them? Do these concerns interfere with your desire and ability to respond to those messages thoughtfully? Moreover, do they distract you from other, more important tasks or relationships?

Organizations provide employees with information technology resources— BlackBerries and iPhones—equipped with instant messaging, text messaging, and e-mail to improve their productivity. Yet, these technologies can tether employees to their work 24 hours a day, seven days a week. Employers now have the ability to "push" e-mail and voice mail messages to employees anywhere, anytime, and employees who fail to draw the line can find themselves overworked and stressed by the constant demands placed on them through technology.

This mentality has even pervaded popular culture—spawning terms like "CrackBerry" for those addicted to their BlackBerries, and movies like *The Devil Wears Prada* and *Two Weeks Notice* about BlackBerry-addicted employees and bosses who expect 24/7 responses to any request and think nothing of pulling employees out of weddings or birthday parties.

WHO CAN REMEMBER LIFE BEFORE MULTITASKING?

Recently, challenges to the ethos of multitasking have begun to emerge. Numerous studies have shown the sometimes-fatal danger of using cell phones and other electronic devices while driving, for example, and several states have now made that particular form of multitasking illegal. In the business world, where concerns about time-management are perennial, warnings about workplace distractions spawned by a multitasking culture are on the rise. In 2005, the BBC reported on a research study funded by Hewlett-Packard and conducted by the Institute of Psychiatry at the University of London that found, "Workers distracted by e-mail and phone calls suffer a fall in IQ more than twice than that found in marijuana smokers." The psychologist who led the study called this new "infomania" a serious threat to workplace productivity. One of the *Harvard Business Review*'s "Breakthrough Ideas" for 2007 was Linda Stone's notion of "continuous partial attention," which might be understood as a subspecies of multitasking: by using mobile computing power and the Internet, we are "constantly scanning for opportunities and staying on top of contacts, events, and activities in an effort to miss nothing."

However, Dr. Edward Hallowell, a Massachusetts-based psychiatrist who specializes in the treatment of attention deficit/hyperactivity disorder argues that multitasking is a "mythical activity in which people believe they can perform two or more tasks simultaneously." He has discovered a new condition, "attention deficit trait" (ADT), which he claims is rampant in the business world. ADT is "purely a response to the hyperkinetic environment in which we live," writes Hallowell, and its hallmark symptoms mimic those of ADD. "Never in history has the human brain been asked to track so many data points," Hallowell argues, and this challenge "can be controlled only by creatively engineering one's environment and one's emotional and physical health."

Adapted from "The Myth of Multitasking" by Christine Rosen, The *New Atlantis: A Journal of Science and Technology*, Spring 2008.

In the workplace, computers and computer training are supposed to help employees organize and manage their work. What employers seldom realize is that they may also be contributing to the employees' sense of **information overload**. When too many forms of communication intersect at one time, we have difficulty making decisions, responding, and prioritizing.

Of course, in a success-oriented, individualist culture, such as the United States, making these resources available carries the implicit message that you should never not be working. Increasingly, we have given up more and more of our leisure time for the allure—as well as the demands—of work. As you will see through the rest of the chapter, the argument is not that technology is bad, but that our uses of technologies can be more streamlined and improved.

CULTURAL AND GENDER DIFFERENCES

The way we use information technology differs from culture to culture and between genders. These differences include how:

- information technology is used
- people think about technology
- technology plays a role in managing professional relationships

Cultural Differences   Understanding how different cultures think about technology is important for managing global business relationships. In some cultures, like in the United States, we have an anxiety about having our work-life and home-life boundaries crossed, yet we've adapted many new technologies and blur that line. For example, in Australia and in Hindi traditions, the work-life and the home-life are kept quite separate.[1]

How a country views **power distance,** or how members of institutions and organizations expect and accept the unequal distribution of power, can give us insights into how a country may view the use of certain information technologies. As you will learn later in this chapter, the advancement of technologies and the Internet has made accessing those in high power easier than ever before. However, just because you can do something doesn't mean you should. Countries with a higher-power distance, like China and Saudi Arabia, would not respond kindly to entry-level employees trying to gain immediate access via e-mail to their top managers. In some cultures, people prefer to communicate with technologies that have more visual cues, such as video conferencing, than communicating with e-mail. The important thing to note is that not all cultures, even within the United States, view the use of information technology in the same way, and it is important to remain conscious of this when communicating with others.

Gender, Class, and "Digital Divide" Differences   Not all of us respond to the need to use information technologies in the same way. Differences are based on gender, social class, and familiarity/willingness to learn to use new forms of digital communication.

---

[1] http://www.intel.com/technology/magazine/research/rs06041.pdf.

As we learned in previous chapters, women and men tend to differ when it comes to communication. But for a long time, researchers did not see a correlation between gender differences and perceptions or uses of information technology. However, important new questions have been asked that highlight how gender differences can be used to better understand decisions about information technology in the workplace (Geffen and Straub, 1997; Matheson, 1991; Witmer and Katzman, 1997).

Gender differences impact the introduction and diffusion of information technologies. Women tend to experience greater levels of anxiety than men do when it comes to implementing new information technologies, and user-friendliness matters more to women than to men. But women tend to adopt characteristically masculine usage patterns once the technology is in place (Matheson, 1991; Geffen and Straub, 1997, p. 397).

Women tend to place information technology within a social context. They have a greater need for "a technological medium to convey 'the presence' of the communicator—her feelings and thoughts" (Geffen and Straub, 1997, p. 397). Women tend to want to express themselves in a medium that allows for greater elaboration of their reasons and feelings, whereas men tend to focus primarily on the instrumental function of mediated speech.

Men and women perceive the modes of communication differently; for example, women tend to perceive e-mail communication as less useful than men do (Tannen, 1994b; Geffen and Straub, 1997). Women and men may have differing perceptions of the "social presence" of e-mail. More misunderstandings may take place between women and men who communicate via e-mail because of the different perceptions of the social meaning of words used in that technological context. This may help explain why women tend to use more graphic accents (such as smiles and frowns) in e-mail than men do (Witmer and Katzman, 1997).

Despite these studies, more recent research indicates that gender differences, at least in the United States, may be disappearing. For example, a study comparing IT use in Japan and the United States (Ono & Zabodny, 2004) found that previous studies from the 1990s (such as those cited above) established gender differences that had all but disappeared by 2001 for women in the U.S. However, for women in Japan who had lower levels of IT use at work, they remained stable. So clearly the issue of gender differences in the use of information technologies is a more complex issue, as it intersects with cultural differences as well.

One trait that has remained relatively stable over time is the relationship between social class associated with the use of information technologies. Studies of college and high school students show that women and men who grow up in families without a computer in the home and/or limited access to the Internet at school or work often don't perform as well as students who do enjoy those advantages. One result is that career paths for high school students often diverge based on access to information technologies. Those without access select occupations that do not require those skills; those with access choose careers that do.

Finally, there can be a "digital divide" based on age as well as on social class or culture. Older workers who have not become accustomed to new information technologies—who may, for example, prefer print versions of e-mail to the online content, and who never use text-messaging—often find that returning to work in an IT rich environment challenging as well as frustrating.

Organizations planning to introduce new or updated information technologies should take into account these gender, culture, social class, age, issues that contribute to "digital divide" differences. Additionally, we should learn to recognize that these differences may significantly influence perceptions of meaning associated with all forms of mediated communication. Marketing specialists make use of this research when putting together focus groups designed to help implement new technologies in the workplace or provide feedback to systems and software designers about user impact and usage.

INFORMATION TECHNOLOGY AND CONSCIOUS COMMUNICATION

How can we better think about, make decisions about, and use the rich information-technology resources available to us? In an informal ethnographic study conducted for this text, we considered the types of personalities typically associated with usage patterns in organizations we've consulted with. The results are displayed in Figure 8.1.

Figure 8.1 shows a range of usage patterns for information technologies, based in part on preferences for communication mode and in part on personality. At the left side of the continuum, we represent people who are least likely to use or respond to technology: "Luddites." A **Luddite** is a person who refuses to adapt to new forms of technology. (The term comes from workers in nineteenth century England who destroyed machines that they thought would threaten their employment.) Typically, people who fail to adapt to technological advances fall behind in their ability to compete successfully, so Luddite behavior is not a good choice for people who work in a business and professional environment.

In the middle of the continuum, we represent a range of users—from the compulsive personality to the employee who just tries to cope day in and day out with information overload. Employees in the middle of the continuum may try to limit the time they spend sending and receiving mediated messages, thus

LUDDITE Refuses or ignores technology	COMPULSIVE Receives and processes compulsively	RITUALIZED Receives and processes at set times during the day	COPING Tries to use technology as adjunct to communication	CONSCIOUS COMMUNICATION CHOICES
Employee receives but does not process or respond to most electronic messages.	Employee is always online or using cell phone, to detriment or neglect of human contact.	Employee will receive and respond to messages only at prescribed times.	Employee thinks about the best channel for messages but doesn't always follow through.	Employee is profoundly aware of the influences of a channel on the meaning of a message.

Mindless Technological Domination ⟶ **Mindful Technological Power**

FIGURE 8.1 | CONSCIOUS COMMUNICATION AND TECHNOLOGY CONTINUUM

risking being thought rigid. Or they may try to make better-informed decisions about channels for exchanging messages but sometimes find themselves unable to carry out their decisions. As you can see, as you become a more conscious communicator, you grow less willing to allow information technologies to control your time or the channels you use to create, maintain, or change relationships with others.

On the far right of the continuum, you see people who make conscious decisions about which technology to use for maximum communication effectiveness with minimal intrusion into their lives. To become a mindful, more conscious user of communication channels, we must adapt our thinking about selecting appropriate channels and consider likely outcomes when selecting technology. Conscious users of technology understand the need to include relational and contextual information when communicating using technology. To reduce the possibility of misunderstanding in communication with coworkers or clients, mindful communicators may limit the amount of information shared via e-mail and phone messages, and they may make more time for personal contact. Mindful communicators are cognizant of Marshall McLuhan's popular axiom, "the medium is the message." It is important to understand how the medium you choose to send a message influences the recipient's interpretation of the message. For example, those of us who use a BlackBerry (or equivalent device) to send e-mail messages often include a "Sent from my BlackBerry" signature line. Why do we do this? We are signaling to the recipient that we are responding from a BlackBerry and we do not have time to write a long message.

The downside to this type of communication is that it is void of many of the pleasantries of face-to-face communication because of the medium. If the message

---

CASE STUDY 7 | **DRAWING THE LINE WITH TECHNOLOGY**

Tori's boss never explicitly told her she was on call 24/7, but she was told shortly after taking the job as an agricultural analyst for a senator in Washington D.C. six months ago that her BlackBerry "shouldn't ever be more than six inches from her reach day or night." At first, it was exciting to get messages at all times of the day and night. It made her feel like part of the club to have her BlackBerry vibrate on Saturday morning when she was running on the treadmill at the gym, or when she was in a movie on Friday night, or when she was riding the Metro into the office on Monday morning. But lately, it was starting to get on her nerves. She was making good money, but not enough to live in D.C. and be on a 24-hour chain to her boss.

At lunch, Tori overheard some of the other staffers who had worked on the Hill for years talking about filing a lawsuit over their BlackBerry use. They loved their jobs and the rush they got working on the Hill,

but the intrusion into their lives had taken a toll. Tori wondered what the alternative was. Could she continue to have this level of intrusion in her life for another year or two? Or should she support her fellow staffers in calling for a Blackberry ban after hours? Or should they request overtime for any work done outside the office? Maybe she should find a job where BlackBerries weren't a requirement. Did those jobs even exist?

Tori wants to be a good staffer, but she knows that have a balance, she needs to draw a line between her professional and personal life. How would you draw the line if you were in Tori's situation? Would you give up working on the Hill even though a few years there would open doors in the private sector that wouldn't otherwise be open to you? Or, would you simply resign yourself to not having a private life until you leave the Hill? Or, are there other options?

you are sending is in response to a misunderstanding or problem that would be handled better in person, you should make a conscious decision to choose a different form of communication. Ideally, the more conscious you become of the influences of technology on communication in business and professional relationships, the more power you gain to define how and when you will select and use technology. In the following section, we provide advice about using technology to change your span of communication.

TYPES OF INFORMATION TECHNOLOGIES

As recently as twenty-five years ago, the words *information technology* were not part of the daily lexicon and desktop computers were a luxury. Cell phones had not yet been invented. Google had not yet been born. Now, it's common for people to own or have access to two or more computers. Many people have a desktop computer at home, one at work, and a laptop to take with them when they travel. In addition to their BlackBerry or iPhone, they can access their company's network over the Internet, making access virtually possible anywhere in the world. They can search on any subject, download information from a wide variety of sources, entertain themselves, and create messages for instantaneous global delivery. This level of access to information technologies requires new forms of communication including:

- mediated communication
- electronic support systems and voice mail
- computer networks
- videoconferencing
- social networking sites

MEDIATED COMMUNICATION TECHNOLOGIES

As modems became faster, PCs more prevalent, and e-mail more sophisticated, sending documents via e-mail became an important business solution. E-mail has replaced much of the interpersonal, face-to-face communication that used to occur in the workplace. We all know people who will send a series of e-mails to someone who works three cubicles away rather than go and talk to that person, even if a simple conversation would take less time. And we have all seen the text messaging addict who won't call to finalize details for dinner or get directions, but rather engages in a volley of messaging to the frustration of everyone around him.

By now it should be clear how important it is to communicate consciously. Just because you *can* send an e-mail or a text message doesn't mean that is the best way to communicate. In many professional contexts, verbal and nonverbal feedback would enhance communication by cutting down on miscommunication, misunderstandings, and reduce the time needed to respond. Before picking up your BlackBerry or typing an e-mail, you need to ask yourself:

- Would this be handled better face-to-face?
- Is the person I am communicating with someone I've had problems dealing with via e-mail or text message in the past?

- Is this a situation where I will not need a written record of the conversation for backup?

If you can answer "yes" to any of these questions, deliver the message in person if possible or over the phone. If you answered "no," then send an e-mail. Below, we offer some tips for using e-mail more effectively:

- Think of e-mail as a virtual conversation rather than a long essay.
- Follow the assumption that each correspondent will have at least one turn in the conversation to make a point or respond to the other person's information.
- Use short, concise statements that offer opportunities for feedback.
- Invite follow-up in the form of person-to-person contact, letters, or a phone call, so that your communication partners can facilitate detailed exchanges.
- Convey emotion. If a posted message appears to have ambiguous meanings or if it could cause an unwanted emotional response, use an "emoticon" to signal the mood or effect intended. For example, a smiley face [:)] after a sentence may signal humorous intent; a wink and smile [;)] can indicate "This is just between us," or a sense of irony; a frown [:( ] can indicate displeasure or unhappiness. Limit your use of these emoticons, to ensure you are taken seriously.
- Make yourself easily recognizable. Attaching a "signature file" to your e-mails helps recipients locate you through other communication channels—phone, fax, physical address, and virtual address via e-mail, or website. It also alerts recipients if you are using a mobile device, explaining a brief message.
- Don't cry wolf. Avoid marking every e-mail message as urgent. Eventually, your audience will catch on and stop reading your e-mail.

E-MAILS ARE *NOT*:

- novels, they are business messages. E-mails should be concise and to the point. Don't beat your audience over the head with your message. If you need to write a lengthy report, write the report, attach it to the e-mail, then and offer a brief summary in the body of the e-mail.
- a place to pick a fight, they are a form of *public* communication. Avoid "flaming" others with critical comments, slurs, or personal attacks. If you have a problem with someone, resolve the problem in person.
- a recycling bin for your junk mail. Avoid sending unsolicited e-mails by making sure the content is of value to the recipient. "Spam" (the Internet term for junk mail) is seldom appreciated and is usually deleted.
- private; they are public documents. There is no such thing as private e-mail. Even if a message is deleted, it can be accessed from the hard drive or network system. Remember, everything you send can be read by your boss.

E-Mail and Text Messaging Shorthand

BRB—Be right back
BTW—By the way
FWIW—For what it's worth
FUBAR—Fouled up beyond all recognition
GD&R—Grinning, ducking, and running (after a snide remark)
GTG—Got to go
INAL—I'm not a lawyer (but...)
IDK—I don't know
IMHO—In my humble opinion
IYKWIM—If you know what I mean
LOL—Laughing out loud

OTF—On the floor
OTOH—On the other hand
PMJI—Pardon my jumping in
TIA—Thanks in advance
TPTB—The powers that be
ROTFL—Rolling on the floor laughing
RSN—Real soon now
SPAM—Stupid person's advertisement
WRT—With respect to
WYSIWYG—What you see is what you get
YWIA—You're welcome in advance

Electronic Support Systems and Voice Mail

Voice mail is any message left on a telephone answering system. All of us have been on the receiving end of phone systems that require us to punch in a series of numbers before we can get our account or a beep to leave a recorded message. Almost everyone who interacts in a business and professional environment routinely uses voice mail systems to screen calls. And, we have all left voice mail on people's voice mail systems. However, before leaving another voice mail message, you should make clear and conscious choices about how and when to use voice mail to ensure that your message is well received and acted upon. Abusing voice mail puts your messages at the mercy of the delete button. Below, we offer tips for using voice mail effectively:

- Be clear and concise.
- Give relevant information, such as the date and time of the communication, and the name of the sender and intended receiver.
- Limit the message to two or three sentences. If additional information or clarification is needed, the receiver can call you back.
- Include the specific date/time by which a response is required, if necessary.
- Do not ramble or mix information or purposes.

Computer Networks

Computer **networks** are two or more computers connected either locally (within a company or building) or widely (across different geographic locations) by cable, phone lines, or satellite. Unlike e-mail and voice mail, computer networks do not facilitate direct communication. Instead, these forms of technology facilitate communication indirectly. Local area networks (LANs), wide area networks (WANs), and the Internet allow us to access files, e-mail, the World Wide Web, and documents stored on another computer, in another room, or even in another part of

Focus on Ethics

Dominick's boss James is frustrated by a drop in productivity over the last year. It amazes Dominick that James, who is the owner of a national outsourcing company, is a bit of a Luddite and blames "technology" for the drop in production. James says that he worked twice as fast and more effectively before "technology invaded everything we do." Ironically, he has contracted with a company that placed productivity software on all the company computers. The software tracks how employees use the Internet, recording what websites they view and how long they spend on a website, and making copies of all the e-mail and text messages they send via the company network. Dominick was charged with going over the reports each week and reporting any anomalies to his boss. At first, he found the weekly reports fascinating. It was shocking what websites people visited while they were at work. While no one was violating the company policy against using company computers to look at pornography or gamble, they did look at health websites, home loan sites, and dating sites. Dominick learned a lot about his coworkers that eventually he wished he didn't know. He also found out that two of his coworkers were carrying on a heated affair on company time and over company e-mail. What responsibility does Dominick have to report his findings to his boss? Should he warn his co-workers about the software? Or, should he refuse to participate in the surveillance? What would you do in Dominick's situation?

the world. Perhaps the biggest impact networks have had on business and professional communication is **telecommuting**: working from your home or another remote site, away from your company's primary location, but connected by telephone, fax, and computer.

Telecommuting, has created a number of communication challenges. How do you communicate, build relationships, deal with conflict, or solve problems with members of a team who you have never met face to face? Although telecommuting has certain advantages (freedom regarding your time and empowerment to do work your own way), the disadvantages (removal from everyday organizational life, lack of person-to-person contact, uncertainty about your place in the organization's culture) are only now being addressed from a communication perspective.

VIDEOCONFERENCING

Often, you will find yourself assigned to a work team or group whose members may not work in the same city, state, or even country. In many cases, virtual teams rely on **videoconferencing** to hold meetings or present ideas. In videoconferencing, two or more participants at different sites conduct a conference by using computer networks or audio and video equipment. As the cost of travel increases, many companies find that videoconferencing is an economical way to provide long-distance training or bring a company together for meetings when its employees are spread across many time zones.

However, without planning and practice, videoconferencing can be confusing and intimidating. Using CCCD—choose, create, coordinate, and deliver—to plan the components of your presentation and adding in elements for videoconferencing will help ensure your success. The tips below were developed with help from Diane

Howard's work on videoconferencing. Howard teaches students and professionals how to present information in a videoconference environment.

Before the Conference

1. Reserve the videoconference facilities for the day of your presentation and for one or two practice sessions, if necessary.
2. Learn to use the equipment. Ask the technology support person at your company to go over all the equipment with you. Ask questions and be sure you understand how everything works. Ask someone who frequently uses the equipment to attend your practice session and give you advice on using the equipment more efficiently.
3. Determine your potential audience in advance. If possible, find out the names of those attending the conference and their affiliations.
4. Keep in mind that videoconferencing is a visual medium. Therefore, *you* become a visual aid. Wear bright colors that project well on screen. Keep your hair, jewelry, and other accessories simple so they do not distract your audience. Make sure the room you are presenting in is free of visual clutter.

At the Conference

1. Present an agenda for the meeting. This could be on a digital slide, or you could e-mail the agenda to your audience in advance.
2. Vary the images on the screen: you, a digital slideshow presentation, back to you, other members of the team at your location (this is possible if you have a cameraperson at your facility or if there are multiple cameras in the room), back to you.
3. Use confident, energetic, and engaging body language. Just because you are speaking into a camera doesn't mean there is no audience.
4. Look into the camera! Don't forget that people are watching. Don't walk out of camera range and continue to talk while your audience stares at a blank screen.
5. Adjust your speech and movement for the time lag that may occur between you and the remote audience. Speak more slowly than normal. Enunciate carefully. Vary the quality of your voice so that your presentation isn't flat or boring.

THINKING GLOBALLY—TECHNOLOGY IN THE GLOBAL WORKPLACE

Get in touch with the technology group at your school or workplace. Ask a person from your technical group to run you through the process of conducting a video conference, doing a PowerPoint presentation using a laptop, and accessing the Internet from a conference room. Getting familiar with this technology now will save you frustration and potential embarrassment in the future. Mastering this technology will allow you to include videoconferencing and other forms of technology as skills on your résumé. These are skills that will be very attractive to employers who are active in the global workplace.

As we have seen, mediated communication technologies provide users the ability to increase the effectiveness of their communication. However, if it is not used correctly or consciously, mediated technology can have a negative impact on you both inside and outside of the workplace. The next section talks about managing your online identity, which is important in your professional and personal life.

MANAGING ONLINE IDENTITY

With so much technology at our disposal, we often adopt it without realizing that how we use technology impacts what others think about us. Regardless of which form of technology you use to send a message, there are common rules of etiquette that apply to all forms of computer-mediated communication. **Netiquette** is the term used to describe the manners we should use when participating in online discussions, using e-mail, or exchanging instant messages. The basic rule is to "think before you type and lurk before you leap" (Trenholm, 2000, p. 323). Netiquette encourages users to demonstrate appropriate entrance and exit rules; check FAQs (frequently asked questions) that are posted on a website to avoid redundant questions; and avoid "flaming" others when you disagree with them. How you communicate when using technology affects people's perception of you in the workplace. Another factor that can influence people's perceptions of you in the workplace is the availability of information about you on the Internet. Even the information you choose to display on social networking sites can be accessed by your boss, potential employers, and competitors.

Social Networking Sites, such as the popular MySpace, Facebook, and LinkedIn, are sites intended to help build communities of users with shared interests and activities. The prevalence of social networking sites in many countries, including the United States, is astounding. MySpace and Facebook are two of the top five most-visited sites in the United States, and are located in the top ten in many other countries, such as South Africa, India, and the United Kingdom.[2] Many of us take advantage of the benefits that these sites offer, such as staying in touch with friends and contacts across the globe, making new business and networking connections, and showing people what we are doing. Making too much information known online, though, can be against your best professional interests. Many companies use social networking sites to research information about current and potential employees. In 2006, one in ten companies reported using social networking sites to research current and potential employees, and this number increased to 25 percent of companies in 2007, with continued growth expected.[3] The other area of growth that more than doubled is the use of search engines, such as Google, Yahoo! and MSN, to search for employees (25 percent in 2006 compared to over 50 percent in 2007). What you put online, then, becomes increasingly important to your

---

[2] http://www.alexa.com/site/ds/top_500.

[3] http://www.idsnews.com/news/story.aspx?id=39784&comview=1 and http://www.itmanagersjournal.com/feature/28732.

GLOBAL PROFILE FOR SUCCESS—BRINGING PROFESSIONALS TOGETHER AROUND THE GLOBE

LinkedIn is an online network with offices located in Mountain View, California. The LinkedIn network connects more than 20 million experienced professionals from around the world, representing 150 industries.

Using LinkedIn, you can track former colleagues, find consultants, recommend others and get recommendations for a job, get hired for consulting jobs, and find clients. LinkedIn also provides company profiles, industry statistics, and job listings.

Explore LinkedIn's website: http://www.linkedin .com.

What can you learn about social networking from the website? What are the benefits of having a profile on a site like LinkedIn? What are the possible negatives? Create a mock LinkedIn profile. Have a friend review your profile and make suggestions. Did you put things in your profile that your friend felt would compromise you? Check out other networking sites. Which site is the best choice for your chosen industry?

professional appearance, and often, your success. The next section talks about how you can be more successful in finding information online. But before you read any further, take a minute and Google yourself. (Be sure to put your name in parenthesis to limit the results, e.g. "Jill Schiefelbein".) You might be surprised what you find.

NEWS YOU CAN USE: DOING WEB-BASED RESEARCH

In addition to opening up opportunities for telecommuting and networking, another major advantage of the Internet is that it allows us to access information quickly and relatively painlessly. One disadvantage is that distinguishing quality information from the rest of the stuff out there can prove to be time-consuming and frustrating. In this section, we recommend ways of using the Internet that can help you distinguish among the quality of information available on websites. First, some general guidelines:

- *Check out your school's library for information about search engines that are unique to your institution.* Librarians are usually the most up-to-date professionals to consult when it comes to Internet research. Many universities sponsor collaborative Internet-based research programs that allow users to search professional journals, magazines, newspapers, and reference sources electronically. In some cases, users can print entire articles and abstracts from these sources at no charge.
- *Use your school's homepage to begin navigating the Internet.* Most universities and colleges in North America sponsor websites with practical links to libraries, research institutions, academic departments, and alumni and student organizations. These sites provide useful search advice and help the novice user become acquainted with what the Internet can offer.

- *Contact the Communication Institute for Online Research (CIOS) to begin your research project.* Go to http://www.cios.org/ and follow the links. This is a very easy-to-use, impressive site designed for students.

Next, we offer advice about finding valuable information posted on websites:

- The official and often the best information for any field of study or profession is likely to be found on the homepage of professional organizations. Check out the National Communication Association (http://www.natcom.org) or the Academy of Management (http://www.aomonline.org). The American Communication Association website (http://www.americancomm.org) offers an online journal and comprehensive links to research sites associated with the communication field.
- Bulletin boards and discussion groups provide formal and informal sources of information, and many sponsor archives that can be searched with keywords or topics. Yahoo! Groups is an easy place to start (http://groups.yahoo.com).
- Popular information relevant to any field of study can usually be found on the websites of commercial magazines and newspapers. They often sponsor searchable archives. For good examples, check out the *New York Times* online (http://www.nytimes.com/), *BusinessWeek* magazine (http://www.businessweek.com/), or the online magazine *Slate* (http://www.slate.com/).
- Wikipedia is quickly becoming the go-to site for someone doing research on any topic. We caution you to not use this information as a primary source or cite the website in your college papers. Instead use it as a way to find out basic information about a topic. Often a good references section is found at the bottom of a Wikipedia page and you can find great links to academic or business articles there.
- You can find information on any topic through search engines such as Google, Yahoo!, Excite, Netscape, AltaVista, or Ask Jeeves. If you haven't already done so, you should be sure to do a search on yourself, using popular search engines. When typing in your name, you can put quotation marks around it to make the returned matches more accurate. Also, Google offers a more academic-specific search engine called Google Scholar (http://scholar.google.com), which tracks research published in scholarly journals and books.

HOW MUCH TECHNOLOGY DO I NEED?

Often, when consulting, we encounter people who do not have the technological skills to keep up with changes in their industry. Their lack of skills frustrates them, their colleagues, and their customers. However, we also regularly encounter the "techno geek," the person who has every gadget, software program, and electronic toy ever made. Sitting with a techno geek in a meeting can be quite painful when the person attempts to juggle a laptop, BlackBerry, iPod, and other devices while talking, texting, typing, and surfing. As with most areas of our life, there needs to be a balance.

In our experience, the most successful users of technology are those who pick a few tools that are appropriate for their jobs and become very proficient with new and changing technology. How much and what type of technology you need depends on several factors:

- *Your business or profession.* Why spend hours or weeks learning a piece of software you will never use? Find out which software is commonly used in your chosen field and learn it—now. Accountants need to be proficient with spreadsheet and tax accounting software. Cartologists (mapmakers) need to know CAD/CAM software. Learning the predominant software for your industry ensures that you will be able to communicate your ideas in the proper format when you need to.
- *The standards set by your industry.* Each industry differs slightly on the specific types of hardware and software that are used. For example, WordPerfect, which is equipped with templates and standard phrases that assist with the creation of legal forms and documents, is still preferred by many law firms. Graphic artists and designers almost exclusively use Macintosh computers. Microsoft Word is widely preferred in business environments. These standards have evolved over time and change slowly. Stick with the technology that is the standard in your industry.
- *The amount of time you are willing to invest in learning.* "Continuous learning," "lifelong learning," and "learning organizations" are phrases you will hear again and again throughout your business or professional life. These terms are especially relevant when it comes to technology in the workplace. Technology changes every day, and it is difficult to keep up with progress in software, hardware, and networking. Invest in and learn only those technologies you are willing to continually use.

SUMMARY

This chapter served as an introduction to technology and communication in the workplace, and examined using types of mediated communication, managing your online presence and finding online resources. We believe it is important to understand how technology impacts your communication in the workplace. To foster that understanding, we looked at the use of technology in business and professional settings and offered tips for using technology more efficiently.

BUSINESS AND PROFESSIONAL COMMUNICATION IN THE GLOBAL WORKPLACE ONLINE

All of the following chapter review materials are available in an electronic format on either the *Business and Professional Communication in the Global Workplace Online* Resource Center or the book's companion website. Online you'll find chapter learning objects, flashcards of glossary terms, InfoTrack® College Edition Activities, weblinks, quizzes, and more.

WHAT YOU SHOULD HAVE LEARNED

Now that you have read Chapter 8, you should be able to do the following:

- Provide a brief history of the evolution of technology in the workplace.
- Describe the downside to technology.
- Discuss the cultural and gender differences associated with technology.

- Explain how we can use technology consciously.
- Discuss the advantages and disadvantages of telecommuting.
- Provide tips for using voice mail and e-mail effectively.
- Discuss social networking sites and their role in the workplace.

- Walk through the process for doing web-based research, including providing sites that you could use.
- Discuss the three elements used to decide how much technology you need in your chosen field.

KEY TERMS

e-mail *167*	Netiquette *177*	telecommuting *175*
information overload *168*	networks *174*	videoconferencing *175*
Luddite *170*	power distance *168*	voice mail *174*

WRITING AND CRITICAL THINKING

The following activities can be completed online or submitted to your instructor.

Choose one of the following activities:

1. You have to set up an important meeting for your group. The meeting will be Monday, October 25, in Conference Room 7 at 9:00 A.M. Each participant needs to be prepared to give a brief update on his or her progress. At the end of the meeting, you will be giving Dension, the foreign exchange student assigned to your group, a going-away party. Write an e-mail that includes the above information.

2. You consistently receive incoherent voice mail messages from Carl. Whenever he calls, he mumbles, forgets to leave complete information, or rambles on about three or four unrelated topics. How do you address the problem with Carl?

3. You are one of the first in your department chosen for the new telecommuting project. The prospect of working at home excites you, but you worry that you may be overlooked for future promotions or special projects. What steps can you take to ensure that you remain part of the company culture?

4. As you are a recognized conscious business communicator, the president of your company has approached you and asked for your advice on the quickest and most

effective way to send crucial information to all employees in the company. Some company divisions are not in your physical location, and some employees telecommute. Prepare a report for the president identifying the advantages and disadvantages of the use of the technologies discussed in the chapter to enhance the reception and understanding of her message. Of the following scenarios, are there any for which you would advise not using electronic information technology?

- the need for employees to contribute an additional 10 percent to their company health insurance next year
- a potential employee cutback due to a downturn in the economy
- announcement of a new multimillion-dollar contract awarded to your company
- relocation of some company departments to better align with their customer base
- your company's merger with another company
- your recent promotion to vice president of public relations
- accepting applications for telecommuting

5. In groups, discuss the ethics of personal use of office equipment and technology (telephones, e-mail, Internet).

PRACTICING COMMUNICATION IN PROFESSIONAL CONTEXTS

Surfing the Net for Information: A Practical Guide

1. Access a search engine and type in the most succinct keywords you think will identify the sites you want to visit. The sites will appear in an order determined by your keywords and the search engine's evaluators. For example, let's assume you want to find up-to-date information on e-commerce. One possible source of information is trade magazines with sites on the Internet. For our purposes, let's say you want to visit *BusinessWeek* magazine online. Type in "BusinessWeek magazine."

2. Once the relevant sites are identified, click on the site you want to visit. If the site contains a lot of graphics, it may take a while to appear on your computer screen, depending on your connection speed. The *BusinessWeek* site is professionally created, so graphic content on its homepage is limited to small items that load fairly quickly. In a few seconds, you will see the entire page. Links generally appear in blue or as underlined text. To explore a topic, click on a link. Or you can use the search engine for the site to locate e-commerce information within the *BusinessWeek* archives.

3. Let's say that a story on e-commerce is available on the *BusinessWeek* homepage. When you click the link it takes you to Intel Corporation's site about starting e-commerce companies, complete with stories from startups. On the Intel site, a link at the bottom of the page takes you to a list of other information resources about e-commerce.

4. Bookmark the site you found. Bookmarking allows you to save the site address for future reference. Click the Bookmarks button on the toolbar at the top of your web browser. Clicking the Bookmarks button while you are on a particular web page automatically prompts you to add the bookmark to a folder. The next time you want to visit this site, click on the Bookmarks button, find the name of the Intel or *BusinessWeek* site, and click on it.

YOUR PERSONAL COMMUNICATION PROFILE

We have talked about technology as an important communication tool that creates a span of communication. For this breakthrough skill development, we would like you to begin investigating the technology associated with your profession or chosen career. What software products are standard in your industry? What computer skills do you need in order to communicate your ideas effectively? What is the learning curve associated with these skills? What steps would you have to take to become proficient?

Create a technology plan that includes the following information:

- the type of software used in your chosen field

- your current level of proficiency with that software
- the learning curve to reach the level of proficiency that is standard for your industry
- the steps you need to take to learn to use the product
- the classes or training available through your current job, at your school, or at community colleges or training locations in your city
- the benefits of learning the software now rather than waiting until you have begun a job or are looking for a job in your field
- the costs involved in becoming a proficient user of the technology
- the costs involved if you *don't* learn the technology

COMMUNICATING IN GROUPS AND TEAMS

CHAPTER 9

In the workplace, a **team** is defined as a group of individuals who share a unifying goal. Organizations use teams to overcome challenges caused by a lack of common understanding and communication, and to bring knowledgeable people together to solve problems. Many teams are put in place as organizations downsize and hierarchies are flattened and as organizations expand globally. Teams allow organizations to bring people together who are responsible for implementing the goals and carrying out an organization's vision. As we saw in Chapter 8, those working in global teams communicate virtually, through a variety of technological means and media.

As you can see from the continuum in Figure 9.1, simply applying the label team does not a team make. Many organizations simply lump people together, calling those collectivities of individuals a team, providing them with little or no training for working as a team. The results, in these cases, are usually dismal. When organizations place people in groups and teams without unifying goals or the training needed to operate successfully as a team, misunderstanding and miscommunication become more likely—and so does conflict. Conflicts may take the form of:

- clashes over contradictory goals for the group
- differences over preferred methods and strategies for carrying out the team's work
- disagreements about perceived individual roles and hierarchy
- frustration with a lack of progress or success by the team or individually
- resentment or anger caused by one person doing the bulk of the work while others get or take the credit

External conflicts can also arise. External conflicts occur when management has not clearly defined a team's goals. This can result in a team's priorities conflicting with those of another team within the organization, setting off **turf battles** within the organization and causing potential organizational chaos. Effective, conscious communication can help bring order to the chaotic environment in which many teams function.

Group of individuals	Group in name only	Collaborative group	Team	Conscious Communication Choices
People who come together occasionally to pass information. Members have a laissez-faire attitude, individual orientation, lack of initiative, and no responsibility for group success.	Members are thrown together with little orientation or clear purpose. Main function of the group is meetings. After group work is done, members return to their individual jobs or departments.	Group members disagree over conflicting goals for the group, cite differences in preferred methods or strategies for carrying out the group's work, but use collaboration and conflict to move the group forward.	Members share a unifying goal. The team succeeds through shared knowledge, diversity of experiences, and collaborative energy. Members realize their individual success depends on the synergy of the team.	Give and take of information by participants who are informed and goal oriented.

Mindless Groups/Teams ⟶ **Mindful Groups/Teams**

FIGURE 9.1 | CONSCIOUS COMMUNICATION AND GROUP/TEAM COMMUNICATION CONTINUUM

Team communication, depicted toward the right of the continuum in Figure 9.1, occurs when a team achieves **synergy**, the stage at which people are truly working together. A synergized team recognizes that shared knowledge, diversity of experiences, and collaborative energy provide the team with powerful resources. When tackling a business or professional problem, what makes the difference between a group and a team are mindful communication processes and practices that improve the likelihood of success for everyone involved.

As we have seen, the CCCD process—choosing, creating, coordinating, and delivering—offers an opportunity to develop skills necessary for successful communication in the global workplace. After reading and studying the material in these sections, you should have a blueprint for communicating with others in groups and teams. However, for the purposes of this discussion, we will focus on teams as the most conscious form of group communication.

CHOOSING: STRATEGIES FOR ORGANIZING TEAMS

There are few organizational experiences as frustrating as being placed on a team or assigned to a group that lacks a core function or specific goal. Much of the frustrations inherent in team participation are avoidable if organizations follow a clear set of team building strategies as soon as teams are appointed. Specifically, team experiences improve when the members *choose* productive strategies for organizing team activities. Successful teams do the following:

- develop effective leadership strategies
- outline strategies for team participation locally and globally
- develop criteria for the selection of team members
- practice adaptive communication skills, such as behavioral flexibility
- create collaboratively stated goals and objectives for group work

In the remainder of this section, we will discuss the first four strategies listed above.

DEVELOPING EFFECTIVE LEADERSHIP STRATEGIES

At its most basic level, *leadership* in groups refers to a set of managerial functions (Barnard, 1938; Gouran, 1970; Hirokawa, 1992). For example, in most business and professional group meetings, the most senior member of the group—the person highest up in the organizational hierarchy—is usually thought of as the leader and is responsible for carrying out managerial tasks. Tasks might include scheduling meetings or sending weekly status reports to an executive team. As important as these management functions are to a group's success, leadership does not end with them. In fact, the real power of leadership emerges from the leader's success with managing the communication of the group, including:

- choosing team members
- clarifying individual and team goals
- facilitating communication
- consensus building
- seeking and providing information
- making assignments
- evaluating, summarizing, and reporting
- celebrating success

This attention to the conscious communication of team members by their team leader allows a group to develop the synergy needed to become a team. Let's take a look at these basic strategies in more detail to see how each is used to create synergy within a team.

Choosing Team Members   Choosing the most appropriate individuals for a team is associated with the team's success (Eisenberg, 1990; Bennis, 1999). A key factor in the success of a team is that each individual understands what he/she brings to the team and what his/her contribution will be. Team leaders should convey the reasons for choosing team members to individuals when they are assigned to a team and to other members of the team once it is established. When team members understand their role on the team, they are more willing to participate and are less apt to feel as if time spent on team projects is wasted.

Clarifying Goals   A **goal** is a concrete, achievable end. **Objectives (sometimes called "benchmarks")** are the tasks required to reach a goal, and those tasks are best articulated when they are associated with reasonable deadlines. Effective team leaders understand that often team members are working on multiple teams, managing a number of projects, and are juggling multiple goals and objectives simultaneously. It is the team leader's responsibility to help the members of his/her team clarify and prioritize their goals and tasks and keep projects on track. To do this, team leaders seek ways to move the team forward. These include:

- conducting a vision meeting when the team is first organized
- introducing team members to one another and highlighting what each team member brings to the project
- emphasizing open and honest communication practices among team members

- holding regular team meetings to review and revise the team's goals and set new milestones
- meeting individually with team members as needed, to clarify what is required to accomplish each member's goals

Team leaders accomplish these tasks by facilitating communication with those throughout the organization.

Facilitating Communication   The team leader's role is to help team members make sense out of the organization's vision, objectives, and activities by facilitating communication within the team and with those outside the team. Team leaders facilitate team communication by:

- sharing the knowledge and information a team needs rather than trying to horde or control information
- making decisions based on the experience and collaborative efforts of the team
- recognizing when the team needs to communicate and initiating the discussions needed to move the team forward
- coordinating with those outside the team and the organization to gather the information and resources required to make the team successful

Seeking and Providing Information   A key element in team leadership is information. Unfortunately too many of those placed in leadership positions try to *control* information, using it as a bargain chip or something to be doled out as they see fit. Leaders who behave in this manner generally fail. By contrast, successful team leaders act as a conduit for information, allowing information to flow freely among team members and with those outside the team while also encouraging transparency in their work. A team cannot function in isolation from other teams or other units of an organization, or from its customers and clients. To be a conduit, the team leader has to learn to *listen* to the myriad of conversations—verbal and electronic—that flow within an organization, and from those conversations take the information that the team needs to make good decisions, meet its goals, and build consensus.

Consensus Building   Although a good team leader recognizes that teams are made up of individuals, he or she also knows that to move forward, the team must move forward *together*. It is the task of the team leader to build understanding among team members. This may require team members, at the team leader's urging, to practice give and take. When conflicts or impasses occur, a team leader needs to:

- address the issue as soon as the conflict arises, rather than waiting until it grows into a serious problem
- ask team members for points of agreement
- ask team members to listen to each other's point of view
- determine if there are reasonable ways to accommodate differing points or expend resources more equitably
- adjust schedules and assignments to alleviate conflict

- realign goals when necessary
- thank team members for working together to get beyond the conflict or impasse

Making Assignments   An important function of the team leader is making and giving the team members' equitable assignments. Too often, team leaders overlook this basic function, expecting team members to instinctively know what they should do. In most cases, they won't. Without direction, team members may step on one another's toes or go off in directions that may not help the team as a whole. And without a sense of equity in the work assigned, individual team members will likely become frustrated with each other and resent the leader's lack of concern for equity.

Team leaders can ask for volunteers for assignments that don't require the skills of a specific team member, but ultimately, it is up to the team leader to ensure that the team stays on task and accomplishes its goals. By making clear assignments and following up to see that assignments are completed in a timely and effective manner a leader demonstrates leadership. This vital function requires team leaders to develop the skills needed to evaluate the contribution of individual team members and the efforts of the team as a whole.

Evaluating, Summarizing, and Reporting   A team cannot succeed within an organization without someone evaluating, summarizing, and reporting the progress of the team. These functions occur in two ways: to individuals and to outside groups who will benefit from or contribute to the team's efforts.

Individuals.   Effective team leaders routinely evaluate the performance of team members. Evaluations can be both formal information, such as reading weekly progress reports or listening to a team member's input in meetings, or through casual conversation or formal reviews. Formal reviews of team members should occur at regular intervals, at a minimum of once a year.

Outside Groups.   A large part of a team leader's responsibility is to keep other teams and management apprised of the team's progress. In their reports, team leaders should provide outside members with an evaluation of the team's progress. They also should identify any additional resources that might be required and any changes in dates associated with the team's project.

Celebrating Success   An often overlooked, but important function of a team leader is celebrating a team's success. Team leaders need to recognize both individual and team success and celebrate it. Celebration may come in any of the following forms:

- a congratulatory e-mail
- an announcement at a team or organization meeting
- a raise, bonus, or other form of compensation
- a party to celebrate completing a project

While it is perfectly acceptable to single out team members who go above and beyond to contribute to the team's success, it is important that all team members feel appreciated for their work.

PHRASES LEADERS SHOULD NEVER USE

The phrases listed below kill participation and creativity. Team leaders should avoid these negative phrases and say things that encourage participation and solutions.

What Leaders Shouldn't Say	What Leaders Should Do
That's not the way we do things here. We tried that once before. Let's just keep doing things the way we always have. Please just stick to your job; I'll worry about everything else.	Know and say that there are many ways to accomplish tasks and they are open to new ideas and innovation.
What were you doing talking to _____ without my consent? We've never gotten any cooperation, buy-in, or help from that department, so why try now?	Understand and demonstrate that communication should be open and they do not try to control the flow of information into or out of the team.
We don't have the resources. Don't you think that's more trouble than it's worth?	Not be dismissive of others' suggestions and try instead to exhaust all possibilities to provide productive team members with the resources they need.
Because I said so. That will cause me way too much work, so forget it!	Do not put themselves ahead of the success of the team.

LEADING VIRTUAL TEAMS

Virtual teams are teams that are located in more than one physical location. The use of virtual teams in the global workplace allows organizations to hire the best people in their industry regardless of their location around the globe. Virtual teams allow organizations to:

* bring people together from across the country or around the globe to work on projects
* develop projects in geographical locations where it isn't practical to put an entire office or large staff
* join together other organizations, non-profits, contractors, scientists and others that might be key to a project's success but may not work for an organization
* reduce travel, lodging, and other costs the organization might incur from relocating employees or others to centralized sights

Organizations form virtual teams when:

* an organization has offices and employees distributed across the country or the globe that need to work together
* a key team member (often a consultant or chief scientist) may be working on other projects and is only available part-time or on a scheduled basis
* an organization is conducting fieldwork or testing in one location, and research and development in another
* workers need to **telecommute,** work from home or a long distance from an organization's headquarters or other physical location

To ensure the success of virtual teams, team leaders need to establish a cohesive virtual environment in addition to following the strategies for managing teams discussed on the previous page. A virtual team environment should:

- provide all team members the electronic equipment, software, and network access needed to fully operate as a team
- provide each team member with the training needed to operate effectively on the team
- set reasonable standards, goals, and objectives that all team members can reach regardless of their geographic location
- provide virtual team members with the information they might need to smooth cross-cultural interactions between team members
- allow virtual team members the same opportunities for advancement available to traditional team members
- hold regular face-to-face meetings with all team members using video conferencing or video chat to ensure everyone is communicating directly and effectively
- circulate information as quickly and widely as possible
- require regular status reports and updates from all members of the team to ensure projects stay on track and goals are met

THINKING GLOBALLY—WORKING IN THE VIRTUAL WORKPLACE

Working virtually requires team members to master software they might not need when working in traditional teams or individually for an organization. Some of these applications will be in-house software developed specifically for an organization, accessed through the organization's network. Other applications are employed on a project-by-project basis. These applications fall into three basic categories:

- Project management—project management software is used by engineers, designer, software developers, and service teams to track each team member's assignments, progress, time spent and dependencies.
  - Two widely used project management applications are Microsoft Project (http://office.microsoft.com) and Tracker (http://www.TrackerSuite.Net/).
- Brainstorming—brainstorming software allows team members to pool ideas. These applications allow ideas to flow freely, without judgment, in a creative and unstructured environment.

- Two widely used brainstorming applications are Open Mind 2 Business (http://www.matchware.com) and Mindmapper (http://www.mindmap perusa.com).
- Document sharing—document sharing applications allow team members to share word documents, spreadsheets, and presentations online. Team members can edit and comment on the documents virtually in real time.
  - Two widely used document sharing applications are Microsoft Office (http://office.microsoft.com) and Google Docs (http://docs.google.com).

Visit the websites above and review the products listed. Download the demo versions of the software and experiment with them to become familiar with these products. Taking a little time now to get accustomed to the applications and skills required for working in virtual teams will make you and your work shine in the future.

CREATING: WORKING IN TEAMS

Choosing effective strategies for your participation as a team member is another way to improve mindful team communication practices. **Participation** refers to what you contribute to the team effort and how you conduct yourself as a team member. One way to become a more mindful team participant is to learn from the mistakes your fellow team members make. Another way to improve your participation is by asking yourself the following questions:

- What does the team expect from me?
- How can I best serve the team?
- Do I have any promises or commitments to the team I haven't fulfilled?
- Is there any reason I cannot succeed?
- What information do I need?
- Is there any way that I can help other members of the team?

We want to underscore the importance of effective team participation. We stress a number of behaviors that contribute to effective participation:

- Be fully committed to the team and its work and remind yourself of this commitment regularly.
- Prepare for dialogue on specific topics by thinking about the contributions you can make in meetings, informal team discussions, and e-mail conversations.
- For any team meeting, prepare a list of personal goals that may serve as your guide for assessing your performance and the team's progress.
- Listen carefully, and without interruptions, to the contributions of others.
- Provide verbal and nonverbal feedback to members of the team.
- Ask relevant questions publicly rather than keeping them to yourself or sharing them only in private with a coworker.
- Be willing to adapt your behavior to the needs and expectations of *individualized* others; avoid stereotypical evaluations of others.
- Avoid taking comments personally or engaging in personal attacks on other team members and thereby contributing to negative conflict.
- Be willing to participate fully in team traditions, rites, and rituals.
- Help the team stay on task by avoiding commentary that leads it astray.
- Trust the team process and the other members of the team.

As you can see from the above-listed characteristics of effective leadership and participation, the coordination of personal goals and attitudes with communication strategies and behaviors increases the conscious effort you put into teamwork. Coordinating your communication with the team's vision and goals is essential to group success. Equally important is the selection of team members.

JAMMING

In part, the success of a team is due to what researchers have come to label **jamming** (Eisenberg, 1990), a term borrowed from musicians. *Jamming* means engaging in a spontaneous, energetic group session. It refers to the positive energies (and fun) that emerge from total group coordination when every individual has a role to play in the team as well as a chance to demonstrate individual skills. The result is usually that the performance of the whole group improves, sometimes dramatically. However, as most musicians recognize, jamming requires that the group members have about the same skill levels. "Stars" detract from team play by intimidating those with less skill, and people who have little skill have a difficult time working at the team's level, which everyone notices. The selection of team members should be accomplished with regard to similar skill levels.

However, Warren Bennis (1999) also points out that good leaders in organizations view teams as places where talented individuals can *develop* new understandings and skills. Part of the team experience is a learning process that requires both listening and learning to improvise. Team members are fully in the flow and jamming when they:

- reserve judgments about other team members until they see what others can contribute to the team
- fully appreciate and acknowledge the skills and talents of their fellow team members
- listen to the ideas of their fellow team members with an open mind
- remain flexible and open to change that is an inevitable part of working in teams and organizations
- work to resolve personal conflicts before they have an impact on the team

ADAPTIVE SKILLS

Team communication requires a higher level of communication, collaboration, and cooperation than working individually as a part of a large department or group. This increase in cooperation occurs when team members develop what researchers call "adaptive skills" (Phillips, Pedersen, and Wood, 1990; Goodall, 1990). **Adaptive skill** refers to the ability of team members to adapt their behaviors to the needs and expectations of others. Adaptive communication skills involve behavioral flexibility, which consists of the following mindful processes (Goodall, 1990, pp. 133–34):

- developing a repertoire of self-presentations that can be used to formulate appropriate responses to situations and to others
- accepting the legitimacy and honesty of others' identities and personalities by learning to expect and adapt to displays of diversity in meeting behavior, by not allowing personal conflicts or past performances to interfere with your ability to share information productively, and by staying on task
- serving as an example of effective collaborative communication by actively demonstrating your desire to work well with others
- showing patience with emergent ideas
- actively listening and providing feedback for the ideas and suggestions of others
- complimenting the work and contributions of group members

Developing these skills gives team members the ability to engage in positive, task-oriented talk that allows team members to move forward together successfully.

These skills provide a foundation for accomplishing the team's goals, because they demonstrate to team members the need to stay on task and on schedule, working together toward a common goal.

CREATING THE VISION, GOALS, OBJECTIVES FOR A TEAM

Teams succeed when they have a clear vision, stated goals, and effective shared communication designed to accomplish commonly perceived objectives. Team members buy into a team's vision, goals, and objectives if they actively participate in defining these elements. In this section, we discuss how to define goals and strategies for teams and options for communicating within teams.

BEGIN WITH A CLEAR AGENDA

Because so much of a vision meeting is about managing perceptions and ensuring that the personal agendas brought to a meeting do not overshadow the team's agenda, creating and managing an **agenda** is central to the success of a vision meeting. An agenda is a functional document that should include the date, time, and place of the meeting and the speaking assignment or role for all participants who are responsible for specific areas of the agenda. There are numerous ways to organize agendas:

- Timed agendas follow strict time spans and limit the length of time available to speakers or presenters. Timed agendas signal to each participant that he or she has a specific time to speak at the meeting. Good team members adhere to the time allotted on the agenda. If you find you require additional time (or less time), contact the person conducting the meeting so that the agenda can be revised and re-sent.
- Old to new agendas begin by recapping issues that still need to be resolved from previous meetings, then move to a discussion of new issues, and, finally, allow time for discussing and making assignments to be completed before the next meeting.

FOCUS ON ETHICS

Leo was one of the first team members selected for a new team being organized to streamline calls into the company's call center. He was selected because he had seven years of call center experience. This time around, the members of the U.S. call center would be teaming up with members selected from the various call centers in India, Ireland, and Mexico. This morning, Leo heard that Shannon, the team leader, was planning a "visioning" meeting for the team's first get together. Leo had been through enough visioning exercises to develop the strong belief that they were a complete waste of time. Before hearing any more, Leo made up his mind he would participate as little as possible. He would take his laptop to the meeting and get some "real" work done, while the others did the visioning.

What is Leo's obligation as a team member? As an employee of the company? Does he owe Shannon an opportunity to make her case for vision? Is mentally checking out of the meeting an ethical option?

- Topically arranged agendas break the meeting into specific topics that are then arranged in the order that best fits the objective of the meeting. Topical agendas may also include time limits if presenters are assigned to each topic.

Figure 9.2 provides an example of an agenda for a visioning meeting for a newly formed virtual documentation and training team.

CREATING A SHARED VISION

Within the context of an organization, a shared **vision** refers to the overall, far-reaching idea of what a team or organization should accomplish and the values that should inform those accomplishments. Each vision statement and the values that define the statement are unique to the team and the project. The steps for creating a vision shown on the following page have been adapted from an exercise outlined in Peter Senge's book, *The Fifth Discipline* (1994, p. 337). These questions are summarized in the box on page 194.

DOCUMENT AND TRAINING TEAM KICKOFF MEETING

Date: January 19, 2009

Time: 9:00 A.M–3:00 P.M

Place: Inverness Conference Center—Pine Room, for participants from the Greensboro, NC, office

Wild Horse Pass Resort—Sedona Conference Room, for participants from the Chandler, AZ, office

AGENDA

9:00–9:30	Opening remarks – Carlos Hayes, president and CEO
9:30–10:00	Introduction of team members – Shannon Green, director of documentation and training
10:00–10:30	Discussion of management team vision and stated objectives – Carlos and Shannon
10:30–10:45	Break
10:45–12:15	Breakout group discussions
12:30–1:30	Catered lunch on site
1:30–2:30	Bringing it all together
2:30–3:00	Wrapup and assignments for next meeting

Please turn off all cell phones, pagers, and e-mail before the meeting begins. You will have short breaks throughout the day to check messages. Lunch is catered, and there will be coffee, tea, soda, water, and light snacks in each conference room.

FIGURE 9.2 | SAMPLE AGENDA

Step 1: The Vision of the Future

One way to create a vision is to create it from the future then backtrack to the present. Begin by envisioning your organization, team, or project five years from today's date. If you could create the perfect situation, what would it be? As a team, describe, as realistically as possible, what you envision. Consider these questions one by one, painting an ever clearer shared vision of your future organization.

Make sure each member of the team has an opportunity to comment on each of the following questions. Write down your ideas or use brainstorming software that everyone has access to in order to capture the ideas. As the team reaches a consensus, note:

1. Who are the stakeholders associated with our team? (Remember, you are five years in the future.)
2. How do we work with each stakeholder group?
3. How do we produce value for them?
4. What are the most influential trends in our industry?
5. What is our image in the marketplace? How do we compete?
6. What is our unique contribution to the marketplace? What is the impact of our work on other teams, the organization, and our customers?
7. How do we make money?
8. What does our team look like? How does our team interact with other teams in the organization?
9. How do we handle good times? How do we handle hard times?
10. In what ways is our organization a great place to work?
11. What are our values? How do people treat each other? How are people recognized?
12. How do we know that the future of our team is secure? What have we done to ensure its future for ourselves?
13. What is our team's role in the organization?

After you answer each question above, ask the following question:

14. How will we measure our progress?

Step 2: Current Reality

Now come back to the current year and look at the organization as it is today.

15. What are the critical forces in place today that will allow us to succeed?
16. Who are the current stakeholders—both inside and outside the organization?
17. What changes do we perceive taking place among our stakeholders?
18. What are the most influential trends in our industry today?
19. What aspects of our team will empower people? What aspects of our team might disempower people?
20. How is the company's vision and objectives statement currently used by other teams?
21. What do we know that we need to know? What don't we know that we need to know?

Step 3: Creating the Vision

Underline the key words in each answer. Did any words reoccur in the answers? Highlight these words. Make a list of the main themes that emerge from the answers. Draft a vision that incorporates the main themes and keywords that you identified from the answers to both sets of questions.

GLOBAL PROFILE FOR SUCCESS—TEAMING WITH VISION

Price Club, a wholesale club strictly for business customers, began in 1976. Part of the Price Club family, the first Costco opened in 1984 and catered to business and individual customers. In addition to its retail stores, Costco Wholesale Industries operates manufacturing businesses, which includes special food packaging, optical laboratories, meat processing, and jewelry distribution. Costco employs over 125,000 full and part-time employees, in over 500 locations in seven countries.

An important part of the Costco vision is its employees. CEO Jim Sinegal believes that "it's important to hire good people and give them good jobs and good wages. They are the people who are going to run your business." Costco employees have salaries that are 40 percent higher than its leading competitor. They also have a full benefits package, including health care, which contributes to an employee turnover rate that is among the lowest in the business. According to the company website, only 5 percent of Costco's employees leave every year, which is 54 percent below the industry average of 59 percent.

Explore Costco's corporate website: http://phx. corporate-ir.net/phoenix.zhtml?c=83830&p=irol-homeprofile.

What can you learn about team building from the Costco website? What skills are necessary to succeed in the global workplace as a member of the Costco team? What does the compensation policy at Costco tell you about working there? Does the compensation policy reflect the vision of Costco?

COORDINATING: WORKING WITH OTHERS

In Chapter 7, Exploring Interpersonal Communication, we discussed how individuals within an organization should interact. In this chapter, we add to the foundation we began in Chapter 7 by listing the communication skills that team leaders and participants need to develop to be successful team members. In this section, we will discuss the skills for communication across teams to coordinate problem-solving efforts within an organization.

Often in organizations, a major communication breakdown occurs when teams must solve problems that affect more than one team. Team members may do a relatively good job of communicating within their team, but if needs, expectations, resource requirements, deadlines, and other pertinent information is not passed from one team to another, one or more teams may be set up for failure.

Effective communication in organizations requires balancing creativity with constraints (Eisenberg, Goodall, & Trethewey, 2008). **Creativity** results from giving people the freedom to explore alternatives to the traditional ways of doing things. However, too often, giving a team license for creativity is interpreted as freeing the team from the natural constraints inherent in any organization. **Constraints** are restrictions or limits, which in an organization may result from factors such as limited resources, such as time or money. Charged with finding a creative solution to a problem, a team might feel free to suspend the need for a written agenda, abandon order in the discussions, or ignore the vision or objectives of the organization or team. Unfortunately, this type of creativity usually doesn't yield productive results.

How do we make cross-team endeavors successful? One way is by encouraging teams to look for creative solutions within the constraints that naturally occur within organizations before they become problems. Without a framework for sharing talk throughout the organization, creativity is unlikely. Organizational theorists such as David Bohm (1980) point out that creativity actually exists *because of* constraints, and that both forces, creativity and constraints, are necessary to produce innovation and change. Just as an artist works within the constraints of her or his materials, budget, and available time, so do problem-solving or planning teams work within the constraints of their own imaginations, budgets that have been given to them, and a projected deadline. Yet the artist still manages to produce great art, and problem-solving groups come up with interesting, if not unique, solutions. How does this happen?

COORDINATING: THE PROBLEM-SOLVING PROCESS

Successful planning and problem solving begin with a shared understanding among team members about problem-solving processes. One of the oldest and most reliable methods for solving problems of any kind is the scientific method. For this reason, researchers and theorists of small-group and team behavior have long advocated adapting the scientific method to human problem solving (Dewey, 1912; Phillips, Pedersen, and Wood, 1979; Goodall, 1990). When applied in a business or professional setting, the problem-solving process consists of eight steps:

1. Understanding the charge
2. Phrasing the question
3. Fact-finding

Mark Richards/PhotoEdit

4. Establishing criteria for a solution
5. Generating alternative solutions
6. Testing each alternative solution against the cr'
7. Formulating a solution
8. Presenting the solution

Each of these steps is more fully discussed below.

Step 1: Understanding the Charge   What must the team accomplish.
stand its charge, the team must outline the problem to be solved. The team ъ.
answer the following questions:

- What is the nature of the problem?
- Who is involved?
- What is each person's stake in the problem and solution?
- What resources (financial, material, technological, and human) are currently available?
- What are the deadlines?

The chart below provides example answers for the questions listed above:

What is the nature of the problem?	The sales teams scheduled two clients for training in the same week.
Who is involved?	The sales teams, the D&T team, and both clients.
What is their stake in the problem and solution?	The sales teams' credibility. Our reputation as being "team players." The clients' trust in that we, as an organization, will deliver what we say we will.
What resources (financial, material, technological, and human) are currently available?	We currently have the human resources to teach classes for both clients; however, we don't have the classroom facilities. If we have to secure off-site training facilities, we will have to ask for a budget increase to cover the rental costs.
What are the deadlines?	We need to have a solution by the end of the week.

Step 2: Phrasing the Question   Once the problem is outlined, the team should determine the issues that will guide the remainder of the team's decision making. To accomplish this goal, the team must phrase the issue as a question, which will be used to guide all future interactions. Keep in mind the following points:

- The wording should be clear.
- The wording shapes the outcome and possible solutions.
- The wording should reflect what is important or relevant for solving the problem.

Step 3: Fact-finding To answer the question phrased in the second step of this process, the team must collect and organize as much relevant information about the issue as possible. In order to collect the necessary information, the team must be willing to share information among team members and with other members of the organization. There are three areas of fact and questions associated with each that the team should investigate:

- *Background.* What decisions were made (and by whom) that led to the current situation? Has this problem arisen in the past? If so, how was it resolved? Was the resolution considered successful?
- *Current state of the problem.* Who are the people involved who have information about the problem? What possible solutions do they have to offer? Is there anything we don't know that they might be able to tell us?
- *Possible outcomes.* What are the customers' expectations? What are the organization's expectations? What are the team's expectations?

The chart below provides example answers for the questions listed above:

Background	
What decisions were made, and by whom, that led to the current situation?	Two separate sales teams promised training to two separate customers for the same week.
Has this problem arisen in the past? If so, how was it resolved?	This is the first time we have encountered this problem, so we don't have a historical solution.
Was the resolution considered successful?	We don't have the data for this question.
Current State of the Problem	
Who are the people involved who have information about the problem?	The sales teams, our group, and the clients.
What possible solutions do they have to offer?	Each sales team wants the other to renege on their promise.
Is there anything we don't know that they might be able to tell us?	We don't know if there are any other dates that might be acceptable for either client.
Possible Outcomes	
What are the customers' expectations?	The customers' expectations are that we will provide training when we promised.
What are the organization's expectations?	The organization's expectations are that we find a solution for delivering training.
What are the team's expectations?	The team's expectations are that the sales teams learn a valuable lesson from this situation and no one promises training for specific dates without first consulting with the D&T team.

Step 4: Establishing Criteria for a Solution Establishing criteria against which to measure possible solutions ensures that the team will settle on the solution that comes closest to meeting the needs of all the stakeholders. After the facts have been

determined, and before a solution is articulated, the group needs to establish the standards that will be used to assess, evaluate, and test possible alternative solutions. To do this, the group should articulate an ideal solution that answers the following questions:

- What would the ideal solution look like?
- What might it include?
- How would it impact the stakeholders?
- What resources are necessary to implement the solution?

The chart below provides example answers for the questions listed above:

What would the ideal solution look like?	The ideal solution would be one that provides both clients with training without making it seem as if we cannot live up to our promises.
What might it include?	It might include incentives for either client to accept a flexible training solution.
How would it impact the stakeholders?	It would provide all the stakeholders involved a positive solution.
What resources are necessary to implement the solution?	A meeting with the sales teams, phone calls to the clients, and time for the D&T to work through possible solutions.

Step 5: Generating Alternative Solutions   The goal of this step is to create as many possible alternative solutions as the team can think of. Generally, the team will use a brainstorming technique to accomplish this purpose, and team members should articulate alternatives without interrupting the flow of talk with comments or criticism. A number of software packages are designed to facilitate the brainstorming process. The basic rules that should be followed when brainstorming include:

- Write everything down. The beginning of a solution may lie within any thought or idea.
- Don't criticize anyone's ideas. There are no bad ideas.
- Keep going until the team is completely out of ideas.
- Link or stream ideas to encourage creative, unique thinking. For example, one team member may say "classes," which leads to "new scheduling options," and the next may say "staggered classes," to which a third might add "joint membership."
- After brainstorming, use clustering to group ideas together.

Step 6: Testing Each Alternative Solution against the Criteria   The team should expose each alternative to the criteria posed in the fourth step of the problem-solving process. When doing so, the team should fairly and accurately consider the merits and limitations of each proposed solution. Be sure to test all the alternatives, even if the first alternative seems to be a solution. The team may find a better solution in the third or fourth alternative.

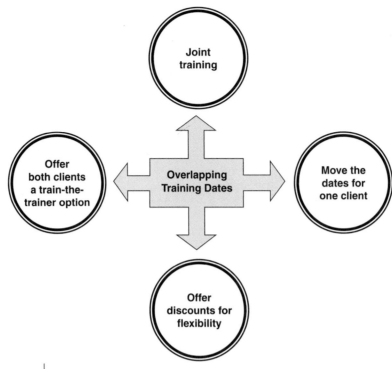

FIGURE 9.3 | BRAINSTORMING RESULTS

If none of the alternative solutions clearly meets the criteria, combine two or more of them until you create a solution that does. Or you may need to go back to Step 5 and generate additional alternatives.

The chart below provides example criteria and solutions:

Solution Criteria	Allows us to live up to our agreement?	Allows for incentives if a flexible training solution is accepted?	Provides all the stakeholders a positive solution?	Can be implemented with minimal impact?
Move dates	No	Yes	Possibly, need more information	?
Train the trainer	Yes and No	Yes	Possibly, need more information	Yes
Joint training	Yes	Yes	Yes	Yes

Step 7: Formulating a Solution   Once you have found a solution that meets the criteria, clearly state the solution so that all the team members understand the direction the team will take. This statement will be used to create your report or presentation.

Step 8: Presenting the Solution The goal of the final step in the problem-solving process is to present a convincing argument to the charging authority or stakeholder in the organization. Presentation of the solution will be made in person, by written report, or via e-mail. Rarely does anyone have the time or patience to read a long report in business today. Frequently, solutions to a problem are offered in an e-mail response. To be certain your audience is familiar with all of the components of the problem, you should include the following information:

- a recap of the background
- who is affected by the problem and the solution

CASE STUDY 8	WORKING AS A TEAM, ALL ON YOUR OWN

Robyn had never minded working in teams before. As the newest member of a sales and marketing team charged with increasing customer subscriptions to the company's newest website offering, Robyn was excited about the project. His last job had been with a travel publisher. While there, Robyn had helped launch an online travel service that incorporated the travel publications the publisher was known for and a number of new and emerging luxury travel services offered to an upscale clientele, so he had experience in this area and had something to offer. Although Robyn didn't know much about investing or financial services, he knew a lot about how to market ideas and services.

The team included people from across the company—account executives, financial analysts, customer support, and web designers. The website offered upscale customers advice on the stock market, investing, and other financial services the company specialized in. The team members came from across the company and represented most of the company's locations and all aspects of the company's business. Most of the people serving on the team had been with the company for years. Robyn, who had only been with the company for a few months, was surprised and pleased when they elected him the team leader at the first meeting. He had shown the website he worked on at his previous company to give everyone an idea of what he was bringing to the table. And it seemed that everyone was enthusiastic about what he had to offer. Now, Robyn was beginning to think that the enthusiasm his team members had shown was simply relief that they had someone to pawn all the work off on. In the past month, Robyn had reviewed the current website and drafted a detailed plan of the changes that were needed to make the

old website easier to use and more accessible to the market. He created a list of the sites that their website should be linking to and drafted a plan for getting links for their site on other prominent websites that catered to their client base. And he created a marketing plan for an official launch of the website services, something that wasn't done when the website was originally launched. All of these efforts were met with enthusiasm, but Robyn seemed to be the only member of the team doing anything. To add insult to injury yesterday at the biannual company meeting, May Chien, the vice president of sales and marketing, congratulated the "team" for coming up with a plan that significantly enhanced the website and increased subscriptions 12 percent in the last three months alone. Robyn was stunned as the other members of the team rose to accept the applause offered to them. After the meeting, a couple of people from the team shook his hand and slapped him on the back, but no one acknowledged that Robyn had been the person who did all the work.

We have included the example of Robyn because team equity tends to be one of the biggest issues for those working in a team. Team members often complain that either one or two people end up doing the majority of the work or that there is one team member who refuses to carry his or her weight. Did Robyn bring the situation on himself by jumping in and carrying the bulk of the load? Were there things Robyn could have done differently to encourage the participation of others? Should the members of the team acknowledge that Robyn did the bulk of the work? How would you have handled the situation? Would you ask your boss for recognition or would you simply let the situation go and try to learn from it?

- the time frames involved (deadlines, how long the problem has been going on, and so forth)
- the relevant facts gathered during the fact-finding phase
- a brief summary of the alternative solutions and the criteria used to weigh the alternatives
- the recommended solution, including the cost, resources, and time frames required to implement the solution

DELIVERING: AS A TEAM

Most people think that teamwork is delivered primarily in formal meetings. However, organizations increasingly realize that meetings drain resources and time. Most informal team communication occurs in clusters of team members working around someone's computer or at a whiteboard. In addition to formal meetings and presentation, teamwork is delivered using:

- memos and reports
- staff briefings and weekly sessions
- planning and problem-solving meetings
- virtual meetings
- conferences, workshops, and seminars

Let's examine each of these delivery methods in more detail.

MEMOS AND REPORTS

With the rise in popularity of e-mail and its prevalence in organizations, most memos and reports are delivered online. In fact, we cannot remember the last time someone handed us a paper copy of a memo or report. One of the benefits of conveying reports and memos online is that it allows the reader to determine if the information needs to be printed, thus reducing the daily paper load. Another advantage is that information gets to the recipient quickly and responses are generally received quickly.

Memos Memos are quick snippets of information. They should focus on one concept, and the information in them should be direct and easy to follow. The format for memos is fairly standard, but memos should allow for style variations that reflect the information relayed. An example of an e-mail memo is show in Figure 9.4 on page 203.

Reports Reports convey detailed information about a topic or a group of related topics. In today's busy organizations, few people have the time or the desire to read a long, detailed report. Before you begin drafting a detailed report, ask yourself the following questions:

- Who is my audience?
- What do they need to know?

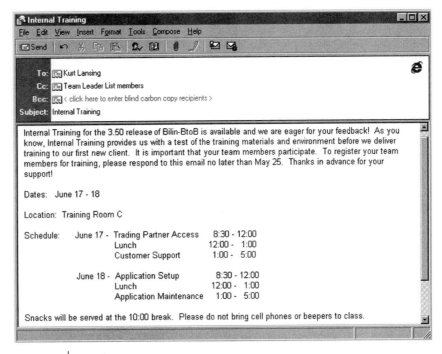

FIGURE 9.4 | SAMPLE ELECTRONIC MEMO

- How will they use the information I am providing?
- When will the action need to occur?
- Am I including information that is irrelevant to or unnecessary for my audience?

Depending on its length and intended audience, a business report may include the following elements:

- cover page
- executive summary
- table of contents
- list of illustrations (usually included in technical or scientific reports)
- abstract (usually included in technical or scientific reports)
- text (should be seven to twelve pages long)
- references
- appendixes

STAFF BRIEFINGS AND WEEKLY SESSIONS

The most common type of meeting in a business or professional setting is the weekly staff briefing. Generally, these group meetings are organized for the purposes of sharing information and making plans for organizing work. They are typically held in a conference room, with each group member seated around a large table. Meeting leaders should do the following:

- provide an agenda for the meeting in advance.
- call the meeting to order.
- follow the agenda and not allow the meeting to get off course.
- acknowledge the efforts of team members.
- ask questions.
- recap the main points.
- recap points of consensus.
- make assignments.

The briefing or staff meeting ends when the leader, manager, or facilitator terminates it. In most cases, these meetings occur on an established schedule (for example, Mondays at 9:00 a.m. or Wednesdays at noon).

PLANNING AND PROBLEM-SOLVING MEETINGS

Most organizations recognize planning and problem-solving meetings as an important part of their everyday operations. Planning sessions are held to create a shared vision and mission, to establish core business values, and to organize the development, manufacturing, marketing, and delivery of new services or products. Problem-solving meetings are used when gaps appear between the organization's vision or core values and the actual daily operation of the business, or when a particular issue arises that may negatively influence the development, marketing, manufacturing, or delivery of the service or product. (The elements of a problem-solving meeting were detailed in the section on Coordinating the Problem-Solving Process, page 271.)

VIRTUAL MEETINGS

Virtual meetings (for example, videoconferencing, networks, telephone conference calls, and online chat) may occur across a wide geographical space. They use technology as the principal delivery system. They may include members of your team, members of cross-functional teams, vendors, suppliers, or customers. As the technology for virtual meetings has improved, the reasons and possibilities for conducting virtual meetings have increased.

Virtual meetings may not be defined by the standards applied to traditional face-to-face meetings. In virtual meetings you may find the following to be true:

- Members include people from inside and outside the organization.
- Teams using virtual meetings may form, break up, and reform as a need arises.
- Participants in virtual meetings have reporting responsibilities to different parts of the organization.
- Participants in virtual meetings may have goals and objectives that are different from or at odds with the goals and objectives of other participants.

In order to be successful, participants of virtual meetings and teams need to follow these guidelines:

- It isn't the technology that should influence the team, but rather the way the technology is used and for what purpose.
- Avoid substituting a virtual meeting for a face-to-face meeting if the face-to-face meeting is possible.
- If participants have multiple goals and objectives, the goals of a virtual meeting should be collaboration and communication rather than total agreement consensus.

CONFERENCES, WORKSHOPS, AND SEMINARS

Conferences are large group meetings designed to facilitate talk about a specific topic or area of common interest. Workshops and seminars are smaller group meetings designed to improve knowledge and skills associated with task performance.

Conferences, workshops, and seminars often make use of panel presentations as a preferred format or agenda. Panels of three to six participants or experts are assembled, and each panel member presents a brief individual talk before opening up the session for general questions and remarks from others in attendance. Seminars and workshops also make use of specialized formats, such as problem-solving and brainstorming techniques. Many divide time between brief oral overviews (usually accompanied by computer-assisted slideshows) of a skill or idea delivered by the seminar or workshop leader, followed by actual practice in that skill or application of the idea by the participants.

SUMMARY

In this chapter, we discussed the communication skills needed to be both an effective team member and leader. We discussed the difference between traditional and virtual teams and the skills needed to be a successful team member either on site or virtually. We placed these skills in the context of CCCD—choose, create, coordinate, and deliver. We examined the need to choose strategies that provide team leaders and members with ways to help the team accomplish its goals. We discussed creating a vision and objectives that allow team members to feel vested in the team and the organization. We looked at coordinating as a means for problem solving in teams and across teams. We talked about the importance of coordinating with all the teams within an organization. Finally, we discussed ways that teams deliver information both within the team and to outside team members.

BUSINESS AND PROFESSIONAL COMMUNICATION IN THE GLOBAL WORKPLACE ONLINE

All of the following chapter review materials are available in an electronic format on either the *Business and Professional Communication in the Global Workplace Online* Resource Center or the book's companion website. Online you'll find chapter learning objects, flashcards of glossary terms, InfoTrack® College Edition Activities, weblinks, quizzes, and more.

What You Should Have Learned

Now that you have read Chapter 9, you should be able to do the following:

- Understand the differences between groups and teams.
- Apply the eight strategies for effective team leadership.
- Apply strategies for effective participation in teams.
- Develop criteria for selecting team members.
- Discuss adaptive skills and behavioral flexibility as an adaptive communication skill.

- Develop agendas for team meetings.
- Discuss the concepts of vision, goals, and objectives and how they affect a team.
- Discuss the concepts of creativity and constraint in problem solving.
- Use the scientific method for team problem solving.
- Use brainstorming as a team skill.
- Determine the best method for delivering team communication.

Key Terms

adaptive skill *195*	jamming *190*	team *183*
agenda *192*	memo *202*	turf battles *183*
constraints *195*	objectives *185*	vision *193*
creativity *195*	report *202*	virtual meeting *204*
goal *185*	synergy *184*	virtual teams *188*

Writing and Critical Thinking

The following activities can be completed online or submitted to your instructor.

Choose one of the following activities:

1. Break into teams. Your assignment is to create a criteria list for team participation in a group presentation. Think about your experience in other groups and teams. What are your needs and expectations? How do they mesh with those of other members of your team? Generate criteria for your team that will balance the needs of the individual with the needs of the team.
2. Think about a leadership experience you have had. Write a paper discussing how you did or did not apply the eight strategies for becoming an effective leader. What would you have done differently, now that you have this information?
3. As a team, create a vision for your final presentation. Go through each of the stages of creating a vision. Share your vision

with the class. How are your visions similar?

4. As a team, develop a list of communication challenges each of you have experienced in another team and how the team dealt with it. Each team member is then to interview a person who leads a team in a business environment and find out the most challenging communication problems he or she encounters and how he or she deals with them. Compare the two lists for similarities and differences and generate a master list of team challenges and criteria for dealing with problems. Next, your team is to draw up an agreement that specifies the criteria for interacting as team members for the team project.

5. Think of a supervisor you have worked for whom you view as a leader and one you do not view as a leader. Write an essay describing the traits you found in the

leader but that the nonleader supervisor lacked. How did the leader approach decision making, delegation of tasks, and team communication? How many of the eight strategies identified in the chapter were evident or missing in each leader's communications? What are the most important lessons you have learned about team leadership as a

result of working under the two supervisors?

6. Your team has been invited by the administration department to give a presentation of life on your campus to visiting student candidates. Brainstorm with your team to develop visual aids that would accurately portray academic and social life on your campus.

PRACTICING COMMUNICATION IN PROFESSIONAL CONTEXTS

Problem Solving as a Team

Break into teams and solve the following problem using the any of the problem-solving tools provided in this chapter:

Student parking has been slashed by 25 percent because of an aggressive new campus building plan. Although everyone agrees the new buildings are necessary, a solution to the limited student parking must be found.

PRESENTATIONS AND PERSUASION

UNIT

5

Presentations in a Global Workplace

Public speaking is one of the most highly valued as well as one of the most highly feared activities engaged in by people around the globe. It is highly valued because effective speakers exemplify habits of mind and habits of character that are both intelligent and inspiring. They offer listeners useful information, calls to action, even entertainment, but they do so in a way that compels attention and respect.

That said, public speaking also often appears at the top of the list when people are asked what they most fear. But there is good news. While a fear of spiders and heights might take nerves of steel or years of therapy to overcome, for most people, a fear of public speaking is much easier to overcome once you develop the presentational skills discussed in this chapter.

For some, the task of public speaking is further complicated when you are presenting to a diverse global audience. But there is good news. What many people don't realize is that, whether you are speaking locally or globally, a little planning, organization, and preparation refocuses your attention away from your fear of speaking and onto your presentation.

There is a secret to effective and enjoyable public speaking. The secret is being *organized, prepared,* and *practiced.* Most people find that when they have organized their presentation properly and are thoroughly prepared and practiced, giving a speech becomes natural and a *fear-free,* or at least a far less fear-inducing, experience. As with the other types of communication we have discussed in previous chapters, we will refer to the CCCD process—choose, create, coordinate, and deliver—to help guide the development of your presentation and ensure a more positive outcome.

In this chapter, we focus on the components of informative and persuasive presentations in the global workplace and discuss the differences between informative and persuasive presentations. In addition, we show you how to design effective presentations using presentation software, such as Microsoft PowerPoint. By the end of this chapter you will have all of the tools you need to construct informative and persuasive presentations and to evaluate their success.

CHOOSING: THE GOAL FOR YOUR PRESENTATION

The first step for preparing a successful presentation is to choose the goal(s) and desired outcome(s) that will guide it. There are five components to choosing the goals for a business presentation. They are:

- selecting a speech purpose and type
- developing an audience profile
- establishing outcomes
- establishing your credibility
- developing criteria that allow you to measure success

We discuss each of these components in detail below.

SELECTING THE PURPOSE AND TYPE OF YOUR PRESENTATION

To determine your goal(s), you should ask the following questions:

- Are you trying to disseminate information?
- Or, are you trying to move people to action?

These questions help you determine the purpose of your presentation. If you answered "yes" to the first question, and the overall purpose of your presentation is to present straightforward facts to an audience, which will increase the audience's knowledge on a subject or train audience members for a specific task, then you will develop an **informative presentation.**

If, however, you answered "yes" to the second question and the overall purpose of your presentation is to instill sympathy, motive, or to influence your audience to act in a certain way, you will develop a **persuasive presentation.** Let's look at each type of presentation in more detail.

Informative Presentations Informative presentations explain or describe facts and information in an objective manner with the ultimate goal of educating listeners about a topic. Speakers presenting information in an informative manner *do not* pressure their audience to make a decision, take an action, or change a position.

There are three types of formats used for informative presentations: briefings, reports, and training presentations. Each format has specific uses, preferred lengths of speaking time, and other considerations (e.g., physical location, organizational context, number of people in the audience, availability of support for laptop or visuals, etc.) that allow you to make choices about how to present and support your topic.

Briefings allow a speaker to disseminate a concise number of facts in a short amount of time. Briefings are best used when it is important to get information out quickly so that it can be acted upon. Generally, you do not need to go into the history, background, or impetus of a project or a problem because people are already familiar with the situation.

For example, if an engineer needs to update the members of his team on the progress he has made on a project, he would use the briefing format.

Briefings are:

- short—generally lasting between 5–15 minutes
- concise—covering one specific aspect of a topic in a concise manner
- oral—while you can use presentation software like PowerPoint, generally it isn't necessary
- non-contextual—more often than not, the audience for a briefing will be familiar with the context of the topic

Reports allow a speaker to introduce and explain information over an expanded period. Reports are best used when information needs to be presented in greater detail or when background, history, and context, are required by the audience.

For example, if an HR manager is introducing insurance options for employees, and each option has a number of components that people need to know about before they make a decision, the best format would be a report. In this format, rather than simply stating the new policy, as one would do in a briefing, the HR manager can *explain the costs, comparative advantages, and benefits* of the options and compare and contrast the policy with existing policies. The HR manager might also want to prepare (a) a PowerPoint presentation to go along with the oral presentation and/or (b) handouts for employees to review at their convenience.

Reports are:

- longer—generally lasting between 15 minutes and one hour (reports lasting longer than one hour should be rare and broken into discrete segments with scheduled breaks)
- multifaceted—covering one or more related topics or multiple aspects of a single topic
- oral and visual—usually include a PowerPoint presentation or a handout of relevant materials
- contextual—may require providing the audience with a review of the history, background, or impetus of a project or a problem

Training presentations are most often used when participants require examples, exercises, and practice to grasp the information being presented. Training often occurs over a period of hours or days and is usually accompanied by a visual component and extensive supplementary materials, which can be accessed online and/or in hardcopy.

Many organizations are turning to e-Learning, or electronic learning systems, to deliver training presentations to geographically dispersed employees and customers. If a company does not have the ability to gather all of its employees from locations across the globe for a training session, the company may opt for an informative briefing or report alerting employees about a new software package or sales plan. The briefing or report then may be delivered via the web or through teleconferencing. Following the initial meeting the company would provide e-Learning activities and training presentations so that employees have an opportunity to learn how to use the software or perform according to the sales plan. A training presentation is:

- long—often running from an hour to several days
- focused on learning—it covers the information needed to master a new process, software, or concept

- oral and visual—it usually includes presentation software and may require printed training materials
- contextual—it may require a brief review of the history, background, or impetus of a project or a problem that the new process, software, or concept is designed to help

If you find that an informative presentation does not fit your purpose, you should investigate the components and goals for persuasive presentations, discussed next.

Persuasive Presentations   The purpose of a persuasive presentation is to lead the members of the audience to make a decision, to change their minds, or to encourage them to take action. Speakers who need to persuade their listeners use different kinds of arguments and appeals to strengthen the power of their presentation. Persuasive presentations may incorporate more than one type of appeal or argument in the presentation.

There are three ways to appeal to an audience: logical appeals, emotional appeals, or appeals based on one's status, celebrity, or character. Each appeal has specific advantages and uses.

Logical appeals use facts and figures, as well as cite authorities already widely accepted by the audience to bring them to an understanding of the problem or situation and what action should be taken. If a logical appeal is well-crafted, it will also increase the ethos (character) of the speaker. For example, the movie *An Inconvenient Truth* relies on a logical appeal, presenting scientific data using a series of charts, graphics, and quotes to build the case for global warming and what action needs to be taken to save the planet. It relies on the character of the presenter, Al Gore. In turn, the logical appeal of the movie increases the ethos of the movie's narrator.

Emotional appeals are those that appeal to the audience's emotions or sympathies. These appeals are usually delivered passionately and are tied to the underlying values of the audience. For example, a mother who has lost a child in a drunk-driving accident, and who uses that accident to make her case while speaking to teens about drinking and driving is relying on an emotional appeal. The mother is passionate about the topic and the audience shares an underlying value that drunk driving is wrong. In this example, because the speaker has direct experience with the tragedy of losing a child to drunk driving, she would also be making an argument based on her *character*.

Character appeals rely on the reputation and experience of the speaker to build a foundation for the appeal. Character appeals are generally made by those who are recognized as experts in a particular field, or by those who are extremely knowledgeable on a particular subject. However, they may also be derived from cultural heroes and celebrities, if the person's status as a hero or celebrity *is directly relevant to the topic*. Character appeals may be subtle or the speaker might cite educated opinions and expertise to make a more overt appeal to the audience. For example, a well-renowned cardiac surgeon speaking to a group about heart disease and what action needs to be taken to prevent the disease is making a character appeal. The surgeon may also employ a logical appeal by citing statistics, facts, and other recognized sources. Similarly, a well-known celebrity who suffered a heart attack and whose public stance about heart disease is well established may also be employed as support for the claims being advanced.

Once you have decided if your presentation is informative or persuasive, and have chosen the format or types of appeal(s) you will use, the next step is to create an audience profile so you can customize your presentation to your audience's needs and expectations.

DEVELOPING AN AUDIENCE PROFILE

An early step in organizing a presentation is to develop an audience profile. This step is particularly important with global audiences because you want them to get the most out of your presentation. A good audience profile allows you to:

- determine the needs and expectations of the audience
- establish the desired outcomes for each audience
- determine the best way to establish credibility with your audience
- establish criteria by which you can measure your success after the presentation

Each of these concepts is discussed below in greater detail.

Audience Needs and Expectations   The needs and expectations of an audience and those of the speaker are rarely the same. Do not make the mistake of assuming that your own needs, as the speaker, should come first. They do not. After all, you are not trying to educate or convince yourself. Instead, the focus must be primarily on the needs and expectations of your audience.

By taking into account the needs and expectations of your audience while you prepare, *your* primary need—to make a successful presentation—will be met. Successful communicators recognize that although it is important to know what you personally expect to get out of giving a presentation, it is even more important to understand what your listeners expect to gain from listening to your presentation. As in every other aspect of doing business, meeting the needs of your customers or clients should be a primary goal.

An audience assessment should include the answers to the following questions:

Audience needs—What does the audience need from me? Does the audience require that I display a certain level of expertise before they can accept my presentation? Or is there another form of credibility that is important to this audience?

Audience expectations—Is the audience expecting to receive information? Or do they need to learn that action needs to be taken, and how to act? Do they expect me to stick to the facts or do they expect me to sympathize with them? Do they want a short precise presentation or a presentation with more detail? Do they expect to learn something? Or do they expect to be motivated in some way?

Audience history—Has anyone in my firm or company presented to this audience before? What can I learn from that person about my audience? What ideas and strategies have worked in the past with this particular audience?

Audience authority—What reasons, authorities, examples, and "truths" does this audience regularly refer to, to justify a position or explain their goals? Do I have friends or business contacts who might have valuable information to add?

Audience research—What information can I gain from outside sources that will help me better understand my audience? Do any recent publications quote or feature the people, department, or organization? Does the group that I am speaking to maintain a website with useful information about their culture and values?

Collecting information about an audience's needs and expectations allows you to determine how your audience might evaluate your presentation. Once you have gathered this information you can:

- develop your presentation in a way that will satisfy the needs and expectations of your audience
- adjust your presentation to the cultural values or norms of your audience
- anticipate areas of concern or disputes you might not have considered without the audience profile

After you assess the needs and expectations of the audience, the next step is to establish outcomes for your presentation.

ESTABLISHING OUTCOMES

Outcomes are what you want to achieve as a result of your presentation. What do you want your listeners to know, believe, or do after listening to your presentation? In an informative presentation, the outcomes you are working toward should be to educate or inform. Additionally, you can work toward outcomes that increase your credibility or reputation as well as provide useful and necessary information for audience members. For example, if you are a broker charged with educating your company's clients about a change in the tax rules governing specific investments, the outcomes you are working toward may be to:

- educate your audience on the tax changes
- ensure your audience understands the differences between the old and new tax laws
- assure clients that the company is aware of the changes and is on top of the tax laws
- enhance your own credibility as a resource for applying or interpreting these tax changes

If you find your goal is to convince or persuade audience members, then you need to consider persuasive presentation outcomes. For example, if your company needs to choose between two software programs for a new initiative and you believe that one is better than the other, you may need to convince the group to adopt that program. The outcomes you may be working toward are to:

- explain the differences between the software programs
- demonstrate the weaknesses of the other program
- demonstrate the strengths of your program
- make a logical appeal with your demonstrations
- enhance your credibility as a knowledgeable resource on this topic

Once you have your presentation outcomes, you need to determine the best way to establish or enhance credibility with your audience. Five ways to establish credibility are described below.

ESTABLISHING CREDIBILITY

Both types of presentations—informative and persuasive—rely on the credibility of the speaker to be truly effective. **Credibility** is derived from a speaker's perceived status, believability, and trustworthiness with an audience. If a speaker has high credibility, the audience will likely feel that they can believe the information presented to them, and that they can trust the speaker to provide all of the important facts. If a speaker demonstrates low credibility, his or her message is easily dismissed.

A speaker develops credibility with the audience by demonstrating knowledge of a subject and a positive presence as a speaker. There are five ways to establish credibility:

- education
- expertise
- empathy
- enthusiasm
- appearance

Let's take a look at how each of these areas contribute to a speaker's perceived credibility and which form of credibility works for an informative versus a persuasive presentation.

Education   Education includes your formal education, the workshops, seminars, and, courses you have attended, as well as any specialized training you have received. Degrees, honors, and awards also fall into this category. It is not necessary to give a laundry list of *all* of the accolades you have received, nor do you need to recite your entire résumé to your audience to build your credibility. If your resume is extensive, you run the risk of boring your audience or alienating those who feel you are being vain or self-indulgent.

Instead, refer only to the education that is *directly* related to the topic of your presentation. For example, an accountant who is trained in CPR does not need to tell her audience about her education in accounting if she is instructing them in CPR. Nor, would she inform an audience attending an accounting seminar that she is trained in CPR because it would not be relevant.

Education is a source of credibility for both informative and persuasive speakers.

Expertise   Expertise includes your length of time in a particular field or with a specific company. When talking about expertise, you should include research or conference panels you have participated in, articles or books you have written, projects (individual and group) where you made a significant contribution, and any other experience that is directly related to your topic. In some cultures, education is valued more than expertise; in others, the reverse might be true.

Most of the time, presenting a well-balanced mix of education and expertise will help establish your credibility with your audience. As with education, less is often more. It is not necessary to recite every paper, panel, or project you have contributed to. Today, it is not uncommon for people to have three to five careers over their lifetimes. You should pick and choose, selecting those experiences that highlight your knowledge, but not so many that you appear arrogant, flighty, or unorganized. For example, a woman who starts her professional life as a third-grade school teacher and then goes back to school to become a lawyer, should not refer to her time as a schoolteacher in a legal presentation unless her experience as a teacher was relevant to the presentation and enhances her credibility with the audience.

Expertise is a source of credibility for both informative and persuasive speakers.

Empathy   Empathy involves demonstrating to an audience that you have their best interests in mind or that you understand, perhaps share, and always respect the experiences they have in relation to the topic. In some cultures, developing empathy may first require that you establish rapport with the audience. **Rapport** is created by showing sympathetic understanding, emotional affinity, or mutual trust for the concerns of the audience. In any case, you have to make it clear that the information you are presenting is useful and important to your audience and you should make it clear that you understand their goals.

Building common ground, or demonstrating shared goals, can go a long way in accomplishing credibility through empathy. For example, a doctor speaking to an audience of diabetics about a new device for glucose monitoring could create rapport with his audience by disclosing that he too is a diabetic, and struggles daily to control his diabetes.

Empathy is a source of credibility best reserved for persuasive speakers. A note of caution: if you use empathy to boost your credibility, the empathy you display should be genuine and based in truth!

Enthusiasm   Actively showing an audience that you are interested in and excited about the information you are presenting is what enthusiasm is all about. That interest is reflected in your tone of voice, your facial expressions, your gestures, and body movement. Enthusiasm is contagious and can help engage and energize your audience. When you successfully engage and energize your audience, your credibility as a speaker is increased. Think of it in this way: If you don't care about your topic, why should your audience? If you aren't excited by it, why should they be?

That said, enthusiasm can be interpreted in different, and not always positive, ways. Be sure to understand your audience and their expectations of you before being overly enthusiastic. For example, an inventor who is presenting his creation to a group of potential investors needs to be enthusiastic about his invention and the possibilities it creates. An overly-enthusiastic training manager teaching nurses about a new procedure for taking blood might appear ghoulish.

Enthusiasm is a source of credibility best reserved for persuasive speakers. Showing mild enthusiasm in an informative presentation is fine, but displaying more than mild enthusiasm might be interpreted by your audience as subtle persuasion.

Appearance   Finally, dress for the show. Appearance—whether we like it or not—is not only important, but is often one of the first things our audience evaluates. Appearance includes choices made about clothing, hair, makeup, nails, shoes, habits, etc. It includes all of the nonverbal physical cues you send to your audience before, during, and after you speak.

If the majority of your audience consists of successful business leaders who are likely to show up for your presentation neatly groomed in standard business attire, you might have difficulty gaining credibility if you arrive un-showered and in torn jeans, a band t-shirt, and flip-flops. On the other hand, if you are hosting a seminar for a group of young, newly admitted college students, you could safely lean toward more casual attire.

How an audience interprets your appearance can vary from culture to culture. If you are speaking to global audiences and are unsure what to wear, it is better to dress more conservatively and professionally rather than to take a chance that "business casual" is acceptable.

Dress can also vary from climate to climate. For example, we have a friend who is a top attorney at an international law firm based in San Diego, California. He wears a suit when he goes to court and when he is in the Washington D.C., New York, or London offices, but when he is in the San Diego office, he wears khakis and a golf shirt. In San Diego, business casual is acceptable on an everyday basis; in Washington, D.C., it is not. In the United States, business casual attire is common and widely acceptable in all but a few business environments; however, in the United Kingdom, business casual dress is less common and frowned on in many business environments.

- Appearance can be a source of credibility for both informative and persuasive speakers. An unkempt appearance or outfit that does not meet the expectations of your audience can detract from the credibility of both informative and persuasive speakers.

GLOBAL PROFILE FOR SUCCESS—KEYNOTE SPEAKER SPANS THE GLOBE

Gerald Celente, founder and director of the Trends Research Institute and renowned public speaker, travels the globe and discusses trends for global business. In order for businesses to get ahead in the global marketplace, action rather than reaction is key. According to *The Economist*, Celente now heads a group of 25 experts whose range of specialties would rival many university faculties.

Celente and his associates regularly deliver keynote addresses and seminar presentations at business, government, professional, and academic conferences worldwide. In order to be successful and reach global audiences, Celente and his associates must establish their credibility, have clear goals, create a localized message, coordinate with members of the conference planning committees, and deliver an informative and engaging message that helps each respective organization reach its global business goals.

Explore Trends Research Institute's website: http://www.trendsresearch.com/.

What can you learn about presenting to global audiences from the Trends Research Institute website?

DEVELOPING CRITERIA TO MEASURE SUCCESS

A list of criteria for success allows you to gauge whether you have accomplished your goals. What feedback will your audience give you if the presentation is a success? What feedback might you receive if the presentation is a failure? It is important to establish measurable outcomes so that you know if your presentation is successful. The **S.M.A.R.T.** method allows you to align your outcomes with criteria for success that are specific, measurable, achievable, realistic, and time-bound. Each component is described below:

Specific   Think of who, what, where, when, why, and how. Specific goals can answer all of these questions. It isn't enough to simply say, "I want to do a good presentation." For example, your outcomes should focus on meeting with your clients on the appointed day and time to inform them about the changes in the tax laws so that they retain their confidence in the firm and your company's ability to handle their investments.

Measurable   How will you measure your progress? How will audiences let you know they appreciate the information? This might occur with client retention or it might be through the specific feedback you receive from your clients.

Achievable   Set achievable outcomes that match your goals. If your goal is to inform, it is unrealistic to expect the outcome to be a substantial increase in sales. An achievable goal might be business retention or an increase in trust between your clients and their brokers.

Realistic   Make sure that the goals you set are realistic. In order to be realistic, you need to be sure that you have all of the tools and resources you need to achieve the outcome. Striving to increase customer loyalty with an informative presentation that focuses on sharing information is realistic, striving to increase investments by 25 percent is not.

Time-Bound   When will you know that you have reached your goal or achieved the outcome you hope to achieve? Outcomes are generally obvious within a short period of time: a few days, weeks, or at the longest a month. Goals may take longer to reach.

The chart on the following page provides an example of a completed goal chart for a presentation on changes in tax laws.

Purpose Inform clients about a change in tax laws that might affect their investments.

Type Informative Presentation

Objective Report that explains the current law, the new law, and the types of investments that are impacted by the change.

Audience	Needs and Expectations	Outcomes	Credibility	Criteria
Existing clients	• Become informed about changes in the tax laws without any pressure to take any immediate action. • Gather as much information as possible, in the shortest amount of time, from an informed source.	• Receive information about the new tax changes in a non-pressure environment. • Be able to make confident and informed decisions about their investments. • Feel that their investments are in the hands of knowledgeable and informed advisors.	• Education • Expertise • Appearance	• Not being surprised by tax changes or the result. • Feeling as if those they entrust to take care of their investments are forthcoming about information. • Walking away from the presentation with more answers than questions.
Brokerage firm	• Introduce the tax changes to clients. • Gain the client's confidence in the firm's expertise and ability to handle their investments after the changes take place.	• Increased client loyalty to the firm. • Retain clients after the tax changes take place. • Receive positive feedback from clients after the meeting.	• Education • Expertise • Appearance	• Having few (if any) clients leave the firm after hearing about the tax changes. • Not having to spend individual time with more than a handful of clients after the presentation. • Not receiving complaints after the tax changes that clients were uninformed or misled about the changes and the impact on their investments.
Speaker	• Make a professional presentation that is well received by both the clients and the other brokers in the audience. • Make a favorable impression on the boss and stand out a bit from the other brokers at his level.	• Having my boss be happy with the presentation. • Receiving positive feedback from my fellow brokers. • Receiving positive feedback from clients.	• Not applicable	• Not receiving questions from the audience that reflect that the material was not adequately covered. • Having a feeling of confidence and calm after the presentation. • Not second-guessing the information, delivery, or style of the presentation.

CASE STUDY 9 | DEVELOPING A PROFILE FOR MULTIPLE AUDIENCES

After three years as an investment broker at an investment firm with offices around the globe, Gerald was asked to develop a presentation about a new product for the brokers located in the company's offices in the U.S., Europe, and Japan. Gerald's goal was to inform the brokers about the retirement investment program the company was offering. The product would be tailored to fit the needs of clients in each location, but the bulk of the product could be adopted with just a few changes. Gerald was picked to present the new program because he spoke Spanish, French, and Japanese and had served on the team that developed the new product offering.

While Gerald felt honored to be asked to present the program to his fellow brokers and was excited to be traveling to the company's offices abroad, he knew there was a lot at stake. This was his first international assignment and the first opportunity he had to use both his language skills and his knowledge of the company and its products. This assignment was also challenging because he had to find a way to present information about the new plan so different audiences would understand.

Gerald knew he had to take a step back before creating the presentation itself and learn more about the audiences he would be presenting to. Instead of concentrating on what made each audience different, Gerald thought it made more sense to design one presentation that focused on what the audiences had in common. He made a list of the audiences' common characteristics. They were:

- savvy, experienced brokers
- very busy people with short attention spans
- listeners who would not respond well to being bored or talked down to

He felt that the overall tone of his presentation would be crucial, and decided that an informative briefing—rather than a long, boring report or training session—would be the best way to disseminate the information.

After a good bit of preparation, Gerald went off to Japan to deliver his first presentation. Because he would have to go straight from the airport to the office, Gerald thought it made sense to dress in khakis, a button-down shirt, and a jacket, opting to be comfortable on the long flight but presentable for his audience.

When he walked into the expansive boardroom of the Tokyo office, he realized that everyone was in full business attire, and neatly groomed and pressed. Gerald, on the other hand, appeared rumpled and casual. "Maybe," he thought, "I should have planned my flight better so I could have put on a fresh suit. Oh, well, it won't matter how I'm dressed if my presentation goes well." But halfway through the presentation, it was obvious that things were not going as Gerald had planned. Gerald felt that his audience did not respect him, and that he might have made a mistake in his assessment of them. The Tokyo brokers seemed put off by his presentation. They quickly left the room after Gerald had finished, avoiding eye contact, and not bothering to thank him for coming so far to talk to them.

When Gerald got back to the home office, his boss called him in to share some of the feedback he had received from the brokers in Japan. Most of the brokers who attended his presentation had decided not to begin pushing the new retirement option. They felt that they didn't have enough information to discuss the program and, because Gerald had spent so little time on the presentation, they felt the product might not be ready. "I don't understand. I spent a lot of time preparing for the presentation. What went wrong?" Gerald asked. "Well," his boss said, "It sounds to me like you approached the Japanese brokers like you would have approached brokers working in the American office. Here, the concept of a retirement plan is nothing new, but the brokers in the Asian office need more context." Gerald was floored. He had spent so much time focusing on what the audiences had in common, he had completely missed their differences and what each needed from the presentation.

We have included the example of Gerald in the following case study to highlight how important it is to develop an audience profile when you are presenting to global audiences. In Gerald's initial profile, he did an adequate job examining what his audiences had in common, but failed to realize how they might be different. Although not all differences have an impact on a presentation, Gerald's mistake cost his company potential sales and revenue. In addition, his poor audience assessment led to the unfortunate consequence of a poorly received presentation, which caused him to lose face with his boss.

CREATING: THE BUSINESS PRESENTATION

Once you have set your goals and assessed your audience, it is time to begin creating your message. When you create any presentation—persuasive or informative—it is important to follow a sound organizational structure. The organizational structure for a presentation contains the following components:

- a clear purpose
- a thesis statement
- a preview
- main points and subpoints
- support for each point
- transitions from one main point to the next
- an effective introduction and conclusion

PURPOSE AND THESIS STATEMENT

As we have learned, one of the most important aspects of developing a presentation is having a clear and articulated purpose in mind. The purpose of your presentation should reflect the goals and audience profile developed using the information provided earlier. Boiling this information down into a **purpose statement** allows you to define the primary goal for your message. You can then use the purpose statement to write the **thesis statement**, which is a simple declarative sentence that:

- introduces your audience to your message
- announces your intentions

In most business and professional contexts, the thesis statement sets up expectations that the listeners will use to evaluate the effectiveness—and the truthfulness—of the message. For this reason, it is vital that you craft your thesis statement carefully because it will guide the remainder of your presentation. For example, if you have determined that your goal is to encourage people between the ages of 18 and 24 to vote in an upcoming state election, your purpose statement might read: My presentation will provide new voters a reason to go to the polls by telling them what is at stake and getting them excited about the power of exercising their vote. Your thesis statement might read: Tonight, I will share with you some of the reasons it is important that you vote and how casting your vote in the upcoming election can change our state and your future.

DETERMINING THE MAIN POINTS OF THE MESSAGE

Generally speaking, business and professional presentations contain two to five major points. The number of points depends on the organizational pattern that best accomplishes your purpose. However, research demonstrates that if you use more than four main points, chances are very good your listeners will forget some of them and much of your message (Ehninger, 1974). Let's examine the relationship between your choice of organization pattern and the number of main points that work best with each structure.

There are four basic organization patterns speakers use to structure a business presentation:

- **cause/effect**—offers a cause and its resulting effect
- **problem–solution**—states a problem and then offers one or more solutions
- **chronological**—details the sequence of events
- **topical**—follows topically from the main idea through a logical topical sequence

Some thesis statements naturally lend themselves to causal or problem–solution reasoning. Others require a chronological sequence that provides a historical overview and the development of an idea. Others suggest that a logical series of topics be presented to guide listeners' understanding. When you outline your presentation, you should try different organization patterns to determine which one is best. Sometimes it isn't clear which pattern will work for the information you are presenting or which is best suited for your audience.

ORGANIZATIONAL PATTERNS FOR MESSAGES

Basic Organizational Patterns

Two Main Points	Three Main Points	Four Main Points
Causal Pattern	Chronological	Topical
• Cause>>>Effect	• Past	• Basic idea
Problem—Solution	• Present	• Implementation of the idea
• Problem>>>Solution	• Future	• Budget for implementation
		• How it all works

Now that you have determined your organizational structure, you can begin to lay out the main points of your presentation. Use the table above to determine how many points you will have, and the order in which your points should appear. Each of your main points may require sub-points and support. We discuss how to develop support for your sub-points later in this chapter. The outline below shows an example of how to structure your main points and sub-points.

I. Main Point 1

    (a) Sub-point

        Support

    (b) Sub-point

        Support

II. Main Point 2

    (a) Sub-point

        Support

(b) Sub-point

    Support

(c) Sub-point

    Support

OUTLINING, DRAFTING, OR COMPLETING A PRESENTATION

One of the most frequently asked questions we get about doing presentations is, "How far do I go? Should I just do an outline, write a draft, or write a finished and polished presentation?"

And the answer is it depends. How much you need to prepare for a presentation depends on:

1. How well you know your subject—if you are extremely familiar with your subject and you are comfortable speaking about the topic, you may only need an outline. On the other hand, if you are just developing your knowledge of a subject and you're not comfortable speaking about your topic, you are better off completing a final draft of your presentation.

2. However, having a final draft of your presentation does not mean that you should read your presentation verbatim from your paper. The audience will know you are reading to them and unless you are particularly eloquent, they will begin to squirm. Later in this chapter, we will discuss delivering your presentation with confidence.

WRITING A PREVIEW

After you have determined an organizational structure and written out your main points and subpoints, you are ready to create a preview for your audience. A **preview** is a review of what you will be discussing in your presentation. A basic, but boring preview is as simple as:

> First, I will discuss the history of the Puritans in Leyden, Holland. Then I will discuss why the period the Puritans spent in Leyden is no longer discussed in the historical record. Finally, I will explain why it is important to recapture this part of the history.

A better preview looks something like this:

> Few people know that the Puritans, who are also known as the Pilgrims or our founding fathers, spent twelve years in Leyden, Holland, before traveling on to the New World. After the Civil War, American historians felt it was important to develop a heroic story about the beginning of America that could be widely embraced and would begin to eliminate the rancor and division of the Civil War. The revised history of the Puritans began with the journey across the ocean not from Leyden, but from England, eliminating twelve years from their history. It is important to recapture the missing twelve years in the Puritan's history to shed light on why the Puritans ultimately decided to leave the safety and comfort of Europe and travel to the New World and begin life in an undeveloped and uncivilized country. Let us begin with the journey not from England to the New World, but from England to Leyden.

DEVELOPING SUPPORTING MATERIALS

Supporting materials add interest, visual impact, and credibility to your message. How many presentations, team meetings, or group discussions have you attended where the speaker droned on and on, mostly repeating the same points over and over and offering little support for his or her claims or ideas? Is it any wonder that the audience's attention began to wander shortly after the speaker began talking? In today's high-tech, visually driven world, few people will sit still long enough to listen to anyone who isn't an incredibly captivating speaker, or who doesn't use interesting and engaging graphics to support the message.

There is a difference between verbal and visual examples. **Verbal examples** are comparisons that help make a point within your presentation. **Visual examples** walk an audience through a complex concept, often with images or supplementary materials, such as handouts or PowerPoint slides.

However, just because you can have a graphic, does not mean that you need to use a visual example for every point or subpoint in your speech. In this section, we will discuss using the four types of verbal and visual support in your presentations. They are:

- examples and narratives
- facts and statistics
- authoritative sources
- visual cues

Examples and Narratives   Examples and narratives provide memorable elaboration for main points and subpoints. Although these can be an extremely effective form of support, they may require time to develop, a higher level of confidence on the part of the speaker, and a close, personal identification between listeners and the example or story.

Example and narratives require additional rehearsal time to find the most effective way to deliver the story. However, when used well, examples and narratives humanize information and build rapport between a speaker and an audience.

Speakers doing informative presentations should limit the use of personal examples or narratives to the attention-getting portion of the presentation or for their conclusions. To use examples and narratives effectively they should be:

- carefully chosen with regard to the cultural, professional, gender, racial, and socioeconomic considerations of your audience
- appropriate for the purpose and topic
- fresh rather than overused and trite examples

Authoritative Sources   Authoritative sources include research citations or testimonials by reputable sources that are recognized by your audience. Including a compelling citation in your presentation can lend authority and credibility to your talk. References should be used to clarify a point or to underscore the importance of a point. To use authoritative sources effectively they should be:

- from sources your audience will find credible

- tied directly to your topic—don't drop names simply for the sake of name-dropping
- short and to the point—don't use a long and confusing quote if one sentence will do

Facts and Statistics   Facts are pieces of basic, empirically verifiable information. **Statistics** are empirically verifiable information presented in the form of numbers, such as percentages and averages. By "empirically verifiable," we mean that the statistic or statements represented as facts are drawn from credible sources and can be verified by the audience.

Facts and statistics have benefits and drawbacks. If used effectively, they offer quick, credible support for your message. However, they are often overused. As a result, many people have developed the attitude that "you can find a statistic or fact to support any position" (which by and large is true). To use facts and statistics effectively and ethically, they should be:

- used when they are needed to clarify or strengthen your talk, not merely for shock value
- readily apparent and relevant to the point or subpoint you are making
- presented in a numerical format that can be easily understood by your audience
- presented as simply as possible, rather than in the form of complicated graphs and charts that take the focus away from what you are saying
- used only if they accurately reflect the type of information being presented

Visual Cues   The number one rule when designing any type of visual aid—but especially PowerPoint or Keynote presentations—is to remember that the visual aids are *supplements* to the talk, and do not represent nor take the place of the entire talk.

The biggest mistake you can make when employing visual aids is to cram every word you plan to say onto them and then read from them. This practice is especially bad if you turn your back to your audience *and* read directly from your visual aids. Not only will you bore your audience, you risk losing credibility. Many audiences find this type of presentation offensive and will shut down before the presentation has gotten very far.

FOCUS ON ETHICS

Too often presentations are given in which the speaker knowingly or accidentally exaggerates or inflates the significance of a statistic. This practice is often done for emphasis or dramatic effect designed to influence an audience.

What are the ethical consequences behind manipulating statistics? Is a small statistical "white lie" ever justified? What would you do if your boss or a coworker asked you to exaggerate the statistics used in your presentation?

Instead, think of visual cues as enhancements for your talk that, done creatively and correctly, enhance your credibility on the subject. **Visual cues** are the statements, quotes, or other information placed within the presentation to emphasize or strengthen a point. An audience may receive a message more clearly if they see the words or concepts as well as hear about them.

PowerPoint slides (or others drawn from other software packages) should be used sparingly and only for special emphasis. You do not need to have a slide for every fact, statistic, or citation you use in your presentation. Figures 10.1 and 10.2 are examples of how to use visual cues effectively in your presentations.

Start with a Blank Slate   Many people begin their PowerPoint presentation with a slide that displays the title or subject of the talk and the speaker's name. A typical reaction from the audience is a long groan accompanied by, "Not another PowerPoint presentation!" Before you have even begun to talk, your audience is preparing to be bored.

You can change the audience's expectations by using the following strategies:

1. Begin your talk with a blank screen.
2. Introduce yourself and your topic, stating the main points in an outline.
3. Bring up the first slide only when you reach a point in the talk that requires that visual aid.
4. When you have finished explaining the slide, bring up another blank screen, rather than leaving the last slide on the screen (which can be a distraction).

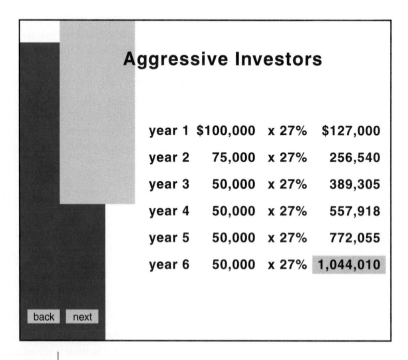

FIGURE 10.1

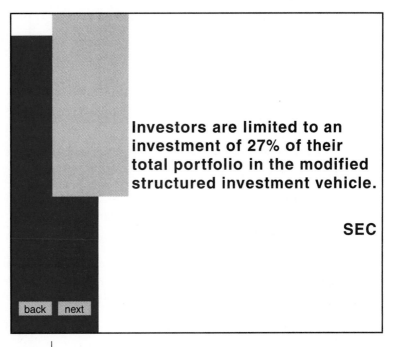

Investors are limited to an investment of 27% of their total portfolio in the modified structured investment vehicle.

SEC

back   next

FIGURE 10.2

5. Continue through the presentation, using the slides where necessary to *enhance* your talk, and using blank screens between visuals.

Used sparingly, your audience will take notice of the slides when you use them and will appreciate your ability to incorporate those visual enhancements into your presentation.

Limit the Number of Slides   One of the biggest mistakes a speaker can make when using presentation software is to have too many slides that contain too much information. Follow these basic rules:

- Use only one slide per main point or subpoint.
- Include no more than four to six lines of text on one slide—this can be one quote, three bullets that are two lines each, or one example.
- Remember that slides are used to enhance your talk, not replace it.

Use Transitions   PowerPoint programs typically use transitions to switch to a new slide. They range from simply replacing one slide with a blank screen to over-the-top explosions that break one slide into a million pieces that come back together to form the next slide, accompanied by annoying sound effects. Transitions should not be distracting or interfere with the verbal or visual message on the slide. Most business-people have seen so many slideshows that fancy transitions don't stun and amaze them anymore; they are just an annoying waste of time.

Here are the basic rules for transitions:

- Select one transition technique and stick to it all the way through the slideshow. "Cover left," for example, moves the new slide onto the screen from right to left, covering the previous slide.
- Keep whiz-bang transitions to a minimum, if they are used at all.
- Use blank slides while you are talking, so that the audience is not distracted by the slide for the previous point.

Use a Readable Font Size   Font size refers to the size of the lettering you are using for the text elements in your presentation. Choosing the right font size can make the difference between an effective presentation and a useless one; the words must be readable for the audience.

The chart below gives you an indication of the font size you need for the space you are presenting in.

Font typeface refers to the particular style of the text characters, such as Times New Roman or Arial. Simply put, use basic sans-serif fonts such as Arial or Helvetica. Sans-serif fonts (those without curly ends) are the most readable fonts from a distance. On paper, other fonts might be more attractive, but reading these on a screen thirty feet away is very difficult. As you get more proficient, you can try other fonts, but until you gain experience with them, sticking to Arial or Helvetica will ensure a clean, readable presentation.

TABLE 10.1	FONT SIZES
36 Point	This font size can be read from 5 feet away. Unless you are using an LCD projector, which actually magnifies your presentation, this font size is almost useless.
72 Point	This size font can be read from 10 feet away. You can get approximately 10 words of text on the slide using this font size.
144 Point	This size font can be read from 20 feet away. You can get approximately 3 words of text on the slide using this font size.

Use Colors Wisely   Developing your first presentation is not the time to discover your "inner artist." It is amazing how often people turn business presentations into ugly "works of art" that no one can read or really wants to look at. As with many other areas within the world of business communication, apply the acronym "KISS"—Keep it simple, stupid.

Just as is the case with transitions, color can and is often used incorrectly. Messy or cluttered slides are also distracting. Perhaps the most important thing to keep in mind when selecting color is that we all have our favorites; what one person likes, you might dislike, which makes neutral choices the best.

Color also introduces a readability issue. Although some colors work well together on paper, those relationships may not translate well to a light-based medium such as a computer screen. Listed below are a few basics for using color:

- Never use more than three colors per slide.
- Stick to the same three colors for the entire slideshow.

- Remember that white is a color.
- Ten percent of the population has red–green colorblindness, so unless these are the colors in your company's logo, you might want to avoid this combination.
- The greater the contrast between colors, the greater the readability. Using light colors such as white, pale gray, yellow, or cream on a dark background is more readable in a room where the lights will be dimmed.
- Use color to signal a key point or to highlight significant information.
- Use blocks of color to set off important information.

Use Clip Art Wisely   **Clip art** consists of all the prepackaged, ready-to-use pictures, cartoons, and graphics that people add to their presentations. When it comes to clip art, less is more—or better yet, use none at all. However, if you feel you must use clip art, here are some things to keep in mind:

- Use one style of clip art on all your slides. Don't switch from animation to pictures to graphics.
- Use clip art only if it enhances a given slide.
- Be very selective about the clip art you use. If you can't find exactly the right image, don't use anything.

The bottom line is that PowerPoint is a visual presentation aid that should be used to add emphasis, support a point, and build interest in your talk. Before using presentation software in front of an audience, practice your talk using your slides, preferably in front of a colleague or two who you trust to give you useful feedback.

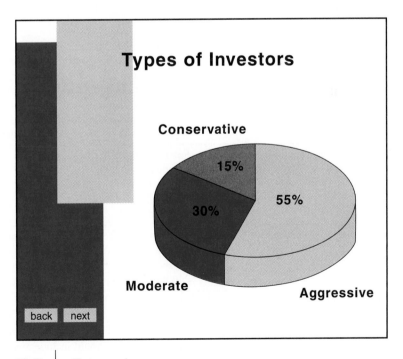

FIGURE 10.3 | TYPES OF INVESTORS

MAKING TRANSITIONS

Transitions connect one topic or point to another. Transitions are useful in presentations because they signal a change in the point being made or summarize what has been said and signal what is to come. Think of transitions as signposts that signal that one section of the presentation has ended and another is beginning.

While good transitions can enhance listeners' abilities to follow the progression of a presentation, poor transitions can lead to:

- Confusion—this occurs when a speaker moves to a new point, but a listener is still on the previous point because there was no transition.
- Boredom—this occurs when the speaker relies on the same transitional device, such as saying "Next, I will ..." over and over.
- Withdrawal—this occurs when a speaker relies on unplanned fillers, such as "okay," or "you know," or "well" rather than effective transitions.

To avoid these problems, good speakers make use of several types of transitional devices. These are shown in Table 10.2 below.

TABLE 10.2 | TYPES OF TRANSITIONAL DEVICES

When you need to:	Use this type of transition:
Introduce or preview topics in the speech	First, second, third One, two, three A, B, C
Signal topic changes in cause–effect, problem–solution, and chronology patterns during the body of the speech	"Now that we have seen how X occurred, let's examine its influences on Y." "Now that we understand the problem, it is time to explore solutions." "The past has provided us with X. The present has given us Y. If you are like me, you are wondering what the future holds."
Offer extended explanations of key definitions or ideas	For example... To illustrate... Simply put... Allow me to clarify... In other words...
Alert listeners to spatial relationships	Think of the face on a clock. At one o'clock we see X; at four o'clock we find Y; at eight o'clock we locate Z. To the east ... ; to the west... Alongside, behind, in front of, next to, below, above.
Remind your audience of your main points prior to moving to your recommendations	"We have seen that there are three causes of our problem. They are: one, which is caused by X; two, which is brought about by Y; and three, which is generated by Z. Now let's see what a solution should include and how we can work to implement it."

WRITING YOUR INTRODUCTION AND CONCLUSION

The beginning and ending of a presentation are uniquely interrelated: done well, an introduction and conclusion are circular. The conclusion should always tie back to the introduction so your audience feels that your presentation has come full circle.

An effective **introduction** achieves three main goals: 1) it gets your audience's attention, 2) it states your thesis or purpose statement, and 3) it previews what is to come. To come full circle, then, an effective **conclusion**: 1) summarizes your main points, 2) restates your thesis or purpose statement, and 3) ties back into the attention-getter used in your introduction.

Let's look at each part of the introduction and conclusion in more detail.

Attention-Getters   An attention-getter draws your audience into your presentation. For either informative or persuasive presentations, the attention-getter may be a startling statistic, an interesting fact, a quotation, or a question.

An attention-getter can be:

- an interesting question
- a startling statement or quotation
- a personal example that relates directly to the topic
- a story that develops suspense
- a funny story or a joke
- a captivating or a startling image

Thesis or Purpose Statement   The thesis statement provides a clear and concise articulation of the topic of your presentation.

Preview of the Main Points   A preview of the main points provides the audience with 2–4 signposts they can listen for throughout the presentation. The preview helps the audience know what to expect as well as provides them with a mechanism to help them stay on track with the flow of presentation, rather than wondering where you are headed or why you have moved in a particular direction.

Inducement   An inducement explains to the audience the benefits of listening to the presentation. An inducement describes what they will learn that they didn't know, or what they will be able to do that they couldn't do before listening to your presentation.

Review   A review recaps the main points of your presentation. It allows you to remind the audience what they have heard and allows them to walk away from the presentation with a brief mental summary of your presentation.

Closing   A closing signals that the presentation has come full circle and is ending. Truly effective presentations return to the story, example, statistic, quotation, or other attention-getting device used in the introduction. The "return to the beginning" nature of this strategy is designed to tie the presentation together for the

TABLE 10.3 | CREATING THE MESSAGE—COMPLETED PRESENTATION PLAN

Introduction

- Personal narrative about choosing an advertising agency and my experience starting with the firm.
- Thesis—I will present to you a concept that we believe will help you reach your product sales goals and open your product to additional markets, while remaining within the budget guidelines you specified.
- In this presentation, I will describe our concept and explain why we believe it will appeal to your target market. Next, I will provide a timeline of how we will implement the concept, which I'm sure you will find well within your prescribed parameters. Finally, I will answer any questions or discuss ideas you may have.
- After listening to my presentation, you will clearly see that our company has the ideas, the team, and the resources to make your product a success across America.

Main and Subpoints	Support	Transitions
• Concept • Connection to target market	• Concept—fact and examples • Two examples of successful campaigns from the same target market • Target market—statistics • Current numbers representing the size of the market and target demographics	• Introduction • Preview the flow of the talk • Concept • Simply put, the concept will allow us to reach the target market by...

• Timeline
  • October–January
  • February–April
  • May–August
	• Timeline—fact and examples
	• Which media we will use and examples of how they will be used at each stage in the campaign
		• Timeline
		• Now that you have seen the concept, I would like to take a few minutes to discuss the timeline.

• Total budget
  • Cost breakdowns by category
  • Justification for budget
	• Budget—statistics, authoritative sources, and examples
	• Total budget—statistical breakdown
	• Cost breakdown—statistical breakdown of each category and statements from clients illustrating the cost savings compared to other firms
	• Justification—review examples for each phase and show quality vs. cost
		• Budget—statistics, authoritative sources, and examples
		• Of course, a timeline this rigorous requires an investment...

• Request for questions • Request for business	• Questions and request for business—examples and personal narrative • Review examples to illustrate points brought up during the question period • Return to my experience with the firm, my clients, and why I think the concept and the firm are the best investment for the client	• Questions and request for business • Review main points • Return to introduction

SAMPLE SPEECH OUTLINE

Introduction
(A) Attention-getter
(B) Thesis or purpose statement
(C) Preview main points

Main Body
(A) Main point 1
    (a) Support 1
    (b) Support 2
    (c) Support 3

(B) Main point 2
    (a) Support 1
    (b) Support 2
(C) Main point 3
    (a) Support 1
    (b) Support 2

Conclusion
(A) Summarize main points
(B) Restate thesis or purpose statement
(C) End interestingly

audience and leave them with a satisfying ending. The least effective presentations start with a powerful attention-getter that is never woven into the presentation and leaves the audience wondering (hours or days later) why the presenter told a particular story or used a certain example.

You can organize your speech using Table 10.3 or using a traditional outline. An example of a speech outline is shown above.

COORDINATING: THE BUSINESS PRESENTATION

Conscious communication is mindful of the needs and expectation of others. When we say "others," we mean people beyond just the immediate audience; we refer to everyone who might be impacted by the communication event. Our friend Menyon, the director of technology for a large global apparel firm, made a statement that sums up the coordinating stage of conscious communication:

It doesn't matter if I am promoted, or if I look good, as long as the company can move ahead and meet its goals. As long as the company is moving ahead, I am moving ahead, because I own stock [and] have a stake in the company. My job is to ensure that everyone has the information they need to keep the company moving ahead.

Menyon's attitude epitomizes the "Three Musketeers" approach to communicating in organizations. She learned what some people never learn, that for a project to succeed is for her to succeed, that she doesn't work alone and therefore shouldn't keep information to herself. To be truly successful in today's business environment, Menyon learned that she must provide information to others who may be able to use it, gain feedback from them, and coordinate her communication efforts with their often diverse needs and expectations.

Her statement also recognizes that communication processes move a company forward. Without communication, Menyon's company—or any company—would come to a grinding halt. Sharing what we know (or what we are doing, or what we think was said or heard, or what direction we are taking on a big project or a group initiative) is vital for our own growth, as well as for the growth of the company.

Coordinating our communication also allows us to gain vital insight (feedback) that we cannot get working alone. Feedback tells us that we are on the right track and in sync with the goals and mission of the group, team, department, and company. It allows us to rehearse our message, to try it out on others before making a mistake. With corrective feedback, we learn to edit our errors, modify our information, and become more effective with others.

Finally, coordinating our communication means making sure everyone who should be included in a communication event is notified of the event, and, if possible, reminded again of it on the day it is to occur. This may mean broadly disseminating information and invitations about the presentation well in advance so people can clear their schedules. And, last but never least, it means asking for feedback from those who can help make a communication event successful.

Now that you have created your presentation, you should coordinate with those within your organization who can help you deliver the best presentation possible. It is always a good idea to have others look over your presentation to ensure that your information is correct and you have not forgotten or overlooked anything important. Additionally, if you are presenting to multiple audiences in multiple locations, be sure that your technical needs are met in each venue and that you have identified the number of audience members at each area, should you have handout materials to distribute at the presentation.

DELIVERING: THE BUSINESS PRESENTATION

The payoff for any presentation is successfully delivering in front of the intended audience. The first three components of the CCCD process—choosing, creating, and coordinating—ensure that you will have a professionally developed presentation with strong supporting materials. These steps will help you develop an interesting, informative, and structured message appropriate for your audience and aligned with their needs and expectations. However, even the best message, with strong verbal and visual support and clear goals, will suffer if delivered poorly. The last component in the CCCD process—delivery—begins with practice.

PRACTICE, PRACTICE, PRACTICE

How many times have you listened to someone speak and felt that his or her message was good, but that something was missing? Try as you might, you couldn't quite put your finger on it. Chances are good that what was missing was practice. Few of us are naturally eloquent. Fewer still feel really comfortable giving a speech without any practice—which is why practice is essential to delivering an effective message.

There are no research studies demonstrating an optimal amount of preparation and rehearsal time for presentations. However, most teachers of speech communication agree that the amount of practice time needed depends on these factors:

- the amount of prior speaking experience
- the number and complexity of presentational aids
- familiarity with the topic and audience
- confidence regarding speaking abilities
- the degree of formality for the occasion or context

Rehearsal of a message is not limited to presentational speaking. We have found that most people feel more confident if they practice a formal presentation at least three times before delivering it. For important presentations (those that will get you noticed within an organization), you may want to practice more often, and before an audience of friends or coworkers before you go public.

Depending on how familiar and comfortable you are with the presentation and with public speaking, you can use an outline, or limited notes, or refer to a written copy of your presentation. However, you must remember that you *cannot read your presentation* to your audience. Print out the notes for your presentation using a 24- or 28-point font and highlight the important concepts or words. Use the highlighted words as prompts to guide you through the presentation. Do not print out your speech to use as a crutch during your delivery. It gives you a crutch, yes, but it will be one that is often too tempting to ignore, thus reducing you to reading from a script instead of interacting with your audience.

Each practice session should be timed (so that adjustments to the length of the speech can be made, if necessary), and you should try to make less and less use of the outline or notes each time. Practicing your presentation will help you achieve four speaking characteristics that make the difference between a good presentation and a great presentation: fluency, naturalness, vivacity, and nonverbal competence. Let's look at each of these characteristics in more detail.

FLUENCY

Fluency refers to the smooth or effortless articulation of the words that comprise a speech. With practice, fluency naturally increases. You become more and more familiar with what you intend to say, in what order, and, as you practice, a comfortable speaking style will emerge, helping you to feel more confident and sound more fluent. Practice also helps you avoid saying "um" or "ah" or "like, you know," or any other form of speech that will make you appear less articulate. You will no longer rely so heavily on the terms "and" or "so" or "uh" to connect thoughts. These sources of in-articulation disappear and are replaced with natural vocal pauses.

Achieving fluency allows you to focus on the *flow of ideas* rather than on specific words. When you speak fluently, your message is clear and you deliver it smoothly and with confidence.

NATURALNESS

Naturalness refers to an easy, genuine, conversational manner of speaking. Although your aim is not to re-create the Oprah Winfrey show, think about how natural she appears when speaking before a large audience. Natural speakers draw us into the message, making us feel that we're a part of the presentation. They are fluent in their subject and comfortable talking about it.

You should aim to be yourself, and then to work a little higher than that. Be your *best* speaking self. Avoid affectation; your attitude toward your audience should always be one of collaboration and equality, not superiority and distance. Stand up straight, be precise yet poised, and reflect a positive, helpful posture toward your listeners.

SKILL BUILDER WORKSHOP

Select a topic for your informative speech. Ask yourself the following questions:

- Which format would work best for my topic—a briefing, report, or training presentation?
- Who is the audience for my presentation?

- Will my topic allow me to demonstrate credibility (do I have experience with the topic), or does my credibility need to be developed from my research and knowledge of the subject?
- What type of research should to conduct to ensure I have the best information for my presentation?

VIVACITY

Every day in boardrooms, conference rooms, and training facilities around the world, people are forced to listen to seemingly endless streams of flat, lifeless, boring talk. **Vivacity** refers to the energy and enthusiasm used and generated among audience members when speaking. High-energy speakers display a positive attitude toward their topics and their audiences, which has an infectious quality. This energy comes through in their enthusiasm for the subject and the opportunity to tell the audience about it.

However, do not confuse being vivacious with being overly emotional or falsely passionate. In most cases, audiences will reject the ideas of overly emotional or passionate speakers because they don't seem reasonable.

NONVERBAL COMPETENCE

Nonverbal competence refers to the ability of a speaker to (a) maintain an appropriate level of eye contact with listeners; (b) use gestures without making them appear repetitive or redundant; (c) use purposeful body movement, particularly during verbal transitions in the speech; and (d) incorporate visual aids smoothly in the presentation. The more confident you become in voicing your speech, the more attention you can place on these aspects of effective delivery.

Practice helps you develop each of the characteristics described above. With ample practice, your delivery will be fluent, natural, vivacious, and competent. Your nonverbal cues will reflect a level of assurance that can come only when you feel confident and prepared.

SUMMARY

In this chapter we discussed the basics of preparing a business presentation. We contrasted informative and persuasive presentations. We also explained how to use presentation software and provided tips for preparing an effective PowerPoint presentation. Finally, we emphasized the importance of coordinating and practicing your presentation, which we cannot emphasize enough.

BUSINESS AND PROFESSIONAL COMMUNICATION IN THE GLOBAL WORKPLACE ONLINE

All of the following chapter review materials are available in an electronic format on either the *Business and Professional Communication in the Global Workplace Online* Resource Center or the book's companion website. Online you'll find chapter learning objects, flashcards of glossary terms, InfoTrack® College Edition Activities, weblinks, quizzes, and more.

What You Should Have Learned

Now that you have read Chapter 10, you should be able to do the following:

- Distinguish between an informative and a persuasive presentation.
- Discuss the types of informative presentations.
- Discuss issues of credibility and develop ways to build credibility.
- Determine the best types of support to use during an informative presentation.
- Use PowerPoint or other presentation software effectively.
- Understand the importance of coordinating your efforts and practicing presentations.

Key Terms

briefings 232
cause/effect 224
character appeals 214
chronological 224
clip art 231
conclusion 233
credibility 238
expertise 214
empathy 217
emotional appeals 214
facts 227
fluency 237
font size 230

font type 230
informative presentations 212
introduction 223
logical appeals 214
naturalness 237
needs and expectations 215
nonverbal competence 237
outcomes 212
persuasive presentation 212
preview 223

problem/solution 224
purpose statement 233
reference 226
reports 212
S.M.A.R.T. 220
statistics 226
thesis statement 233
topical 224
training presentations 212
transitions 223
visual cues 226
vivacity 237

Writing and Critical Thinking

The following activities can be completed online or submitted to your instructor.

For each of the activities listed below, you should pick a topic for an informative presentation. Be sure to choose a topic you already know something about and have an interest in developing further.

1. What makes you a credible speaker for this topic? Go through each of the types of

credibility discussed in this chapter and describe how you can demonstrate your credibility. Make a list of your sources of credibility.

2. Brainstorm in your group the goals for a presentation on a particular topic. Remember that your job is to inform, not persuade. After twenty minutes, stop and discuss your results. Is your goal an informative one?

3. Pick an informative presentation you have heard recently. You can select a speech, a news story, or a class lecture. Were there elements that were more persuasive than informative? What were they? How did this affect you as a listener? How did these elements affect the speaker's credibility? What could the speaker have done differently?

4. Using the CCCD worksheet, develop a thesis statement and suggest visual aids you would use for the following speech topics:

   • the magic of television ads
   • how to become a smart consumer
   • what is a liberal arts education?
   • the difference between formal and informal business communication

   • how to eat well on a college student's limited budget

5. Collect and examine informative charts, graphs, and other visuals in a popular national newspaper (such as *USA Today*) or in your local paper and charts from a scientific or professional business journal. Prepare a short class presentation comparing the use of verbal and visual information presented in each publication. Is there a difference in how the publications address their reading audiences? Which rules for developing charts and graphs and statistical information are employed by the publications? If a chart or graph is unclear, what changes would you make to aid comprehension?

PRACTICING COMMUNICATION IN PROFESSIONAL CONTEXTS DEVELOPING AN INFORMATIVE PRESENTATION USING THE CCCD WORKSHEETS

This exercise is your opportunity to apply much of what you have learned throughout this course. In addition, you have the opportunity to create a well-planned and practiced presentation in a classroom setting, before your job or career success depends on your presentation ability. Take full advantage of this opportunity by treating it as if you were speaking to a group of professional peers. Think of your instructor as your boss. The grade you receive might reflect how well you would do in this type of situation in the workplace.

Select a topic within your chosen major and prepare a ten-minute informative presentation using the CCCD worksheets provided. Keep the topic focused on either a business or professional aspect of the field you are pursuing. For example, if you are nursing student, you could make a presentation on giving injections or a new drug. If you are an accounting major, you could give a presentation on a new tax law.

Whatever topic you choose, remember that your aim is to inform, not to persuade. You should also use presentation software. If this technology is not available for your classroom, mount enlargements of your slides on foam board or provide handouts.

Make sure that you think about ways to demonstrate your credibility to your audience. Dress for your presentation exactly as you might in the workplace. Don't forget to practice, practice, practice.

Persuasive Communication in a Global Workplace

Many theorists claim that any act of communication is indeed an act of persuasion. While we don't believe that *every* act of communication is inherently persuasive, many business and professional communication situations involve some form of persuasion. In a global business environment, where competition is steep, it is important to understand how and when persuasion occurs in the workplace.

For example, for two years, as a student member of the university governance committee on staff benefits, you have been trying to get the Provost to consider flex scheduling. The Provost views flex scheduling as frivolous and he believes that staff members will take advantage of the system. After a meeting, you casually mention to the Provost that you recently read an article touting the environmental and financial benefits of flex scheduling, which has become more popular since gas prices soared. You know he is opposed to flex scheduling, but you also know he is a penny-pincher and an environmentalist. You hope that by couching your argument in economic and environmental terms you might subtlety change his mind on flex schedules. This example demonstrates how those trained in *mindful* persuasion can use persuasion to accomplish their goals in the workplace.

In Chapter 10, we discussed the elements of a persuasive *presentation* given to an audience. This chapter discusses persuasive *communication* in non-presentational settings. The goal of this form of persuasive communication is to induce listeners, co-workers, and organizational superiors or subordinates to make a decision or to perform an action. Persuasive communication is an everyday occurrence and therefore may be experienced in interpersonal, group, team, or public situations. In this chapter, we discuss the strategies for persuasive communication and how to use them in the global workplace.

No matter what position you have in an organization, you encounter and use persuasive communication on a daily basis. Even if your position doesn't have the word "sales" in the title, you may need to sell an idea to multiple audiences every day, often with the intent of encouraging your audience to come to a decision or take action. For example, as students, you attempt to persuade your instructor and your classmates every time you make a point in class. In a job interview, you are persuading the interviewer you are the best person for the job. Positions in management require even more persuasion, as you persuade your employees to complete tasks, follow directions, organize their work around a common vision, and produce quality products. As you can see, persuasive communication plays a large role in our everyday lives. Let's look at some of the ways these everyday forms of persuasion may be used in the workplace.

CONCIERGE PERSUASION

To succeed in business, we need to adopt an attitude of "concierge" persuasion. **Concierge persuasion** is a persuasion "of discrete problem-solving and assiduous service" (Bennet, 2000). For example, a concierge in a fine hotel might provide one hotel guest with theater tickets, another a table in a good restaurant, and another the assurance that his dog will get walked at noon every day. The purpose of having the concierge provide all these services is to convince guests that they have selected the best hotel and that they should stay there again.

This concierge concept also applies at work. In everyday situations, you will find that you have to persuade your audience that you have the best approach to solving a problem, to applying knowledge to the fulfillment of duties and responsibilities, and/or to demonstrating how or why your firm offers the highest quality product at the most reasonable price. To be able to persuade the target audience in each of those situations, you have to meet both the needs and the expectations of your listeners. In today's global business environment, the concept of concierge persuasion is even more important, because we not only have to persuade a local audience but we have to persuade multiple audiences and cultures simultaneously.

We found the flyer shown in Figure 11.1 in an elevator on our campus. The University Technology Office posted the flyers to remind computer technicians that they weren't just "fixing computers"; they were persuading their customers that not only were they were doing a good job fixing computers but moreover they were showing customers that they "cared" about their needs and could meet their expectations.

Just as the hotel concierge adapts to each hotel guest's needs, we must adapt our communication strategies to each situation, and preferably, to each person with whom we do business. This requires crafting a personal connection between yourself and others, as well as developing an understanding of the persuasive strategy that works best in each type of situation, person, and with each type of culture.

For example, one way to gauge which persuasive strategy will work best is by examining whether a business culture tends to be more masculine or feminine. A masculine culture values assertiveness and competition and may be better served with a masculine communication style, which is more direct and blunt. A feminine culture, on the other hand, values nurturing and collaboration and may be best served by a feminine communication style, which tends to be more subtle. These are, of course, generalizations. Individual representatives of business cultures may differ from the general rule, but general rules do provide starting places for analysis. The important thing is to assess how well your strategy is working and make adjustments based on the responses you receive.

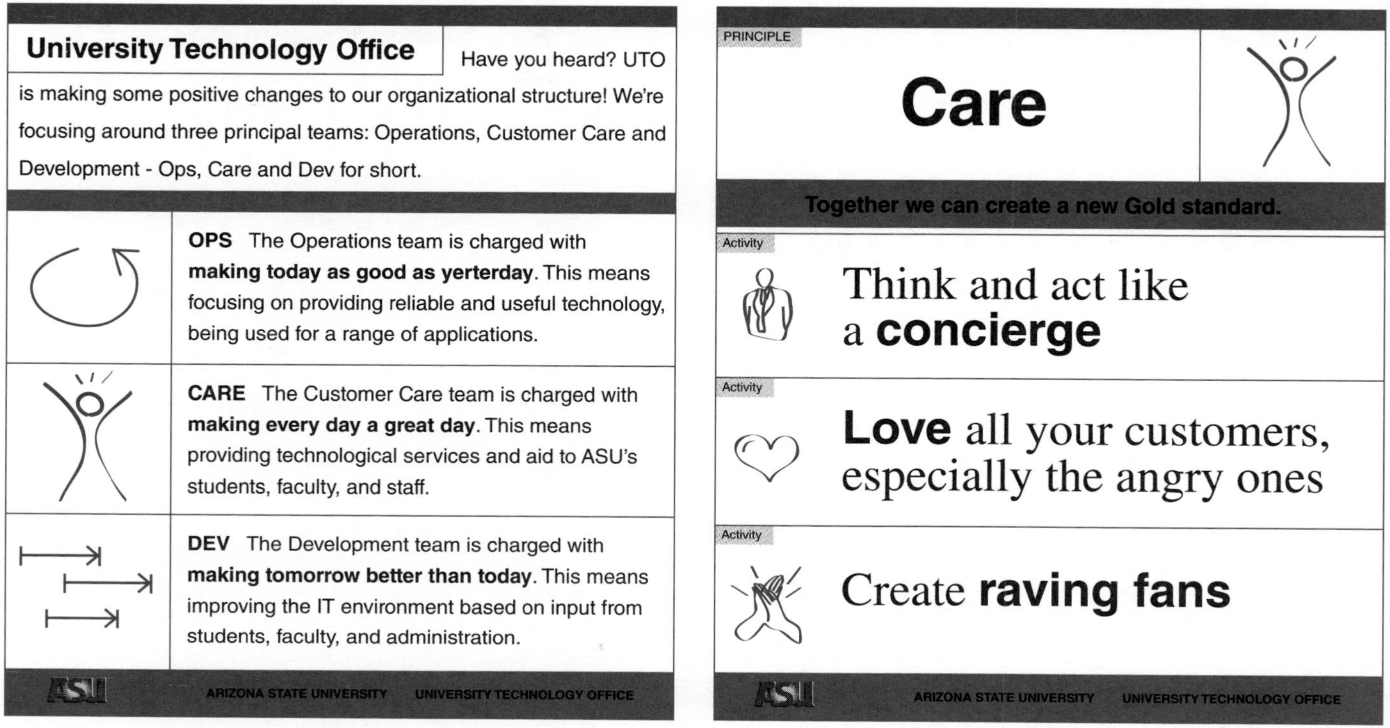

Courtesy Arizona State University.

Care

PRINCIPLE

Together we can create a new Gold standard.

Activity

Think and act like a **concierge**

Activity

Love all your customers, especially the angry ones

Activity

Create **raving fans**

ASU   ARIZONA STATE UNIVERSITY   UNIVERSITY TECHNOLOGY OFFICE

University Technology Office

Have you heard? UTO is making some positive changes to our organizational structure! We're focusing around three principal teams: Operations, Customer Care and Development - Ops, Care and Dev for short.

OPS The Operations team is charged with **making today as good as yesterday.** This means focusing on providing reliable and useful technology, being used for a range of applications.

CARE The Customer Care team is charged with **making every day a great day.** This means providing technological services and aid to ASU's students, faculty, and staff.

DEV The Development team is charged with **making tomorrow better than today.** This means improving the IT environment based on input from students, faculty, and administration.

ASU   ARIZONA STATE UNIVERSITY   UNIVERSITY TECHNOLOGY OFFICE

FIGURE 11.1   CONCIERGE COMMUNICATION AT WORK.

Remember, you should use a persuasive approach and a communication style that fits with the cultural expectations of the person with whom you are dealing. Again, the CCCD model can help you make successful and effective communication decisions.

CHOOSING A PERSUASIVE COMMUNICATION STRATEGY

After determining the needs and expectations of your target audience, you need to choose a communication strategy that fits with that audience and situation. The persuasion continuum in Figure 11.2 illustrates when a particular persuasive strategy should be used. These strategies can be applied to a variety business and professional communication situations—conversations, sales meetings, small groups, teams, or presentations.

As you can see from the continuum, the persuasive strategies available range from "brutal" to "mindful." There is a place in the global workplace for each type of persuasion. That said, relying on one strategy for all your business communication is sure to backfire. As we move across the continuum, from brutal to mindful, notice that as a speaker, you become more focused on the needs of the target audience and less focused on the simple goal of compliance. Notice also that the decision-making choices available to the target audience shift with the strategy employed.

Our goal should always be to become more mindful in business situations. But occasionally one of the less mindful persuasive strategies may be more expedient or simply necessary. Not every business situation is about choice. There may be only one option for a given situation and the communication goal must therefore be to get your audience to comply as quickly and efficiently as possible. Other situations may call for you to discuss with your audience all of the possible choices available

Brutal	Rational	Rational/ Emotional	Mindful	CONSCIOUS COMMUNICATION CHOICES
Characterized by one-sided persuasion. Uses the hammer method of persuasion. Provides the listener with no choice.	Characterized by two-sided exchanges. Uses the pro vs. con method of persuasion. Allows listener to test alternatives before coming to a conclusion.	Characterized by mass appeal to a large audience. Uses Monroe's Motivated Sequence to persuade. Presents listener with attention-getter, need, solution, and call to action.	Characterized by a connection between the audience and the speaker. Uses an understanding of the needs of the audience and a personal commitment to satisfy those needs as persuasion. Emphasizes personal choice in decision-making.	A mindful approach to persuasion; appropriate in any context, but it takes more work by all parties.
Strong pathos	Logos	Pathos	Ethos	

Mindless Persuasion ━━━━━━━━▶ Mindful Persuasion

FIGURE 11.2 | PERSUASION BY PERSONAL CONNECTION

to them, or be willing to engage them in a dialogue about options. Throughout the remainder of this chapter, we examine how you can use each persuasive strategy in a business context. We end the chapter with an examination of organizational crisis, and show you how to interpret during crisis situations to help you choose the most appropriate persuasive strategy.

THE TYPES OF PERSUASIVE STRATEGIES

Not all persuasive situations are created equally. The strategy selection criteria chart shown in Figure 11.3 will help you to determine which type of persuasive strategy works best in a given situation. Let's examine each of these strategies in more detail.

CHOOSING THE BRUTAL STRATEGY

Choosing a **brutal strategy** (Covino and Jolliffe, 1995; Woods, 1997) is appropriate when the following conditions apply:

- You are not offering the target audience a choice, yet you want to convince them that compliance is in their best interest or is the only option available.
- Your target audience has a history of being resistant or closed to your ideas or products.
- The needs of your target audience are less important than the outcome you are presenting.
- You need to make the presentation in a one-on-one setting to avoid publicly embarrassing or undermining your target audience.
- Your ability to persuade your target audience lies more with your position of organizational authority than with your personal credibility.
- All other forms of negotiation and persuasion have failed.
- Your main goal is compliance, in the form of agreement with your position or proposal.

For example, imagine your boss just told you that the company is reorganizing and is closing its customer service location in Tempe, Arizona. Employees working in Tempe will have the option of relocating to the Las Vegas, Nevada, office. It is your job to persuade the best-trained and most valuable employees from the Tempe office to relocate to Las Vegas. In this case, the employees don't really have a choice—they either relocate or lose their jobs. The most effective communication strategy in this situation is brutal honesty.

CREATING THE BRUTAL MESSAGE

While you might empathize with your target audience, the fact is they do not have a choice when it comes to a brutal message. You need to create a message that is as clear as possible so there is no confusion or hope for a different outcome. The evidence you use to support your case should clarify that the situation is non-negotiable and not subject to change. Any future action required by the audience should be stated clearly and should then be confirmed by the audience. When creating a message using the *brutal strategy* you should:

- Clearly state the problem.
- Cite any supporting evidence for your case.
- Clearly state the actions required by your audience.

FIGURE 11.3 | STRATEGY SELECTION CRITERIA WORKSHEET

Strategy	Brutal	Rational	Rational/Emotional	Mindful
What type of presentation would work best?	• One-on-one	• One-on-one small groups large audiences	• One-on-one small groups large audiences	• One-on-one small groups large audiences
What are the needs of your audience?	• Not considered	• Clearly definable	• Somewhat definable/ somewhat fluid	• Clearly definable
What type of choices will your audience be presented with?	• None or either/or	• Multiple with best alternative presented	• Call to action	• Choice that reflects personal responsibility and organizational accountability
How open to your position, product, or idea has your audience been in the past?	• Closed or resistant	• Somewhat open	• Persuadable	• Open
What method of persuasion would work best?	• Strategic control—the use of authority to warrant compliance	• **Logos**—an appeal that is based in evidence and logic	• **Logos/pathos**—a logical appeal that induces the emotions of the audience	• **Ethos**—an appeal that is based on the credibility of the speaker and his or her ability to follow through on commitments
What personal trait does your argument rely on: organizational authority, personal credibility, knowledge, or expertise?	• Authority	• Knowledge or expertise	• Credibility and Empathy	• All
What is your goal?	• Compliance	• Consensus	• Action	• Commitment

For example, it has come to your attention that an employee is sending e-mails that some of his fellow employees view as offensive. Sending jokes or sexually explicit e-mails over the company's e-mail system is strictly prohibited. This policy is clearly stated in the employee manual. In the past week, five female employees have complained about the e-mails and two have told you they are considering filing a sexual harassment complaint with the Equal Employment Opportunity Commission (EEOC). You should call the employee into your office and:

- Have him read the section on e-mail abuse in the employee manual.
- Have him sign a statement that you prepared in advance, stating that he has read the section on e-mail and understands it.
- Inform the employee that the statement will go into his employee file, and that he will be dismissed if he sends any more non-business-related e-mail.

This is an example of brutal communication. There are no options and no room for niceties or coddling in this situation.

COORDINATING THE BRUTAL MESSAGE

When coordinating persuasion using a *brutal strategy* it is best to notify anyone who may be affected by your decision. While the delivery of a brutal message is generally done one-on-one, coordination with others in the organization prior to delivery may be necessary. However, do not go beyond those who have a direct stake in either the delivery of the message or the outcome. Gossip and rumors can easily circulate in an organization, especially when bad or negative news is being delivered. Once the message is delivered, you should inform those who need to know of any complications. For example, if you fire an employee and the employee makes threats against you, fellow employees, or the company, you need to inform your superiors, security at your company, and, if necessary, the police.

DELIVERING THE BRUTAL MESSAGE

Delivering a message using a *brutal strategy* should be done one-on-one to minimize any resulting embarrassment or discomfort. However, in some cases, you may need a witness or even a security officer. For example, if you are meeting with an employee who has a habit of making offensive or threatening remarks, it may make sense to have a witness present.

Make sure the environment supports your message. For example, it would be cruel and unprofessional to tell an employee he is being laid off at his desk, with his coworkers looking on. Just as the environment should fit the message, the tone of the message should fit the environment. To ensure you are using the appropriate tone you should:

- **Be sure.** Be absolutely certain before you walk into the room that a brutal strategy is the only choice you have to affect change or gain acceptance for your position. Use the brutal strategy only when all else fails. This should be the last method of persuasion you try.

- **Be prepared.** Lay out your case before your meeting. Have your reasons firmly in hand and present your case in a clear and reasoned manner to your audience.
- **Be kind.** Just because you are using a brutal strategy doesn't mean you have license to embarrass, belittle, or humiliate someone. Use the brutal strategy only in one-on-one settings. If it is necessary to use this strategy with a team or a department, consider presenting your decision to the team leader or department head and allowing that person to present it to the rest of the group. Or present your decision in a closed-door session with only those who are directly affected.
- **Be considerate.** Give your audience some time to absorb your idea or proposal. They will need time to think about what you have said. They may also need time to develop a way to agree without losing face or looking bad in the process. Have a box of Kleenex on hand.
- **Be firm.** You will lose all credibility and authority with your audience if you cave in or back-pedal once you have stated your case in a brutal manner.

CHOOSING THE RATIONAL STRATEGY

Choosing a **rational strategy** (Covino and Jolliffe, 1995) is appropriate when the following conditions apply:

- You want to lead your target audience to consensus by presenting alternatives and then ultimately the best alternative.
- Your target audience is somewhat open to your ideas.
- Your ability to persuade your target audience relies on both your knowledge of the subject or product and your personal credibility.
- Your main goal is consensus for your position or proposal.

For example, imagine you are the owner of a medium-sized company that designs logos and prints clothing for sports teams. Most of your sales people and graphic designers don't work out of the shop. All of the design work and orders are handled over the company's Intranet, which can be accessed from anywhere. In fact, two of your graphic designers live a few hours away and only come to the office a few times a year. Most of your shop workers—stockers, embroiders, and packers—live in the neighboring county where the taxes are lower and the housing prices are more reasonable.

You and your wife recently purchased a vacation home on a lake that you would like to make into your full-time home in the next few years. Once that occurs, you know you won't want to make the 45-minute-to-an-hour drive from the lake every morning and every evening. After making the drive from the lake a few times after long weekends, you realize what a toll in gas and time long drives take on those in your company who often make the least amount of money and who in most cases have the most physically demanding jobs. While it was the choice of these employees to live outside the metropolitan area, you see that you could do something beneficial for a portion of your workforce while accomplishing your dream of living at the lake that much sooner.

After scouting real estate outside of the city, you find a location that would be perfect for your business. You decide to relocate your business within six months.

You realize that you may lose a few employees and the tiny percentage of walk-in business that you have at your current location, but the upside is that the company will save money in rent and taxes, you'll be closer to home, and the move will benefit a significant portion of your employee base.

You have a high level of credibility with your employee base. They think of you as kind and caring boss who looks out for his people and makes good business decisions. You decide to use a rational message strategy to present the alternatives to your employees. Although you have already made up your mind to move the shop, you want your employees to understand your decision and agree with you.

Some business owners would simply move their business without discussing the matter with their employees. However, by taking the time to present the alternatives—staying in the current location or moving outside the metro area—you will more likely not only gain the consensus of your employees but also retain and deepen your **reputation** as a caring boss who makes sound business decisions.

CREATING THE RATIONAL PERSUASIVE MESSAGE

Think back to Chapter 10 and the ways in which you can establish credibility with an audience. The first two, education and expertise, are often combined to increase a speaker's credibility, which is key to a rational communication strategy. Reputation is also a source of credibility. Before you choose a rational strategy, review what makes you a credible speaker on this topic by answering the following questions:

- Do you have the expertise, education, and/or experience that will demonstrate to your audience that you know what you are talking about and can be trusted?
- What is your reputation with this audience? Do they know you as a leader, a person who does what she says she will do? Someone who is fair? Or honest?
- What is the best way to convey your credibility to the audience?

Typically, when using a *rational* message strategy, you present your audience with two or more alternatives, and then explain why you feel a certain alternative is the best option or direction to take. When using this strategy, a speaker should present each alternative and then the evidence that both supports and refutes that alternative as a viable option. Then, the speaker presents the best alternative along with evidence that clearly supports it as the best alternative. Speakers using a rational strategy are using persuasion in a subtle, careful, and respectful way that allows the audience to move toward consensus rather than a brutal message, which requires compliance, or an emotional strategy, which requires the audience to take action.

COORDINATING THE RATIONAL PERSUASIVE MESSAGE

When coordinating persuasion using a *rational strategy*, check, check, and recheck your facts. A rational message strategy relies heavily on credibility so it is very important that your facts are correct and verified. As with any communication strategy, it is imperative that you coordinate your message with anyone who may be affected by it.

DELIVERING THE RATIONAL PERSUASIVE MESSAGE

While it is often difficult to practice for a conversation that relies on a brutal message strategy, as you may not anticipate the reactions of someone being fired or reprimanded, it is essential that you know and anticipate your audience's responses in advance when using a rational strategy. You should anticipate these responses when you create your message and, if you plan well, you should be able to respond to any alternatives your audience might come up with. This process will go much more smoothly and fluidly if you practice your message before you deliver it. Seek the advice of someone in the company you trust to give you honest and helpful feedback. This preparation will ensure that you have taken into account the potential alternatives, and that your message will cover all the necessary persuasive bases.

A rational message strategy depends on a rational and unemotional delivery. A rational delivery should not be too dramatic; however, you don't want to speak in a monotone, either. This type of delivery takes practice, but you will be sure to strike the right balance if you:

- Select an organizational pattern that allows you to present your case in a logical and organized manner. Organizational patterns are discussed in detail in Chapter 10.
- Prepare an outline or use the chart at the end of Chapter 10 to organize all the elements of your message.
- Practice your presentation in front of your team, a coworker, or a friend. Ask for feedback about any gaps they may perceive in your preparation or planning. Ask them how these gaps might be filled.
- Develop visual support that enhances your message, but only if it makes sense to do so. (See Chapter 10 for tips on developing visual support.)
- Dress in a way that enhances your credibility and doesn't distract from your message.
- Deliver your presentation with confidence.
- Show the appropriate enthusiasm for the alternative you present as the best option or direction.

FOCUS ON ETHICS

You know that a coworker feels very strongly about expanding into the European market. He has done all the research and has a sound argument for the expansion. He is scheduled to present his information to the CEO on Monday. You are concerned that if he presents his expansion ideas, and the CEO accepts them, it could set back your career. You know that the CEO of the company has reservations about expansion. While playing golf with the CEO on Saturday, you bring the conversation around to the European expansion. When he asks your opinion, you do your best to discourage the expansion. Do you have an ethical obligation to tell your coworker about your conversation with the CEO before his meeting? Is it more important to treat people fairly in the workplace, or to protect your career?

CHOOSING THE RATIONAL/EMOTIONAL STRATEGY

Choosing a **rational/emotional strategy** is appropriate when the following conditions apply:

- Your goal is a call to action.
- Your target audience is open and receptive to your ideas.
- You need to persuade your target audience that you can meet their needs, especially when they might be unaware of what their needs are.
- Your ability to persuade your target audience lies with your ability to meet their emotional needs and to rely on your personal credibility with them.

For example, you work for your university's foundation raising money for special campus programs. The chancellor of the university has created an initiative that will fund research for alternative fuel sources. You know a major donor wants to give a substantial gift to the university, but is undecided about how the gift should be used. The donor already has a building named after her and has endowed a number of scholarships and faculty chairs. She is looking for a substantial project that has long-term benefits to the university and society.

You would like to use her gift to seed the chancellor's alternative fuel research initiative. You present her with three alternative programs but reserve your emotional appeal for the long-term benefits of alternative fuel and an explanation of how research in this area will benefit every man, woman, and child on the planet.

Asking people to part with money often requires more than a straightforward, rational appeal. It requires "showing" donors or contributors how their money will benefit those they care most about. In this case, the donor cares about the university, its growing reputation, and society as a whole. Making a rational/emotion appeal is a good strategy that allows you to show the donor the long-term benefits of her gift.

CREATING THE RATIONAL/EMOTIONAL MESSAGE

Creating a rational/emotional message requires that the speaker make a rational appeal to his or her target audience's emotions in order to move them to a particular action. This is done by:

- Demonstrating to target audience members that you understand their needs.
- Explaining how those needs can be satisfied.
- Helping them visualize how a product or service can meet those needs.

When creating the *rational/emotional* message, it is important to create your message using an organizational structure that follows this pattern and is easy for your audience to follow. You can use one of the organizational patterns discussed in Chapter 10. Or you can use **Monroe's Motivated Sequence**, discussed on the next page, to organize your message (McKerrow, Grombeck, Ehninger, and Monroe, 2000).

STEPS IN MONROE'S MOTIVATED SEQUENCE

STEP 1: Attention-getter

The **attention-getter** is a story, joke, or the first line of a message, designed to pull the audience into your message. Your attention-getter should relate to your topic in some way. Telling an entertaining story that isn't related to the topic may briefly entertain your audience, but then they may spend the remainder of the talk wondering why you told the story or joke and where it is leading.

STEP 2: Need

The **need** is the part of a message that details the audience's need or problem. This is where your audience needs and expectations assessment comes in, as you can use the information you gleaned about your audience. This part of the message should also include your rational appeal, along with support that is appropriate for the topic and your audience.

STEP 3: Satisfaction

The **satisfaction** is the part of a message that conveys the solution to the audience's need(s) or problem(s). This part of your message begins your emotional appeal. When using an emotional appeal, it is important that you show, rather than tell, the audience about the solution in order to persuade them.

STEP 4: Visualization

Visualization allows your audience to see the need and provides them with the solution to their problem or a remedy for a situation. This can be done literally, using visual aids, or figuratively, painting a picture with words.

STEP 5: Call to Action

The **call to action** is a direct or indirect statement of action that you want the audience to take as a result of listening to your message. A direct statement of action would be, "Now go out there and vote for X candidate." An indirect statement of action would be, "We think the best investment for your donation is the alternative fuel initiative; however, the other projects we describe are also worthwhile projects."

DELIVERING THE RATIONAL/EMOTIONAL MESSAGE

Although you may be excited and enthusiastic about delivering a message, if you begin too energetically, you can hurt your credibility. Keep an eye on your target audience while you deliver the message. Look for feedback: a nod, a smile, a bored look. You can gauge how to adjust the enthusiasm of your delivery based on your audience's feedback.

Make sure your nonverbal delivery matches your verbal delivery: Don't make serious comments with a smirk and or funny comments geared toward lightening the mood of the audience with a deadpan face or delivery. Practicing your message ensures that your verbal and nonverbal delivery is in sync and that you are not overly emotional. Review the section on fluency, naturalness, vivacity, and nonverbal competence in Chapter 10 before delivering a rational/emotional message.

It is also important to:

- Keep your purpose firmly in mind and don't allow your emotions to take you off topic.
- Develop visual support for your presentation that enhances the visualization portion of the presentation and draws your audience toward the call to action.
- Deliver your presentation with confidence. If you don't have confidence in your message, why would your audience?
- Use words that help generate the emotions you want to elicit from the audience.

Choosing the Mindful Strategy

A **mindful strategy** (Covino and Jolliffe, 1995) is appropriate when the following conditions apply:

- Your goal is for the target audience to make a *commitment* to your position, product, contract, or candidate.
- Your target audience has a history of being open to your concept, idea, or product.
- The needs of your target audience are vital to the outcome you are presenting.
- Your ability to persuade your target audience lies as much with your position of personal credibility as it does with your organizational authority and knowledge of the situation or product.

For example, you are a sales manager for a successful furniture manufacturer located in High Point, North Carolina. Your company recently introduced a line of high-end linens and accessories. You have been charged with selling the new line to clients in Europe. Your clients are already familiar with your company, which has a good reputation for quality and reliability, so they are open to hearing about the new line. You want a commitment from each client that it will carry the new line of linens and accessories in their showrooms alongside your furniture.

Your strategy is to meet with each client, listen to their concerns about investing in the new line, and overcome any hesitation they might have. This is a good strategy to use when each client might have concerns that are specific to their market or geographic location. One client might be concerned that the new line is too expensive for their market, while another client might be concerned that the new line will require additional showroom space they simply do not have. Being mindful of each client's concerns will increase the level of commitment you receive for the new line.

CREATING THE MINDFUL MESSAGE

When creating the mindful persuasive message, it is important to do the following:

- Analyze the situation.
- Adapt your message to your audience.
- Evaluate feedback as it occurs.
- Be willing to take risks that might lead to better understanding.
- Listen consciously to what was said during the meeting.
- Provide feedback.

Aside from using a solid organizational structure for your message, you should also take opportunities throughout the meeting to evaluate feedback. It is a good practice to put a reminder in your notes to stop and listen. This can help you establish credibility in the form of empathy with your audience (see Chapter 10).

COORDINATING THE MINDFUL MESSAGE

As with any presentation, make sure any technology you need for your presentation will be available. It might not be practical to take samples of all the items in a line of linens and accessories with you, but you could show the line on a laptop. You might also want to leave a catalog with the client. How you deliver the catalog—hard copy, DVD, or over the Internet—will depend on the technology available. Don't assume that every client has access to technology simply because that is the way we do business in the United States. A small shop owner in Italy or France may still write receipts and balance the books by hand.

DELIVERING THE MINDFUL MESSAGE

Be sure to run your message by others who can give you feedback before you deliver it. Additionally, coordinate your message and the facts with your supervisors and coworkers, if necessary. This will ensure that *nobody is taken by surprise* when you deliver your message. If your company has not agreed on a discount schedule for large purchases of the new line, don't offer discounts until you are sure they are possible. It is perfectly acceptable to say, "We are still working on the discount schedule and as soon as I have it, I'll be happy to send it to you."

Don't promise what you cannot deliver.

We've said it before, and we'll say it again...practice, practice, practice! When delivering the mindful message, it is important to be wholly engaged. This means that your verbal message needs to match your nonverbal delivery in all aspects. Be sure to collect feedback from your target audience during and after your delivery and respond accordingly. When using a mindful strategy, follow these steps:

- Analyze the situation before you begin. Develop a deep understanding of the positions of each party before you enter the conversation.
- Listen. You cannot be mindful if you aren't listening to the other parties involved. Listen for intention, position, objections, and emotion.

- Recap. Make sure you understand the positions of the other parties by recapping what they have said. Then ask for confirmation before moving on.
- Give feedback. Make sure that the other parties understand your position by giving them accurate and clear feedback.

CASE STUDY 10 | **WHAT TYPE OF PERSUASION WILL WORK?**

One of the few things William disliked about being a vice president was dealing directly with other people's conflicts. For the past three months, Ivan, the head of implementation, and Mary, the head of product development, had been fighting like small children. Every meeting was the same. Ivan would accuse Mary of meddling in implementation, and Mary would accuse Ivan of being stubborn. William had repeatedly asked the two of them to work through their problems, but Ivan and Mary couldn't seem to meet without an argument.

Over time, William had come to the conclusion that this was not a business process conflict, but a personal conflict, and the root of the problem was Ivan's resistance to change. Ivan, a longtime employee of the company, had been head of implementation for seven years and was stuck in a "This is how I have always done things" frame of mind. He resisted Mary's ideas, as well as any efforts to compromise. Ivan was a

valuable employee but his resistance to change was hurting his department, his relationships with other department heads, and the organization.

After much thought, William decided to place Ivan in charge of the new custom development area for an emerging market in Spain. This department was just getting started and would require a good bit of product and implementation knowledge, something Ivan certainly had. However, it was a much smaller department than implementation, so the move could be viewed as a demotion. How should he tell Ivan about the transfer?

William needed to choose a persuasive strategy that was appropriate for the situation and for Ivan. After consulting the strategies for persuasive messages, William decided that a brutal strategy would be best. Was this the right choice? How might William have handled the situation differently? Was there a better persuasive strategy?

GLOBAL PROFILE FOR SUCCESS—MULTIPLE THEATERS AND MULTIPLE AUDIENCES

Levick Strategic Communications manages an organization's communication during a crisis situation. Levick recognizes that during a crisis, multiple theaters are available for communication to multiple audiences. Understanding which theater to use for which audience is what makes Levick successful.

Explore Levick Strategic Communications' website: http://www.levick.com.

What can you learn about persuasive communication during a crisis from Levick's site? Explore the different sections of the site. Were any persuasive strategies used in the creation of those areas? If so, what strategies were used?

PERSUASION AND ORGANIZATIONAL CRISIS

An **organizational crisis** is a traumatic situation triggered by a natural disaster (a tornado, flood, or hurricane), an unforeseen event (a terrorist attack, explosion, or fire), or human cause (a product recall, hiring someone with a criminal record, showing poor judgment, acting dishonestly or unethically) that requires the organization to implement a crisis strategy before resolution or restoration of the company's image can occur. When a crisis occurs, it is important to develop a well-planned, well-supported crisis strategy that is coordinated across audiences and delivered through a variety of media that addresses the situation and offers a solution or a plan of action.

During a crisis situation, you may need to use multiple persuasive communication strategies to meet the needs of multiple audiences. Audiences can be broken down into primary and secondary audiences. A **primary audience** is the audience from which you have the most to lose if your message is not delivered effectively—your employees, customers, clients, or suppliers, and those who offer your company any type of financial support (bankers, stockholders, lien holders). The **secondary audience** is any group that is not immediately affected by the crisis—the media, your competitors, those living in the city or town who are not in danger, but who are concerned about the crisis. For each message you create, you need to choose a primary audience and adopt your message toward that group. Multiple messages may be created for any crisis, each one having a different primary and secondary audience.

During the pet food recall of 2007, Menu Foods was a company in crisis. Menu Foods manufactured pet food for PetSmart, Safeway, Walmart, and other retailers in the U.S. and Canada. In March of 2007, Menu Foods issued the largest pet food recall in history. Family pets were getting sick and dying after ingesting tainted food. Stores removed products from their shelves, while veterinarians desperately tried to learn the cause of the symptoms and how to treat infected pets to avoid future fatalities. Rather than feed tainted food to their pets, consumers stopped using store-bought pet food because no one was sure which brands of food were affected. Stockholders were wondering if they should sell their stock. News organizations were running stories about tainted pet food in every newscast or newspaper.

In this brief overview of the Menu Foods recall crisis, we can identify multiple primary audiences: consumers, retail stores, and veterinarians. Secondary audiences include Menu Foods shareholders and members of the press. Obviously one message cannot effectively deliver all the information required for each of these audiences. Effective crisis management required more than one message to respond to multiple audiences.

As with any communication episode, the CCCD model can improve the outcome by helping you choose the best strategy, create a message streamlined for a particular audience, coordinate your message, and align the delivery of your message with the communication strategy selected. However, in crisis situations, *how you communicate* is further complicated by the need to communicate continuously throughout the crisis and adapt your message to four stages identified in most crisis situations. The four stages include: emerging, understanding, action, and repair. Each of the stages and the persuasive strategy that works best to address each stage is discussed below.

EMERGING

The emerging stage marks the beginning of a crisis. In this stage, people in the organization are just starting to realize that they have a crisis on their hands. In the emerging stage, choosing your goals and your words carefully are critical.

Before you offer *any* response, you need to gather as much information as possible. To do this, you should ask the following questions:

- **What** caused the crisis? What is the origin? Was the crisis a natural disaster or was it brought about through human causes? What can be done *right now* to assure our customers, clients, and stockholders that we understand the problem and are dealing with it?
- **Who** do we need to talk to in order to gather as much information as possible about the situation? Do we need to talk to experts outside the company? Are there specific agencies that we need to call in (the Centers for Disease Control, the Food and Drug Administration, or the Federal Emergency Management Association)?
- **When** do we need to respond? Does the crisis require an immediate response? Has news about the crisis broken? Or is the crisis only beginning to come to light?
- **How** should we respond? Do we need a full-scale media plan? Would a letter to customers, clients, and stockholders contain the situation? Or is this a situation where simply not responding at this time makes the most sense?
- **Where** should our response be made? At the scene of a disaster? From corporate headquarters? Or should the response be delivered in a neutral location?

While gathering this information might seem to be a daunting task in the middle of a crisis, not gathering all the information you need to respond appropriately may result in a further lack of trust or confidence in your company's ability to respond. Once you have gathered this information, you can choose the best persuasive strategy to move you from the *emerging* stage and to the *understanding* stage of the crisis.

For example, you find that the chief financial officer of your company is involved in an embezzlement scheme that has left your company open to multiple lawsuits, criminal investigations, and a potentially devastating loss of clientele. Your response in the *emerging* phase might be to use the brutal strategy. Using this strategy, your company might draft a press release announcing that the company has become aware of an embezzlement scheme run by the CFO and is cooperating with the FBI in order to recover company assets and restore the financial integrity of each and every client. The president of the company might announce the discovery, pledge to make things right, and then end the press conference. The purpose of the announcement and the use of a brutal strategy is to release the story in a way that is advantageous to the company and to forestall additional questions until an action plan is developed.

UNDERSTANDING

In the *understanding* phase, you pull together all the information gathered in the emerging phase in order to develop a complete picture of the crisis. After asking all of the questions posed in the emerging phase, and developing a full understanding of how the crisis occurred and who was responsible for the crisis, you can begin to develop a plan of action.

As you did in the *emerging* stage, it is necessary to select a persuasive strategy to convey any additional information to your audience(s). The goal in the understanding phase may be to convey additional information as it is gathered in order to keep those who may have a stake in the crisis informed and to forestall rumors or speculation that might further damage the image, stock, or viability of the company.

In the *understanding* stage, you might employ a rational strategy. To be successful, the speaker chosen to represent the company would need to be an expert or someone who can display credibility and appeal to the audience(s) using a logical reasonable argument supported by strong evidence.

Unfortunately, the best way to understand how an organization should handle a specific stage in a crisis is to look at an example of how *not* to handle a specific stage in a crisis. Many of you may remember the initial response of FEMA and the Department of Homeland Security after Hurricane Katrina hit the Louisiana and Mississippi coasts. The lack of response in the early days of the crisis, and the clueless nature with which Michael Chertoff, the secretary of Homeland Security, Michael Brown, the director of FEMA, and the Louisiana state and local officials dealt with the natural disaster have become textbook examples of how *not to* respond to a crisis. Rather than gather their facts and compile a complete understanding of the crisis, spokespeople for numerous state and local agencies presented information at press conferences and in interviews that was either immediately questioned by the press or other agencies as inaccurate.

The number one, unbreakable rule of the *understanding* phase is that *unless you are absolutely certain something is true, accurate, and verified, do not speak.* After you have issued an initial statement in the *emerging* stage, you have time to gather information and get your facts straight. When you are sure of the facts, you can confidently provide updates and additional information.

ACTION

In the *action* stage, the company develops a plan of action and then announces it. It is vital that any action plan takes into account all of those hurt or damaged by the crisis. When presenting the action plan, the company should appoint a speaker who has credibility and is capable of displaying the appropriate sympathy for those injured.

If the crisis is a result of natural disaster, it is vital to:

* Acknowledge that people are suffering.
* Show that your organization understands what is needed *and* what will be done to alleviate that suffering.
* Explain exactly what steps will be taken to distribute aid, supplies, funds, and other resources.
* Explain the actions the company will take to alleviate suffering.

For example, the press release from Harrah's Entertainment, Inc. exemplifies the tone and structure for delivering an action plan after a crisis. Within five days of Hurricane Katrina, one of the largest natural disasters in American history, Harrah's Entertainment launched the Harrah's Employee Recovery Center and had a plan of action in place to help its 8,000 employees who lived and worked in the area hardest hit by Katrina. In addition to continuing to pay many of its employees for 90 days after the hurricane, the company offered the following action plan for employee recovery. It is important to keep in mind that this plan was separate from the plans to rebuild the company's business interests in the area.

SEPTEMBER 6: HURRICANE KATRINA EMPLOYEE RECOVERY TASK FORCE, GULF COAST REGION ASSISTANCE CENTER

Date: September 6, 2005

To: All Harrah's Entertainment Employees

From: Gary Loveman

Subject: Hurricane Katrina Employee Recovery Task Force, Gulf Coast Region Assistance Center

On behalf of our senior management team, I first want to express my deepest appreciation to the hundreds of Harrah's employees who have been working around the clock to assist our colleagues in the Gulf Coast region. The extent of the destruction I witnessed during a visit to the area late last week was almost incomprehensible, and yet I've been genuinely moved by the fact that our employees from Memphis to Las Vegas to Atlantic City have not allowed a nearly endless stream of heartbreaking news and dire predictions to slow the momentum of our recovery efforts.

Despite the range and scope of relief initiatives our company was able to announce last week, it has become increasingly clear that the scale of this disaster will require that we do even more. As a result, this past weekend I formed the Harrah's Hurricane Katrina Employee Recovery Task Force to ensure that relief-related issues receive the immediate attention of leaders in our company with the authority to make critical corporate decisions quickly. I will chair the task force; its other member will be: Senior Vice President and Treasurer Jonathan Halkyard; Jan Jones, Senior Vice President of Communications and Government Relations; Central Division President Anthony Sanfilippo; Jerry Boone, Senior Vice President of Human Resources; and Steve Brammell, Senior Vice President and General Counsel. While they also have been actively involved in recovery work, I have asked Chief Financial Officer Chuck Atwood and Chief Operating Officer Tim Wilmott to concentrate primarily on our company's overall day-to-day operations as we continue to absorb the largest acquisition in our industry's history.

The Task Force will take input from, and provide direction to, a much larger team of regional company operations and support personnel based out of Memphis. This latter group will be dedicated exclusively to employee relief and recovery for the foreseeable future. Its goal, quite simply, is to see that aid and assistance reach employees impacted by the hurricane as quickly as possible.

To that end, this Thursday, Harrah's will open the Gulf Coast Region Employee Assistance Center in the Mid-South Service Center building in Gulfport, Miss. This facility will serve as a local support center to address our employees' most urgent needs: financial and benefits assistance, logistics (including shelter, transportation, and communication) and delivery of on-site health care. We anticipate opening a second Assistance Center in New Orleans shortly.

Under current circumstances, we at Harrah's cannot treat hurricane relief as an issue demanding anything less than this sort of unique and focused effort. I will continue to communicate directly with you about the work we're doing on behalf of our displaced colleagues; I hope you, in turn, will not hesitate to contact me with your suggestions for how we can maximize the effectiveness of our relief work.

If the crisis is a result of human error, in addition to the elements listed above for natural disaster, it is vital to:

- Remain contrite—do not try to erase the past with bravado or by trying to move beyond the crisis too quickly. Having a "Whew, aren't we all glad that's over" attitude may backfire with audiences who are not quite ready to forgive or move on.
- Repeat the company's apology or acknowledgment that errors were made—do not try to cover up the company's responsibility or displace the responsibility to others.

For example, in 2007, RC2, the manufacturer of Thomas the Tank Engine toys, published the following press release announcing an additional recall from the Thomas & Friends line of toys. In the press release, RC2 executives both assume responsibility for the recall and express regret that the recall has placed a "burden" on parents who now must question the safety of their children's toys. In the action plan, the company clearly identifies the toys in question and offers parents numerous ways to contact the company in the event they have purchased one of the toys on the list. The press release also offers parents the assurance that it has implemented a new "Multi-Check Toy Safety System." While it would have been easy to push the problem off onto its Chinese production company, RC2 takes responsibility for its toy safety and offers parents a series of actions the company will take to regain their confidence.

RC2 RECALLS FIVE ADDITIONAL THOMAS & FRIENDS™ WOODEN RAILWAY ITEMS

Extensive Retesting Helps Assure Safety of Existing Toys;

RC2 Announces Multi-Check Toy Safety System to Strengthen New Toy Safety

OAK BROOK, IL, September 26, 2007—RC2 Corporation (NASDAQ:RCRC) today announced that it is voluntarily recalling five Thomas & Friends Wooden Railway items due to levels of lead in surface paint that may exceed U.S. Consumer Product Safety Commission requirements. Since the Company's recall announced in June of 2007, more than 1,500 individual Thomas & Friends toy styles have been retested to ensure their safety. This testing led to five additional discoveries that have prompted this voluntary recall. In total, this recall affects up to 200,000 units in the United States and an additional 69,000 units distributed outside the U.S. There have been no reports of illness or injury related to any of the recalled toys. The recalled toys were all manufactured before April 30, 2007.

"On behalf of everyone at RC2, let me personally apologize for the worry an additional recall creates for parents everywhere," said Curt Stoelting, RC2's chief executive officer. "We deeply regret the burden that recalling toys creates for parents, but we believe parents should be assured of two things: First, that the Thomas & Friends Wooden Railway toys they already have are safe and, second, that the new toys in stores are safe."

The items subject to recall include two toy vehicles and three accessories:

- The all-black cargo car included in the Brendam Fishing Dock Set. No other cargo cars are included in the recall, including all-black cargo cars sold in sets other than the Brendam Fishing Dock Set. Recalled all-black cargo cars from the Brendam Fishing Dock Set can be identified by either the absence of a tracking code or one of the following tracking codes on the car's underside.

26833i

28233i

23243i00

24643i00

25343i00

27443i00

32043i00

34743i00

01553i00

04553i00

13353i00

14753i00

15453i00

18353i00

- A Toad vehicle with a brake lever, which can be identified by a single tracking code, 1656OW00, on its underside. No other Toad vehicles are included in the recall, as each of these vehicles has a different tracking code.
- An olive green Sodor cargo box accessory included in the Deluxe Cranky the Crane Set. This accessory did not in the past carry a tracking code. RC2 is asking consumers to return any olive green Sodor cargo box produced as part of the Deluxe Cranky the Crane Set between January 2006 and December 2006.

  Current production of this accessory has a tracking code on the underside and is not included in the recall. Therefore any olive green Sodor cargo box with a tracking code on it is not subject to the recall. No other Sodor cargo boxes are included in the recall, including those sold in sets other than the Deluxe Cranky the Crane Set.
- The all-green maple tree top and signal base accessories included in the Conductor's Figure 8 Set.

  Because these accessories did not in the past carry tracking codes, RC2 is asking consumers to return any all-green maple tree tops and signal bases produced as part of the Conductor's Figure 8 Set from March 2006 to April 2007. Current production of these accessories has tracking codes and if the tree or signal base has a tracking code on it then it is not included in the recall.

Parents and care givers are urged to immediately remove the recalled toys and return them to RC2. Each consumer participating in the recall will receive a replacement at no charge for each recalled toy that is returned and a free gift. For pre-paid shipping labels and help identifying and returning the recalled toys, consumers are encouraged to visit

RC2's recall website, http://www.recalls.rc2.com. Concerned parents may also e-mail recalls@rc2corp.com or call RC2's Consumer Care Center toll-free at (866) 725-4407 for assistance in identifying and returning the recalled toys.

"To assure that the toys families already have are safe, more than 1,500 individual Thomas & Friends Wooden Railway toy styles were retested," added Stoelting. "By casting this wide net, we discovered that five additional items were potentially unsafe, and they are being recalled today." The company worked in full cooperation with the U.S. Consumer Product Safety Commission to voluntarily recall the five additional Thomas & Friends Wooden Railway items.

"We've learned from our own experience and that of other toy companies and have established significant additional safeguards to ensure that our toys are safe," Stoelting said, "Since June, RC2 has instituted its Multi-Check Toy Safety System to reduce potential future risks to children and preserve parents' trust."

The *Multi-Check Toy Safety System*, which helps assure parents that new toys are safe, includes:

- Increased scope and frequency of testing of both incoming materials and finished products, including testing of finished products from every production run
- Tougher certification program for contract manufacturers and paint suppliers, including evidence that toy safety standards and quality control procedures are in place and operating effectively
- Mandatory paint control procedures for contract manufacturers, including certified independent lab test results of every batch of wet paint before the paint is released for production
- Increased random inspections and audits of both manufacturers and their suppliers, including semi-annual audits and quarterly random inspections for key suppliers
- Zero tolerance for compromise on RC2 specifications reinforced by mandatory vendor compliance seminars and signed agreements

"And we're not finished. We know that every day we must earn the faith that parents place in us and in the quality and safety of our toys. That's why we will continue to look for and explore new ways to further improve the safety of our toys," said Stoelting. "We take our toy safety responsibilities very seriously and measure our success by the trust parents place in us and in our toys. Many of us at RC2 are parents, so knowing that we're taking the right steps to protect children is very important to us personally as well as professionally."

Complete recall information and assistance in identifying the recalled toys is available on RC2's recall website, http://recalls.rc2.com, or from RC2's Consumer Care Center, which can be reached toll-free at (866) 725-4407.

As part of its public outreach efforts, RC2 is notifying retailers to remove the recalled items from their inventories and also is sending letters to families who may have received one or more of the recalled items directly from the Company.

You can view the press release in its entirety at http://recalls.rc2.com

REPAIR

In the *repair* stage, companies work to revive their reputations if the crisis was caused by human error or if their initial response to a natural disaster was insufficient or ineptly handled. In business, a company's **reputation** is both a record of its past and resource for the future and is based on a number of factors, such as:

- Quality—are the company's products safe, well-made, and worth the price? Is the company concerned about the customer or the client's experience? Are their stores clean? Are their salespeople friendly and well-trained? Is customer support accessible and a priority?
- Credibility—does the company do what it says it will do? If it has made a commitment to treat employees fairly, give back to society, or act in an environmentally or sustainable way, has it followed through on those commitments?
- Fiscal responsibility—is the company financially successful? Does it take unnecessary risks? Are executives overpaid compared to those at the bottom of the corporate ladder? Has its stock taken hits because of poor business decisions or misstatements by those in charge?

If a company's reputation is sullied by a crisis or because it handled a crisis poorly, the final stage in crisis management is to repair the company's reputation. Those charged with repairing the company's reputation should answer all of the questions listed above. If a question cannot be answered in a way that is positive for the company, that issue needs to be addressed in the repair plan.

Reputation is no longer simply a local or a national consideration. Reputations, like products and services, are global commodities. A repair plan needs to take into consideration multiple audiences and if those audiences span across multiple countries, it must adapt to the cultural requirements of each country. Repairing a company's reputation takes:

- Time—while a reputation can be ruined overnight, it can take months and even years to repair.
- Consistency—to restore a company's reputation, the actions of its employees and the messages associated with the company need to be consistent.
- Credibility—for a company to regain its reputation, it must first regain its credibility. To do that, the company needs to put forth policies that encourage and reward honesty, truthfulness, and trust.
- Mindfulness—repairing a company's reputation requires a mindful persuasive strategy that reflects the personal responsibility of its employees and leadership, as well as organizational accountability at every level.

For example, when Microsoft faced anti-trust charges, the global repercussions of the courts' decision had a serious impact on the company's reputation. This prompted newswire stories like the one on the following page that quotes officials in Europe commenting on the blow the decision had on Microsoft's reputation.

Wednesday, June 7, 2006

MICROSOFT'S REPUTATION AT STAKE, EU SAYS

BLOOMBERG NEWS

European Competition Commissioner Neelie Kroes said Tuesday that Microsoft Corp. should be concerned about its reputation as well as the financial impact of antitrust rulings.

Kroes, who will decide before the end of July whether to impose daily fines of $2.6 million on Microsoft, said the software maker should take account of its image.

"It's not only a matter of financial aspects in such cases, it's also a matter of reputation," Kroes said at a European Parliament meeting in Brussels, Belgium.

The European Commission, the European Union's antitrust regulator, is threatening to fine Microsoft unless it licenses information on the way its Windows operating system shares printers and files to rival software developers. The regulator says the company hasn't provided "complete and accurate" information to rivals.

Microsoft, whose Windows operating system runs on about 95 percent of the world's personal computers, was fined in March 2004 for abusing its dominant market position by failing to make technical information available and for bundling its media player with Windows.

As part of the antitrust decision, the commission ordered Microsoft to license so-called network protocols, which would allow developers to make competing products. Rivals and the EU have said Microsoft has resisted complying.

Microsoft, which is appealing the antitrust decision, has maintained that it is already meeting the EU's demands.

SUMMARY

In this chapter, we explored persuasive communication and the notion of concierge persuasion—persuasion through personal connection that is intended not only to meet the immediate needs of a situation, but to develop long-term relationships. We discussed four strategies of persuasion: brutal, rational, rational/emotional, and mindful.

We laid out the reasons for using each type of strategy and provided ways to organize messages for each strategy. We also showed how you can use the CCCD process to guide persuasion in the workplace. Finally, we showed you how to effectively handle persuasive communication during an organizational crisis.

COMMUNICATING IN PROFESSIONAL CONTEXTS ONLINE

All of the following chapter review materials are available in an electronic format on either the *Communication in Professional Contexts* Resource Center or the book's companion website. Online you'll find chapter learning objects, flashcards of glossary terms, InfoTrack® College Edition Activities, weblinks, quizzes, and more.

WHAT YOU SHOULD HAVE LEARNED

Now that you have read Chapter 11, you should be able to do the following:

*   Discuss the concept of concierge persuasion and how choosing the right persuasive strategy helps build relationships.

- List the four persuasive strategies and the uses for each strategy.
- Discuss a situation for which a brutal strategy might be required.
- Discuss the criteria for choosing a brutal strategy.
- Give examples of situations for which a rational strategy might apply.
- Discuss the criteria for choosing a rational strategy.
- Discuss situations for which a rational/emotional strategy might be required.

- Discuss the criteria for choosing a rational/emotional strategy.
- Discuss situations for which mindful persuasion might be required.
- Discuss the criteria for choosing a mindful persuasive strategy.
- Use the worksheets provided in this chapter to create a persuasive message.
- Use Monroe's Motivated Sequence to organize a presentation.
- Discuss the four stages of responding to an organizational crisis.

KEY TERMS

attention-getter *252*

brutal strategy *245*

call to action *252*

concierge persuasion *242*

ethos *246*

logos *246*

mindful strategy *253*

Monroe's Motivated Sequence *251*

need *252*

needs assessment *266*

organizational crisis *255*

pathos *246*

persuasive communication *241*

primary audience *256*

rational strategy *248*

rational/emotional strategy *251*

reputation *249*

satisfaction *252*

secondary audience *256*

visualization *252*

WRITING AND CRITICAL THINKING

The following activities can be completed online or submitted to your instructor.

Choose one of the following activities:

1. Jon is required to pass a certification test before he can use a specific piece of machinery. He has failed the test three times and refuses to take the test again. You want to keep Jon as an employee, and eventually you would like to promote him to a team leader position, but you can't do this until he passes the test. What persuasive strategy would you use to persuade Jon to retake the test? Write a three-to-five-page paper discussing your choice of strategy and the possible outcome.

2. In your group, share a recent situation in which you used persuasion. Analyze the persuasive strategy you used. How successful

were you? What would you do differently, having read this chapter?

3. Select a television, Internet, or print ad. Analyze the ad using Monroe's Motivated Sequence. Identify the attention-getter, need, satisfaction, visualization, and call to action used in the ad. Was the ad successful? Why or why not?

4. Working in groups of three, develop three short presentations, each with a different focus. The first appeal will focus on logic (*logos*), the second on emotion (*pathos*), and the third on expertise (*ethos*) to support or argue the statements listed below. Each member delivers one of your group's speeches to the class using the appeal. As an audience member, identify each speaker's appeal through the statements

made, and evaluate how effective the appeal was.

- Some lyrics in rap music should be banned because they incite violence.
- Women are better suited to be caregivers than to be corporate executives.
- The grading system at our school should be a simple pass/fail rather than letter grades.
- In order to vote, citizens should be able to demonstrate knowledge of the issues.

Practicing Communication in Professional Contexts

Before communicating in a professional context, it is often a good idea to do your research first. Complete the following activities to gain a better idea of how persuasive communication fits into your chosen career path.

1. Identify the position or professional field you plan to enter after you graduate. Enter the position name and *persuasion* as keywords in the search engine or InfoTrack College Edition (for example, enter *sales and persuasion*, or *education and persuasion*). Write a report on the influence of persuasion in your field and situations in which you would employ each of the strategies listed in the chapter.

2. Enter the words *logos*, *pathos*, and *ethos* in a keyword search. Select two or three articles to read. How did what you found improve your understanding of the strategies discussed in this chapter?

3. Enter the term **needs assessment** in a keyword search. Browse through the websites and articles provided by the search. Print out a few examples of assessments that you can use to create your own needs assessment.

APPENDIX

CCCD Worksheets for Persuasive or Informative Presentations

Step 1: CHOOSING A GOAL

Audience	Needs and Expectations	Outcomes	Criteria
Audience one:	•	• •	• •
Audience two:	•	• •	• • •
Self	•	• •	• •

CCCD Worksheets for Persuasive or Informative Presentations

Step 2: CREATING THE MESSAGE

Introduction			
• Attention-getter			
• Statement of thesis			
• Preview of main points			
• Inducement			

Purpose and Thesis Statement	Main Points	Support	Transitions
• Purpose • Thesis Statement	Main Point 1 • Subpoint • Subpoint Main Point 2 • Subpoint • Subpoint Main Point 3 • Subpoint • Subpoint	• Support for Main Point 1 • Support for Main Point 2 • Support for Main Point 3	• Transition Transition 1 between Main Point 1 and Main Point 2 • Transition Transition 2 between Main Point 2 and Main Point 3

Conclusion	
• Review of main points	
• Return to the attention-getter and wrap up	

Motivated Sequence Organization Chart

Introduction	Attention-getter	
Purpose and Thesis Statement	**Main Points**	**Support**
• Purpose • Thesis Statement	• Need • • •	• • •
	• Satisfaction • • •	• • •
	• Visualization • • •	• • •
	• Action • •	• •
Conclusion	Call to Action	

Types of Visual Support and Audiences

Type of Visual Support and Audiences	Should Be Used To:	Don't:	Things to Keep in Mind
Slide presentations (see Chapter 10 for tips on using presentation software)			
Appropriate for: • Business and professional groups that are familiar with technology or operate in a technologically comfortable environment	• Stay on agenda • Provide transitions between multiple speakers • Present statistical support in the form of graphs, or graphic charts, or pictures	• Create elaborate complicated slide-shows that distract from your message • Get bogged down in moving the slides along and forget to speak to your audience • Develop or use without practice, practice, practice	• Make sure that the technology to support your slideshow is available at the talk site or plan to bring your own • Develop a backup plan in case something goes wrong with the technology • Be prepared to veer from your use of the slideshow if your audience shows signs of boredom or visual fatigue
Internet-based presentations			
Appropriate for: • Audiences doing business on the Internet • Audiences that will access your Internet site • Internal customers that will access the company Intranet site	• Demonstrate the capabilities of your site • Demonstrate the type of information available on your site • Highlight the advantages of your site vs. other sites	• Get bogged down in the features of a site and forget the important points of your presentation • Get bogged down in the technical aspects of the site, especially if your audience is not technical • Deliver a presentation based on Internet technology without practice, practice, practice	• Make sure that the technology to support your Internet-based presentation is available at the talk site • Develop a backup plan in case something goes wrong with the technology • Be prepared to veer from your use of the Internet if your audience shows signs of boredom or visual fatigue

Types of Visual Support and Audiences

Type of Visual Support and Audiences	Should Be Used To:	Don't:	Things to Keep in Mind
Videotape Appropriate for: • Audiences that require visual demonstration of a sales technique, product, or competitor's product or service • Audiences that are geographically dispersed • Cases where the featured speaker (CEO, president, or motivational speaker) is unavailable for an appearance	• Demonstrate the capabilities of your product or service • Demonstrate a technique or process • Deliver personal message from a CEO, motivational speaker, or other source not available for a personal appearance	• Simply turn on the videotape and walk away. Videotape should be used to enhance a presentation, not substitute for one • Use poor-quality video. If you can't find or develop a video that has high audio and video quality, find another type of support • Deliver a presentation based on video technology without practice, practice, practice	• Make sure that the technology to support the portion of your videotape presentation is available at the talk site • Develop a backup plan in case something goes wrong with the technology
Models Appropriate for: • Presentations that require a 3-D or visual demonstration of a product or idea • Cases where a visual representation is important or will improve understanding. For example, architects often use models to present building concepts	• Illustrate or clarify points that are confusing. For example, crime scene models are often used in court cases to help with a witness's testimony • Create excitement about a product or idea that is in the development stage	• Use models that have not been professionally prepared • Rely on the model to make your case or sell your idea. The model is a support for the presentation, not the presentation	• Should be professionally prepared • If model is a large visual model, be sure that it is backed on foam board. Foam board is more stable than poster board and doesn't buckle when placed on an easel

Types of Visual Support and Audiences

Type of Visual Support and Audiences	Should Be Used To:	Don't:	Things to Keep in Mind
Flip charts Appropriate for: • Audiences that will be brainstorming or generating ideas on the fly • Audiences that are less formal in nature, like teams or groups, or for meetings • Audiences meeting in places where technology is not available • Training classes	• Brainstorm or draw • Collate the ideas or views of a group or meeting	• Allow flip charts prepared in advance to become dated or soiled • Use poor-quality flip charts in professional situations. With the availability of technology, few audiences have any tolerance for hand-drawn charts or hand-labeled graphics • Use flip charts in a technological environment. Learn the technology that is appropriate for the audience you are speaking to	• Make sure you have an easel or other way to display the charts • Use charts big enough for the space you are speaking in. If you are speaking to more than twenty people, chances are someone in your audience will not be able to see your flip chart
Whiteboards Appropriate for: • Audiences that will be brainstorming or generating ideas on the fly • Audiences that are less formal in nature, like teams or groups, or for meetings • Audiences meeting in places where technology is not available • Training classes	• Brainstorm or draw • Collate the ideas or views of a group or meeting	• Use whiteboards as your primary visual aid for a formal presentation	• Write legibly and large enough for everyone to read what you put on the board • Erase completely • Bring markers and erasers with you if you aren't sure they will be available

Types of Visual Support and Audiences

Type of Visual Support and Audiences	Should Be Used To:	Don't:	Things to Keep in Mind
Transparencies Appropriate for: • Audiences meeting in places where higher levels of technology are not available • Training classes	• Collate the ideas or views of a group or meeting • Present training points • Back up higher technology options when technology fails or is unavailable	• Keep using transparencies that have become dated or faded • Use transparencies simply because you don't want to learn new technology	• Make sure an overhead projector is available at your site. These have become rare in most business environments • Use overheads big enough for the space you are speaking in. If you are speaking to more than 30 people, chances are someone in the back of your audience will not be able to see your transparaency
Handouts Appropriate for: • Audiences meeting in places where higher levels of technology are not available • Cases where supplemental materials are necessary • Training classes or where hard-copy supporting materials are needed	• Provide hard-copy supporting materials • Provide graphics to large groups where technology is not available or would not be clearly viewed by the entire audience • Back up higher technology options when technology fails or is unavailable	• Distribute your materials unless what is on the paper is highly valuable. We all have too much paper to deal with • Dump your entire presentation to a handout that you then read from • Pass out the handout when you are speaking	• Distributing your handout while you speak is distracting • Wait till the end of the presentation to hand out materials

Chalkboards—Seen one lately?

Tips for Successful Interpersonal Communication

Type	Definition	Tips for Success
Downward Communication	Communication flows from the top of the organizational chart down. Some examples are: • Goals, values, and vision • Tasks • Schedules • Policies and procedures • Performance appraisals and raise information	1. When communicating tasks to subordinates, tell them how to do a task and why the task is important or fits into the overall scheme of the business. 2. When discussing a problem or conflict, stay on the topic and deal with the employee's behavior, rather than the person. 3. Use written messages only when appropriate and with follow-up and feedback.
Upward Communication	Communication flows from the bottom of the organizational chart up. Some examples are: • Task reports, monthly memos, and status reports • Suggestions for improvement • Complaints about working conditions or coworkers • Problems to be resolved • Feedback about messages from a supervisor	1. Don't conceal or sugarcoat bad news or problems. Eventually, your supervisor will discover the problem and you will lose credibility. 2. Do not distort the facts about a situation that occurs with a coworker. State the facts and give your manager time to respond to the situation. 3. Keep your supervisor aware of your and your team members' significant achievements.
Peer Communication	Communication flows from side to side, between team members, work groups, or department members. Some examples are: • Task coordination • Job-sharing scheduling • Invitations to lunch	1. Keep gossip out of the workplace. Gossip is not only detrimental, it is unethical professional behavior. 2. Be helpful, be kind, and be smart. Never say or write anything you don't want repeated.

Tips for Successful Written Communication

Type	Definition	Tips for Success
E-mail	Short, brief written conversations that call for a quick decision, impart specific or general knowledge, or provide opportunities for networking. Some examples are: • Request for a decision • Directions to a customer's site • Appointment confirmations • Invitation to a group lunch • Follow-up on a memo or report	1. Don't send memos in e-mail form. Studies show that people have limited time in the day to respond to e-mail messages. E-mails that contain detailed information or complex instruction sets may not be given the attention they deserve. Write a brief e-mail describing the memo and requesting the reader print and read the attached memo. 2. Don't abuse e-mail. You will lose credibility if you send e-mails without purpose or substance. 3. Purge and archive e-mails regularly to avoid becoming overwhelmed by your inbox.
Memos	Official company messages that impart specific information or a specific request. Examples are: • Changes in policies or procedures • Changes to schedules • Sales reports • Status reports • Requests for equipment or staff	1. Memos should be one to five pages long. Beyond five pages, the memo becomes a report. 2. Memos should cover one to three specific and related topics. 3. Memos should contain a request for feedback where necessary. 4. Use subheads for memos that are longer than two pages to orient your audience.
Reports	Informational messages that contain large amounts of complex or detailed knowledge. Examples are: • Corporate prospectuses • White papers • Quarterly and annual sales reports • Needs assessments • Requests for equipment or staff	1. Begin by outlining the purpose, scope, and major headings for the report. 2. Analyze the audience for the report. 3. If you are preparing a report for the first time, request copies of previous reports to use as an example. 4. If you are stating a problem, end with recommendations for improvement. 5. Provide only the information that is necessary to inform, educate, and lead your audience to an appropriate decision or conclusion.

Tips for Successful Group and Team Communication

Type	Definition	Tips for Success
Groups	Work groups, departments, or units formed for specific projects. In groups, the operation is more informal, jobs are less connected, and the charge of the group is less specific than in teams. Some examples are: • Committee formed to plan the 25th anniversary celebration of a school • Managers that meet once a month to discuss customer complaints • Committee formed to review a faculty member for tenure	1. Help your group define its purpose and stay on track. 2. Don't belittle other group members' ideas or contributions. 3. Complete group assignments on time and with a high level of quality. 4. Keep information about the group in the group unless all group members agree to make the information public.
Teams	Formally appointed groups of employees whose jobs cut across departments, function, or capability. Teams are given a specific charge to solve a problem, design a product, or change a procedure. Examples are: • Reengineering group charged with redesigning the accounting department • A team charged with bringing your organization into compliance • Product design team charged with creating a car for the 2010 auto show	1. Don't allow conflict or disagreements to interfere with the effectiveness of the team. 2. Ask team members for feedback to ideas you offer and be open to the feedback received. 3. Keep team meetings short and to a minimum. 4. Recognize when your team has accomplished its goal and is no longer needed.

STRATEGY SELECTION CRITERIA WORKSHEET

Strategy	Brutal	Rational	Rational/Emotional	Mindful
What type of presentation would work best?	• One-on-one	• One-on-one • Small groups • Large audiences	• One-one-one • Small groups • Large audiences	• One-on-one • Small groups • Large audiences
What are the needs of your audience?	• Not considered	• Clearly definable	• Somewhat definable/somewhat fluid	• Clearly definable
What type of choices will your audience be presented with?	• None or either/or	• Multiple with best alternative presented	• Call to action	• Choice that reflects personal responsibility and organizational accountability
How open to your position, product, or idea has your audience been in the past?	• Closed or resistant	• Somewhat open	• Persuadable	• Open
What method of persuasion would work best?	• Strategic control—the use of authority to warrant compliance	• Logos—an appeal that is based in evidence and logic	• Logos/pathos—a logical appeal that induces the emotions of the audience	• Ethos—an appeal that is based on the credibility of the speaker and his or her ability to follow through on commitments
What personal trait does your argument rely on: organizational authority, personal credibility, knowledge, or expertise?	• Authority	• Knowledge or expertise	• Credibility and Empathy	• All
What is your goal?	• Compliance	• Consensus	• Action	• Commitment

Sample Interview Script

Establish rapport	These questions should put the interviewee at ease and break the ice. Examples are: • How was your flight? • Did you have trouble finding us?
Define the interviewee's experience	These questions arise from the cover letter, résumé, and references. Examples are: • I see that you majored in communication. How has your major prepared you for this job? • Tell us a little about your current position. • What are two things about your current job that you find challenging? • What are two things about your current job that you dislike? • What has been your biggest accomplishment at your current position? • What will you miss most about the company you work for? • Of all the jobs you have had, which has been the best fit, and why?
Clarify the requirements for the position	These questions zero in on the requirements for the position. Examples are: • This position requires hiring and developing a team of writers and trainers. How would you go about doing that? • In this position, you will be required to manage a team. What qualities do you think are important in a team environment? • As a manager, you will be required to report the progress of your team. How do you feel about providing regular status reports? • An important function of this position is liaison to other teams. What skills do you have that will facilitate this function? • How would this position further your career goals?
Present the organization	These questions open a discussion of the organization. Examples are: • What do you know about Bilin.com? • How do you feel about working for an Internet startup, coming from such an established company? • Bilin is a small, young company and we can't offer the benefits some organizations can. Is that a problem? • We have just signed three major contracts, which has tripled our deliverables overnight. To meet our schedules, we know that we have to work extremely long hours. Is there anything to prevent you from working long hours when necessary?
Provide closure	These questions signal the end of the interview and allow for a final opportunity to clarify information. Examples are: • Do you have any additional questions? • If offered the position, when could you start?

Tips for Conducting Performance Reviews

Before the review	• Ask for a written evaluation from the employee of his or her performance.
	• Carefully read the employee evaluation before you complete your evaluation.
	• Review (if a record exists) the employee's past two performance appraisals.
	• Outline the areas of the employee's performance that exceeded expectations, met expectations, and fell short of expectations for the appraisal period.
	• Indicate areas that have fallen below expectations over the past two review periods.
	• Outline a course of action for the employee to follow that will meet expectations.
	• Document the course of action in a memo for both you and the employee to sign.
During the review	• Present the evaluation to the employee beginning with areas that exceeded expectations, followed by those that met expectations, and ending with those that were below expectations.
	• Keep the focus on the employee's job performance and team and group interactions.
	• Avoid making vague references to the employee's "attitude" or other subjective references.
	• Present the course of action for improvement.
	• Ask the employee if he or she has have questions.
	• Offer the employee a brief period to think about the evaluation and respond either in writing or in person.
	• Ask the employee to sign the review memo documenting the course of action. Indicate that you will expect the memo to be signed by the employee by a specific date and that a nonresponse on the part of the employee indicates agreement with the memo as is.
After the review	• Follow up on the memo if the employee has not signed it by the date specified.
	• Continue to document problems as they arise, but don't harp on problems that have been discussed and solved.
	• Praise the employee for changes and progress made.
	• Follow up with additional reviews as needed at three-month intervals.

Tips for Preparing and Participating in Performance Reviews

Before the review	• Prepare a written evaluation of your work prior to the manager's evaluation. • If you are not asked for a self-evaluation, check with your manager two weeks before your review date and request the opportunity to provide a self-evaluation. • In your evaluation, give an honest assessment of your performance. Include the areas where you believe you went above and beyond the requirements of the job and the areas where you need improvement. • Outline goals for the next review cycle. The goals you outline should reflect your individual and team goals. • Submit a well-thought-out, well-reasoned, organized appraisal of your work.
During the review	• Listen, listen, listen. By now, your manager knows what you think. Now, it is his or her turn. Listen carefully to everything your manager has to say. • Take notes. • Be gracious when given praise or high marks for doing well. • Acknowledge areas you know need improvement. • Ask for a period to reflect on and respond to areas that may be in dispute. • Walk away from the appraisal without being defensive, negative, or closed to suggestions offered by your manager.
After the review	• Spend some time honestly thinking about your appraisal. • Don't talk about your review with coworkers. Submit a well-thought-out, well-reasoned, organized assessment of your appraisal if you believe any areas were unfair. • Indicate areas of agreement and areas seem unfair or too harsh. Suggest ways to remedy the disagreement. Indicate that you are willing to work on your performance and toward an amicable conclusion. • Give your manager an opportunity to respond.

GLOSSARY

adaptive skill *The ability of team members to adapt their behaviors to the needs and expectations of others.*

agenda *The tool used to organize a meeting.*

ambiguity *Expressing yourself in terms that are unclear or open to multiple interpretations.*

attention getter *The story, joke, or first line of a persuasive message, based on Monroe's Motivational Sequence, designed to pull the audience into your message.*

bookmarks *A way of tagging information on the Internet so you can return to it quickly for future reference.*

breakthrough skill *A skill, or skill set, that allows people to act purposefully and competently with others in a global environment.*

briefings *A type of speech that allows a speaker to disseminate a concise number of facts in a short amount of time.*

brutal strategy *A one-sided strategy of persuasion that offers the listener little or no choice.*

bureaucracy *A system of organization marked by hierarchy, set rules, and fixed divisions of labor.*

business and professional communication *A shorthand term that refers to all forms of speaking, listening, relating, writing, and responding in the workplace, both human and electronically mediated.*

call to action *The direct or indirect statement of action you want the audience to take that is placed at the end of a message based on Monroe's Motivated Sequence.*

cause/effect *An organizational pattern used to structure a presentation that offers a cause and its resulting effect.*

CCCD *A four-step model for conscious communication that includes: choose, create, coordinate, and deliver.*

channel *The thoroughfare a message takes from sender to receiver including: electronically mediated methods of message delivery such as radio, television, computers, and satellites, as well as the full range of print media such as office memos and letters, as well as newspapers, magazines, advertising flyers and brochures, and books.*

character appeals *Appeals that rely on the reputation and experience of the speaker.*

chronological *An organizational pattern used to structure a presentation that details the sequence of events.*

clarity *Providing messages in the clearest, least ambiguous way.*

clip art *Computer generated art and graphics that can be dropped into a document to add impact or interest.*

closed questions *Questions that require specific, concrete answers and provide little room for elaboration.*

communication history *The cumulative record of communication events between participants.*

concierge persuasion *A way of looking at persuasion that allows a speaker to offer a persuasive message that fits a particular situation. It is persuasion based on discrete problem-solving and assiduous service.*

conclusion *The ending of a presentation that summarizes the main points, restates the thesis or purpose statement and ties back to the attention-getter used in the introduction.*

conflict *Feelings or perceptions of imbalance that arise in a relational setting.*

conscious communication *Awareness of communication as a process, respects diversity, and requires balancing strategy, ethics, and outcomes.*

conscious listening *Listening openly to a speaker's point of view and reflecting on how talk affects the whole.*

constraint *Organizational limits on: resources, time, money, projects, and creativity.*

creativity *What results from giving people the freedom to explore alternatives beyond the traditional ways of doing things.*

credibility *Derived from a speaker's perceived status, believability, and trustworthiness with an audience.*

critical listening *The ability of a listener to deliberate on what is said by exploring the logic, reason, and point of view of the speaker.*

cultural agility *Recognizing that important communication differences exist among people from different cultures.*

culture *The way of life for an entire society, including codes of manners, dress, language, religion, rituals, norms of behavior such as law and morality, and systems of belief.*

details *The area of a résumé that allows you to expand upon the highlights and describe and explain each experience.*

dialectic *The interaction of two arguments that by nature are oppositional.*

dialogue *Communication that focuses on mutuality and relational growth, rather than self-interest.*

dialogue *Balanced communication that allows all participants to speak and voice their opinions and perspectives.*

diversity *Cultural, gender, racial, religious, and socioeconomic differences.*

downward communication *Communication that occurs between you and anyone lower than you within the organizational hierarchy.*

electronically mediated communication *Includes phone conversations, text messages, satellite conferences, e-mail, instant messaging, personal and company web pages, and the use of the Internet for business communication through social networking and e-commerce.*

email *Electronic mail transmitted from your computer instantaneously to anywhere in the world.*

emotional appeals *Appeals that play on the audience's emotions or sympathies.*

empathy *A demonstration by a speaker that they share the feelings or experiences of their audience.*

employment interview *An interview designed to bring together potential employees and employers to test the fit of someone for a position.*

empowerment *The process of enabling and motivating employees, mainly by removing roadblocks, which builds feelings of personal effectiveness and control.*

environment *The integral parts of an organization that overlap to create a space for communication and understanding.*

equity *Give and take between two communication partners.*

ethos *The perceived credibility or expertise of a speaker.*

exclusive message strategies *An autocratic communication style that reveals a "me" oriented pattern of behavior.*

expertise *A demonstration of a high level of skill or knowledge in a particular area.*

facts *A source of basic, empirically verifiable information.*

feedback *Providing others with an evaluation of the effectiveness of their communication, or the response employees give to bosses and to each other to the communication, ideas, and identities they receive.*

fluency *The smooth or effortless articulation of the words that comprise a speech.*

focus groups *A group assembled to help explore an idea or test a product or a concept.*

font size *The size of text as it appears on paper or visually.*

font typeface *A set of letters, numbers, or symbols that appears a particular way when displayed visually.*

formal interviews *An interview that is very structured and centers on closed questions designed to gather very specific information.*

gendered talk *The differences between the ways that men and women communicate.*

global mindset *The ability to work in or lead global organizations that exist*

within a variety of different social, economic, and political environments.

goal *A concrete achievable end or the set and planned accomplishments of an organization.*

haptics *The study of touching as a nonverbal form of human communication.*

headlines *The area of a résumé that contains categories that emphasize the parts of your résumé that stand out the most.*

hearing *The passive and physical process of listening.*

hierarchical noise *The shadings in meaning attributed to rank or status within an organization.*

hierarchy *The system of authority, rank, and status within an organization.*

highlights *The area of a résumé that contains the most important facts you want emphasized under each headline.*

hostile work environment *An environment in which sexually-explicit, intimidating, or offensive verbal or nonverbal communication interferes with someone's work.*

human communication *Includes informal conversations, interviews, group and team meetings, informative briefings and speeches, sales pitches, and persuasive presentations.*

human relations movement *A theoretical movement that viewed employees as sources of group information and skill that could be developed through training and education.*

inclusive message strategies *A democratic form of communication that takes into account the group or culture, thoughts and feelings of others, while valuing other's contributions and differences.*

informal interviews *An interview that is unstructured and covers a wide variety of topics using open questions.*

information overload *What occurs when too many forms of communication intersect at one time, making decision making and response difficult.*

information transfer model *A model that posited information was passed directly from sender to receiver.*

informational listening *The stage in the listening process where meaning is assigned to the words we hear.*

informative presentation *A presentation that attempts to present facts and information in an unpersuasive manner.*

interdependence *The pattern of contingent decision making that understands the need to revise decision making based on new information and the effects of past decisions.*

interrogations *A one-sided form of interviewing that concentrates on the negative aspects of a problem.*

interview scripts *A plan of questions used for an interview.*

introduction *The beginning of a presentation that gets an audience's attention, states the thesis or purpose statement, and previews what is to come.*

jamming *The positive energies that emerge from total group coordination (and fun) when every individual has a role to play in the team as well as a chance to demonstrate individual skills.*

job description *A description of an open position that usually includes experience, salary, and education requirements.*

job goals *The types of positions you want and the outcomes you want from your employment.*

kinesics *The study of body movement including facial expressions, eye contact, and gestures.*

learning organization *An organization marked by conscious systems-based thinking and an ability to continually adapt communication to organizational, cultural, and individual changes.*

listening *The process of hearing and interpreting messages.*

logical appeal *An appeal that makes persuasive use of facts and figures and cited authorities to motivate understanding of a problem or situation.*

logos *The ability of a speaker to sway an audience using logic or reason.*

luddite *A person who refuses to adapt to new forms of technology in their lives.*

memos *Short snippets of information about a specific topic.*

mental models *The images, assumptions, and stories that permeate the minds or the people working in organizations.*

message *What is said and done during a communication interaction, both verbally and nonverbally.*

mindful communication *An approach to communication that is both purposeful and strategic and emphasizes the audience and expected outcomes.*

mindful strategy *A persuasive strategy that emphasizes a deep connection between the speaker and the audience.*

mindless communication *Episodes of small talk or automatic talk that occur in familiar situations.*

monitoring *Checking the accuracy of your perceptions and questioning the factors that lead to those perceptions about your communication.*

Monroe's Motivated Sequence *An organizational pattern that contains five steps: attention-getter, need, satisfaction, visualization, and call to action.*

motivation *The force or reason that drives us to speak.*

narratives *The representation of experience in the form of a story.*

naturalness *An easy, genuine, conversational manner of speaking.*

need *The spoken, written, or visual portion of a message that details the problem or need for the audience in Monroe's Motivated Sequence.*

needs assessment *A survey or questionnaire that is developed to find out what an audience needs or wants from your company or what problems an audience might have.*

netiquette *The rules of etiquette that govern online interaction on the Internet.*

networks (technology definition) *Two or more computers that are connected either locally (within a company or building) or widely (across different geographical locations) by cable, phone lines, or satellite.*

noise *Any sound that disrupts or interferes with the delivery of a message, or the physical, semantic, and hierarchical influences that either disrupt or shape the interpretation of messages.*

non-supportive messages *Messages that appear aloof or superior and are disrespectful of others in the workplace.*

nonverbal competence *The ability of a speaker to maintain an appropriate level of eye contact with listeners, use gestures without making them appear repetitive or redundant, use purposeful body movement and incorporate visual aids smoothly in a presentation.*

objectives *The tasks required to reach a goal and create a vision.*

oculesics *The study of the eyes as a source of communication information.*

open questions *Questions that require more than a yes or no response and that allow you room to discuss your experience or perspective on a topic.*

organizational crisis *A traumatic situation triggered by a natural disaster, an unforeseen event, or human cause that requires the organization to implement a crisis strategy before resolution or restoration of the company's image can occur.*

organizational culture *The histories, habits, values, and rules for conduct that make working in an organization feel unique.*

outcomes *What you want to achieve as a result of your presentation.*

pathos *The ability to sway an audience using feelings or emotions.*

perception *The way we process and interpret cues from a person's outward appearance, voice, and language usage.*

performance review *A review or critique of an employee's work and job performance.*

personal constructs *The specific evaluations we make of people based on our assessment of their habits and behaviors.*

personal mastery *A form of empowerment that emphasizes the need for continuous growth and renewal as vital to both the individual and the organization.*

personal prototypes *The stereotypes we assign to people when we first meet them.*

personal space *The relationship of nonverbal communication and the spatial distance between speakers.*

persuasive communication *Communication with a goal to bring an audience to a decision or action.*

persuasive interviews *A sales oriented form of interviewing intended to convince a client or customer to buy into an idea or make a purchase.*

persuasive presentation *A presentation designed to bring the audience to a decision or action.*

physical diversions *Any physical element that disrupts or interferes with the delivery of a message.*

physical noise *Noise that emanates from the physical environment.*

policies *The guidelines that oversee conduct in the workplace.*

power distance *How members of institutions and organizations expect and accept the unequal distribution of power.*

power *The sources of influence derived by an individual within an organization.*

preview *A review of what will be discussed in a presentation.*

primary audience *The audience from which you have the most to lose if your message is not delivered effectively.*

problem/solution *An organizational pattern used to structure a presentation that states a problem and then offers one or more solutions.*

proxemics *The study of interpersonal space and distance.*

purpose statement *A statement that defines the primary goal for a message.*

quid pro quo *Harassment based on the threat of retaliation or promise of favoritism or promotion in exchange for dating or sexual favors. "This for that."*

rational strategy *A two-sided strategy of persuasion that presents alternatives and a best solution as a persuasive method.*

rational/emotional strategy *A mass appeal as a persuasive strategy, presented to a large audience, that makes use of an attention-getter, need, satisfaction, visualization, and call to action format.*

receiver *The person to whom a message is initially directed.*

reference *A citation of a noted authority which lends credibility to a presentation.*

reports *A type of speech that allows a speaker to introduce and explain information over an expanded period, or detailed coverage of one or more related topics.*

reputation *A record of a company's past and a resource for the future, based on factors of quality, credibility, and fiscal responsibility.*

résumé *A formal statement of who you are. Résumés are part autobiography, part work history, and part sales presentation.*

rewards *The benefits people receive from work (e.g., money, identity, power, support, companionship, a skill set, etc.) in relation to what it "costs" them (physical labor, mental and emotional stress, free time, time away from families, subordinating personal goals, dealing with difficult people, harassment, etc.).*

rules *The taken-for-granted assumptions and formal pronouncements for communication between and among employees.*

S.M.A.R.T. *A method for setting goals that allows you to align your outcomes with criteria for success that are specific, measurable, achievable, realistic, and time-bound.*

satisfaction *The part of a message that conveys the solution to the audience's need(s) or problem(s) in Monroe's Motivational Sequence.*

schemata *The mental pattern recognition plans that help us identify and organize incoming information.*

scientific management *The theory that posited organizations should be operated as efficient machines governed by scientific principles, rules, and laws.*

scripts *The patterned sequences of talk we use everyday.*

secondary audience *Any group that is not immediately affected by the crisis, but who is concerned about the crisis.*

self-disclosure *Providing personal information within a conversation.*

self-reflexive listening *Listening for the way in which a message applies to the listener's life.*

semantic noise *The differences people have for the meanings of words which include the gender, racial, jargon, and cultural biases of the receiver as well as other misunderstandings.*

sender *The originator of a message.*

sensitivity *Taking into consideration the speaking differences of a communication partner.*

sexual harassment *Any form of sexually-explicit verbal or nonverbal communication that interferes with someone's work.*

shared vision *Ownership of an organizational mission and vision that is built upon a foundation of trust, openness, empowerment, and honesty.*

statistics *Empirically verifiable information presented in the form of numbers.*

strategic communication *Communication planned with specific audiences and specific intentions in mind, that is cognizant of individual and cultural differences.*

supportive messages *Messages that communicate concern and respect for others and indicate cooperation.*

synergy *The shared knowledge, diversity of experience, and collaborative energy that results from mindful team communication.*

systems thinking *An organization in which employees and managers understand the interconnectedness of communication between and among individuals and teams.*

team *What exists when group members recognize the synergy that is created from shared knowledge, diversity of experience, and collaborative energy.*

team learning *Represented by the conscious, coordinated action that translates shared vision, mental models, and personal mastery into thinking and acting as a team.*

technical diversions *Any technological element that disrupts or interferes with the delivery of a message.*

telecommuting *Working from your home or other remote location away from your company's primary location.*

thesis statement *A statement that is a simple declarative sentence that introduces an audience to a message and announces the speaker's intentions.*

topical *An organizational pattern used to structure a presentation that follows topically from the main idea through a logical topical sequence.*

training presentation *A type of speech that is used when participants require examples, exercises, and practice to grasp the information being presented.*

transactional process model *A model that posits the idea that power shifts from the managers within hierarchy to the relationship between the manager and the employee.*

transition *The connection of one topic or point to another within a presentation, or, the process of replacing one slide for another in a PowerPoint presentation.*

turf battle *When a team's priorities conflict with those of another team within an organization.*

upward communication *Communication that occurs between you and anyone higher than you within the organizational hierarchy.*

verbal examples *Comparisons that help make a point within a presentation.*

video conferencing *Conducting a conference between two or more participants at different sites by using computer networks, or audio and video equipment.*

virtual communities *Communities that exist primarily on the Internet.*

virtual meetings *Meetings that occur over wide geographical space, that may include inside and outside team members, and use technology as the principal delivery system.*

virtual teams *Teams that are located in more than one physical location.*

vision *The overall far-reaching idea of what a team or organization should accomplish and the values that should inform those accomplishments.*

visual cues *The statements, quotes, or other information placed within the presentation to emphasize or strengthen a point.*

visual examples *Examples that walk an audience through a complex concept, often with images or supplementary materials.*

visualization *The words or images used to create a visual image of the satisfaction portion of a message based on Monroe's Motivated Sequence.*

vivacity *The energy and enthusiasm used by the speaker and generated among audience members when speaking.*

voice mail *Messages left on a telephone answering system.*

REFERENCES

Abernathy, D. J. (1999, May). A chat with Chris Argyris. *Training and Development, 53,* 80–85.

Albrecht, K. (1992). *The only thing that matters: Bringing the power of the customer into the center of your business.* New York: HarperBusiness.

Allen, M., & Caillouet, R. (1994). Legitimation endeavors: Impression management strategies used by an organization in crisis. *Communication Monographs, 61,* 44–62.

Alvesson, M. (1993). *Cultural perspectives on organizations.* New York: Cambridge University Press.

Alvesson, M. (2002). Indentity regulations as organizational control: Producing the appropriate individual. *Journal of Management Studies, 39*(5), 619–644.

Andersen, P. A. (1993). Cognitive schemata in personal relationships. In S. Duck (Ed.), *Individuals and relationships* (pp. 207–230). Newbury Park, CA: Sage.

Andersen, P. A. (1998). *Nonverbal communication.* Mountain View, CA: Mayfield.

Andersen, P. A., Andersen, J. F., & Landgraf, J. (1985). *The development of nonverbal communication competence in childhood.* Paper presented at the annual convention of the International Communication Association, Honolulu.

Andersen, P. A., Todd-Mancillas, W. R., & DiClemente, L. (1980). The effects of pupil dilation in physical, social, and task attraction. *Australian Scan: A Journal of Communication, 7 & 8,* 89–95.

Anderson, J. (1987). *Communication research: Issues and methods.* New York: McGraw-Hill.

Anderson, J. (2003). Forum response: Ethics in business and teaching. *Management Communication Quarterly, 17,* 155–164.

Anderson, R., Cissna, K., & Arnett, R. (1994). *The reach of dialogue.* Cresskill, NJ: Hampton Press.

Anderson, W. T. (1995). *The truth about the truth.* New York: Tarcher/Putnam.

Argyris, C. (1994, July–August). Good communication that blocks learning. *Harvard Business Review,* 77–85.

Argyris, C., & Schon, D. (1978). *Organizational learning: A theory of action perspective.* Reading, MA: Addison-Wesley.

Arnett, R., & Cissna, K. (1996). *The reach of dialogue: Confirmation, voice, and community.* Cresskill, NJ: Hampton Press.

Ashford, S., & Cummings, L. (1983). Feedback as an individual resource: Personal strategies of creating information. *Organizational Behavior and Human Performance, 32,* 370–3.

Atkouf, O. (1992). Management and theories of organizations in the 1990s: Toward a critical radical humanism? *Academy of Management Review, 17,* 407–431.

Axley, S. (1984). Managerial and organizational communication in terms of the conduit metaphor. *Academy of Management Review, 9,* 428–437.

Bales, R., & Strodtbeck, F. (1960). Phases in group problem solving. In D. Cartwright & A. Zander (Eds.), *Group dynamics: Research and theory* (pp. 624–638). New York: Harper & Row.

Banta, M. (1993). *Taylored lives: Narrative productions in the age of Taylor, Veblen, and Ford.* Chicago: University of Chicago Press.

Bantz, C. (1993). *Understanding organizations: Interpreting organizational communication cultures.* Columbia: University of South Carolina Press.

Barker, R. T., & Camarata, M. R. (1998). The role of communication in a learning organization. *Journal of Business Communication, 35*(4), 443–467.

Barley, S. (1983). Semiotics and the study of occupational and organizational culture. *Administrative Science Quarterly, 23,* 393–413.

Barnard, C. (1938/1968). *The functions of the executive.* Cambridge, MA: Harvard University Press.

Barnet, R., & Cavanagh, J. (1994). *Global dreams.* New York: Simon & Schuster.

Barnlund, D. (1994). *Communicative styles of Japanese and Americans.* Belmont, CA: Wadsworth.

Bateson, G. (1992). *Sacred unity: Further steps toward an ecology of mind.* San Francisco: HarperSanFrancisco.

Bavelas, A. (1951). Communication patterns in task oriented groups. In D. Lerner & H. Laswell (Eds.), *The policy sciences* (pp. 193–202). Stanford, CA: Stanford University Press.

Baxter, L. A. (1988). A dialectical perspective on communication strategies in relational development. In S. Duck (Ed.), *Handbook of personal relationships* (pp. 257–273). Chicester, UK: Wiley.

Baxter, L. A., & Montgomery, B. M. (1996). *Relating: Dialogues and dialectics.* New York: Guilford Press.

Bellah, R., Madsen, R., Sullivan, W., Swidler, A., & Tipton, S. (1985). *Habits of the heart.* Berkeley: University of California Press.

Bellah, R., Madsen, R., Sullivan, W., Swidler, A., & Tipton, S. (1991). *The good society.* New York: Knopf.

Benne, K., & Sheats, P. (1948). Functional roles of group members. *Journal of Social Issues, 4,* 41–49.

Bennis, W. (1999). *Managing people is like herding cats: Warren Bennis on leadership.* Provo, UT: Executive Excellence.

Berger, C. R., & Calabrese, R. J. (1975). Some explorations in initial interaction and beyond: Toward a theory of interpersonal communication. *Human Communication Research, 1,* 99–112.

Berger, P., & Luckmann, T. (1967). *The social construction of reality.* Garden City, NY: Anchor.

Berlo, D. (1960). *The process of communication.* New York: Holt, Rinehart & Winston.

Beyer, J., & Trice, H. (1987). How an organizations rites reveal its culture. *Organizational Dynamics, 15,* 4–35.

Bingham, S. (1991). Communication strategies for managing sexual harassment in organizations: Understanding message options and their effects. *Journal of Applied Communication Research, 19,* 88–115.

Birdwistell, R. L. (1970). *Kinesics and context.* Philadelphia: University of Pennsylvania Press.

Blumer, H. (1969). *Symbolic interactionism: Perspective and method.* Englewood Cliffs, NJ: Prentice-Hall.

Bochner, A. (1982). The functions of human communication in interpersonal bonding. In C. Arnold & J. Waite-Bowers (Eds.), *Handbook of rhetorical and communication theory* (pp. 544–621). Boston: Allyn & Bacon.

Bochner, A. P. (1994). Perspectives on inquiry II: Theories and stories. In M. L. Knapp & G. R. Miller (Eds.), *Handbook of interpersonal communication* (pp. 21–41). Newbury Park, CA: Sage.

Bochner, A. P. (1997). It's about time: Narrative and the divided self. *Qualitative Inquiry, 3,* 418–439.

Boje, D. (1991). The storytelling organization: A study of story performance in an office-supply firm. *Administrative Science Quarterly, 36,* 106–126.

Boje, D. (1995). Stories of the storytelling organization: A postmodern analysis of Disney in "Tamara-Land." *Academy of Management Journal, 38,* 997–1035.

Bracci, S. (1999, November). *Visions of community: Ethical issues in public relations and community building.* A highlighted panel, National Communication Association annual meeting, Chicago.

Brown, M., & McMillan, J. (1991). Culture as text: The development of an organizational narrative. *Southern Communication Journal, 57,* 49–60.

Brownell, J. (2002). *Listening: Attitudes, principles, and skills.* Boston: Allyn & Bacon.

Browning, L. (1992). Lists and stories as organizational communication. *Communication Theory, 2,* 281–302.

Browning, L., & Hawes, L. (1991). Style, process, surface, context: Consulting as postmodern art. *Journal of Applied Communication Research, 19,* 32–54.

Buber, M. (1985). *Between man and man* (2nd ed.). New York: Macmillan.

Buck, R. (1979). Individual differences in nonverbal sending accuracy and electrodermal responding: The externalizing-internalizing dimension. In R. Rosenthal (Ed.), *Skill in nonverbal communication: Individual differences* (pp. 111–139).

Cambridge, MA: Oelgeschlager, Gunn & Hain.

Buckman, R. H. (1997). [Interview, vice chairman of Buckman Laboratories International].

Bullis, C., & Bach, B. (1989). Socialization turning points: An examination of change in organizational identification. *Western Journal of Speech Communication, 53,* 273–293.

Bullis, C., & Glaser, H. (1992). Bureaucratic discourse and the goddess: Towards an ecofeminist critique and rearticulation. *Journal of Organizational Change Management, 5,* 50–60.

Burke, K. (1989). *On symbols and society.* Chicago: University of Chicago Press.

Burke, W. (1986). Leadership as empowering others. In S. Srivasta (Ed.), *Executive power* (pp. 51–77). San Francisco: Jossey-Bass.

Buzzanell, P. (1994). Gaining a voice: Feminist organizational communication theorizing. *Management Communication Quarterly, 7,* 339–383.

Calas, M., & Smircich, L. (1993). Dangerous liaisons: The "feminine in management" meets "globalization." *Business Horizons, 36,* 71–81.

Canadian Manager Office Team. (1999). *Canadian Manager, 24*(2), 20.

Cheney, G., & Mumby, D. (1997). Communication and organizational democracy: Introduction. *Communication Studies, 48,* 277–279.

Chiles, A., & Zorn, T. (1995). Empowerment in organizations: Employees' perceptions of the influences on empowerment. *Journal of Applied Communication Research, 23,* 1–25.

Clair, R. (1993). The use of framing devices to sequester organizational narratives: Hegemony and harassment. *Communication Monographs, 60,* 113–136.

Clair, R. (1998). *Organizing silence.* Albany: State University of New York Press.

Clegg, S. (1989). *Frameworks of power.* Newbury Park, CA: Sage.

Coles, R. (1989). *The call of stories: Teaching and moral imagination.* Boston: Houghton Mifflin.

Conger, J., & Kanungo, R. (1988). The empowerment process: Integrating theory and practice. *Academy of Management Review, 13,* 471–482.

Conquergood, D. (1991). Rethinking ethnography: Towards a critical cultural politics. *Communication Monographs, 58,* 179–194.

Conrad, C. (1983). Organizational power: Faces and symbolic forms. In L. Putnam & M. Pacanowsky (Eds.), *Communication and organizations* (pp. 173–194). Beverly Hills, CA: Sage.

Conrad, C. (1991). Communication in conflict: Stylestrategy relationships. *Communication Monographs, 58,* 135–155.

Contractor, N. (1992). Self-organizing systems perspective in the study of organizational communication. In B. Kovacic (Ed.), *Organizational communication: New perspectives* (pp. 39–65). Albany: State University of New York Press.

Corman, S. R., Trethewey, A., & Goodall, H. L. (2008). *Weapons of mass persuasion: Strategic communication to combat violent extremism. Frontiers in political communication, v. 15.* New York: Peter Lang.

Covey, S. (1990). *Seven habits of highly effective people.* New York: Simon & Schuster.

Covino, W. A., & Jolliffe, D. A. (1995). *Rhetoric: Concepts, definitions, boundaries.* New York: Longman.

Csikszentmihalyi, M. (1990). *Flow: The psychology of optimal experience.* New York: Harper & Row.

Csikszentmihalyi, M. (1997). *Finding flow: The psychology of engagement with everyday life.* New York: Basic Books.

Cusella, L. (1987). Feedback, motivation, and performance. In F. Jablin et al. (Eds.), *Handbook of organizational communication* (pp. 624–678). Beverly Hills, CA: Sage.

Czarniawska-Joerges, B. (1988). Dynamics of organizational control: The case of Berol Kemi Ab. *Accounting, Organizations, and Society, 11,* 471–482.

Damasio, A. R. (1999). *The feeling of what happens: Body and emotion in the making of consciousness.* New York: Harcourt Brace.

Dansereau, F., & Markham, S. (1987). Superior–subordinate communication: Multiple levels of analysis. In F. Jablin et al. (Eds.), *Handbook of organizational communication* (pp. 343–388). Beverly Hills, CA: Sage.

Davis, K. (1953). Management communication and the grapevine. *Harvard Business Review, 31,* 43–49.

Deal, T., & Kennedy, A. (1982). *Corporate cultures.* Reading, MA: Addison-Wesley.

Deetz, S. (1991). *Democracy in an age of corporate colonization.* Albany: State University of New York Press.

Deetz, S. (1995). *Transforming communication, transforming business.* Albany: State University of New York Press.

Deetz, S., & Mumby, D. (1990). Power, discourse, and the workplace: Reclaiming the critical tradition. In J. Anderson (Ed.), *Communication Yearbook, 13,* 18–47.

Dillard, J., & Miller, K. (1988). Intimate relationships in task environments. In S. Duck (Ed.), *Handbook of personal relationships* (pp. 449–465). New York: Wiley.

Dillard, J., & Segrin, C. (1987). *Intimate relationships in organizations: Relational types, illicitness, and power.* Paper presented at the Annual Conference of the International Communication Association, Montreal, Canada.

Donnellon, A. (1992). Team work: Linguistic models of negotiating difference. In B. Shepard et al. (Eds.), *Research and negotiations in organizations* (Vol. 4, pp. 71–123). Greenwich, CT: JAI Press.

Dove, L. (1998). CPA standards elevated for complex profession. *Wichita Business Journal, 13*(22), 16.

Dutton, J., & Dukerich, J. (1991). Keeping an eye on the mirror: Image and identity in organizational adaptation. *Academy of Management Journal, 34,* 517–554.

Ehninger, D. (1974). *Influence, belief, and argument: An introduction to responsible persuasion.* Glenview, IL: Scott, Foresman.

Eisenberg, E. (1984). Ambiguity as strategy in organizational communication. *Communication Monographs, 51,* 227–242.

Eisenberg, E. (1986). Meaning and interpretation in organizations. *Quarterly Journal of Speech, 72,* 88–98.

Eisenberg, E. (1990). Jamming: Transcendence through organizing. *Communication Research, 17,* 139–164.

Eisenberg, E., & Goodall, H. L. (2004). *Organizational communication: Balancing creativity and constraint.* New York: St. Martin's.

Eisenberg, E., & Goodall, H. L., & Trethewey A. (2006). *Organizational communication: Balancing creativity and constraint, 5th edition.* New York: St. Martin's.

Eisenberg, E., Monge, P., & Miller, K. (1983). Involvement in communication networks as a predictor of organizational commitment. *Human Communication Research, 10,* 179–201.

Eisenberg, E., & Phillips, S. (1991). Miscommunication in organizations. In N. Coupland, H. Giles, & J. Weimann (Eds.), *"Miscommunication" and problematic talk* (pp. 244–258). Newbury Park, CA: Sage.

Eisenberg, E., & Witten, M. (1987). Reconsidering openness in organizational communication. *Academy of Management Review, 12,* 418–426.

Ekman, P. (1978). Facial expression. In A. W. Siegman & S. Feldstein (Eds.), *Nonverbal behavior and communication* (pp. 79–101). Hillsdale, NJ: Erlbaum.

Ellingson, L. L. (2003). Interdisciplinary health care teamwork in the clinic backstage. *Journal of Applied Communcation Research, 31,* 93–117.

Etzioni, A. (1988). *The moral dimension: Toward a new economics.* New York: Free Press.

Evered, R., & Tannenbaum, R. (1992). A dialog on dialog. *Journal of Management Inquiry, 1,* 43–55.

Fairhurst, G., & Chandler, T. (1989). Social structure in leader–member interaction. *Communication Monographs, 56,* 215–239.

Fairhurst, G., Green, S., & Snavely, B. (1984). Face support in controlling poor performance. *Human Communication Research, 11,* 272–295.

Fairhurst, G., Rogers, E., & Sarr, R. (1987). Manager–subordinate control patterns and judgments about the relationship. *Communication Yearbook, 10,* 395–415.

Fairhurst, G., & Sarr, R. (1996). *The art of framing.* San Francisco, CA: Jossey-Bass.

Farace, R., Monge, P., & Russell, H. (1977). *Communicating and organizing.* Reading, MA: Addison-Wesley.

Farley, L. (1978). *Sexual shakedown: The sexual harassment of women on the job.* New York: McGraw-Hill.

Fayol, H. (1949). *General and industrial management.* London: Pitman.

Feldman, S. (1991). The meaning of ambiguity: Learning from stories and metaphors. In P. Frost et al. (Eds.),

Reframing organizational culture, 145–156. Newbury Park, CA: Sage.

Fisher, A. (1980). *Small group decision making* (2nd ed.). New York: McGraw-Hill.

Fisher, W. (1984). Narration as a human communication paradigm: The case of public moral argument. *Communication Monographs, 51,* 1–22.

Fisher, W. (1987). *Human communication as narration: Toward a philosophy of reason, value, and action.* Columbia: University of South Carolina Press.

Ford, J. D., & Ford, L. W. (1995). The role of conversations in producing intentional change in organizations. *Academy of Management Review, 20,* 541–570.

Ford, R., & Fottler, M. (1995). Empowerment: A matter of degree. *Academy of Management Executive, 9,* 21–31.

Fox, M. (1994). *The reinvention of work.* San Francisco: HarperCollins.

Franz, C., & Jin, K. (1995). The structure of group conflict in a collaborative work group during information systems development. *Journal of Applied Communication Research, 23,* 108–122.

French, R., & Raven, B. (1968). The bases of social power. In D. Cartwright & A. Zander (Eds.), *Group dynamics* (pp. 601–623). New York: Harper & Row.

Friedman, T. L. (1999) *The Lexus and the Olive Tree: Understanding Globalization.* New York: Farrar, Strauss, and Giroux.

Friedman, T. L. (2005). *The world is flat: A brief history of the twenty-first century.* New York: Farrar, Straus and Giroux.

Fritz, J. (1997). Men's and women's organizational peer relationships: A comparison. *Journal of Business Communication, 34(1),* 27.

Fulk, J., & Mani, S. (1986). Distortion of communication in hierarchical relationships. *Communication Yearbook, 9,* 483–510.

Fulk, J., Schmitz, J., & Steinfeld, C. (1990). A social influence model of technology use. In J. Fulk & C. Steinfeld (Eds.), *Organizations and communication technology* (pp. 143–172). Newbury Park, CA: Sage.

Furnham, A. (1999). Gesture politics. *People Management, 6,* 52.

Geertz, C. (1973). *The interpretation of cultures.* New York: Basic Books.

Geffen, D., & Straub, D. W. (1997). Gender differences in the perception and use of e-mail: An extension to the technology acceptance model. *MIS Quarterly, 21,* 389–401.

Geist, P., & Dreyer, J. (1992). *A dialogical critique of the medical encounter: Understanding, marginalization, and the social context.* Paper presented at the Annual Meeting of the Speech Communication Association, Chicago.

Geist, P., & Dreyer, J. (1993). The demise of dialogue: A critique of medical encounter ideology. *Western Journal of Communication, 57,* 233–246.

Gersick, C. (1988). Time and transition in work teams: Toward a new model of group development. *Academy of Management Journal, 31,* 9–41.

Gersick, C. (1991). Revolutionary change theories: A multi-level explanation of the punctuated equilibrium paradigm. *Academy of Management Review, 16,* 10–36.

Gilsdorf, J. (1998). Organizational rules on communicating: How employees are—and are not—learning the ropes. *Journal of Business Communication, 35,* 173.

Goodall, H. L. (1983). *Human communication: Creating reality.* Dubuque, IA: Brown.

Goodall, H. L. (1989). *Casing a promised land.* Carbondale: Southern Illinois University Press.

Goodall, H. L. (1990a). Interpretive contexts for decision-making: Toward an understanding of the physical, economic, dramatic, and hierarchical interplays of language in groups. In G. M. Phillips (Ed.), *Teaching how to work in groups* (pp. 197–224). Norwood, NJ: Ablex.

Goodall, H. L. (1990b). Theatre of motives. In J. Anderson (Ed.), *Communication Yearbook, 13,* 69–97.

Goodall, H. L. (1993). Empowerment, culture, and postmodern organizing: Deconstructing the Nordstrom's employee handbook. *Journal of Organizational Change Management, 5,* 25–30.

Goodall, H. L., Jr. (1995). Work-hate narratives. In R. Whillock & D. Slayden (Eds.), *Hate speech* (pp. 80–121). Thousand Oaks, CA: Sage.

Goodall, H. L., Jr. (1996). *Divine signs: Connecting spirit to community.* Carbondale: Southern Illinois University Press.

Goodall, H. L., Jr. (2000). *Writing the new ethnography.* Walnut Creek, CA: AltaMira.

Goodall, H. L., & Phillips, G. M. (1985). *Making it in any organization.* Englewood Cliffs, NJ: Prentice-Hall.

Goodall, H. L., Wilson, G., & Waagen, C. (1986). The performance appraisal interview: An interpretive reassessment. *Quarterly Journal of Speech, 72,* 74–87.

Gouran, D. S. (1970). A response to the paradox and promise of small group communication research. *Speech Monographs, 37,* 217–218.

Grantham, C. (1995, September–October). The virtual office. *At work: Stories of tomorrow's workplace, 4(5),* 1, 12–14.

Gray, B., Bougon, M., & Donnellon, A. (1985). Organizations as constructions and destructions of meaning. *Journal of Management, 11,* 83–98.

Gray, J. (1992). *Men are from Mars, women are from Venus.* New York: HarperCollins.

Greene, J. O., & Sassi, M. S. (1997). Adult acquisition of message-production skill. *Communication Monographs, 64,* 181–201.

Gronn, P. (1983). Talk as the work: The accomplishment of school administration. *Administrative Science Quarterly, 28,* 1–21.

Gross, Kim J. & Stone, Jeff. (2002). *Chic Simple Dress Smart for Men: Wardrobes that Win in the Workplace.* New York: Grand Central Publishing.

Gross, Kim J. & Stone, Jeff & Kristina Zimbalist. (2002). *Chic Simple Dress Smart for Women: Wardrobes that Win in the Workplace.* New York: Grand Central Publishing.

Hackman, R., & Associates. (1990). *Groups that work (and those that don't): Creating conditions for effective teamwork.* San Francisco: Jossey-Bass.

Hall, E. T. (1968). Proxemics. *Current Anthropology, 9,* 83–109.

Hall, E. T. (1973). *The silent language.* New York: Anchor Books.

Hall, S. (1997). *Representation in media.* Amherst, MA: Media Education Foundation.

Hammer, M., & Champy, J. (1993). *Reengineering the corporation.* New York: HarperCollins.

Harshman, E., & Harshman, C. (1999). Communicating with employees: Building on an ethical foundation. *Journal of Business Ethics, 19(1),* 3.

Hawes, L. (1974). Social collectivities as communication: Perspective on organizational behavior. *Quarterly Journal of Speech, 60,* 497–502.

Hawken, P. (1992). *The ecology of commerce.* New York: HarperCollins.

Hearn, G, & Ninan, A. (2003). Managing change is managing meaning. *Management Communication Quarterly, 16,* 440–445.

Hellweg, S. (1987). Organizational grapevines: A state of the art review. In B. Dervin & M. Voight (Eds.), *Progress in the communication sciences* (Vol. 8, pp. 213–230). Norwood, NJ: Ablex.

Hemphill, B. (2005). *Taming the Paper Tiger at Work.* Washington D.C.: Kiplinger Books

Heslin, R. (1974). *Steps toward a taxonomy of touching.* Paper presented at the annual convention of the Midwestern Psychological Association, Chicago.

Hirokawa, R., & Rost, K. (1992). Effective group decision making in organizations. *Management Communication Quarterly, 5,* 267–388.

Hodson, R. (2004). A meta-analysis of workplace ethnographies: Race, gender, and employee attitudes and behaviors. *Journal of Contemporary Ethnograhpy, 33,* 4–38.

Hofstede, G. (1983). National cultures in four dimensions. *International Studies of Management and Organization, 13,* 46–74.

Hofstede, G. (1991). *Culture and organizations: Software of the mind.* New York: McGraw-Hill.

Holt, G. (1989). Talk about acting and constraint in stories about organizations. *Western Journal of Speech Communication, 53,* 374–397.

Homans, G. (1961). *Social behavior: Its elementary forms.* New York: Harcourt Brace & World.

Huber, G. (1990). A theory of the effects of advanced information technologies on organizational design, intelligence, and decision-making. In J. Fulk & C. Steinfeld (Eds.), *Organizations and communication technology* (pp. 237–274). Newbury Park, CA: Sage.

Isaacs, W. (1993). *Dialogue.* New York: Currency Doubleday.

Jablin, F. (1979). Superior–subordinate communication: The state of the art. *Psychological Bulletin, 86,* 1201–1222.

Jablin, F. (1985). Task /work relationships: A life-span perspective. In M. Knapp & G. Miller (Eds.), *Handbook of interpersonal communication* (pp. 615–654). Newbury Park, CA: Sage.

Jablin, F. (1987). Organizational entry, assimilation, and exit. In F. Jablin, L. Putnam, K. Roberts, & L. Porter (Eds.), *Handbook of organizational communication* (pp. 679–740). Newbury Park, CA: Sage.

Jackson, S. (1983). Participation in decision-making as a strategy for reducing job-related strain. *Journal of Applied Psychology, 68,* 3–19.

James, J. (1996). *Thinking in the future tense: Leadership skills for a new age.* New York: Simon & Schuster.

Janis, I. (1971). *Victims of groupthink* (2nd rev. ed.). Boston: Houghton Mifflin.

Jhally, S. (1997). *Advertising and the end of the world* [Videotape]. Amherst, MA: Media Education Foundation.

Johnson, D., et al. (1993). *Circles of learning.* Edina, MN: Interaction Books.

Kassing, J. W. (2002). Speaking up: Identifying employees' upward dissent strategies. *Management Communication Quarterly, 16,* 193–207.

Kellett, P. (1999). Dialogue and dialectics in managing organizational change: The case of a mission-based transformation. *Southern Communication Journal, 64,* 211–231.

Kellett, P., & Dalton, D. (2001). *Managing conflict in a negotiated world: A narrative approach to achieving dialogue and change.*Walnut Creek, CA: Sage.

Kellett, P., & Goodall, H. L. (1999). The death of discourse in our own (chat) room: "Sextext," skillful discussion, and virtual communities. In D. Slayden & R. K. Whillock (Eds.), *Soundbite culture: The death of discourse in a wired world* (pp. 155–190). Thousand Oaks, CA: Sage.

Kendon, A. (1967). Some functions of gaze direction in social interaction. *ACTA Psychologica, 26,* 22–63.

Keyton, J. (2003). Teaching a pig to sing? *Management Communication Quarterly, 16,* 453–458.

King, P., & Sawyer, C. (1998). Mindfulness, mindlessness, and communication instruction. *Communication Education, 47,* 326.

Kotter, J., & Heskett, J. (1992). *Corporate culture and performance.* New York: Free Press.

Kram, K.E. & Issabella, L.A. Mentoring alternatives: The role of peer relationships in career development. *Academy of Management Journal, 28,* 10–132-.

Kramer, M. (1993). Communication and uncertainty reduction during job transfers: Leaving and joining processes. *Communication Monographs, 60,* 178–198.

Kramer, M. (1995). A longitudinal study of superior–subordinate communication during job transfers. *Human Communication Research, 22,* 39–64.

Kraut, R. E., & Johnson, R. E. (1979). Social and emotional messages of smiling: An ethological approach. *Journal of Personality and Social Psychology, 37,* 1539–1553.

Krippendorff, K. (1985). *On the ethics of constructing communication.* International Communication Association presidential address, Honolulu, Hawaii.

Krivonos, P. (1982). Distortion of subordinate to superior communication in organizational settings. *Central States Speech Journal, 33,* 345–352.

Kuhn, T., & Ashcraft, K. L. (2003). Corporate scandal and the theory of the firm: Formulating the contributions of organizational communication studies. *Management Communication Quarterly, 17,* 20–57.

Kunda, G. (1993). *Engineering culture: Control and commitment in a high-tech corporation.* Philadelphia: Temple University Press.

Lacy, D. (1995). *From grunts to gigabytes: Communication and society.* Urbana: University of Illinois Press.

Langer, E. (1989). *Mindfulness.* Reading, MA: Addison-Wesley.

Langer, E. (1992). Interpersonal mindlessness and language. *Communication Monographs, 59,* 324.

Langer, E. (1997). *The power of mindful learning.* Reading, MA: Addison-Wesley.

Lawler, Jennifer & Ziegler, H. (2003). *Feng Shui Your Workplace for Dummies.* New York: John Wiley and Sons, 2003.

Lizzio, A., Wilson, K. L., Gilchrist, J., & Gallois, C. (2003). The role of gender in the construction and evaluation of feedback effectiveness.

Management Communication Quarterly, 16, 341–379.

Lodge, D. (1997). The practice of writing. New York: Penguin.

Louis, M. (1979). Surprise and sense-making: What newcomers experience in entering unfamiliar organizational settings. Administrative Science Quarterly, 23, 225–251.

Lovitt, C. R., & Goswami, D. (1999). Exploring the rhetoric of international professional communication: An agenda for teachers and researchers. Amityville, NY: Baywood.

Luhmann, A. D., & Albrecht, T. L. (1990). The impact of supportive communication and personal control on job stress and performance. Paper presented at the International Communication Association, Chicago.

Lutgen-Sandvik, P. (2003). The communicative cycle of employee emotional abuse. Management Communication Quarterly, 16, 471–501.

Marshall, A., & Stohl, C. (1993). Participating as participation: A network approach. Communication Monographs, 60, 137–157.

Marshall, J. (1993). Viewing organizational communication from a feminist perspective: A critique and some offerings. In S. Deetz (Ed.), Communication Yearbook, 16, 122–143.

Martin, J. (1992). Cultures in organizations: Three perspectives. New York: Oxford University Press.

Maslow, A. (1965). Eupsychian management. Homewood, IL: Irwin.

Maslow, A. (1970). Motivation and personality (2nd ed.). New York: Harper & Row.

May, S. (1993). Employee assistance program and the troubled workers: A discursive study of knowledge, power, and subjectivity. Unpublished doctoral dissertation, University of Utah.

May, S. (2003). Case Study: Challenging change. Management Communication Quarterly, 16, 419–433.

Mayo, E. (1945). The social problems of industrial civilization. Cambridge, MA: Graduate School of Business Administration, Harvard University.

McGregor, D. (1960). The human side of enterprise. New York: McGraw-Hill.

McKerrow, R., Gronbeck, B. E., Ehninger, D., & Monroe, A. H. (2000). Principles and types of speech communication. New York: Longman.

McPhee, R., & Corman, S. (1995). An activity based theory of communication networks in organizations, applied to the case of a local church. Communication Monographs, 62, 132–151.

Mead, G. (1934). Mind, self, and society. Chicago: University of Chicago Press.

Meyer, G. J. (1995). Executive blues. San Francisco: Franklin Square Press.

Miller, J. G. (1978). Living systems. New York: McGraw-Hill.

Miller, K. (1995). Organizational communication: Approaches and processes. Belmont, CA: Wadsworth.

Miller, K., Ellis, B., Zook, E., & Lyles, J. (1990). An integrated model of communication, stress, and burnout in the workplace. Communication Research 17, 300–326 .

Miller, K., & Monge, P. (1985). Social information and employee anxiety about organizational change. Human Communication Research, 11, 365–386.

Miller, K., & Monge, P. (1986). Participation, satisfaction, and productivity: A meta-analytic review. Academy of Management Journal, 29, 727–753.

Miller, K., Stiff, J., & Ellis, B. (1988). Communication and empathy as precursors to burnout among human service workers. Communication Monographs, 55, 250–265.

Miller, V., & Jablin, F. (1991). Information seeking during organizational entry: Influences, tactics, and a model of the process. Academy of Management Review, 16, 92–120.

Mintzberg, H. (1973). The nature of managerial work. New York: Harper & Row.

Mitroff, I., & Kilmann, R. (1975). Stories managers tell: A new tool for organizational problem-solving. Management Review, 64, 18–28.

Monge, P., Bachman, S., Dillard, J., & Eisenberg, E. (1982). Communicator competence in the workplace: Model testing and scale development. Communication Yearbook, 5, 505–528.

Monge, P., Cozzens, M., & Contractor, N. (1992). Communication and motivational predictors of the dynamics of organizational innovation. Organizational Science, 3, 250–274.

Monge, P., & Eisenberg, E. (1987). Emergent communication networks.

In F. Jablin et al. (Eds.), Handbook of organizational communication (pp. 204–342). Beverly Hills, CA: Sage.

Monge, P., Farace, R., Eisenberg, E., Miller, K., & Rothman, L. (1984). The process of studying process in organizational communication. Journal of Communication, 34, 22–43.

Morgan, G. (1986). Images of organization. Newbury Park, CA: Sage.

Morrison, E., & Bies, R. (1991). Impression management in the feedback-seeking process: A literature review and research agenda. Academy of Management Review, 16, 522–541.

Motley, M. (1992). Mindfulness in solving communicators' dilemmas. Communication Monographs, 59, 306.

Moxley, R. (1994). Foundations of leadership. Greensboro, NC: Center for Creative Leadership.

Mumby, D. (1987). The political function of narratives in organizations. Communication Monographs, 54, 113–127.

Mumby, D. (1993). Narrative and social control. Newbury Park, CA: Sage.

Mumby, D., & Putnam, L. (1993). The politics of emotion: A feminist reading of bounded rationality. Academy of Management Review, 17, 465–486.

Noer, D. (1993). Healing the wounds: Overcoming the trauma of layoffs and revitalizing downsized organizations. San Francisco: Jossey-Bass.

Ochs, E., Smith, R., & Taylor, C. (1989). Detective stories at dinnertime: Problem solving through conarration. Cultural Dynamics, 2, 238–257.

Okabe, R. (1983). Cultural assumptions of East and West: Japan and the United States. In B. Gudykunst (Ed.), Intercultural communication theory (pp. 212–244). Newbury Park, CA: Sage.

Oldham, G., & Rotchford, N. (1983). Relationships between office characteristics and employee reactions: A study of the physical environment. Administrative Science Quarterly, 28, 542–556.

Ono, H. & Zavodny. (2003). Gender and the Internet. Social Science Quarterly, 84, 111–121.

O'Reilly, B. (1994, June 13). The new deal: What companies and employees owe each other. Fortune, 44.

Osborn, J., Moran, L., Musselwhite, E., & Zenger, J. (1990). *Self-directed work teams*. Homewood, IL: Business One Irwin.

Ouchi, W., & Wilkins, A. (1985). Organizational culture. *Annual Review of Sociology, 11*, 457–483.

Pacanowsky, M. (1988). Communication in the empowering organization. In J. Anderson (Ed.), *Communication Yearbook, 11*, 356–379.

Pacanowsky, M., & O'Donnell-Trujillo, N. (1983). Organizational communication as cultural performance. *Communication Monographs, 50*, 126–147.

Papa, M. (1989). Communicator competence and employee performance with new technology: A case study. *Southern Communication Journal, 55*, 87–101.

Papa, M. (1990). Communication network patterns and employee performance with new technology. *Communication Research, 17*, 344–368.

Perrow, C. (1986). *Complex organizations: A critical essay* (3rd ed.). New York: Random House.

Peters, T., & Waterman, R. (1982). *In search of excellence*. New York: Harper & Row.

Pettigrew, A. (1979). On studying organizational cultures. *Administrative Science Quarterly, 24*, 570–581.

Phillips, G. (1991). *Communication incompetencies: A theory of training oral performance behavior*. Carbondale: Southern Illinois University Press.

Phillips, Micheal D., MD & Lowe, Mark J., Ph.D., & Lurito, Joseph T., et al. (2001). Temporal lobe activation demonstrates sex-based differences during passive listening. *Radiology, 202*–207.

Philpott, J. S. (1983). *The relative contribution to meaning of verbal and nonverbal channels of communication: A meta-analysis*. Unpublished master's thesis, University of Nebraska.

Pinchot, G., & Pinchot, E. (1993). *The end of bureaucracy and the rise of the intelligent organization*. San Francisco: Berrett-Koehler.

Poole, M. S. (1981). Decision development in small groups I: A comparison of two models. *Communication Monographs, 48*, 1–24.

Poole, M. S. (1983). Decision development in small groups II: A study of multiple sequences in decision making. *Communication Monographs, 50*, 321–341.

Poole, M. S. (1992). Structuration and the group communication process. In L. Samovar & R. Cathcart (Eds.), *Small group communication: A reader* (6th ed., pp. 147–157). Dubuque, IA: Brown.

Poole, M. S. (1996, February). *A turn of the wheel: The case for a renewal of systems inquiry in organizational communication research*. Conference on Organizational Communication and Change, Austin, Texas.

Poole, M. S., & Desanctis, G. (1990). Understanding the use of group decision support systems: The theory of adaptive structuration. In J. Fulk & C. Steinfeld (Eds.), *Organizations and communication technology* (pp. 173–193). Newbury Park, CA: Sage.

Poole, M. S., & Holmes, M. (1995). Decision development in computer-assisted group decision making. *Human Communication Research, 22*, 90–127.

Poole, M. S., & Roth, J. (1989). Decision development in small groups V: Test of a contingency model. *Human Communication Research, 15*, 549–589.

Powell, G. N., & Graves, L. M. (2004). *Gender and leadership: Perceptions and realities: Sex differences and similiaraties in communication* (2nd ed.). Mahwah, NJ: Erlbaum.

Putnam, L., & Pacanowsky, M. (1983). *Communication and organizations: An interpretive approach*. Beverly Hills, CA: Sage.

Quinn, R. (1977). Coping with Cupid: The formation, impact, and management of romantic relationships in organizations. *Administrative Science Quarterly, 22*, 30–45.

Rafaeli, A., & Sutton, R. (1987). The expression of emotion as part of the work role. *Academy of Management Review, 12*, 23–37.

Rafaeli, A., & Sutton, R. (1991). Emotional contrast strategies as means of social influence: Lessons from criminal interrogators and bill collectors. *Academy of Management Journal, 34*, 749–775.

Ralston, S., & Kirkwood, W. (1995). Overcoming managerial bias in employment interviewing. *Journal of Applied Communication Research, 23*, 75–92.

Ray, E. (1987). Supportive relationships and occupational stress in the workplace. In T. Albrecht & M. Adelman (Eds.), *Communicating social support* (pp. 172–191). Newbury Park, CA: Sage.

Redding, W. C. (1993). *Unethical messages in the organizational context*. Paper presented at the annual convention of the International Communication Association, Chicago.

Redding, W. C. (1985a). Rocking boats, blowing whistles, teaching speech communication. *Communication Education, 34*, 245–258.

Redding, W. C. (1985b). Stumbling toward identity: The emergence of organizational communication as a field of study. In R. McPhee & P. Tompkins (Eds.), *Organizational communication: Traditional themes and new directions* (pp. 15–54). Beverly Hills, CA: Sage.

Rehfield, J. (1994). Cited in D. C. Barnlund, *Communicative styles of Japanese and Americans*. Belmont, CA: Wadsworth.

Richmond, V., & McCroskey, J. (1995). *Nonverbal behavior in interpersonal relations*. Englewood Cliffs, NJ: Prentice-Hall.

Roberts, K., & O'Reilly, C. (1974). Failures in upward communication: Three possible culprits. *Academy of Management Journal, 17*, 205–215.

Roy, D. (1960). Banana time: Job satisfaction and informal interaction. *Human Organization, 18*, 156–180.

Sahlins, M. (1976). *Culture and practical reason*. Chicago: University of Chicago Press.

Sailer, H., Schlachter, J., & Edwards, M. (1982, July – August). Stress: Causes, consequences, and coping strategies. *Personnel, 59*, 35–48.

Salopek, J. (1999, September). Is anyone listening? *Training and Development, 53*, 58.

Salopek, J. (1999, November). Liar, liar, pants on fire. *Training and Development, 53*, 16.

Samovar, L., Porter, R. E., & Jain, N. C. (1991). *Understanding intercultural communication*. Belmont, CA: Wadsworth.

Scheidel, T., & Crowell, L. (1964). Idea development in small discussion groups. *Quarterly Journal of Speech, 50*, 140–145.

Schein, E. (1991). The role of the founder in the creation of organizational culture. In P. Frost et al.

(Eds.), *Reframing organizational culture* (pp. 14–25). Newbury Park, CA: Sage.

Scollon, R., & Scollon, S. (1995). *Intercultural communication.* Cambridge, MA: Blackwell.

Scott, J. (1990). *Domination and the arts of resistance: Hidden transcripts.* New Haven, CT: Yale University Press.

Senge, P. (1991). *The fifth discipline: The art and practice of the learning organization.* New York: Doubleday/Currency.

Senge, P., Roberts, C., Ross, R., Smith, B., & Kleiner, A. (1994). *The fifth discipline fieldbook.* New York: Doubleday/Currency.

Shockley-Zalabak, P., & Morley, D. (1994). Creating a culture. *Human Communication Research, 20,* 334–355.

Shorris, E. (1984). *Scenes from corporate life.* Hammondsworth, UK: Penguin.

Sias, P., & Jablin, F. (1995). Differential superior–subordinate relations, perceptions of fairness, and coworker communication. *Human Communication Research, 22,* 5–38.

Simon, H. (1957/1976). *Administrative behavior* (3rd ed.). New York: Free Press.

Smith, D. (1972). Communication research and the idea of process. *Speech Monographs, 39,* 174–182.

Smith, H. (1995, May 14). *The three faces of capitalism.* Public Broadcasting System.

Smith, R., & Eisenberg, E. (1987). Conflict at Disneyland: A root metaphor analysis. *Communication Monographs, 54,* 367–380.

Sommer, R. (1969). *Personal space.* Englewood Cliffs, NJ: Prentice-Hall.

Sundstrom, E., DeMeuse, K., & Futrell, D. (1990). Work teams: Applications and effectiveness. *American Psychologist, 45,* 120–133.

Tannen, D. (1990). *You just don't understand: Women and men in conversation.* New York: Morrow.

Tannen, D. (1994a). *Gender and discourse.* New York: Oxford University Press.

Tannen, D. (1994b). *Talking from 9 to 5: Women and men in the workplace, language, sex, and*

power. New York: Simon & Schuster.

Taylor, F. (1913). *The principles of scientific management.* New York: Harper.

Taylor, F. (1947). *Scientific management.* New York: Harper.

Tjosvold, D., & Tjosvold, M. (1991). *Leading the team organization.* New York: Lexington Books.

Trenholm, S. (2000). *Thinking through communication: An introduction to the study of human communication.* Boston: Allyn & Bacon.

Trenholm, S., & Jensen, A. (1992). *Interpersonal communication.* Belmont, CA: Wadsworth.

Triandis, H., et al. (1988). *Handbook of industrial and organizational psychology.* Palo Alto, CA: Consulting Psychology Press.

Trujillo, N. (1985). Organizational communication as cultural performance: Some managerial considerations. *Southern Speech Communication Journal, 50,* 201–224.

Turner, P. K. (2003). Paradox of ordering change: I insist that we work as a team. *Management Communication Quarterly, 16,* 434–439.

Van Maanen, J. (1991). The smile factory: Work at Disneyland. In P. Frost et al. (Eds.), *Reframing organizational culture* (pp. 58–76). Newbury Park, CA: Sage.

Van Maanen, J., & Barley, S. (1984). Occupational communities: Cultural control in organizations. In B. Staw & L. Cummings (Eds.), *Research in organizational behavior* (Vol. 6, pp. 265–287). Greenwich, CT: JAI Press.

Varner, I., & Beamer, L. (1995). *Intercultural communication in the global workplace.* Chicago: Irwin.

Victor, D. A. (1994). *International business communication.* New York: HarperCollins.

Von Bertalanffy, L. (1968). *General systems theory.* New York: George Braziller.

Vroom, V. (1964).*Work and motivation.* New York: Wiley.

Waldron, V. (1991). Achieving communication goals in superior–subordinate relationships: The

multifunctionality of upward maintenance tactics. *Communication Monographs, 58,* 289–306.

Walster, E., Walster, G. W., & Bersheid, E. (1978). *Equity theory.* Boston: Allyn & Bacon.

Watzlawick, P., Beavin, J., & Jackson, D. (1967). *The pragmatics of human communication: A study of interactional patterns, pathologies, and paradoxes.* New York: Norton.

Weber, M. (1946). *From Max Weber: Essays in sociology.* In H. Gerth & C. Wright Mills (Eds.), New York: Oxford University Press.

Weick, K. (1979). *The social psychology of organizing* (2nd ed.). Reading, MA: Addison-Wesley.

Weick, K. (1980). The management of eloquence. *Executive, 6,* 18–21.

Weick, K. (1995). *Sensemaking in organizations.* Newbury Park, CA: Sage.

Wellins, R., Byham, W., & Wilson, J. (1991). *Empowered teams.* San Francisco: Jossey-Bass.

Wenberg, J., & Wilmot, W. (1973). *The personal communication process.* New York: Wiley.

Wheatley, M. (1992). *Leadership and the new science.* San Francisco, CA: Berrett-Koehler.

Wilkins, A. (1984). The creation of company cultures: The role of stories and human resource systems. *Human Resource Management, 23,* 41–60.

Wilson, G., & Goodall, H. L. (1991). *Interviewing in context.* New York: McGraw-Hill.

Witmer, D., & Katzman, S. L. (1997). On-line smiles: Does gender make a difference in the use of graphic accents? *Journal of Computer-Mediated Communication 2*(4). http://www.ascusc.org/jcmc/vol2/issue4/.

Wood, J. (1977). Leading in purposive discussions: A study of adaptive behavior. *Communication Monographs, 44,* 152–165.

Wood, J. (1996). *Gendered relationships.* Mountain View, CA: Mayfield.

Wood, J. (1997). *Communication as a field of study.* Belmont, CA: Wadsworth.

INDEX